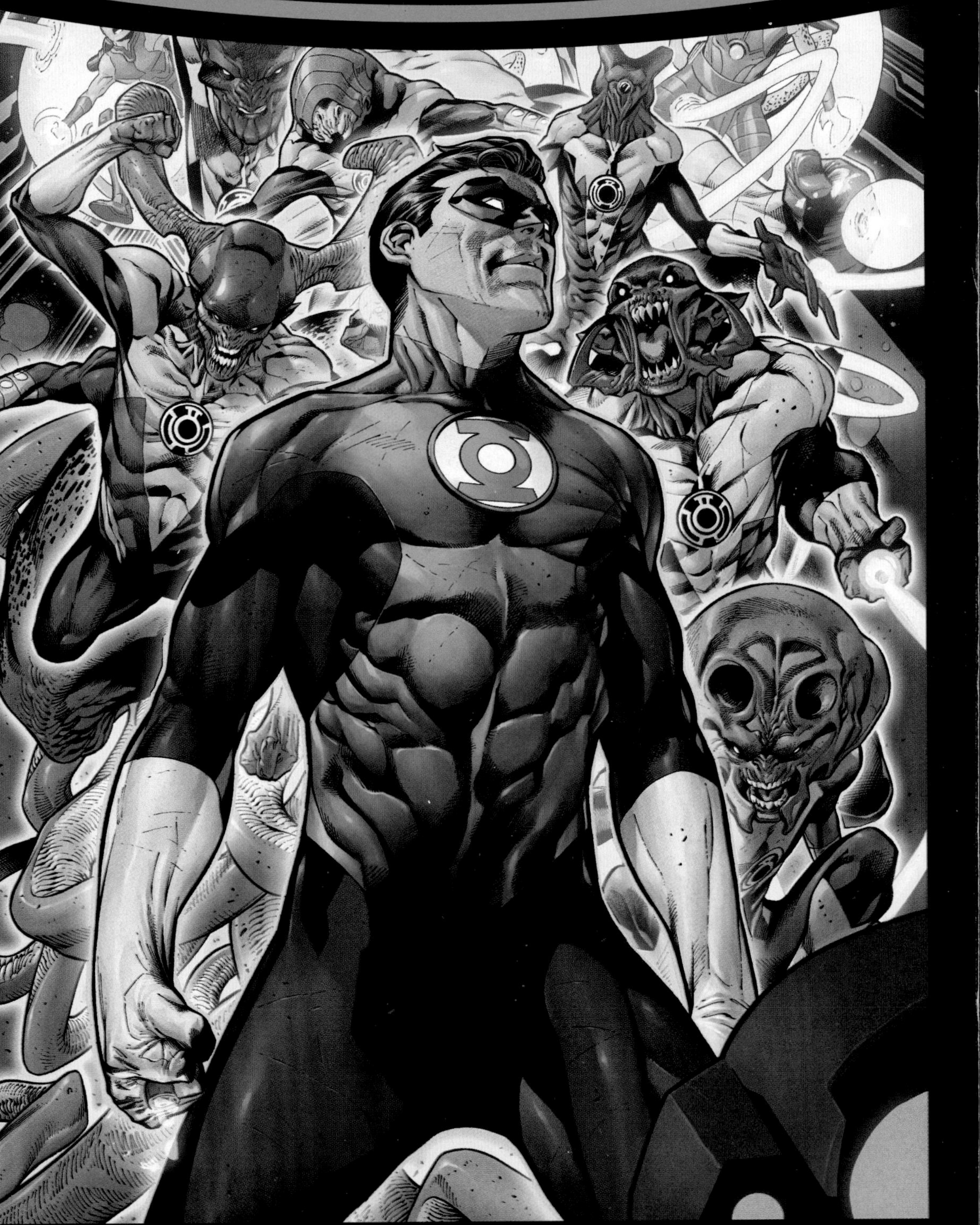

HAL JORDAN AND THE GREEN LANTERN CORPS

VOL.1 SINESTRO'S LAW

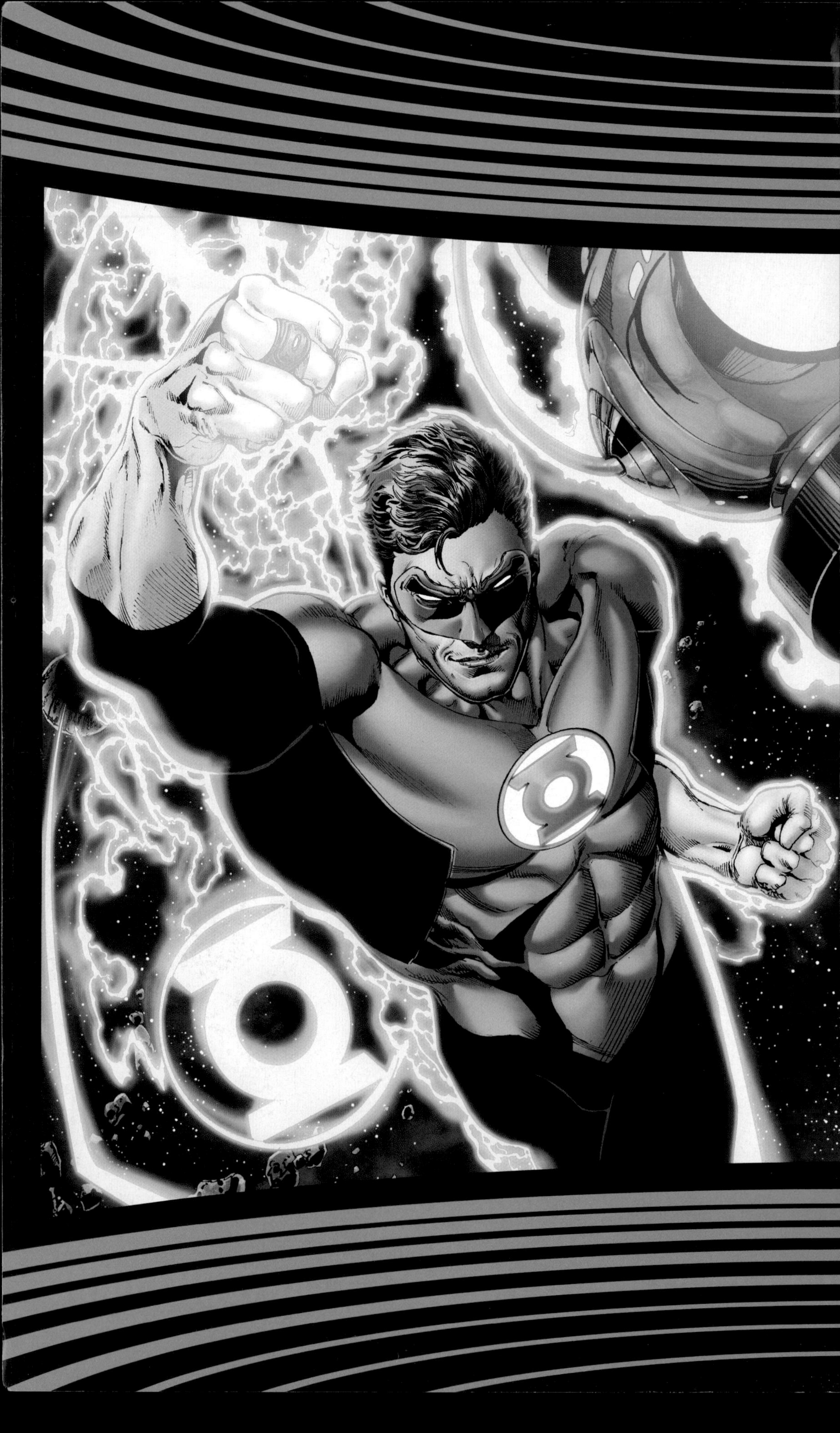

HAL JORDAN AND THE GREEN LANTERN CORPS

VOL.1 SINESTRO'S LAW

ROBERT VENDITTI
writer

RAFA SANDOVAL
ETHAN VAN SCIVER
pencillers

JORDI TARRAGONA
ETHAN VAN SCIVER
inkers

JASON WRIGHT
TOMEU MOREY
colorists

DAVE SHARPE
letterer

ETHAN VAN SCIVER and **JASON WRIGHT**
collection cover artists

Fountaindale Public Library
Bolingbrook, IL
(630) 759-2102

MIKE COTTON Editor – Original Series ✻ **ANDREW MARINO** Assistant Editor – Original Series ✻ **JEB WOODARD** Group Editor – Collected Editions
PAUL SANTOS Editor – Collected Edition ✻ **STEVE COOK** Design Director – Books ✻ **CURTIS KING JR.** Publication Design

BOB HARRAS Senior VP – Editor-in-Chief, DC Comics

DIANE NELSON President ✻ **DAN DiDIO** Publisher ✻ **JIM LEE** Publisher ✻ **GEOFF JOHNS** President & Chief Creative Officer
AMIT DESAI Executive VP – Business & Marketing Strategy, Direct to Consumer & Global Franchise Management
SAM ADES Senior VP – Direct to Consumer ✻ **BOBBIE CHASE** VP – Talent Development ✻ **MARK CHIARELLO** Senior VP – Art, Design & Collected Editions
JOHN CUNNINGHAM Senior VP – Sales & Trade Marketing ✻ **ANNE DePIES** Senior VP – Business Strategy, Finance & Administration
DON FALLETTI VP – Manufacturing Operations ✻ **LAWRENCE GANEM** VP – Editorial Administration & Talent Relations
ALISON GILL Senior VP – Manufacturing & Operations ✻ **HANK KANALZ** Senior VP – Editorial Strategy & Administration
JAY KOGAN VP – Legal Affairs ✻ **THOMAS LOFTUS** VP – Business Affairs ✻ **JACK MAHAN** VP – Business Affairs
NICK J. NAPOLITANO VP – Manufacturing Administration ✻ **EDDIE SCANNELL** VP – Consumer Marketing
COURTNEY SIMMONS Senior VP – Publicity & Communications ✻ **JIM (SKI) SOKOLOWSKI** VP – Comic Book Specialty Sales & Trade Marketing
NANCY SPEARS VP – Mass, Book, Digital Sales & Trade Marketing

HAL JORDAN AND THE GREEN LANTERN CORPS VOLUME 1: RAGE PLANET

Published by DC Comics. Compilation and all new material Copyright © 2017 DC Comics. All Rights Reserved. Originally published in single magazine form
in Hal Jordan and the Green Lantern Corps: Rebirth 1 and Hal Jordan and the Green Lantern Corps 1-7 Copyright © 2016 DC Comics. All Rights Reserved.
All characters, their distinctive likenesses and related elements featured in this publication are trademarks of DC Comics. The stories, characters and
incidents featured in this publication are entirely fictional. DC Comics does not read or accept unsolicited submissions of ideas, stories or artwork.

DC Comics, 2900 West Alameda Ave., Burbank, CA 91505
Printed by Vanguard Graphics, LLC, Ithaca, NY, USA. 1/6/17. First Printing.
ISBN: 978-1-4012-6800-8

Library of Congress Cataloging-in-Publication Data is available.

MIX
Paper from
responsible sources
FSC® C016956

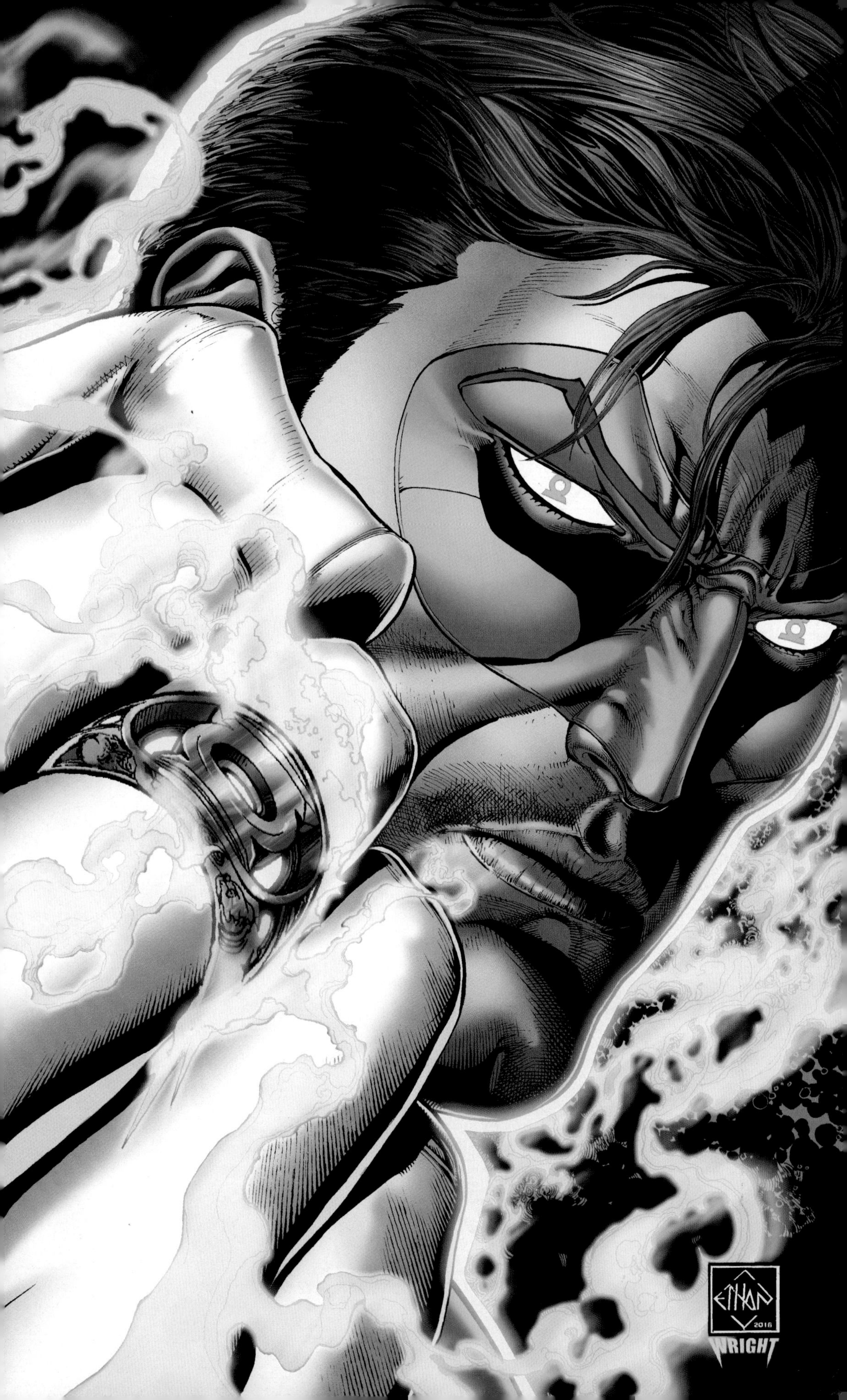
2016
WRIGHT

FORGED

ETHAN VAN SCIVER artist * JASON WRIGHT colorist * ETHAN VAN SCIVER and JASON WRIGHT cover artists

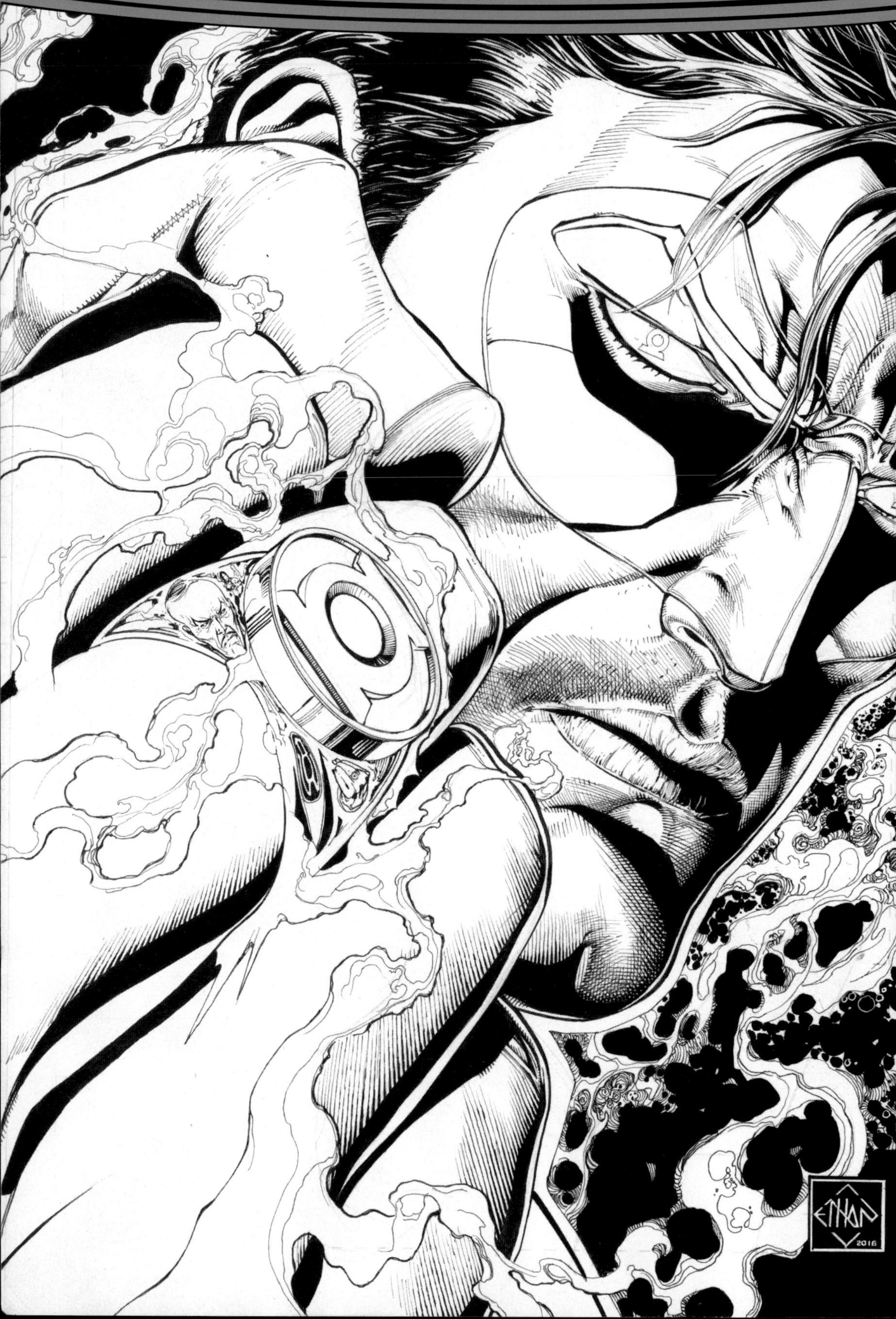

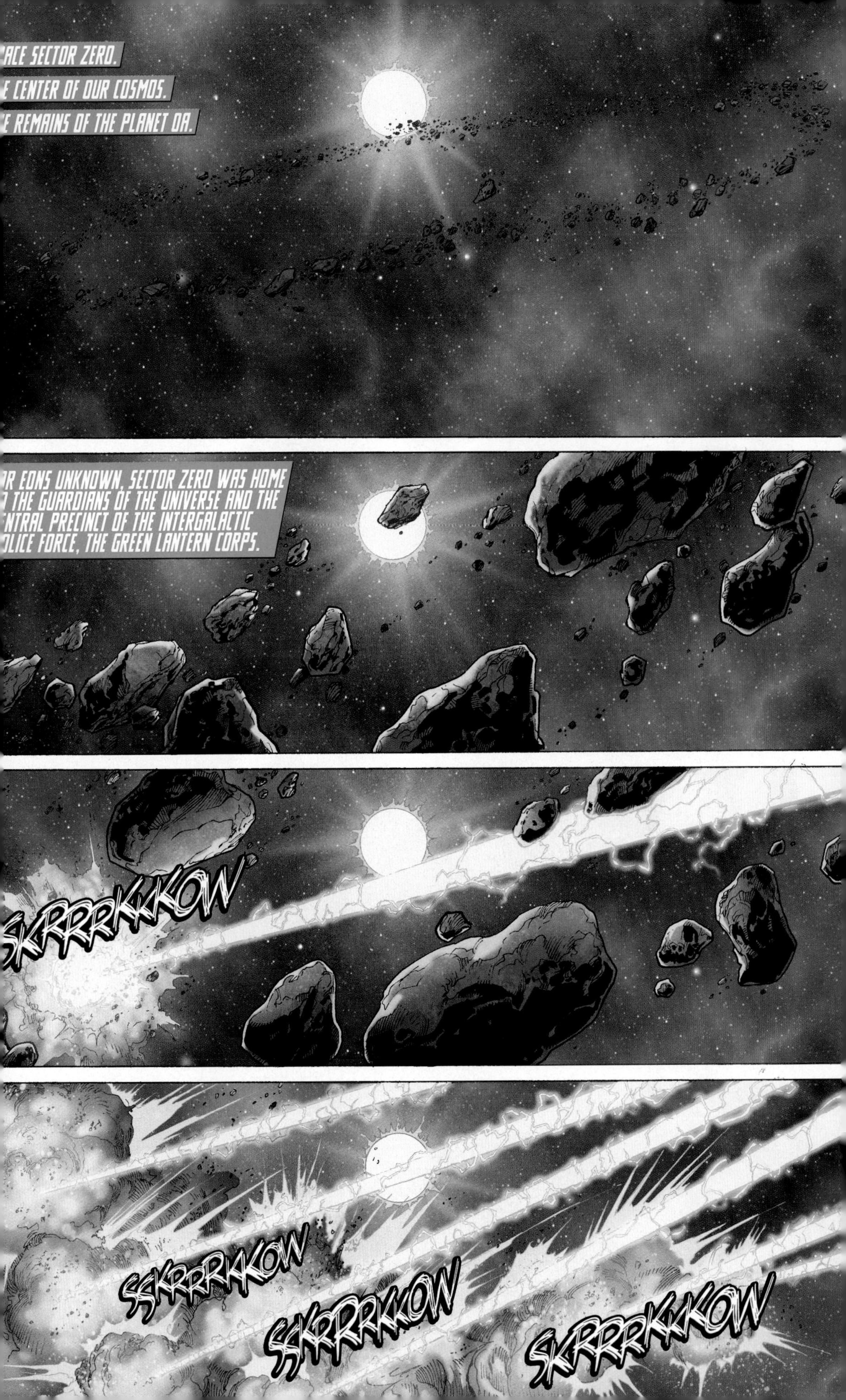
ACE SECTOR ZERO.
E CENTER OF OUR COSMOS.
E REMAINS OF THE PLANET OA.
OR EONS UNKNOWN, SECTOR ZERO WAS HOME O THE GUARDIANS OF THE UNIVERSE AND THE ENTRAL PRECINCT OF THE INTERGALACTIC OLICE FORCE, THE GREEN LANTERN CORPS.
SKRRRKKKOW
SSKRRRKKOW
SSKRRRKKOW
SKRRRKKKOW

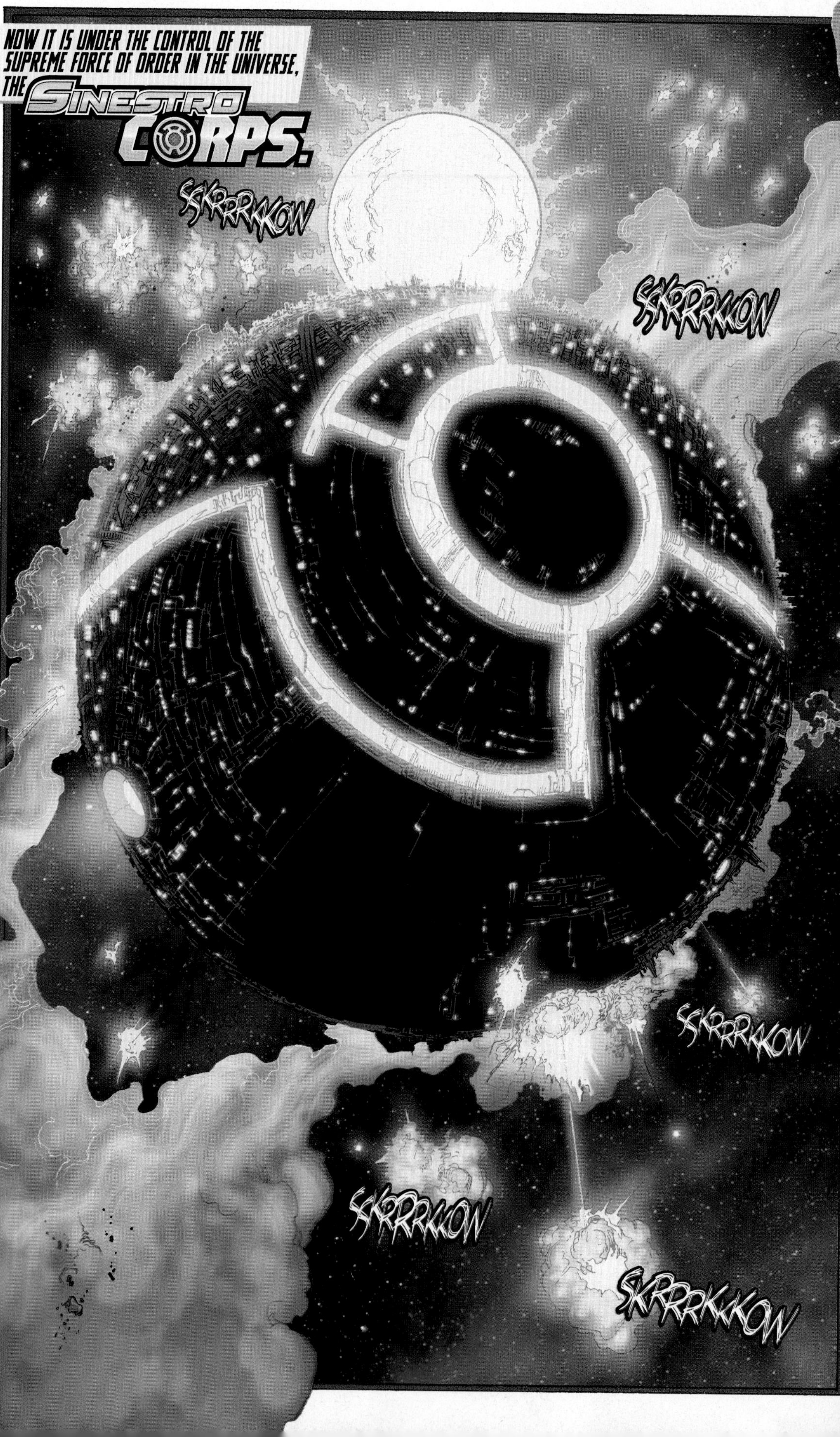
NOW IT IS UNDER THE CONTROL OF THE SUPREME FORCE OF ORDER IN THE UNIVERSE, THE SINESTRO CORPS.
SSKRRRKKOW
SSKRRRKKOW
SSKRRRKKOW
SKRRRKKOW
SKRRRKKKOW

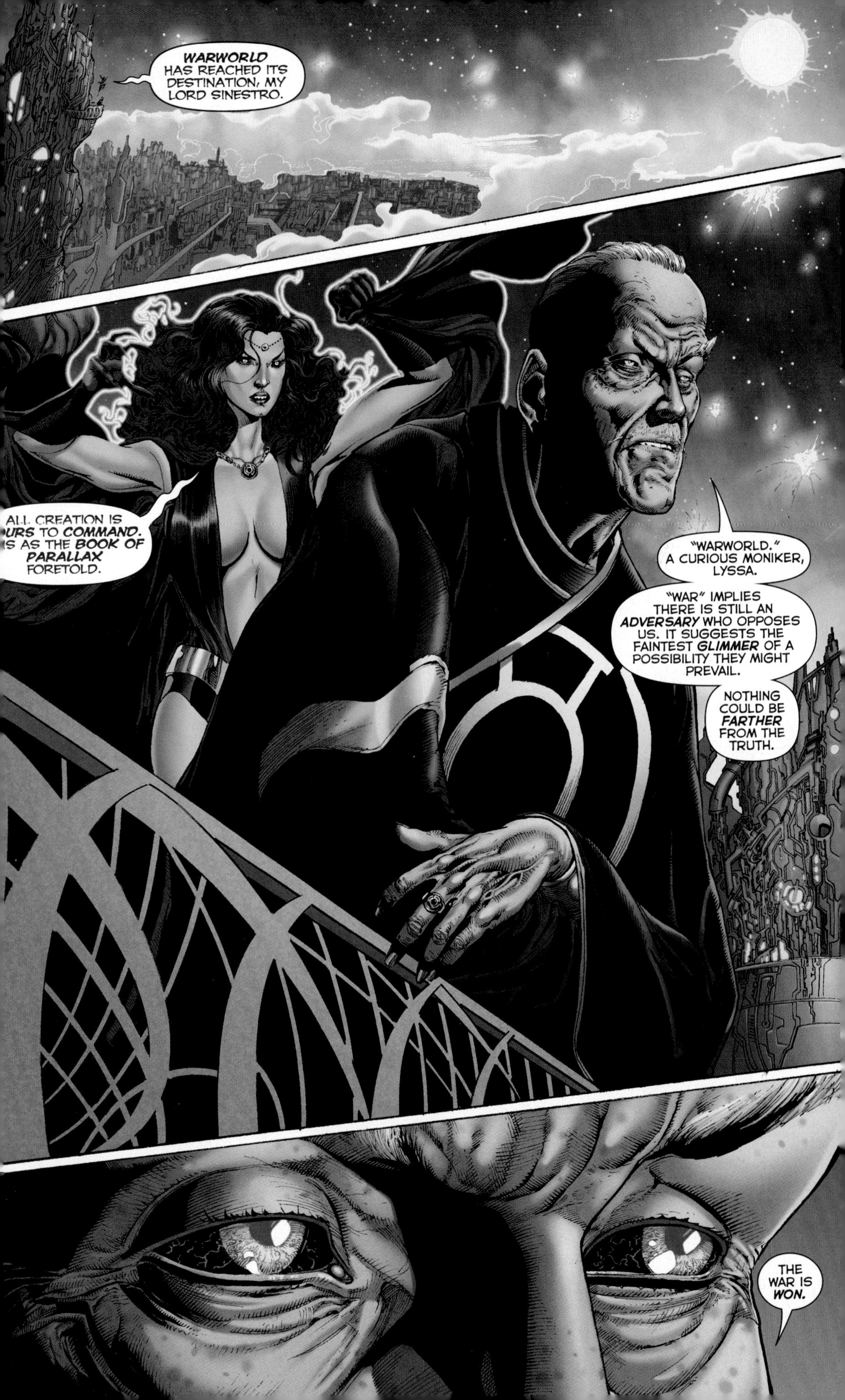
WARWORLD HAS REACHED ITS DESTINATION, MY LORD SINESTRO.
ALL CREATION IS URS TO COMMAND. S AS THE BOOK OF PARALLAX FORETOLD.
"WARWORLD." A CURIOUS MONIKER, LYSSA.
"WAR" IMPLIES THERE IS STILL AN ADVERSARY WHO OPPOSES US. IT SUGGESTS THE FAINTEST GLIMMER OF A POSSIBILITY THEY MIGHT PREVAIL.
NOTHING COULD BE FARTHER FROM THE TRUTH.
THE WAR IS WON.

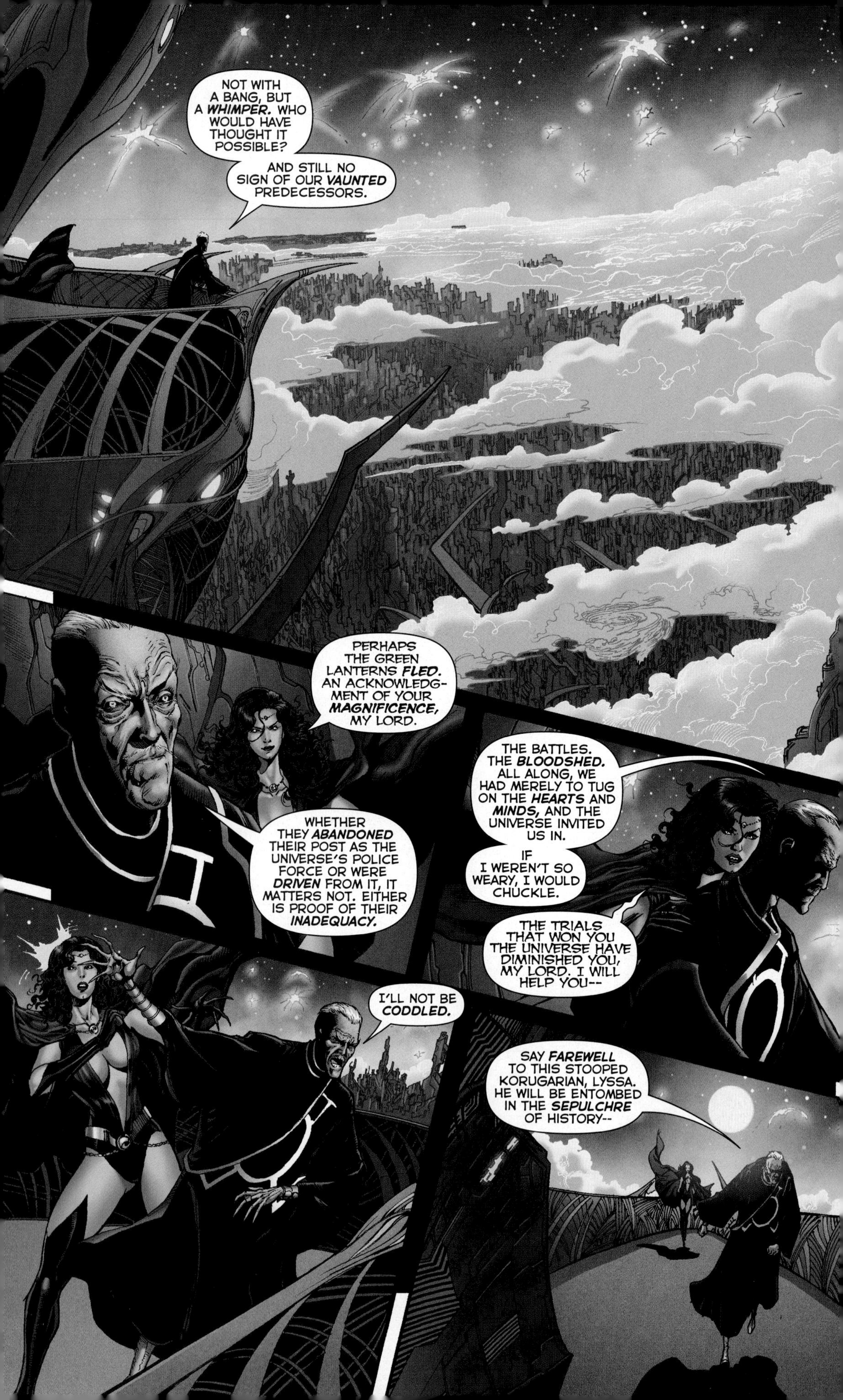
NOT WITH A BANG, BUT A WHIMPER. WHO WOULD HAVE THOUGHT IT POSSIBLE?
AND STILL NO SIGN OF OUR VAUNTED PREDECESSORS.
PERHAPS THE GREEN LANTERNS FLED. AN ACKNOWLEDGMENT OF YOUR MAGNIFICENCE, MY LORD.
WHETHER THEY ABANDONED THEIR POST AS THE UNIVERSE'S POLICE FORCE OR WERE DRIVEN FROM IT, IT MATTERS NOT. EITHER IS PROOF OF THEIR INADEQUACY.
THE BATTLES. THE BLOODSHED. ALL ALONG, WE HAD MERELY TO TUG ON THE HEARTS AND MINDS, AND THE UNIVERSE INVITED US IN.
IF I WEREN'T SO WEARY, I WOULD CHUCKLE.
THE TRIALS THAT WON YOU THE UNIVERSE HAVE DIMINISHED YOU, MY LORD. I WILL HELP YOU--
I'LL NOT BE CODDLED.
SAY FAREWELL TO THIS STOOPED KORUGARIAN, LYSSA. HE WILL BE ENTOMBED IN THE SEPULCHRE OF HISTORY--

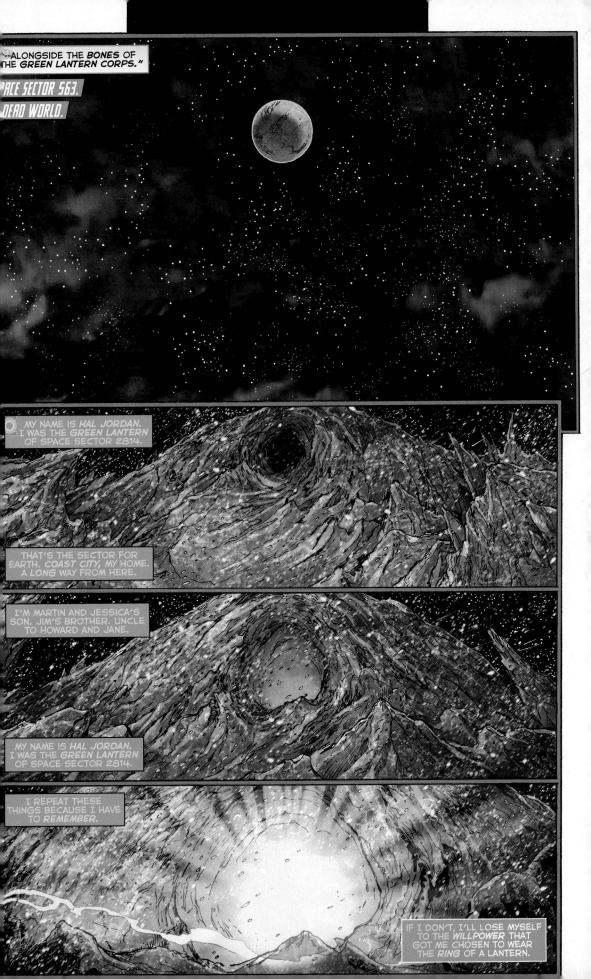

"—ALONGSIDE THE *BONES* OF THE *GREEN LANTERN CORPS.*"

SPACE SECTOR 563.
DEAD WORLD.

MY NAME IS *HAL JORDAN.* I WAS THE *GREEN LANTERN* OF SPACE SECTOR 2814.

THAT'S THE SECTOR FOR EARTH. *COAST CITY,* MY HOME. A *LONG* WAY FROM HERE.

I'M MARTIN AND JESSICA'S SON. JIM'S BROTHER. UNCLE TO HOWARD AND JANE.

MY NAME IS *HAL JORDAN.* I WAS THE *GREEN LANTERN* OF SPACE SECTOR 2814.

I REPEAT THESE THINGS BECAUSE I HAVE TO *REMEMBER.*

IF I DON'T, I'LL LOSE MYSELF TO THE *WILLPOWER* THAT GOT ME CHOSEN TO WEAR THE *RING* OF A LANTERN.

MY DAD WAS A TEST PILOT. MY *HERO.*

WHEN I WAS JUST A KID, HE *CRASHED* AND *DIED* RIGHT IN FRONT OF ME.

I GREW UP AND BECAME A TEST PILOT, TOO.

A GREEN LANTERN NAMED *ABIN SUR* FOUND ME. CRASHED AND DYING, JUST LIKE DAD. HIS LAST ACT WAS TO GIVE ME HIS RING, SO I COULD TAKE HIS PLACE IN THE *GREEN LANTERN CORPS.*

THERE USED TO BE 7200 GREEN LANTERNS. IN TIME, I BECAME THEIR LEADER.

BUT WE WERE IN TROUBLE. *MISTRUSTED* AND *HATED* BY THE UNIVERSE WE'D SWORN TO PROTECT.

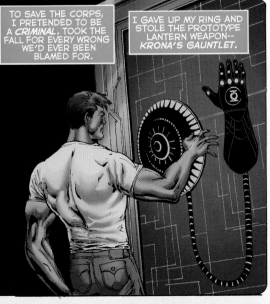

TO SAVE THE CORPS, I PRETENDED TO BE A *CRIMINAL.* TOOK THE FALL FOR EVERY WRONG WE'D EVER BEEN BLAMED FOR.

I GAVE UP MY RING AND STOLE THE PROTOTYPE LANTERN WEAPON-- *KRONA'S GAUNTLET.*

THEN I RAN...

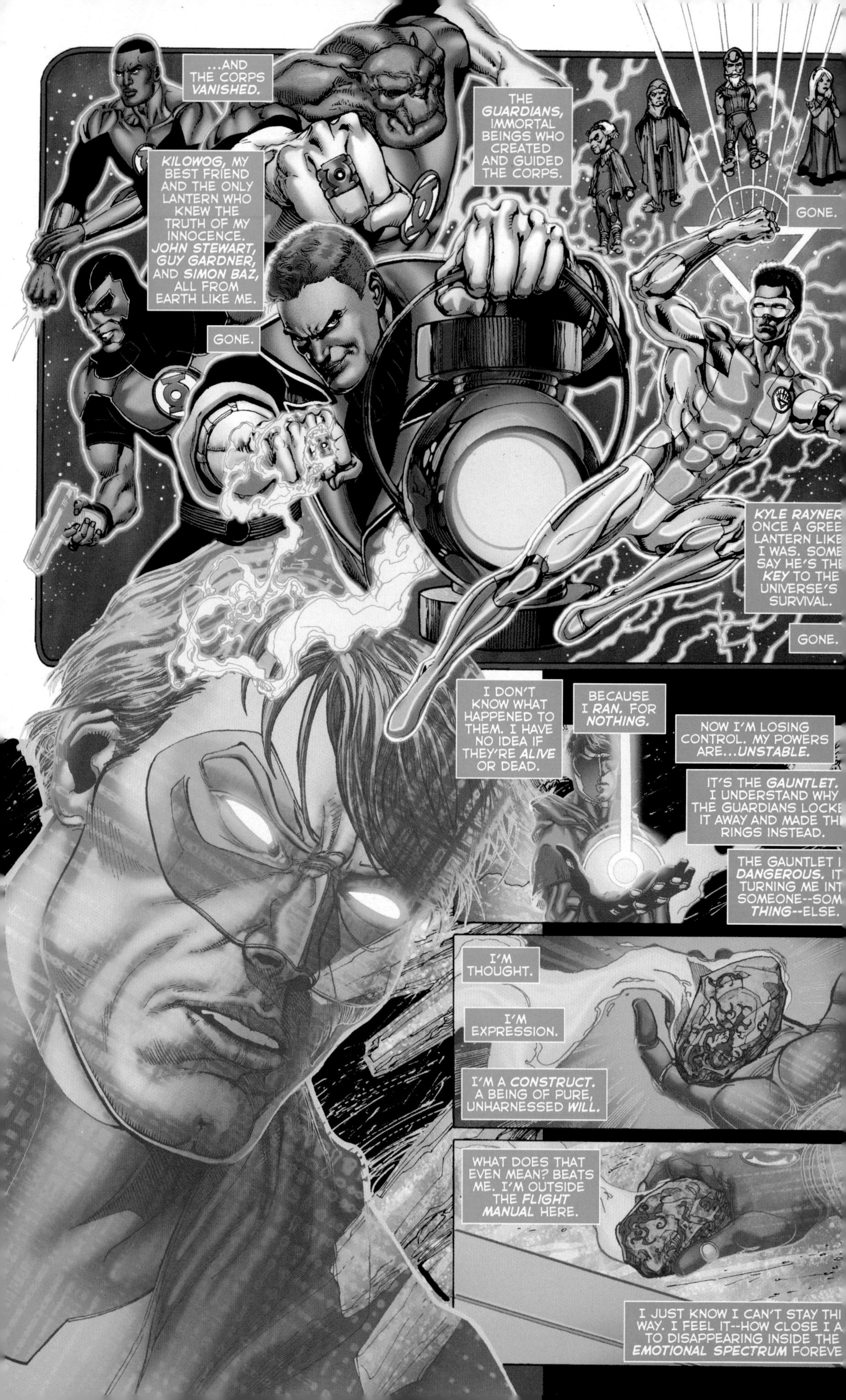
...AND THE CORPS VANISHED.
KILOWOG, MY BEST FRIEND AND THE ONLY LANTERN WHO KNEW THE TRUTH OF MY INNOCENCE. JOHN STEWART, GUY GARDNER, AND SIMON BAZ, ALL FROM EARTH LIKE ME.
GONE.
THE GUARDIANS, IMMORTAL BEINGS WHO CREATED AND GUIDED THE CORPS.
GONE.
KYLE RAYNER ONCE A GREE LANTERN LIKE I WAS. SOME SAY HE'S THE KEY TO THE UNIVERSE'S SURVIVAL.
GONE.
I DON'T KNOW WHAT HAPPENED TO THEM. I HAVE NO IDEA IF THEY'RE ALIVE OR DEAD.
BECAUSE I RAN. FOR NOTHING.
NOW I'M LOSING CONTROL. MY POWERS ARE...UNSTABLE.
IT'S THE GAUNTLET. I UNDERSTAND WHY THE GUARDIANS LOCKE IT AWAY AND MADE TH RINGS INSTEAD.
THE GAUNTLET I DANGEROUS. IT TURNING ME INT SOMEONE--SOM THING--ELSE.
I'M THOUGHT.
I'M EXPRESSION.
I'M A CONSTRUCT. A BEING OF PURE, UNHARNESSED WILL.
WHAT DOES THAT EVEN MEAN? BEATS ME. I'M OUTSIDE THE FLIGHT MANUAL HERE.
I JUST KNOW I CAN'T STAY THI WAY. I FEEL IT--HOW CLOSE I A TO DISAPPEARING INSIDE THE EMOTIONAL SPECTRUM FOREVE

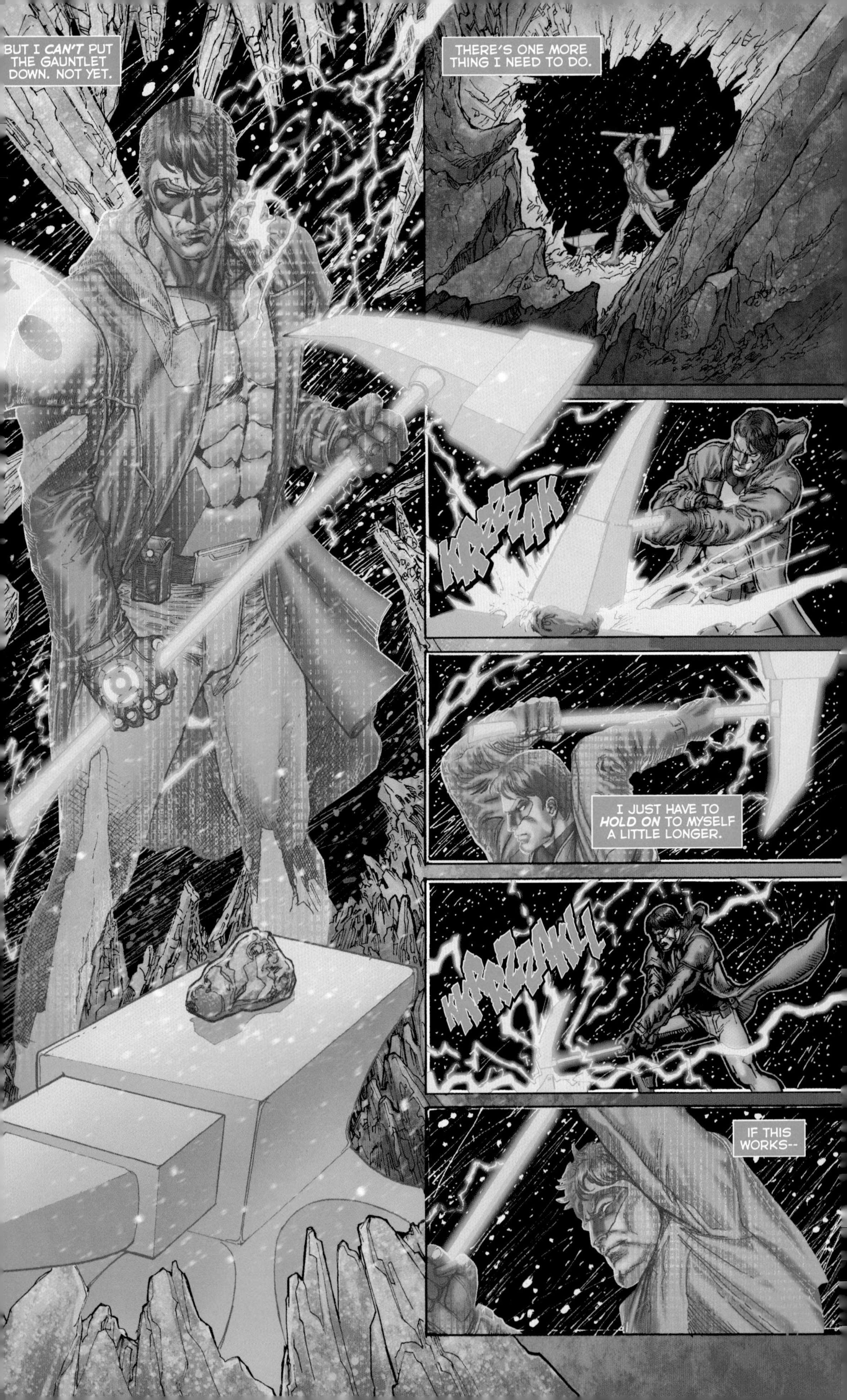
BUT I *CAN'T* PUT THE GAUNTLET DOWN. NOT YET.
THERE'S ONE MORE THING I NEED TO DO.
KRRZZAK
I JUST HAVE TO *HOLD ON* TO MYSELF A LITTLE LONGER.
KKRRZZAKK!
IF THIS WORKS--

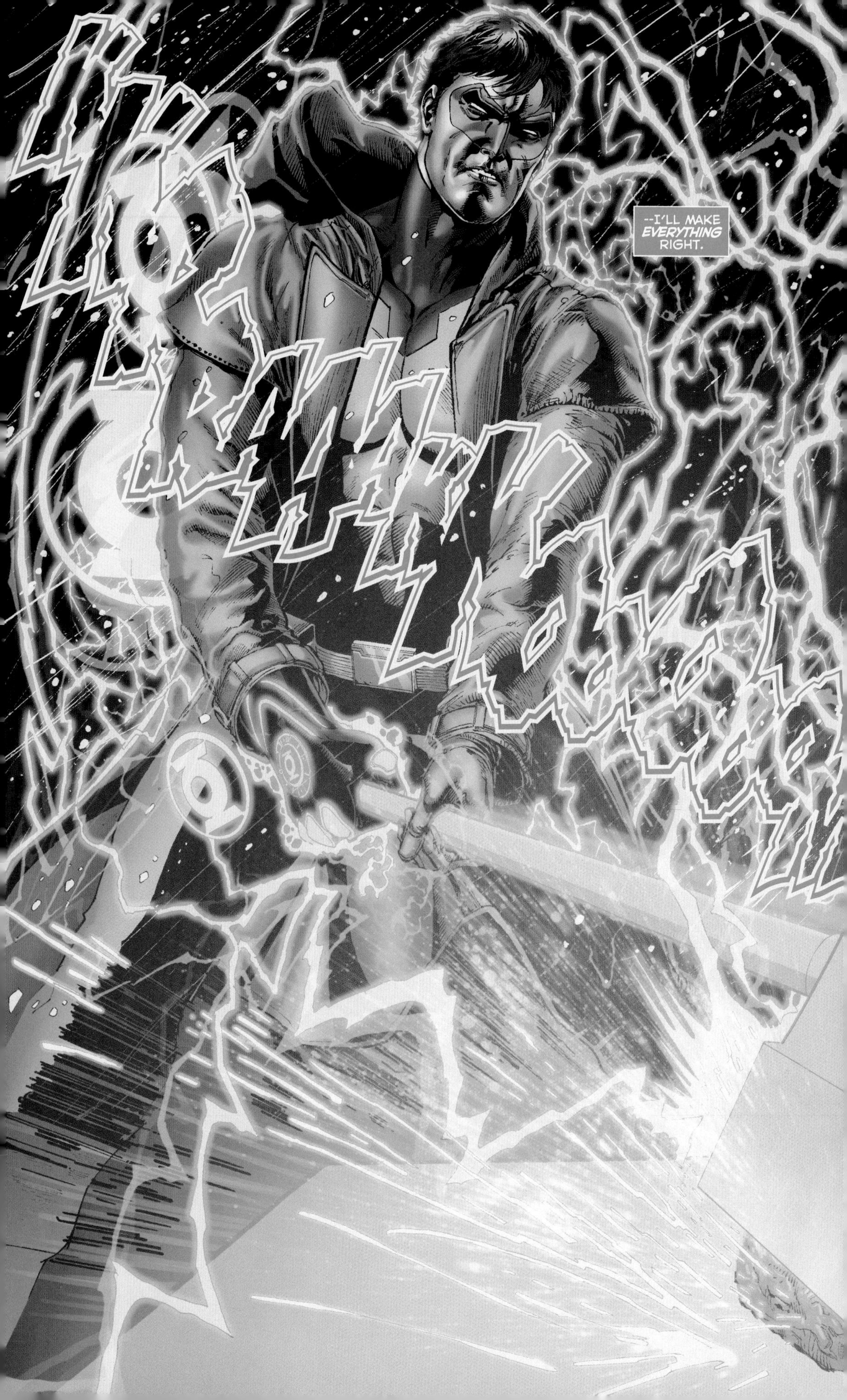
--I'LL MAKE *EVERYTHING* RIGHT.

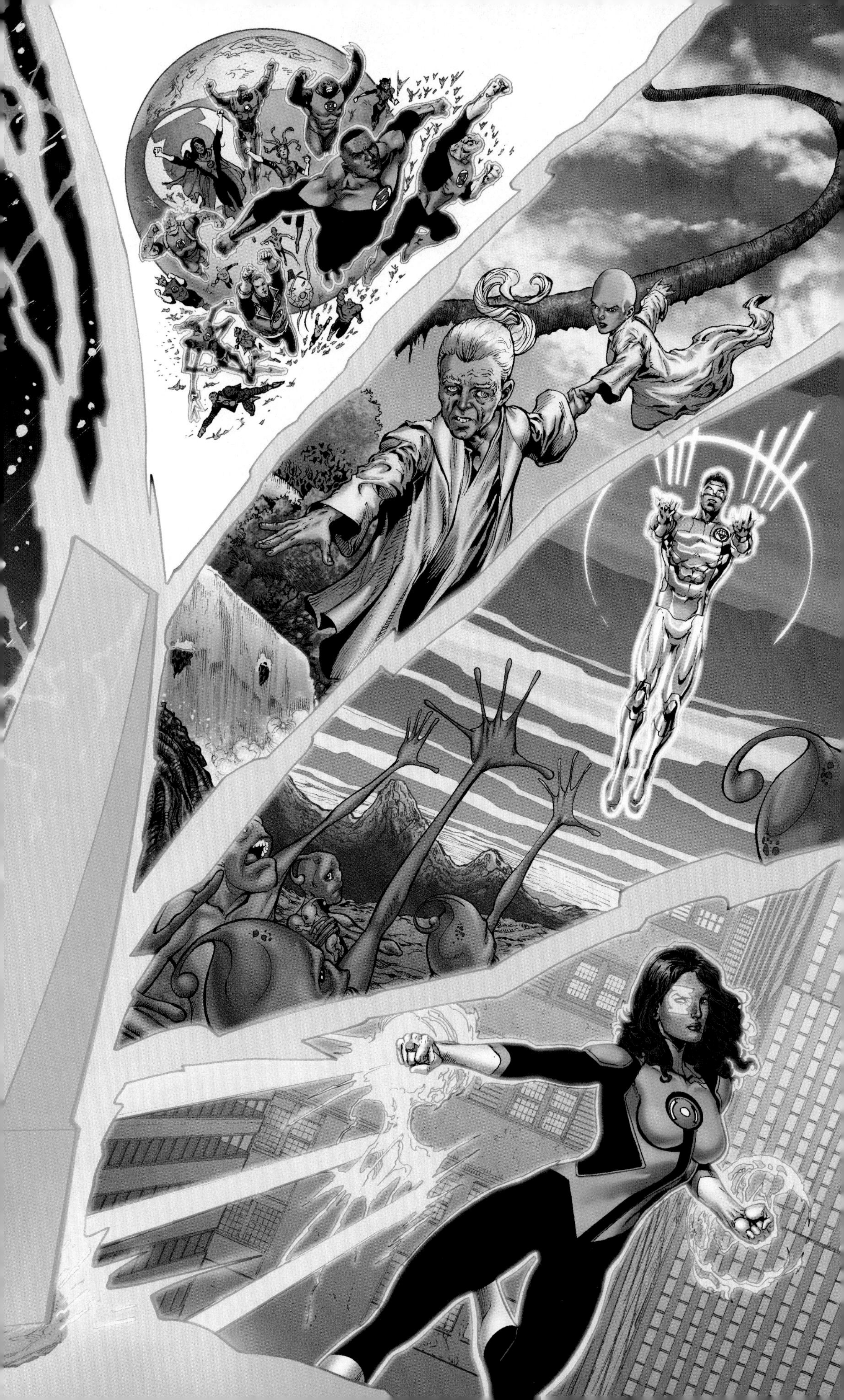

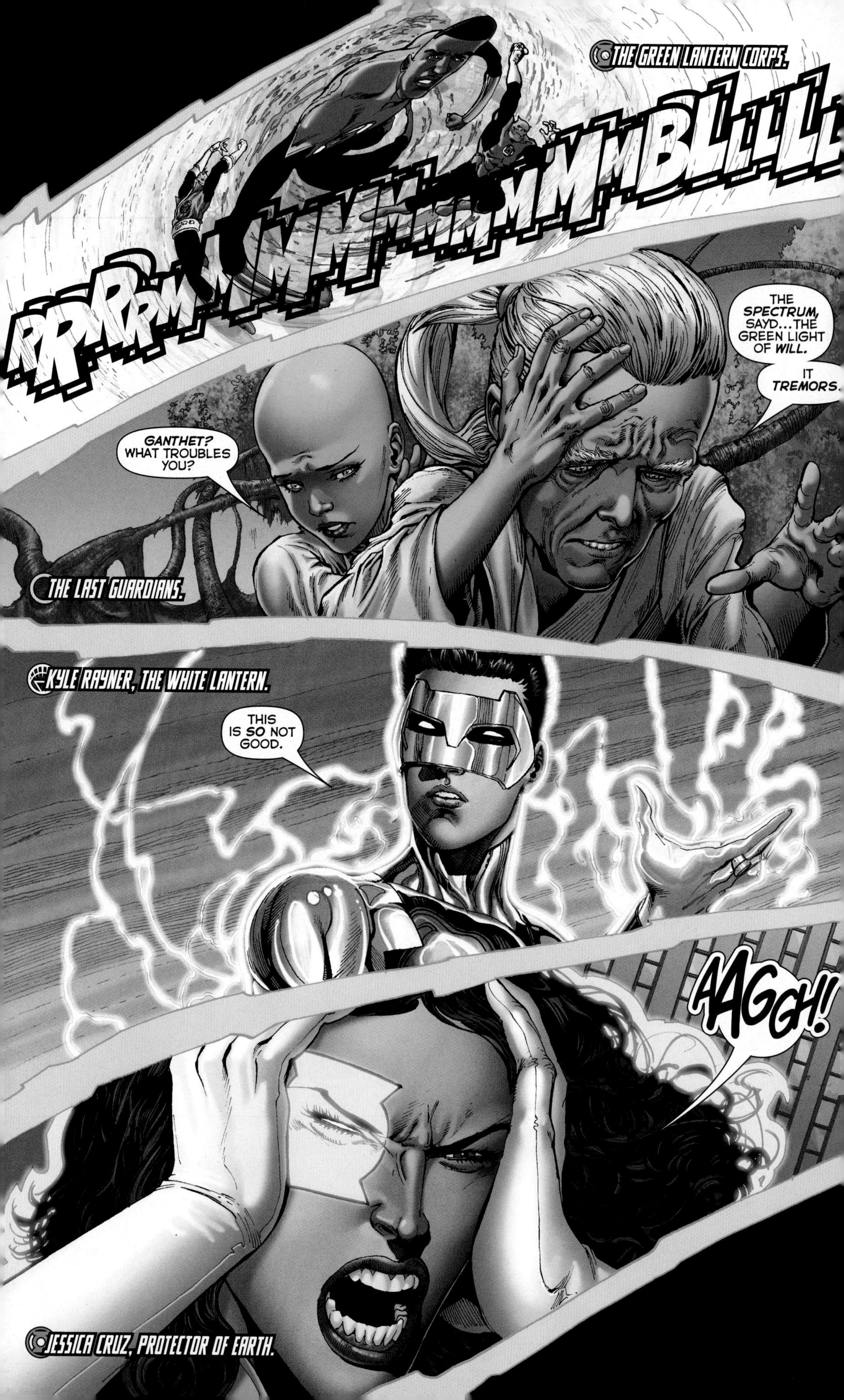

THE GREEN LANTERN CORPS.
RRRRMMMMMMMMMMBLLLL
THE SPECTRUM, SAYD...THE GREEN LIGHT OF WILL.
IT TREMORS.
GANTHET? WHAT TROUBLES YOU?
THE LAST GUARDIANS.
KYLE RAYNER, THE WHITE LANTERN.
THIS IS SO NOT GOOD.
AAGGH!
JESSICA CRUZ, PROTECTOR OF EARTH.

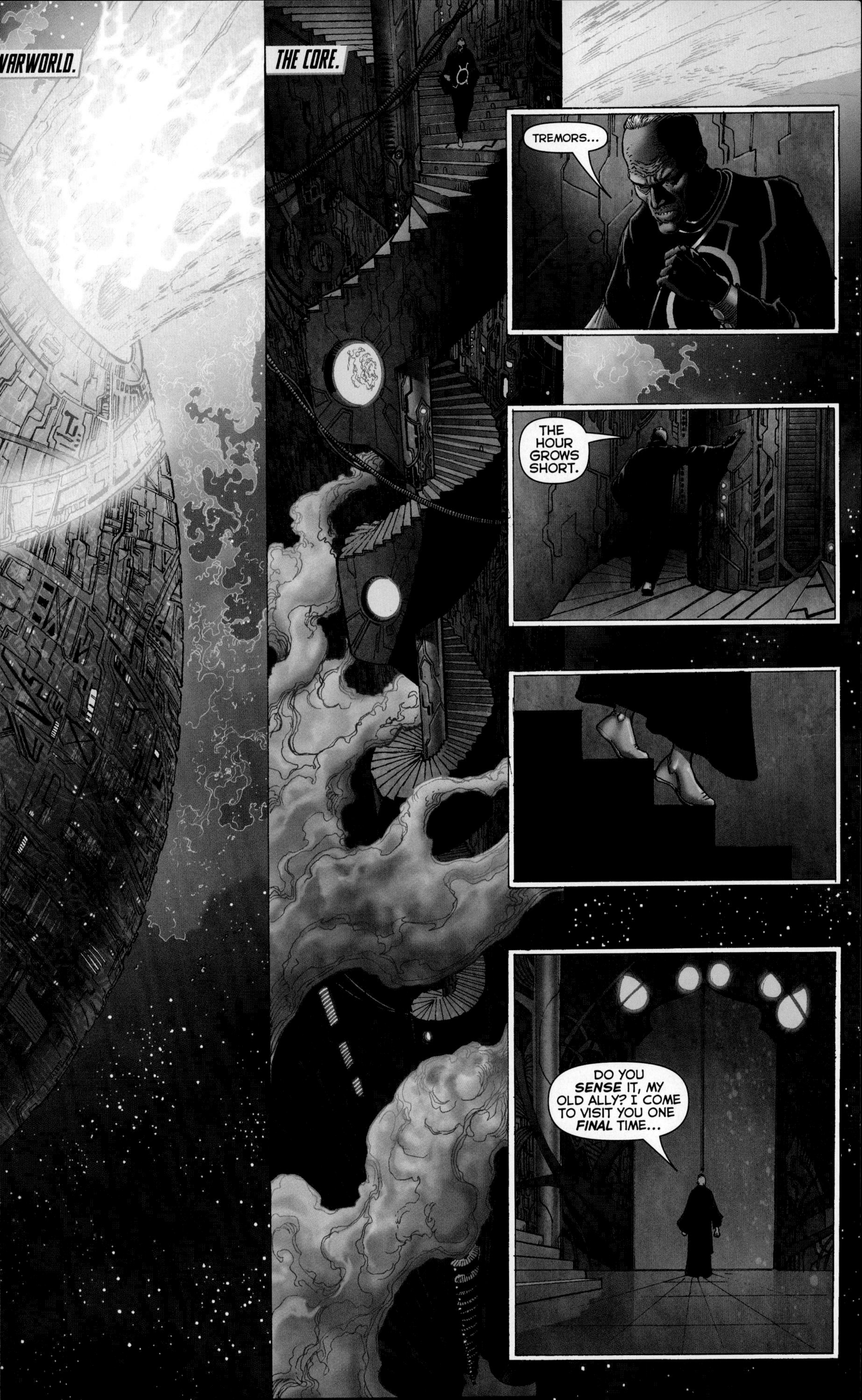
WARWORLD.
THE CORE.
TREMORS...
THE HOUR GROWS SHORT.
DO YOU SENSE IT, MY OLD ALLY? I COME TO VISIT YOU ONE FINAL TIME...

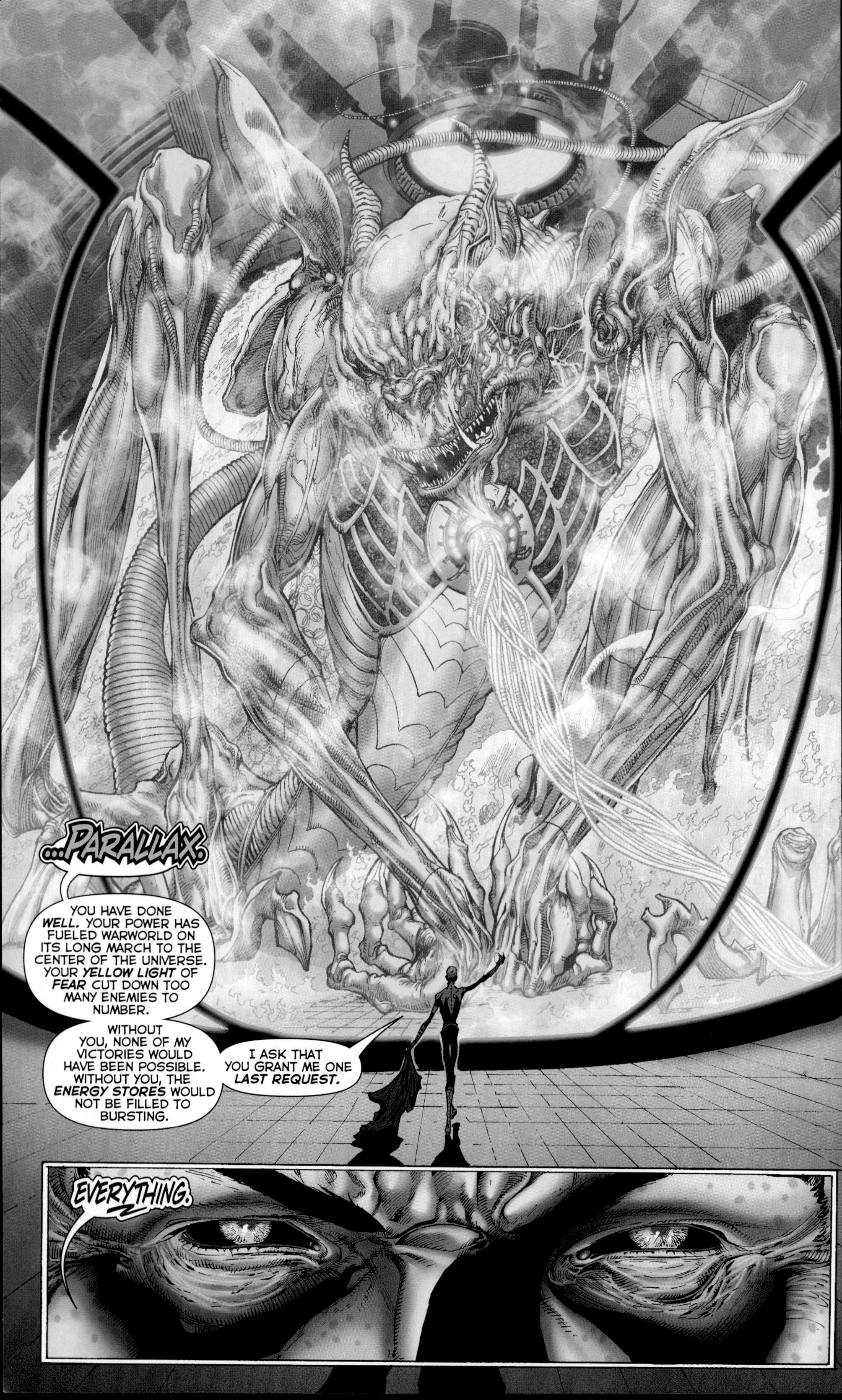
...PARALLAX.
YOU HAVE DONE WELL. YOUR POWER HAS FUELED WARWORLD ON ITS LONG MARCH TO THE CENTER OF THE UNIVERSE. YOUR YELLOW LIGHT OF FEAR CUT DOWN TOO MANY ENEMIES TO NUMBER.
WITHOUT YOU, NONE OF MY VICTORIES WOULD HAVE BEEN POSSIBLE. WITHOUT YOU, THE ENERGY STORES WOULD NOT BE FILLED TO BURSTING.
I ASK THAT YOU GRANT ME ONE LAST REQUEST.
EVERYTHING.

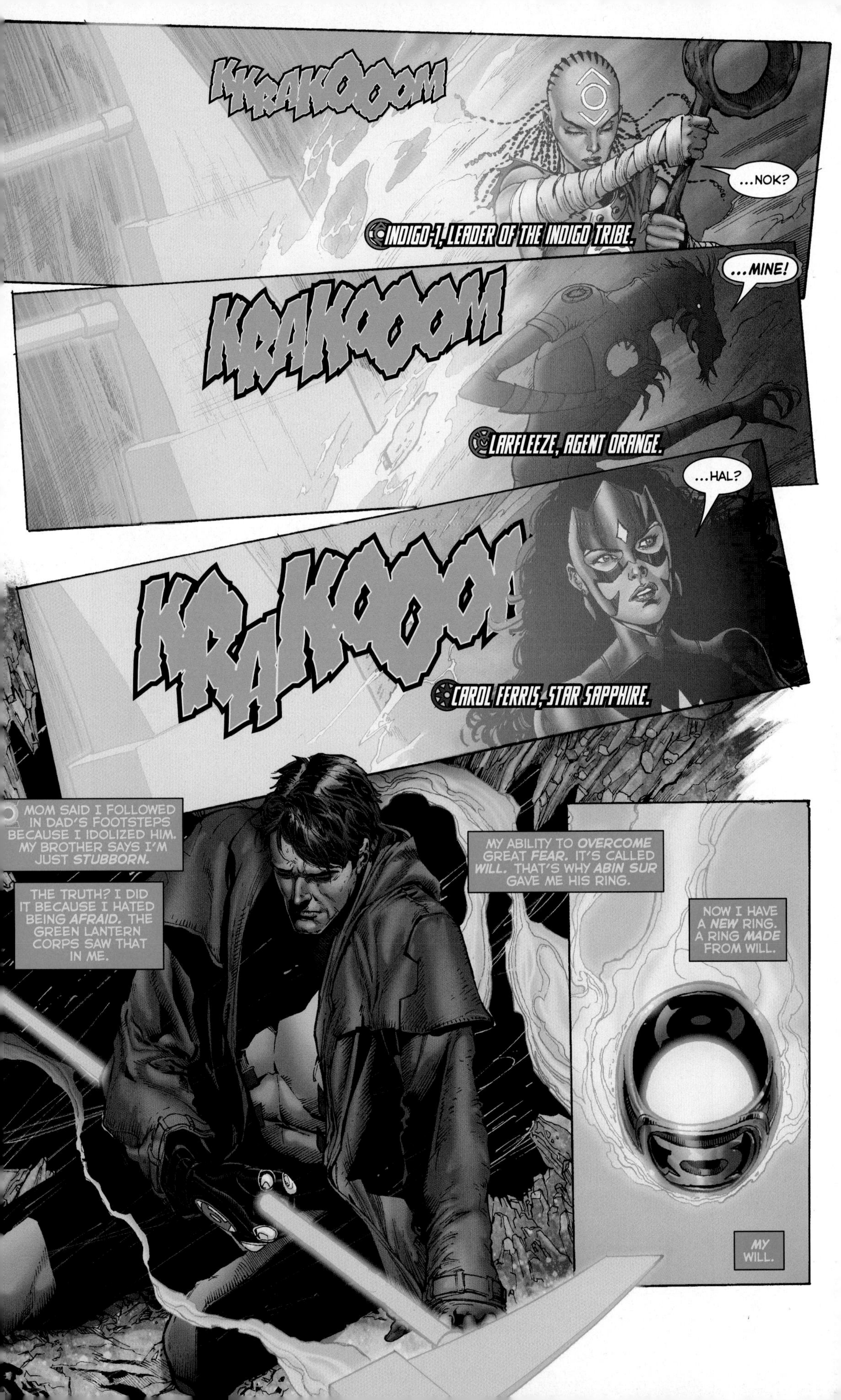
KKRAKOOOM
...NOK?
INDIGO-1, LEADER OF THE INDIGO TRIBE.
...MINE!
KRAKOOOM
LARFLEEZE, AGENT ORANGE.
...HAL?
KRAKOOOM
CAROL FERRIS, STAR SAPPHIRE.
MOM SAID I FOLLOWED IN DAD'S FOOTSTEPS BECAUSE I IDOLIZED HIM. MY BROTHER SAYS I'M JUST STUBBORN.
THE TRUTH? I DID IT BECAUSE I HATED BEING AFRAID. THE GREEN LANTERN CORPS SAW THAT IN ME.
MY ABILITY TO OVERCOME GREAT FEAR. IT'S CALLED WILL. THAT'S WHY ABIN SUR GAVE ME HIS RING.
NOW I HAVE A NEW RING. A RING MADE FROM WILL.
MY WILL.

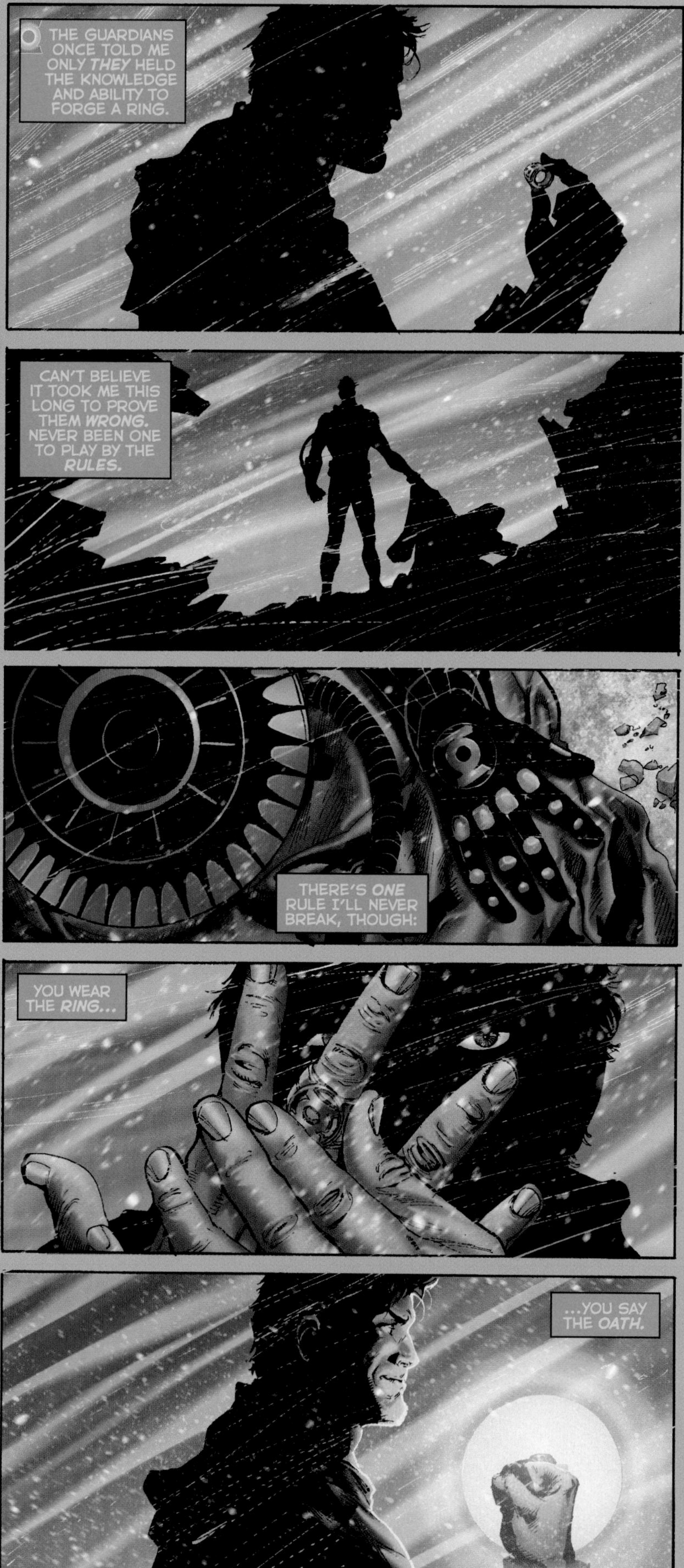
THE GUARDIANS ONCE TOLD ME ONLY *THEY* HELD THE KNOWLEDGE AND ABILITY TO FORGE A RING.
CAN'T BELIEVE IT TOOK ME THIS LONG TO PROVE THEM *WRONG.* NEVER BEEN ONE TO PLAY BY THE *RULES.*
THERE'S *ONE* RULE I'LL NEVER BREAK, THOUGH:
YOU WEAR THE *RING...*
...YOU SAY THE *OATH.*

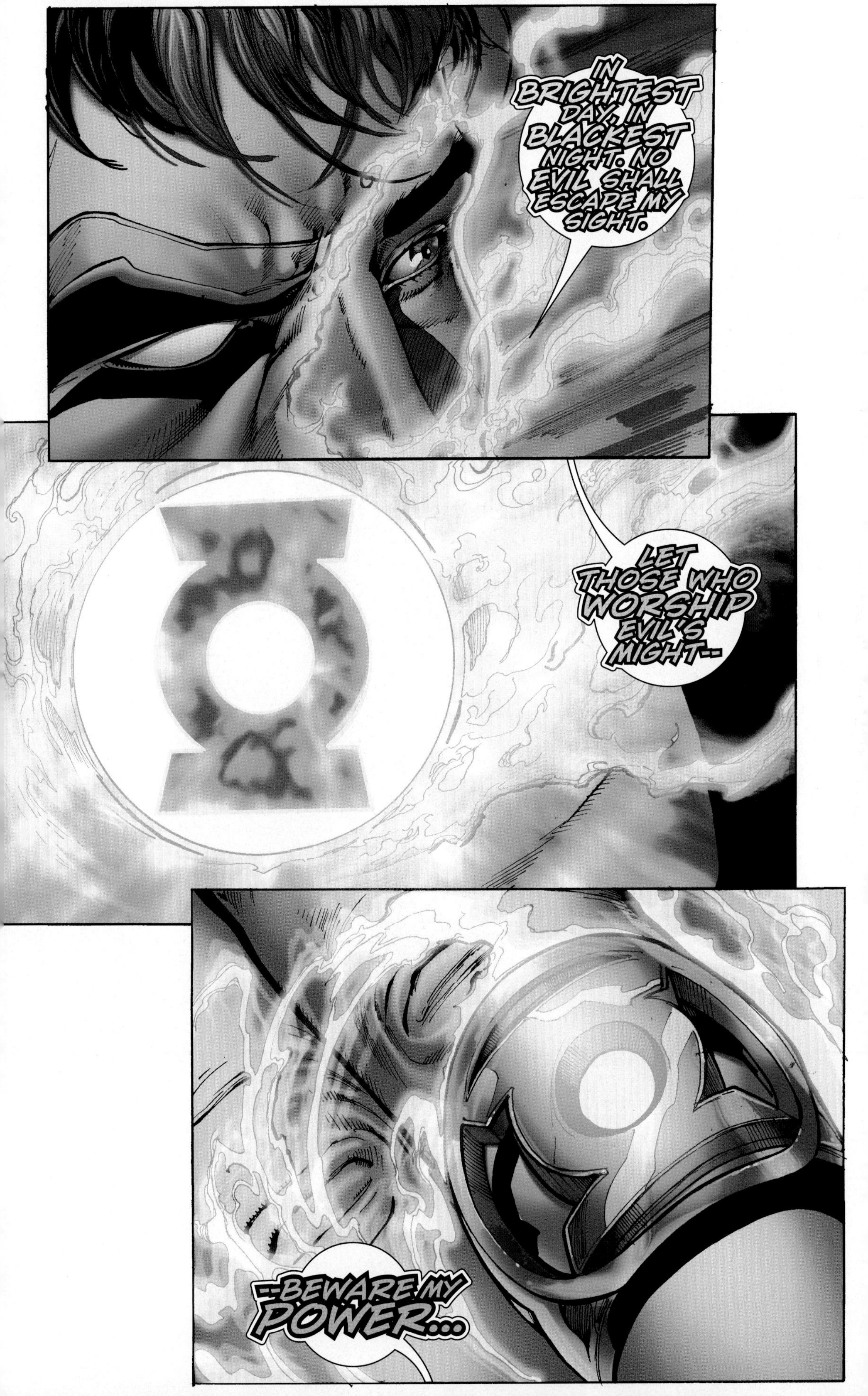
IN BRIGHTEST DAY, IN BLACKEST NIGHT. NO EVIL SHALL ESCAPE MY SIGHT.
LET THOSE WHO WORSHIP EVIL'S MIGHT--
--BEWARE MY POWER...

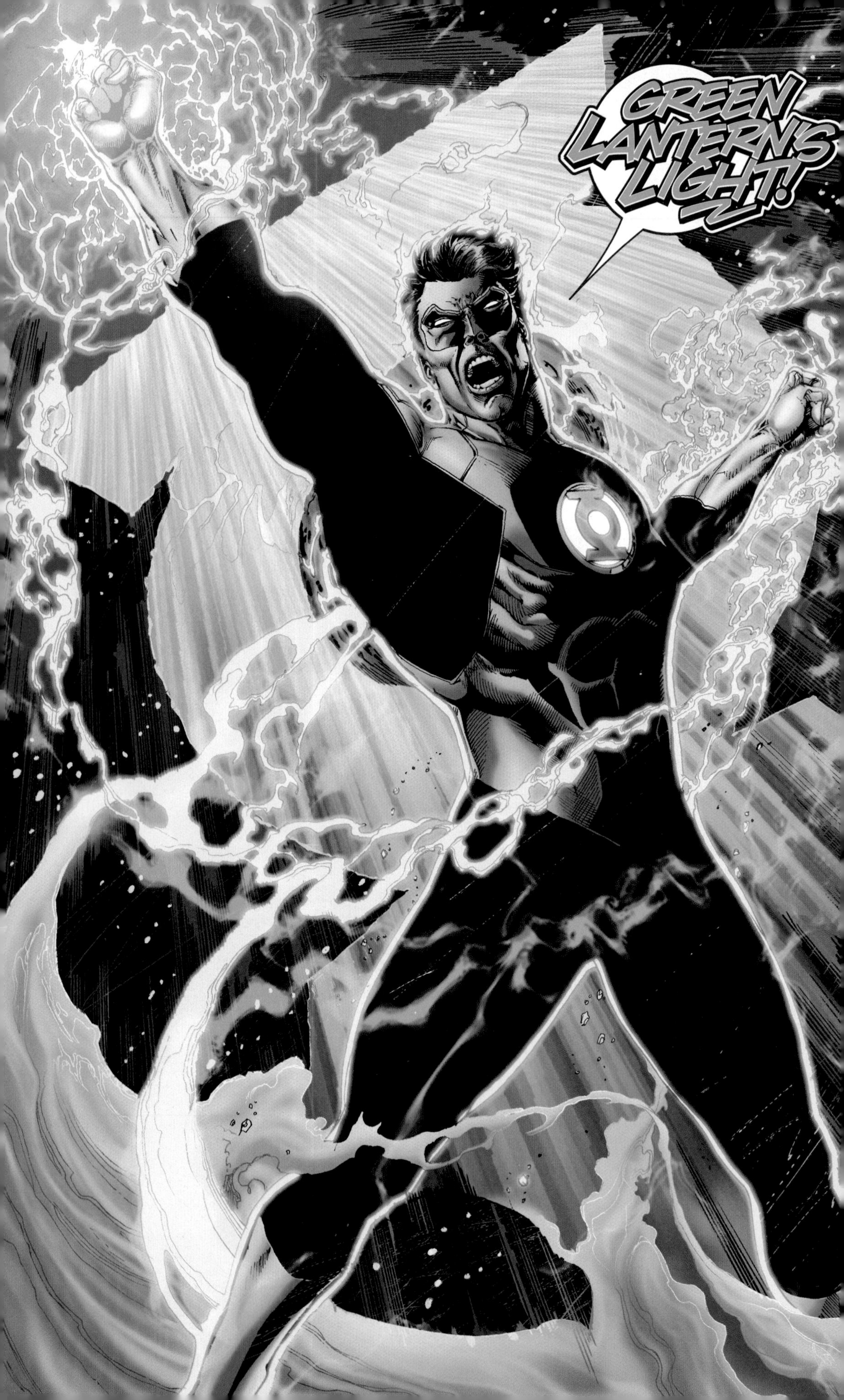
GREEN LANTERN'S LIGHT!

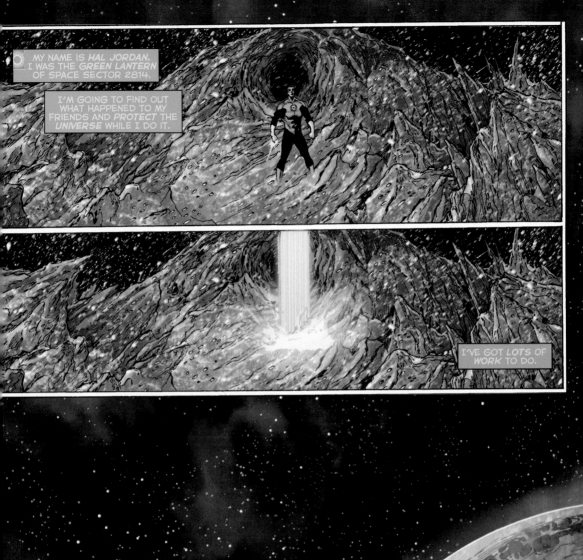

MY NAME IS *HAL JORDAN*. I WAS THE *GREEN LANTERN* OF SPACE SECTOR 2814.

I'M GOING TO FIND OUT WHAT HAPPENED TO MY FRIENDS AND *PROTECT* THE *UNIVERSE* WHILE I DO IT.

I'VE GOT *LOTS* OF *WORK* TO DO.

THE *GOOD* WILL SEE THE GREEN LANTERN SYMBOL AND KNOW THERE'S STILL SOMEONE WITH THE *WILL* TO FIGHT FOR THEM.

THE *BAD* WILL SEE IT AND *RUN*.

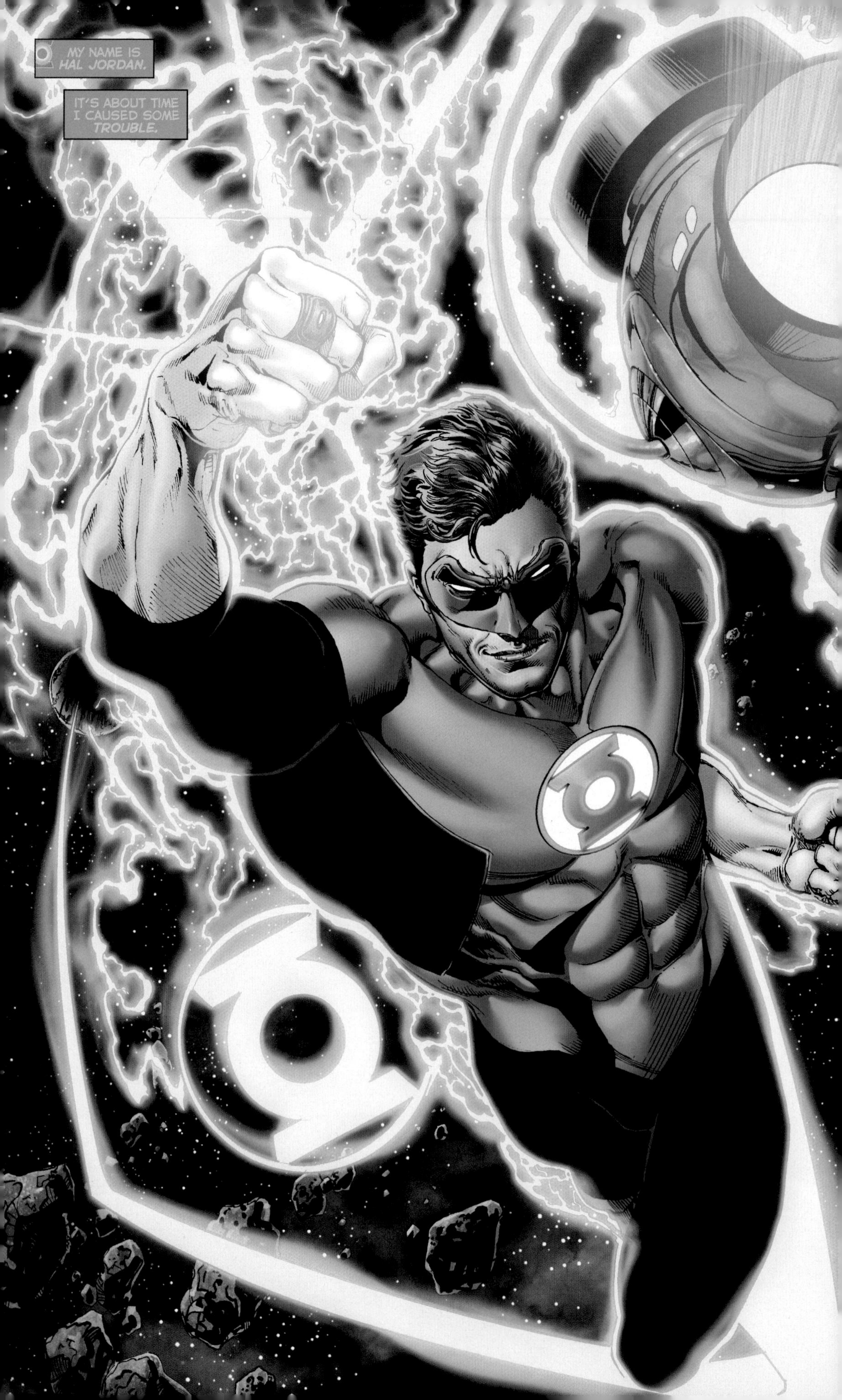
MY NAME IS HAL JORDAN.
IT'S ABOUT TIME I CAUSED SOME TROUBLE.

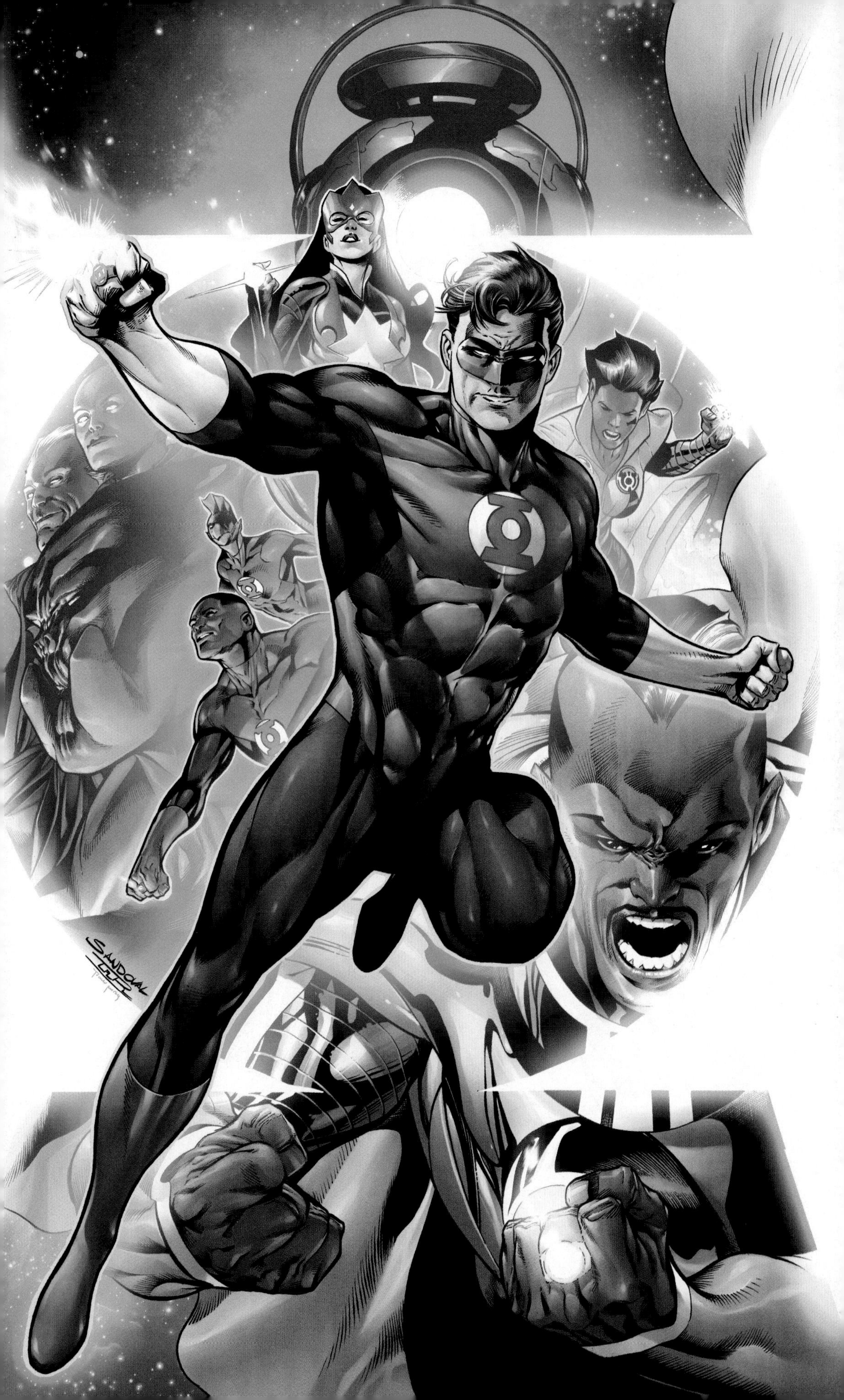
SANDOVAL

SINESTRO'S LAW PART 1: THE LAST LANTERN

RAFA SANDOVAL penciller * **JORDI TARRAGONA** inker * **TOMEU MOREY** colorist
RAFA SANDOVAL, JORDI TARRAGONA and **TOMEU MOREY** cover artists

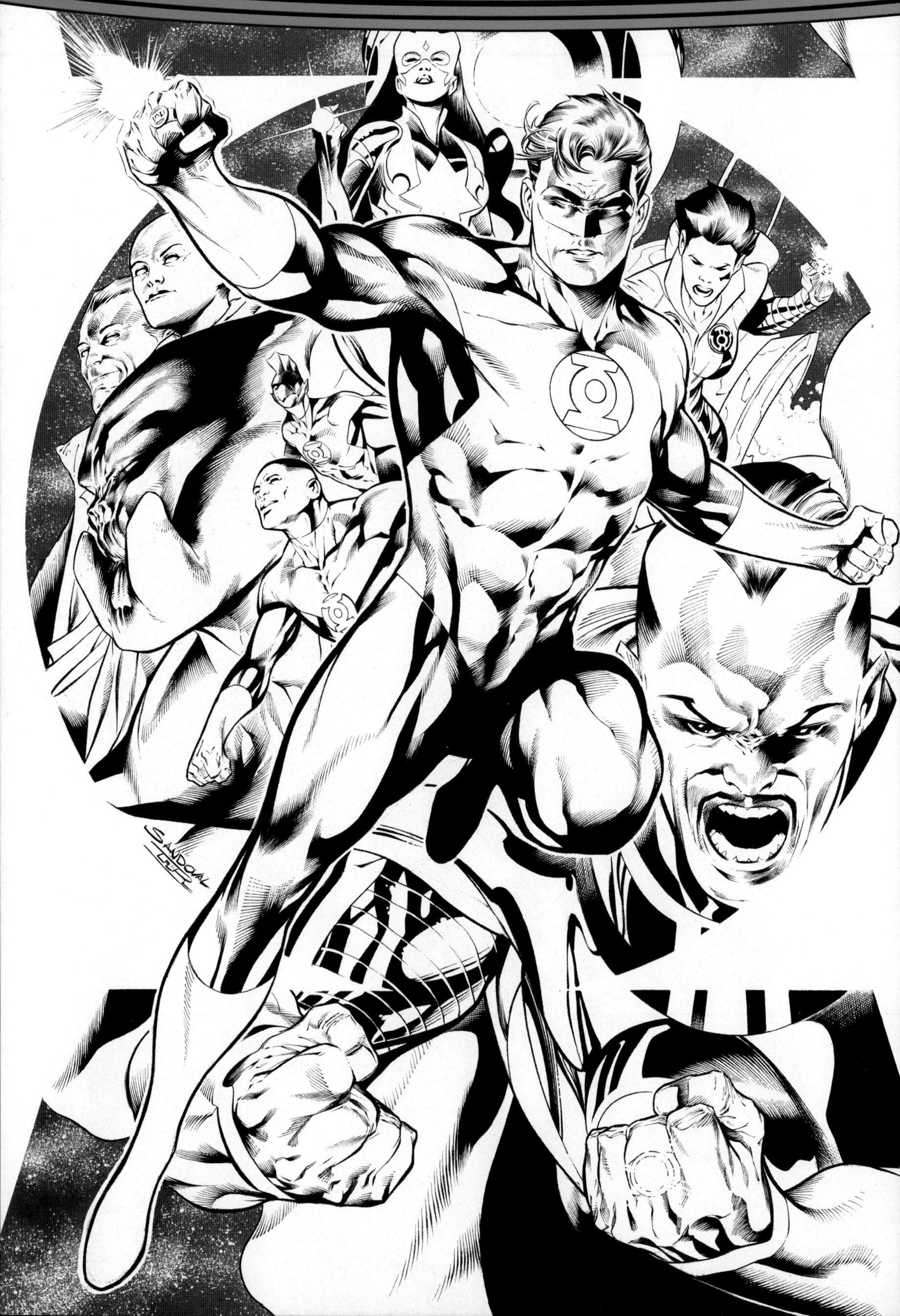

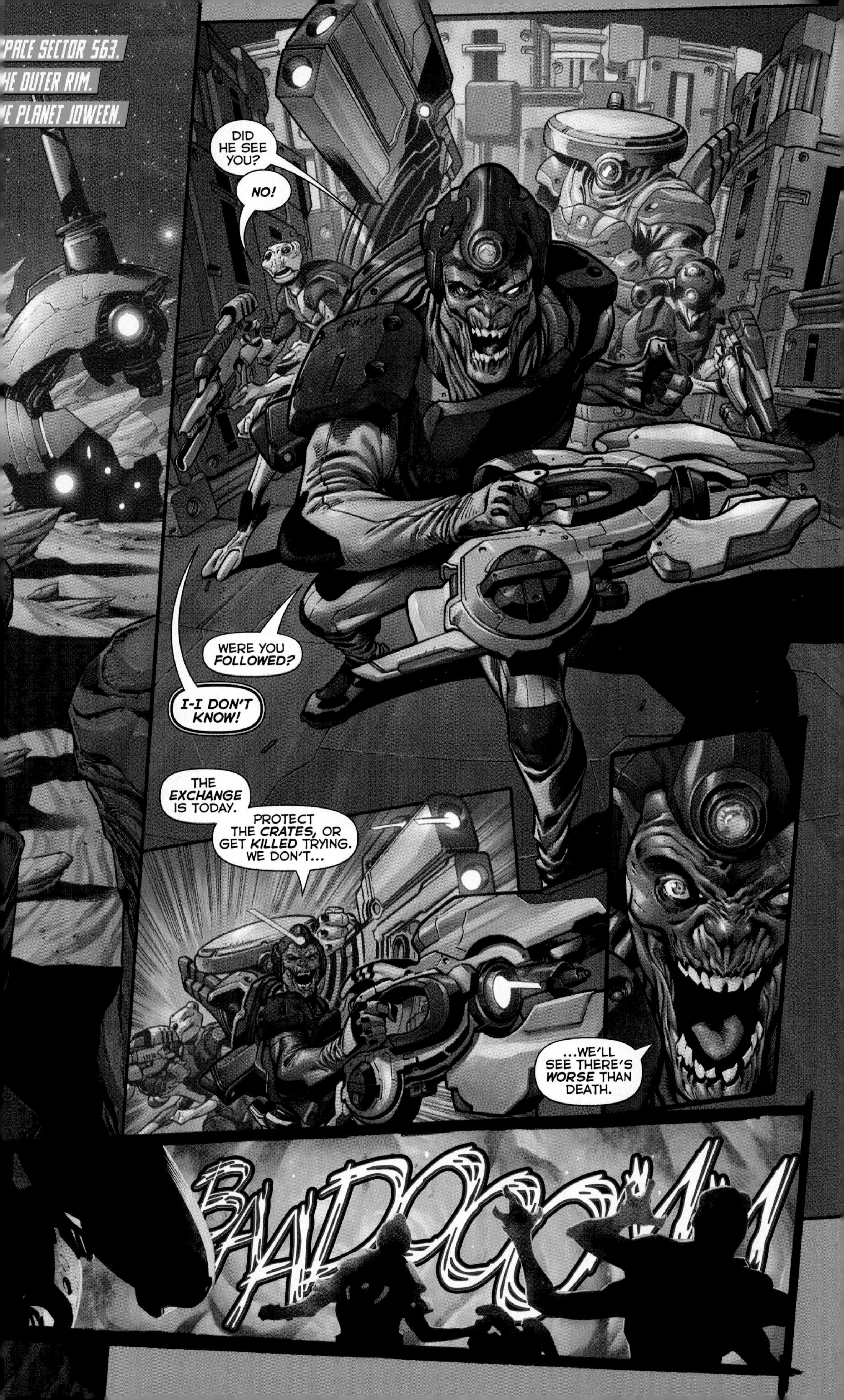
PACE SECTOR 563.
HE OUTER RIM.
E PLANET JOWEEN.
DID HE SEE YOU?
NO!
WERE YOU FOLLOWED?
I-I DON'T KNOW!
THE EXCHANGE IS TODAY.
PROTECT THE CRATES, OR GET KILLED TRYING. WE DON'T...
...WE'LL SEE THERE'S WORSE THAN DEATH.
BAADOOOM

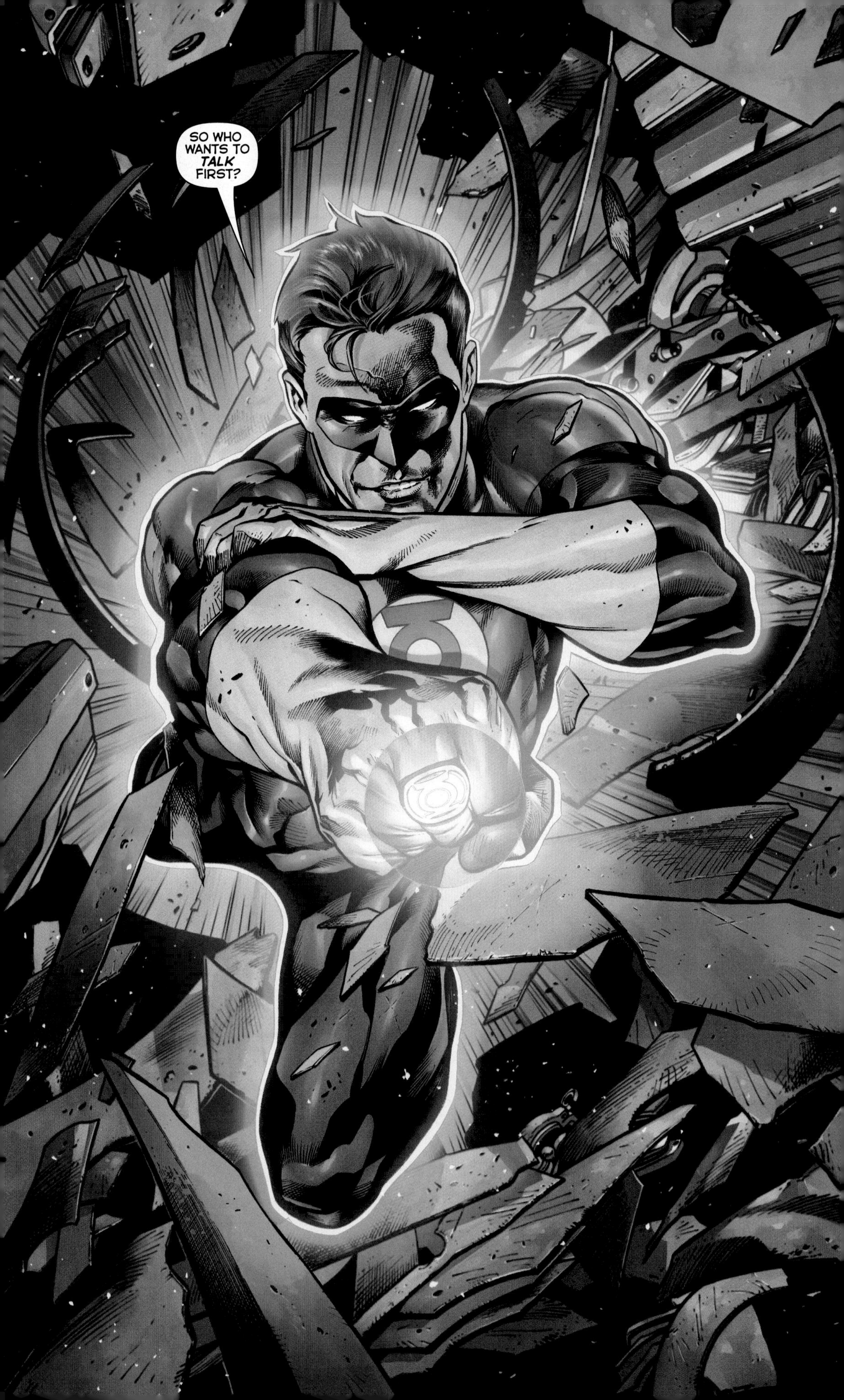
SO WHO WANTS TO *TALK* FIRST?

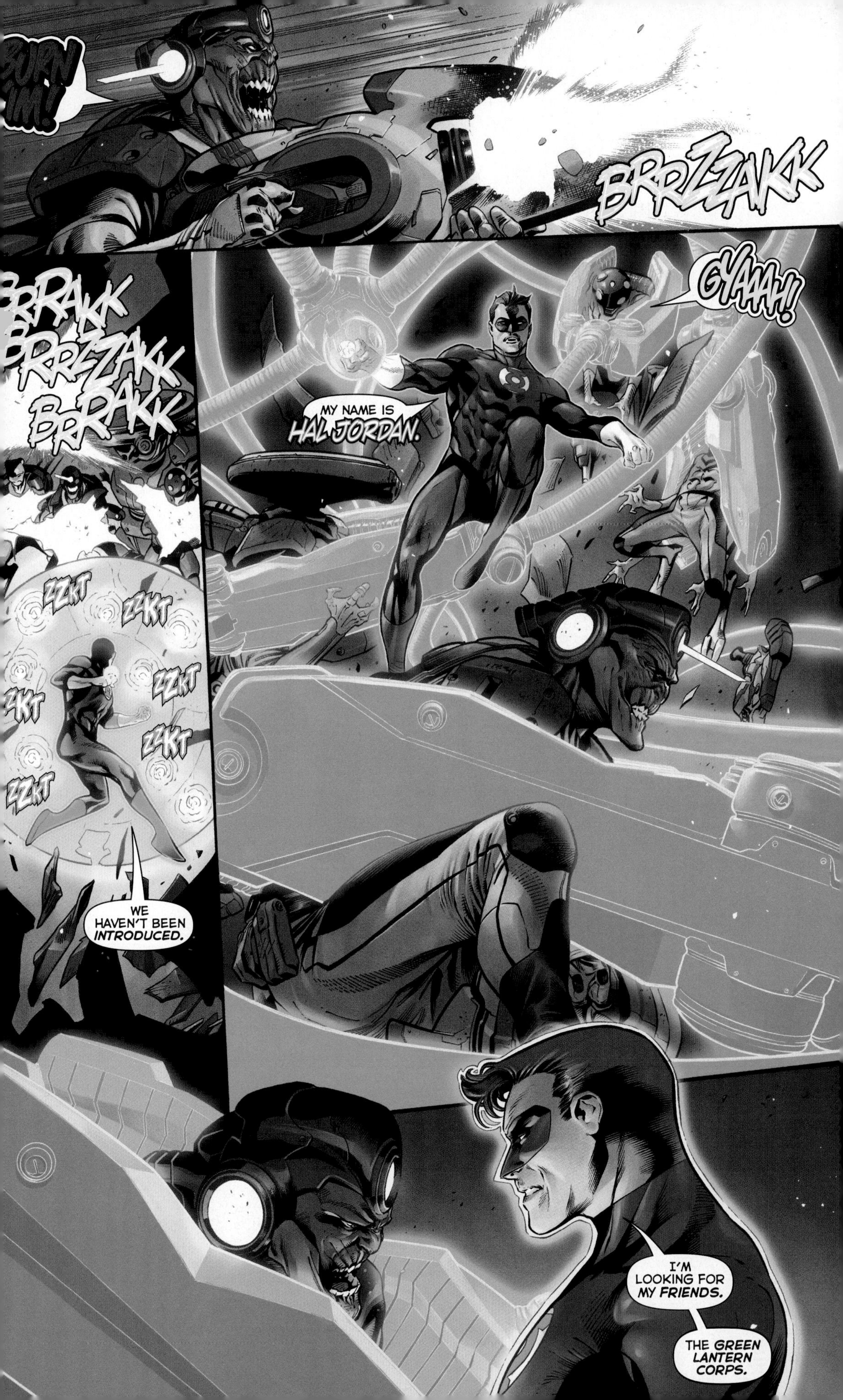
BURN HIM!
BRRZZAKK
BRRAKK
BRRZZAKK
BRRAKK
GYAAAH!
MY NAME IS HAL JORDAN.
ZZKT
ZZKT
ZZKT
ZZKT
ZZKT
ZZKT
WE HAVEN'T BEEN INTRODUCED.
I'M LOOKING FOR MY FRIENDS.
THE GREEN LANTERN CORPS.

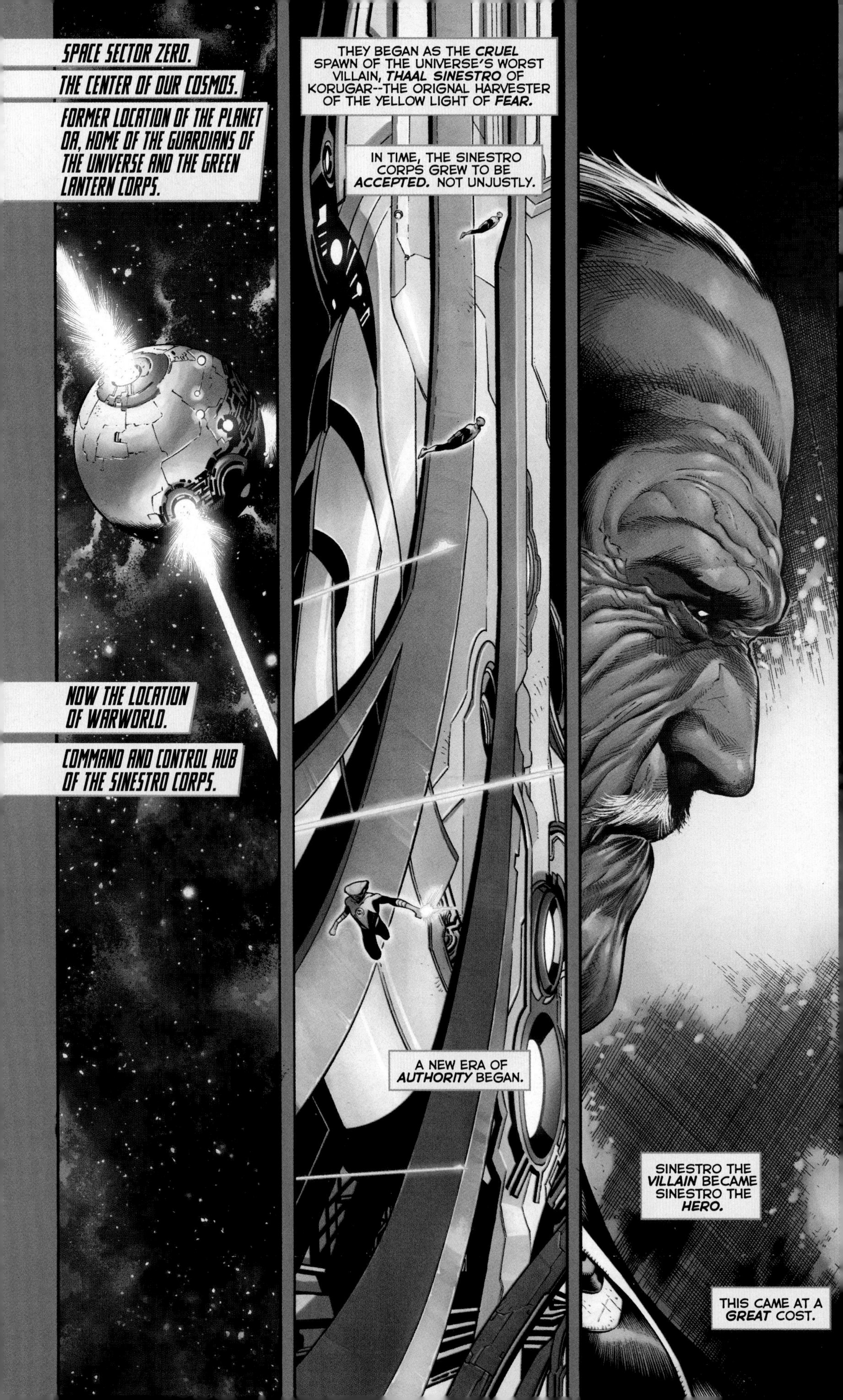
SPACE SECTOR ZERO.
THE CENTER OF OUR COSMOS.
FORMER LOCATION OF THE PLANET OA, HOME OF THE GUARDIANS OF THE UNIVERSE AND THE GREEN LANTERN CORPS.
NOW THE LOCATION OF WARWORLD.
COMMAND AND CONTROL HUB OF THE SINESTRO CORPS.
THEY BEGAN AS THE CRUEL SPAWN OF THE UNIVERSE'S WORST VILLAIN, THAAL SINESTRO OF KORUGAR--THE ORIGNAL HARVESTER OF THE YELLOW LIGHT OF FEAR.
IN TIME, THE SINESTRO CORPS GREW TO BE ACCEPTED. NOT UNJUSTLY.
A NEW ERA OF AUTHORITY BEGAN.
SINESTRO THE VILLAIN BECAME SINESTRO THE HERO.
THIS CAME AT A GREAT COST.

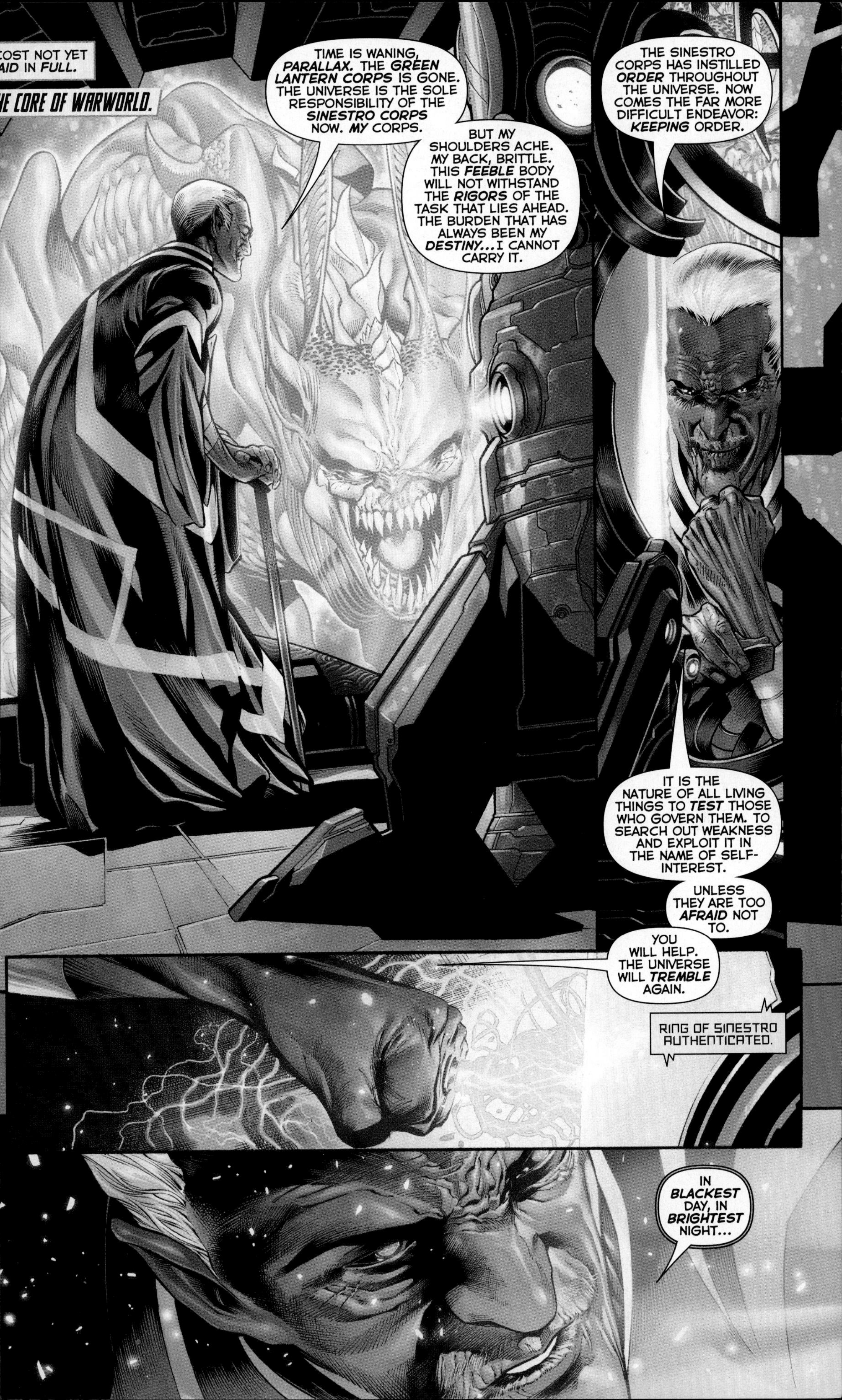

COST NOT YET
AID IN FULL.
HE CORE OF WARWORLD.
TIME IS WANING, PARALLAX. THE GREEN LANTERN CORPS IS GONE. THE UNIVERSE IS THE SOLE RESPONSIBILITY OF THE SINESTRO CORPS NOW. MY CORPS.
BUT MY SHOULDERS ACHE. MY BACK, BRITTLE. THIS FEEBLE BODY WILL NOT WITHSTAND THE RIGORS OF THE TASK THAT LIES AHEAD. THE BURDEN THAT HAS ALWAYS BEEN MY DESTINY...I CANNOT CARRY IT.
THE SINESTRO CORPS HAS INSTILLED ORDER THROUGHOUT THE UNIVERSE. NOW COMES THE FAR MORE DIFFICULT ENDEAVOR: KEEPING ORDER.
IT IS THE NATURE OF ALL LIVING THINGS TO TEST THOSE WHO GOVERN THEM. TO SEARCH OUT WEAKNESS AND EXPLOIT IT IN THE NAME OF SELF-INTEREST.
UNLESS THEY ARE TOO AFRAID NOT TO.
YOU WILL HELP. THE UNIVERSE WILL TREMBLE AGAIN.
RING OF SINESTRO AUTHENTICATED.
IN BLACKEST DAY, IN BRIGHTEST NIGHT...

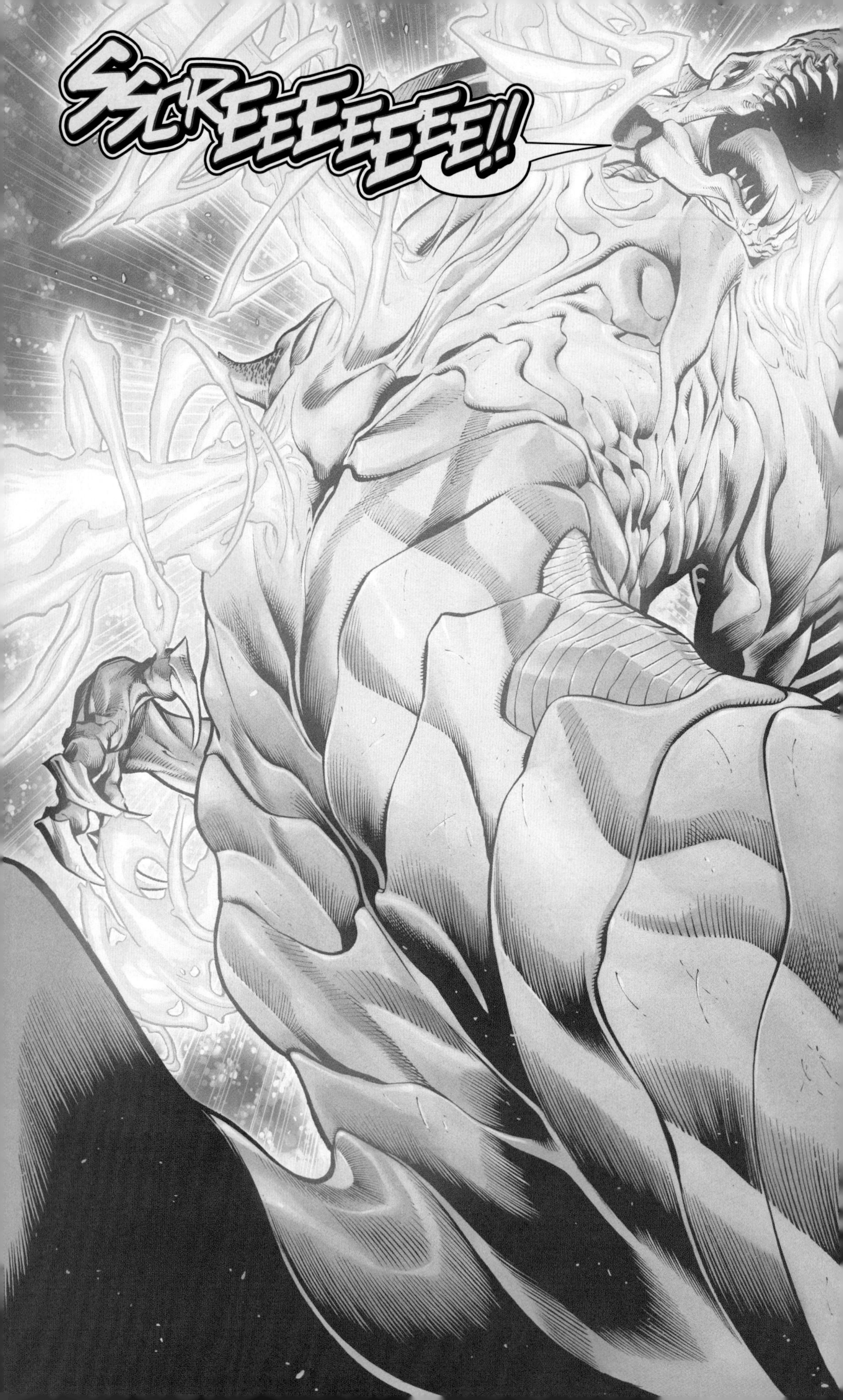
SSCREEEEEEEE!!

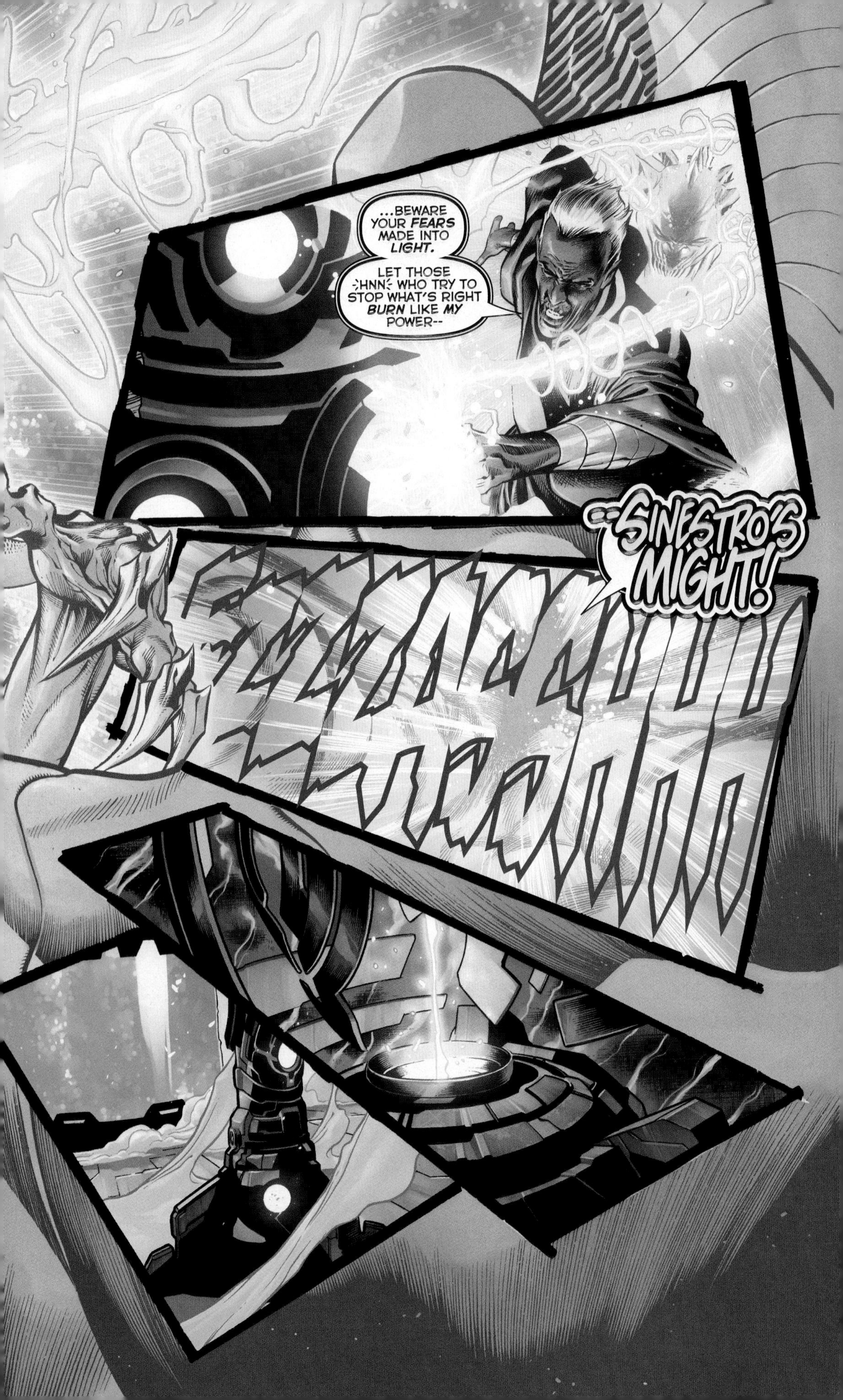
...BEWARE YOUR FEARS MADE INTO LIGHT.
LET THOSE -HNN- WHO TRY TO STOP WHAT'S RIGHT BURN LIKE MY POWER--
--SINESTRO'S MIGHT!

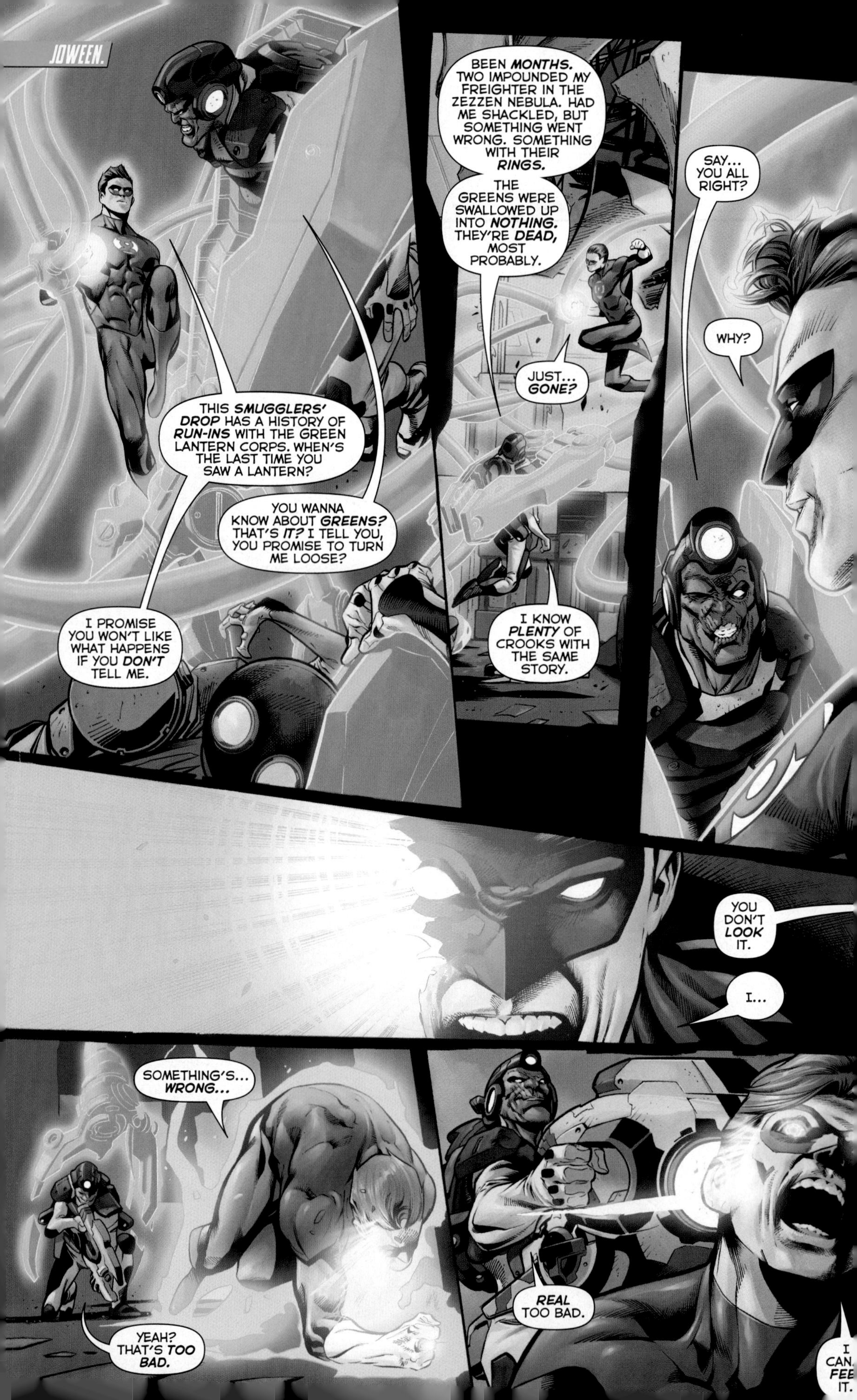
JOWEEN.
THIS SMUGGLERS' DROP HAS A HISTORY OF RUN-INS WITH THE GREEN LANTERN CORPS. WHEN'S THE LAST TIME YOU SAW A LANTERN?
YOU WANNA KNOW ABOUT GREENS? THAT'S IT? I TELL YOU, YOU PROMISE TO TURN ME LOOSE?
I PROMISE YOU WON'T LIKE WHAT HAPPENS IF YOU DON'T TELL ME.
BEEN MONTHS. TWO IMPOUNDED MY FREIGHTER IN THE ZEZZEN NEBULA. HAD ME SHACKLED, BUT SOMETHING WENT WRONG. SOMETHING WITH THEIR RINGS.
THE GREENS WERE SWALLOWED UP INTO NOTHING. THEY'RE DEAD, MOST PROBABLY.
JUST... GONE?
I KNOW PLENTY OF CROOKS WITH THE SAME STORY.
SAY... YOU ALL RIGHT?
WHY?
YOU DON'T LOOK IT.
I...
SOMETHING'S... WRONG...
YEAH? THAT'S TOO BAD.
REAL TOO BAD.
I CAN FEE IT.

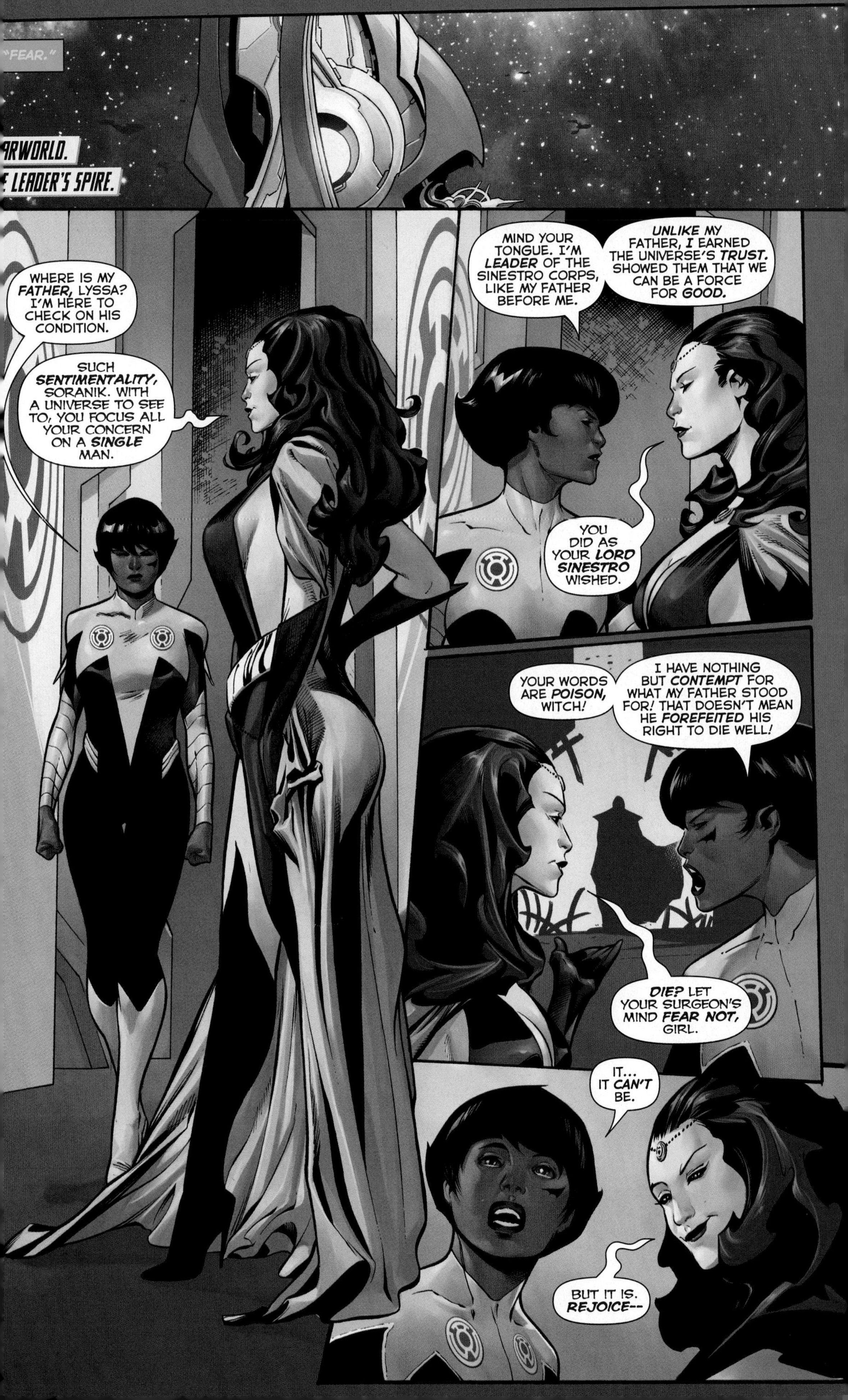
"FEAR."
ARWORLD.
E LEADER'S SPIRE.
WHERE IS MY FATHER, LYSSA? I'M HERE TO CHECK ON HIS CONDITION.
SUCH SENTIMENTALITY, SORANIK. WITH A UNIVERSE TO SEE TO, YOU FOCUS ALL YOUR CONCERN ON A SINGLE MAN.
MIND YOUR TONGUE. I'M LEADER OF THE SINESTRO CORPS, LIKE MY FATHER BEFORE ME.
UNLIKE MY FATHER, I EARNED THE UNIVERSE'S TRUST. SHOWED THEM THAT WE CAN BE A FORCE FOR GOOD.
YOU DID AS YOUR LORD SINESTRO WISHED.
YOUR WORDS ARE POISON, WITCH!
I HAVE NOTHING BUT CONTEMPT FOR WHAT MY FATHER STOOD FOR! THAT DOESN'T MEAN HE FOREFEITED HIS RIGHT TO DIE WELL!
DIE? LET YOUR SURGEON'S MIND FEAR NOT, GIRL.
IT... IT CAN'T BE.
BUT IT IS. REJOICE--

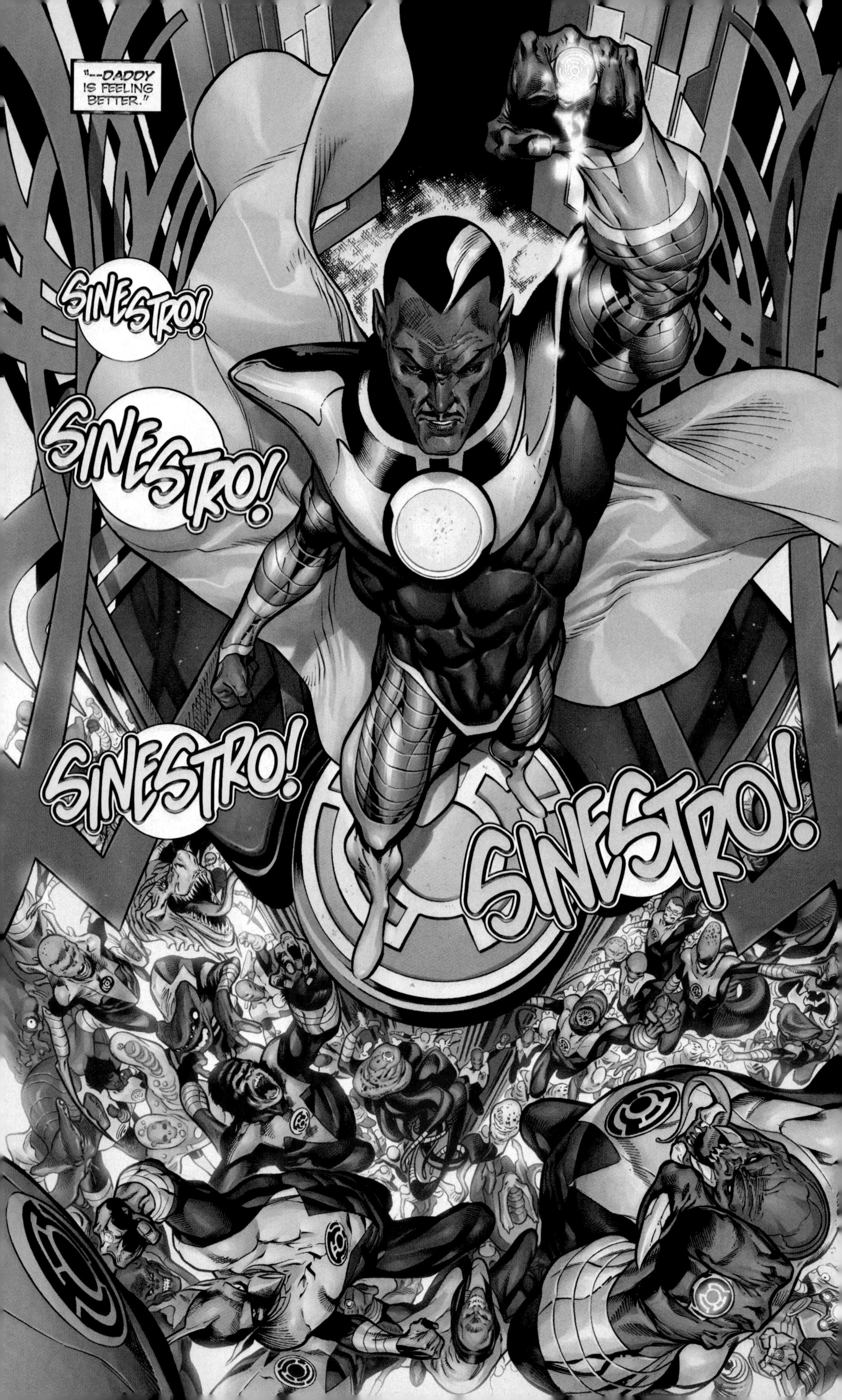
"--DADDY IS FEELING BETTER."
SINESTRO!
SINESTRO!
SINESTRO!
SINESTRO!

SINESTRO!

SILENCE.

MY LOYAL *SINESTRO CORPS*. I STAND BEFORE YOU RENEWED IN *STRENGTH* AND *POWER*. POWER BEYOND EQUAL.

POWER BEYOND *MEASURE,* CONSUMED FROM THE *PARALLAX ENTITY* ITSELF.

WITH THIS POWER, I WILL *RULE* AND *GUIDE* YOU INTO THE FUTURE.

THE *GREEN LANTERN CORPS* IS NO MORE.

THE GREEN LIGHT OF WILL IS *EXTINGUISHED* AT LAST.

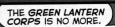

WE FOUGHT HARD TO TAKE OUR *RIGHTFUL* PLACE AT THE CENTER OF THE UNIVERSE. BUT WITH THE END OF THAT CONFLICT COMES A *NEW* WAR.

A WAR WITH NO END.

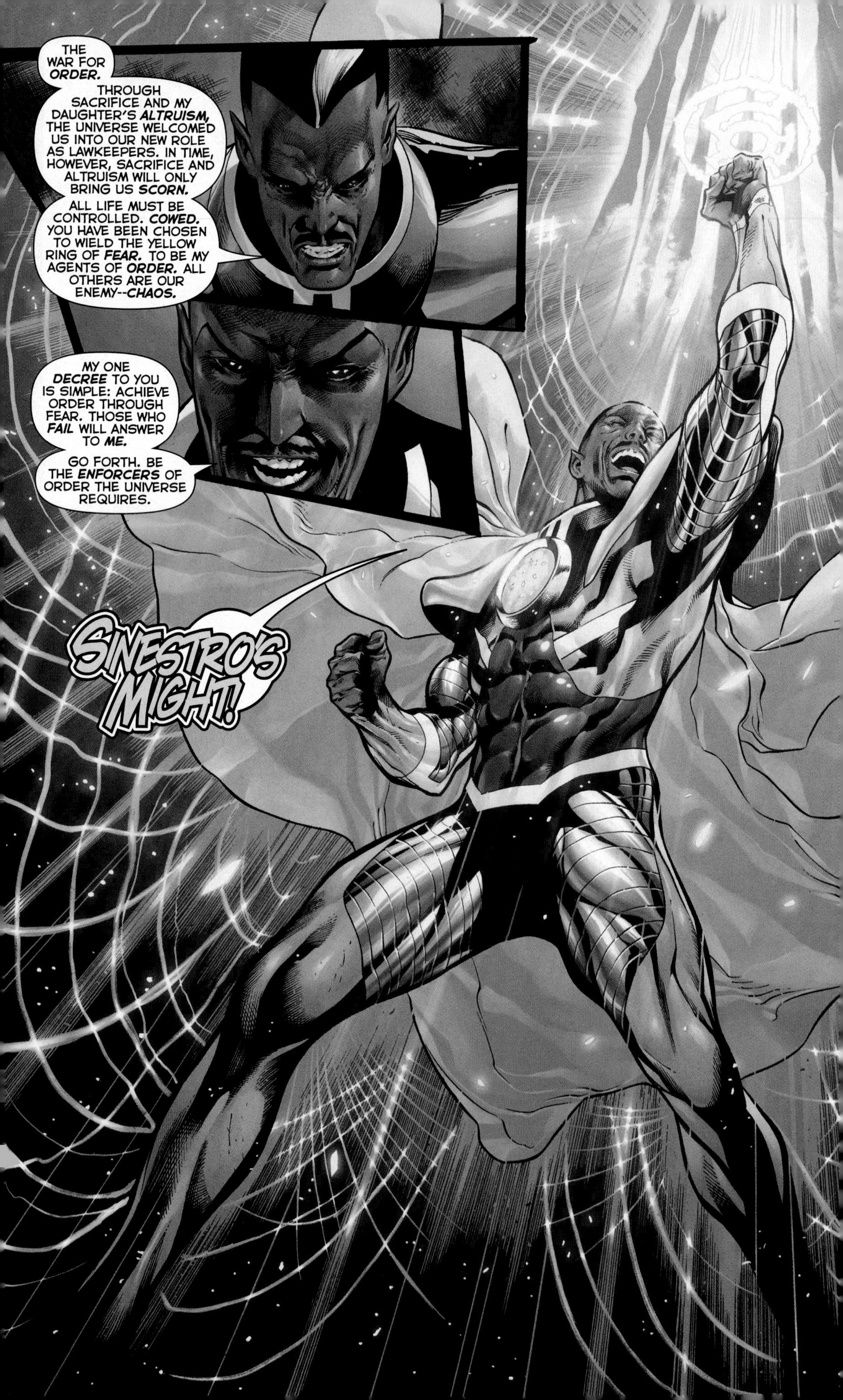
THE WAR FOR ORDER.
THROUGH SACRIFICE AND MY DAUGHTER'S ALTRUISM, THE UNIVERSE WELCOMED US INTO OUR NEW ROLE AS LAWKEEPERS. IN TIME, HOWEVER, SACRIFICE AND ALTRUISM WILL ONLY BRING US SCORN.
ALL LIFE MUST BE CONTROLLED. COWED. YOU HAVE BEEN CHOSEN TO WIELD THE YELLOW RING OF FEAR. TO BE MY AGENTS OF ORDER. ALL OTHERS ARE OUR ENEMY--CHAOS.
MY ONE DECREE TO YOU IS SIMPLE: ACHIEVE ORDER THROUGH FEAR. THOSE WHO FAIL WILL ANSWER TO ME.
GO FORTH. BE THE ENFORCERS OF ORDER THE UNIVERSE REQUIRES.
SINESTRO'S MIGHT!

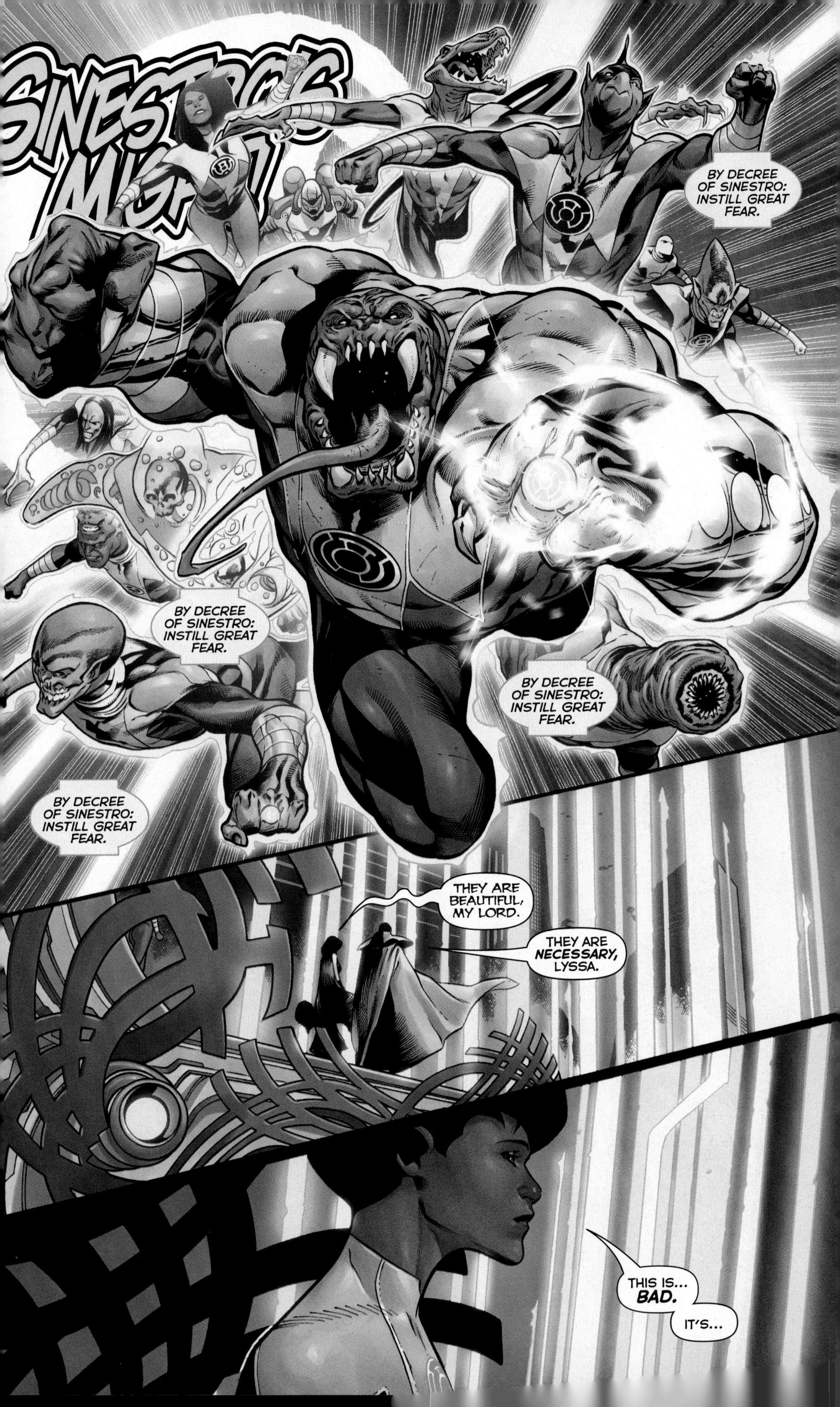
BY DECREE OF SINESTRO: INSTILL GREAT FEAR.
BY DECREE OF SINESTRO: INSTILL GREAT FEAR.
BY DECREE OF SINESTRO: INSTILL GREAT FEAR.
BY DECREE OF SINESTRO: INSTILL GREAT FEAR.
THEY ARE BEAUTIFUL, MY LORD.
THEY ARE NECESSARY, LYSSA.
THIS IS... BAD.
IT'S...

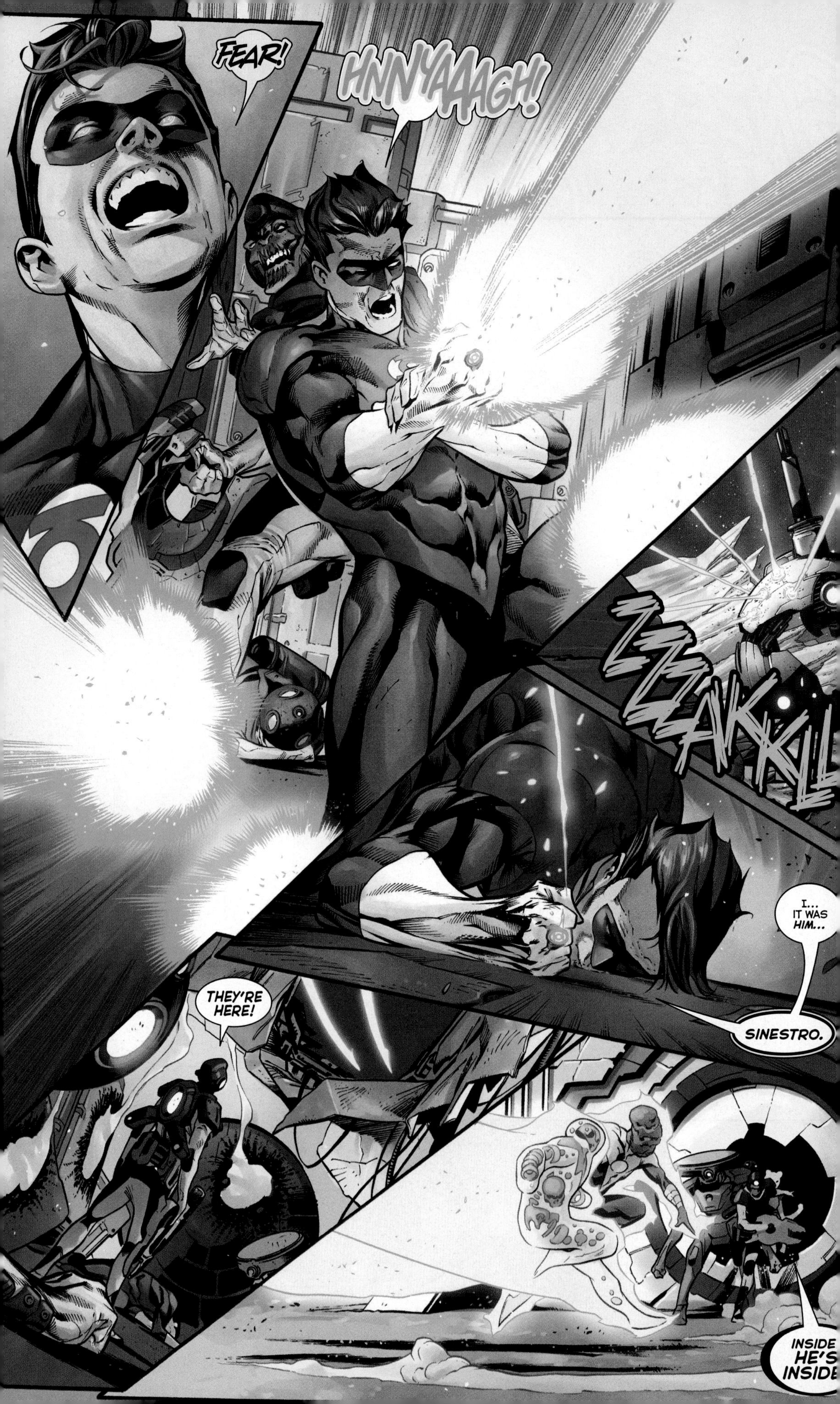

FEAR!
HNNYAAAGH!
ZZZAKKLL
I... IT WAS HIM...
SINESTRO.
THEY'RE HERE!
INSIDE HE'S INSIDE

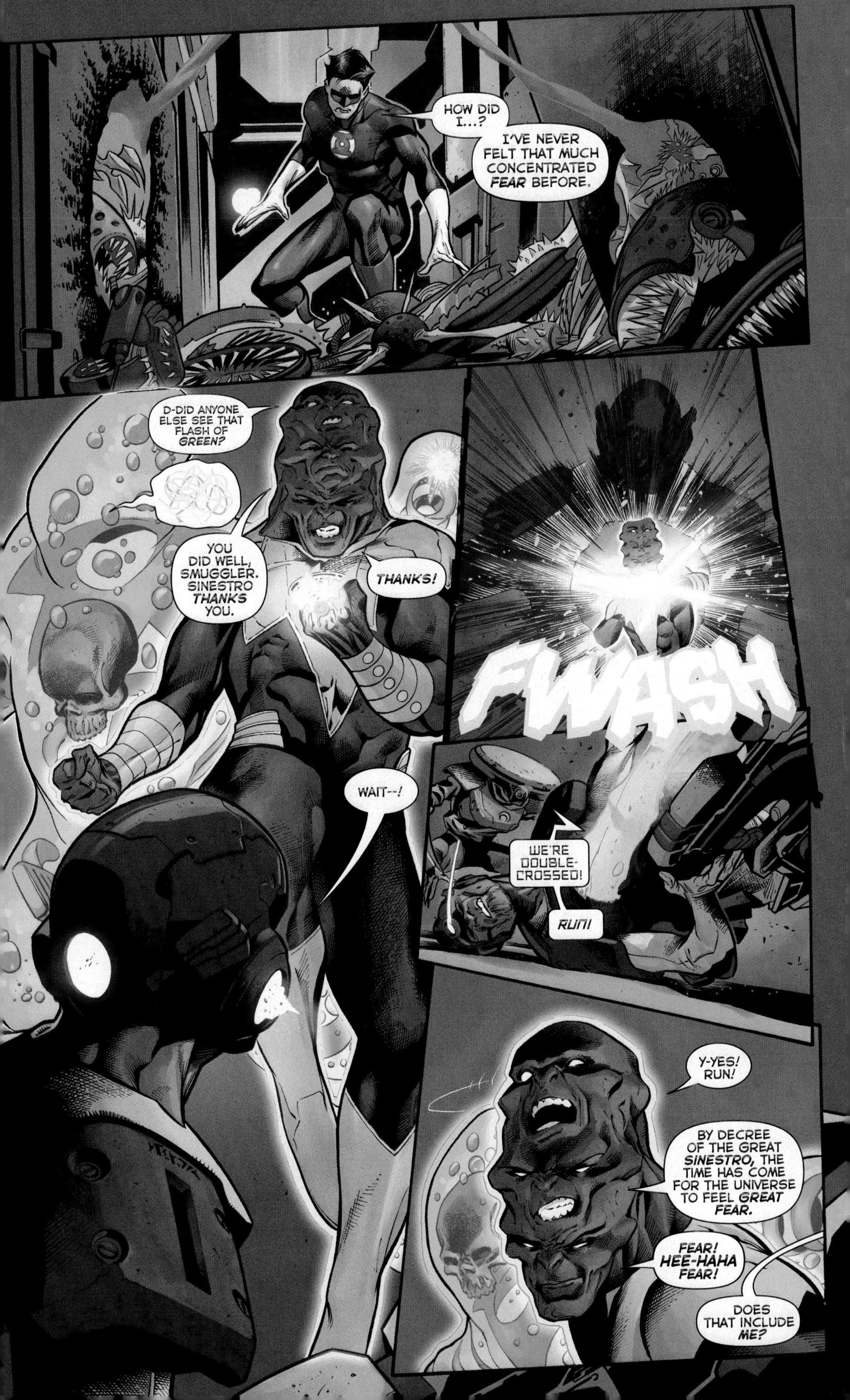
HOW DID I...?
I'VE NEVER FELT THAT MUCH CONCENTRATED FEAR BEFORE.
D-DID ANYONE ELSE SEE THAT FLASH OF GREEN?
YOU DID WELL, SMUGGLER. SINESTRO THANKS YOU.
THANKS!
FWASH
WAIT--!
WE'RE DOUBLE-CROSSED!
RUN!
Y-YES! RUN!
BY DECREE OF THE GREAT SINESTRO, THE TIME HAS COME FOR THE UNIVERSE TO FEEL GREAT FEAR.
FEAR! HEE-HAHA FEAR!
DOES THAT INCLUDE ME?

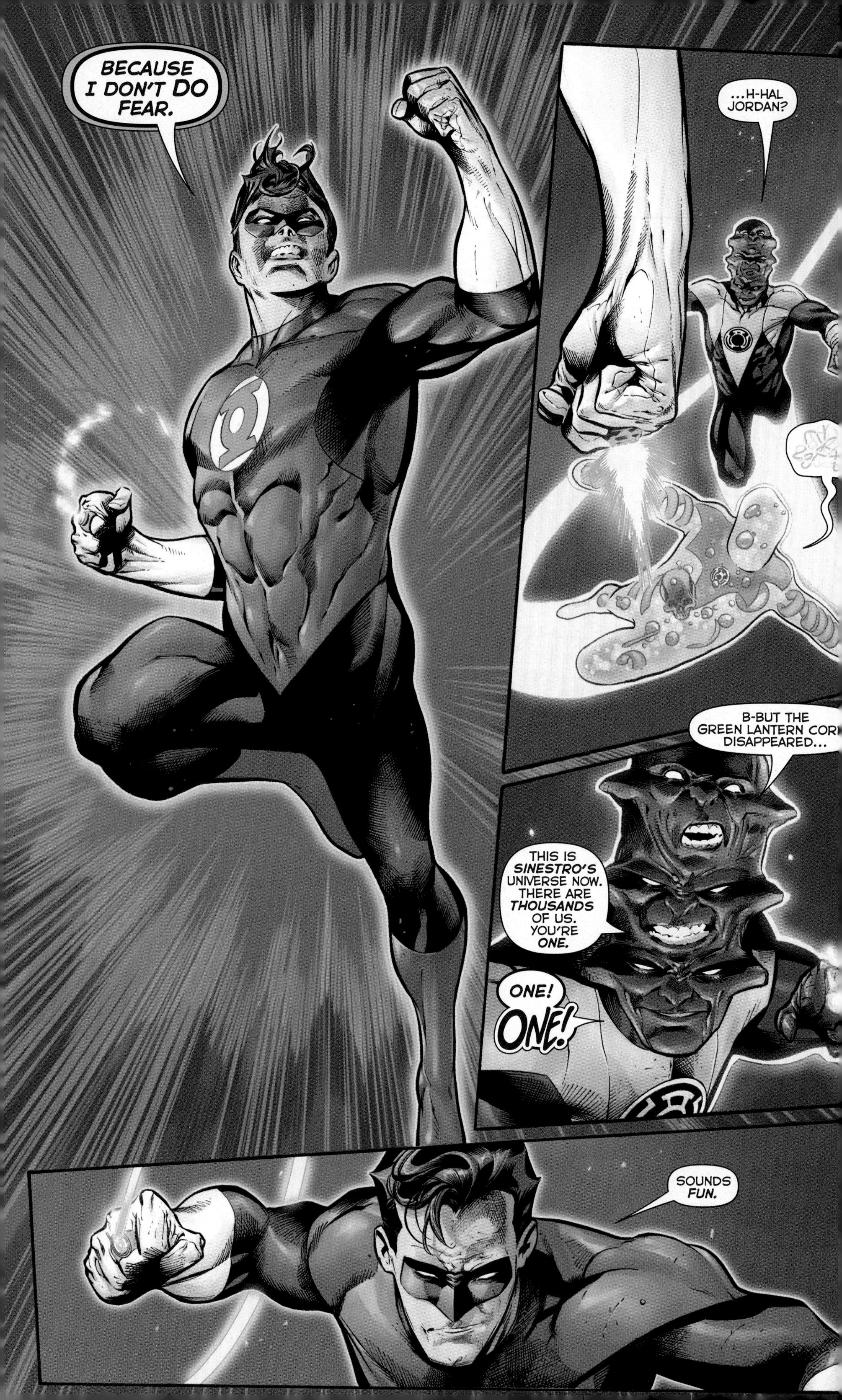
BECAUSE I DON'T DO FEAR.
...H-HAL JORDAN?
B-BUT THE GREEN LANTERN COR DISAPPEARED...
THIS IS SINESTRO'S UNIVERSE NOW. THERE ARE THOUSANDS OF US. YOU'RE ONE.
ONE! ONE!
SOUNDS FUN.

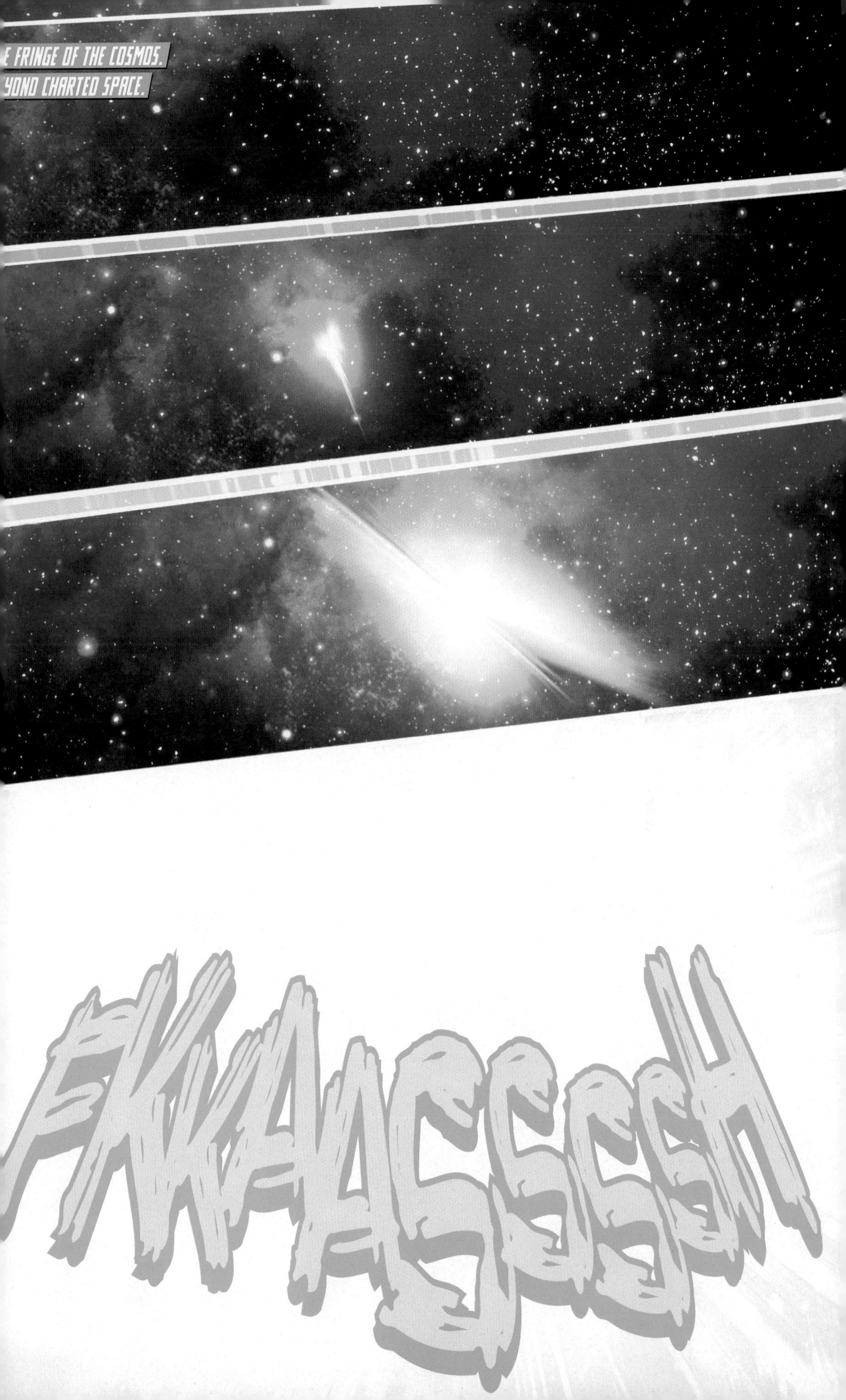
E FRINGE OF THE COSMOS.
YOND CHARTED SPACE.
SKAASSSSH

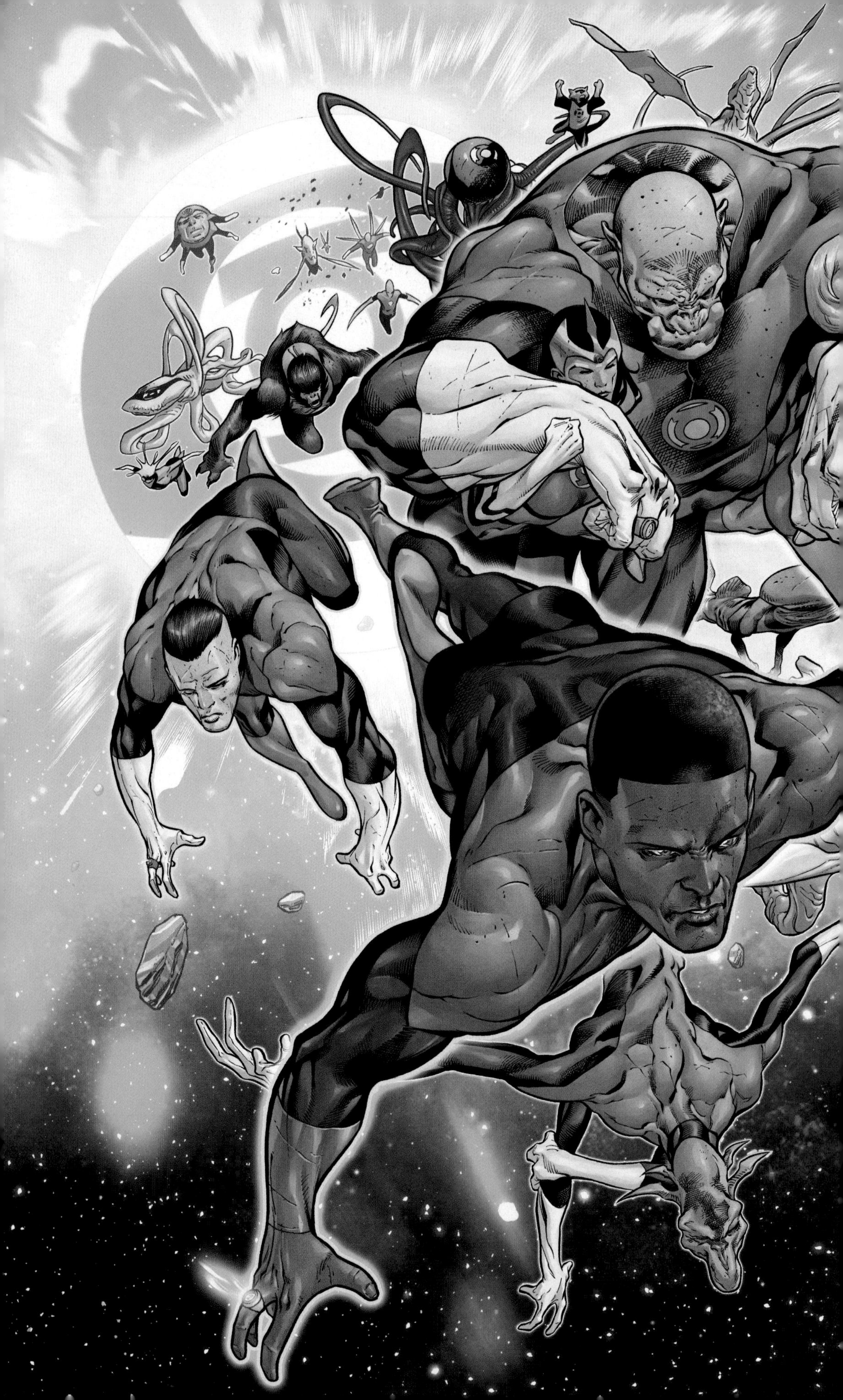

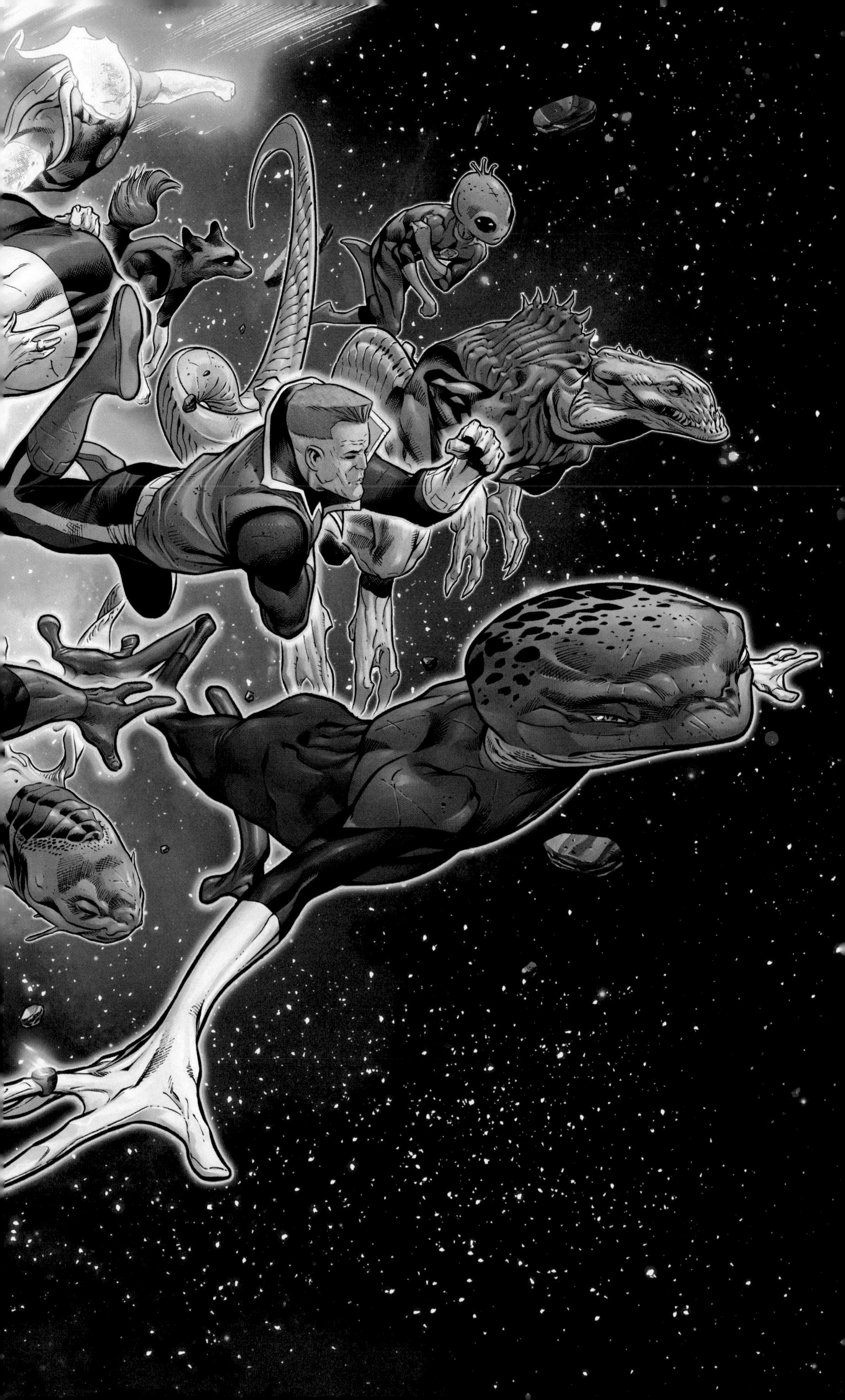

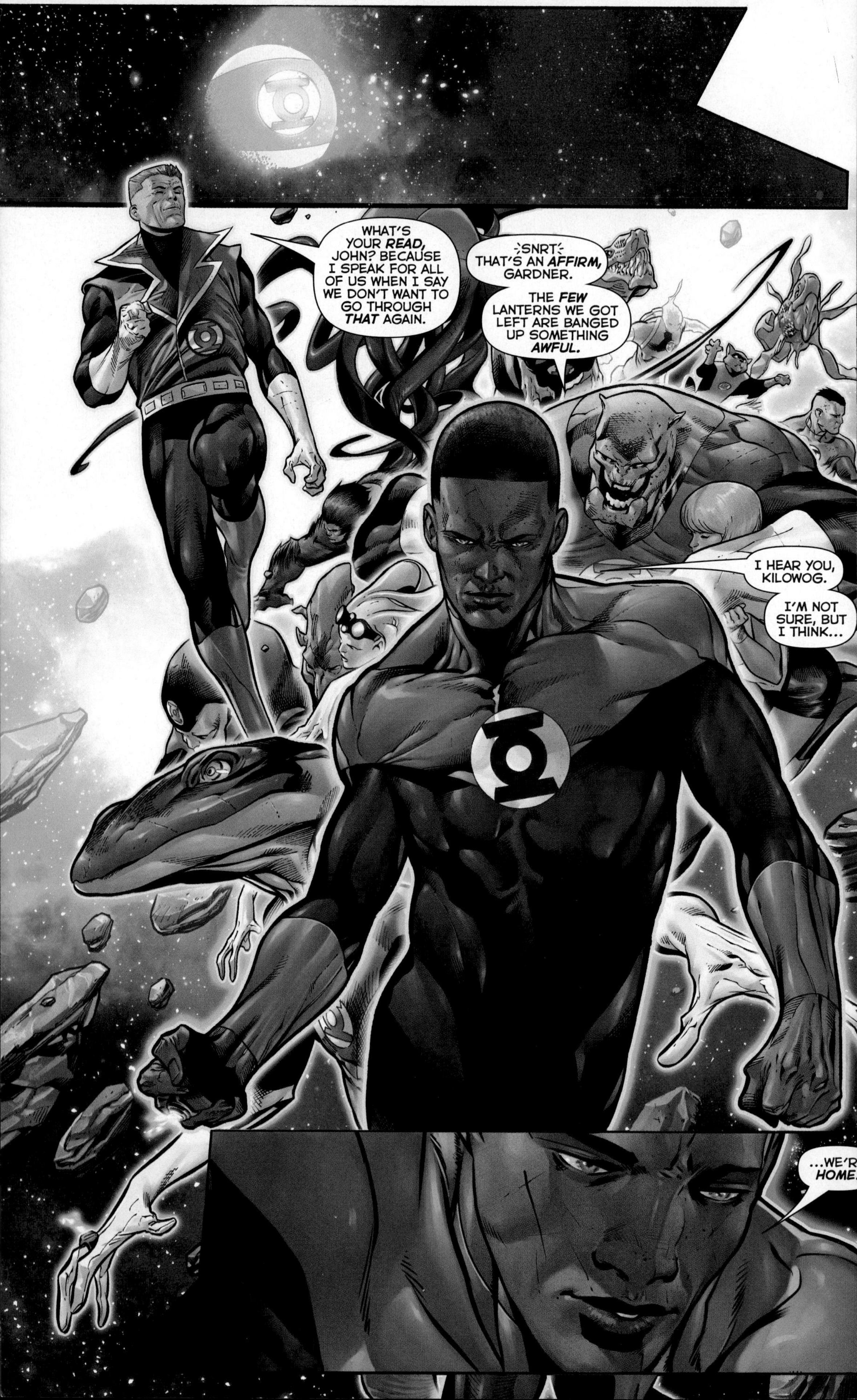
WHAT'S YOUR READ, JOHN? BECAUSE I SPEAK FOR ALL OF US WHEN I SAY WE DON'T WANT TO GO THROUGH THAT AGAIN.
SNRT THAT'S AN AFFIRM, GARDNER.
THE FEW LANTERNS WE GOT LEFT ARE BANGED UP SOMETHING AWFUL.
I HEAR YOU, KILOWOG.
I'M NOT SURE, BUT I THINK...
...WE'R HOME.

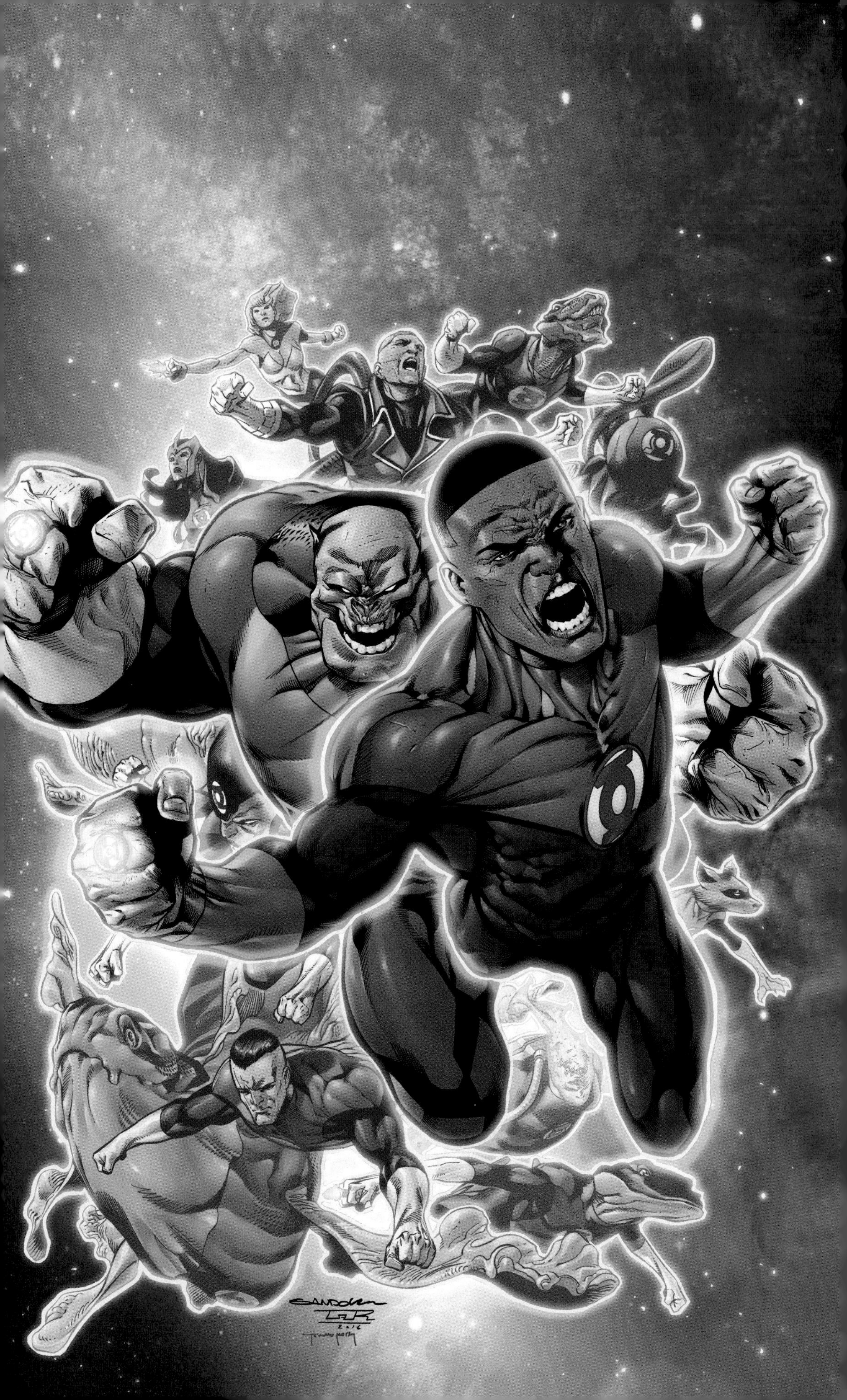

SINESTRO'S LAW PART 2: RECON

RAFA SANDOVAL penciller * JORDI TARRAGONA inker * TOMEU MOREY colorist

RAFA SANDOVAL, JORDI TARRAGONA and TOMEU MOREY cover artists

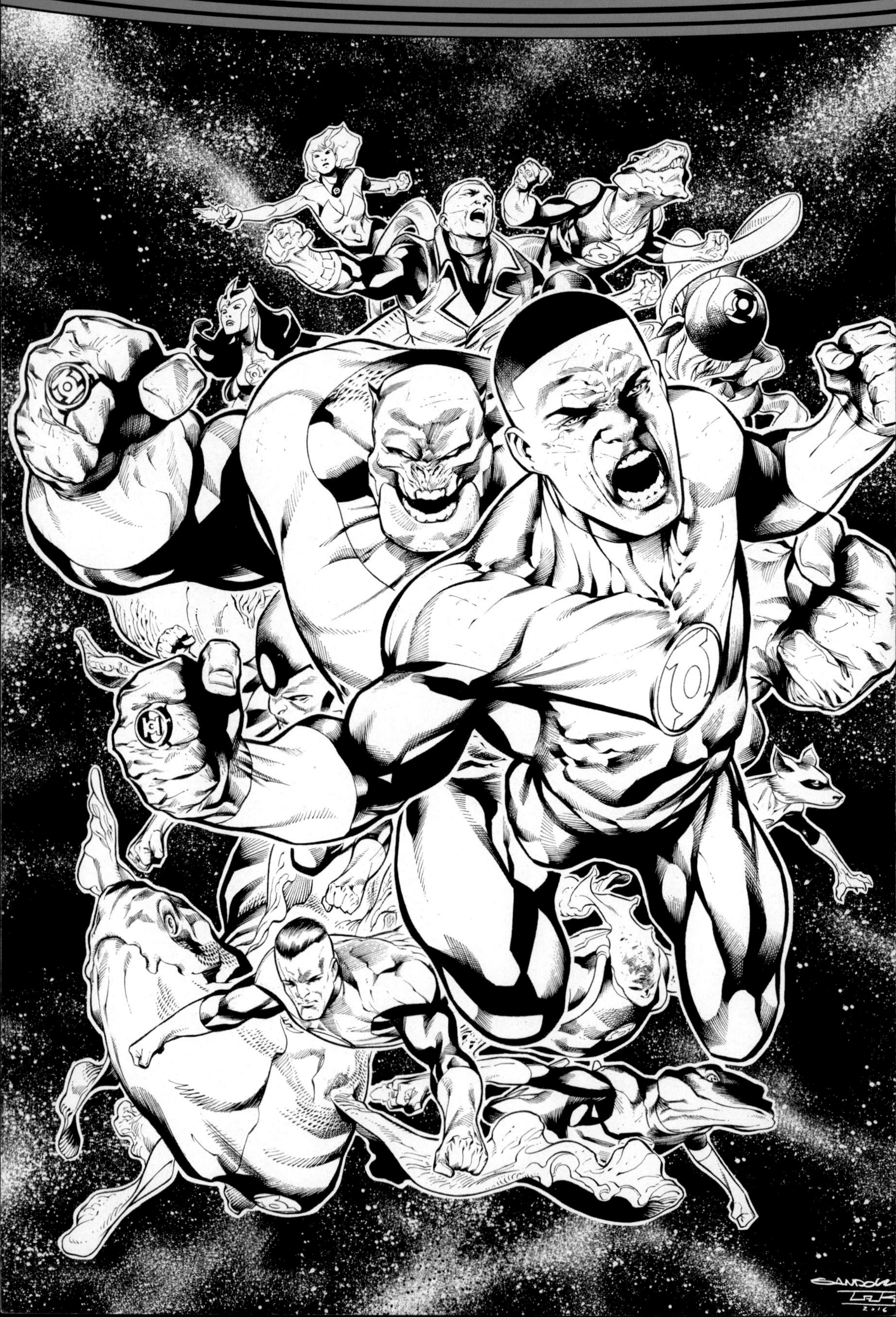

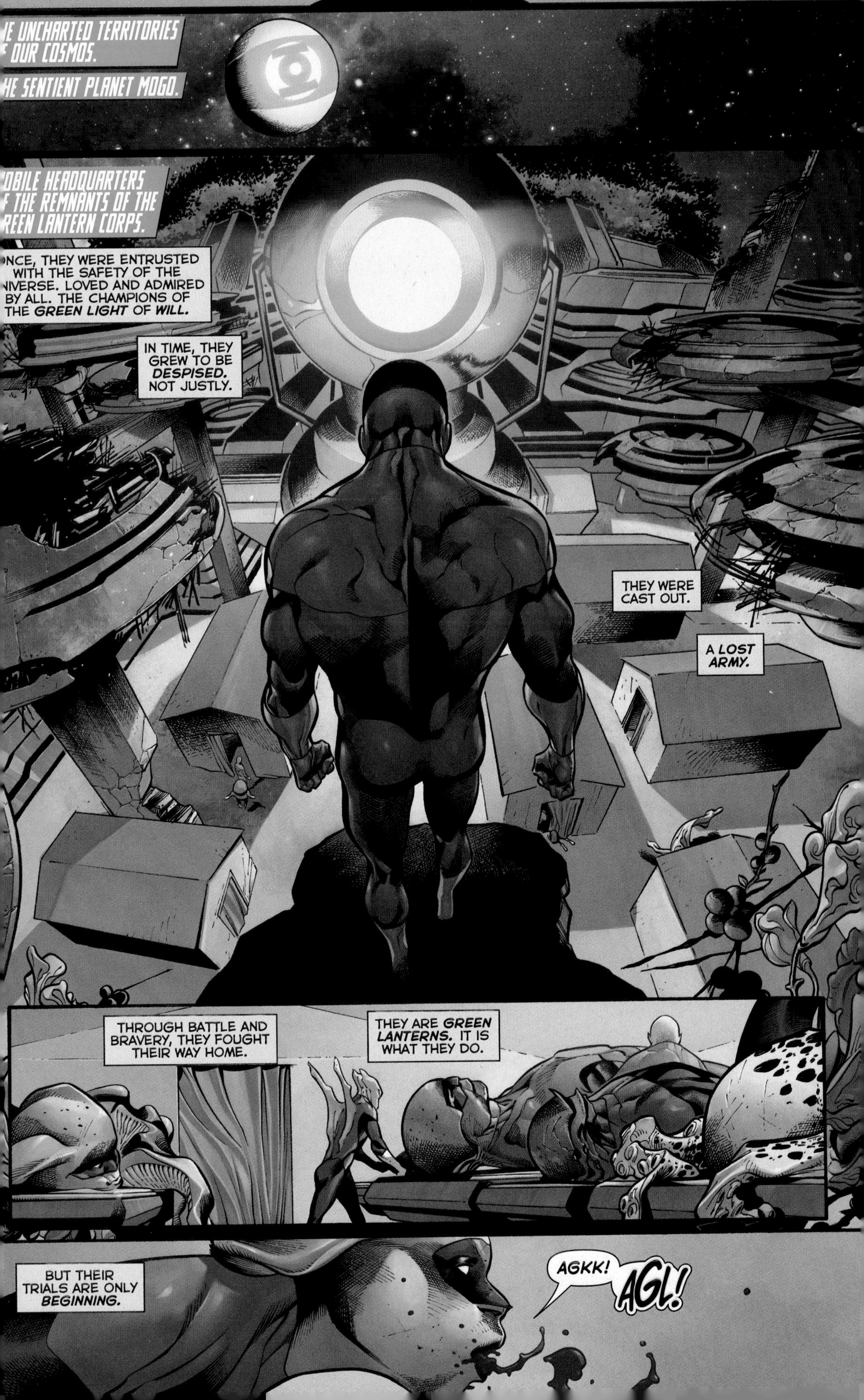
E UNCHARTED TERRITORIES
OUR COSMOS.
HE SENTIENT PLANET MOGO.
OBILE HEADQUARTERS
F THE REMNANTS OF THE
REEN LANTERN CORPS.
NCE, THEY WERE ENTRUSTED WITH THE SAFETY OF THE NIVERSE. LOVED AND ADMIRED BY ALL. THE CHAMPIONS OF THE GREEN LIGHT OF WILL.
IN TIME, THEY GREW TO BE DESPISED. NOT JUSTLY.
THEY WERE CAST OUT.
A LOST ARMY.
THROUGH BATTLE AND BRAVERY, THEY FOUGHT THEIR WAY HOME.
THEY ARE GREEN LANTERNS. IT IS WHAT THEY DO.
BUT THEIR TRIALS ARE ONLY BEGINNING.
AGKK!
AGL!

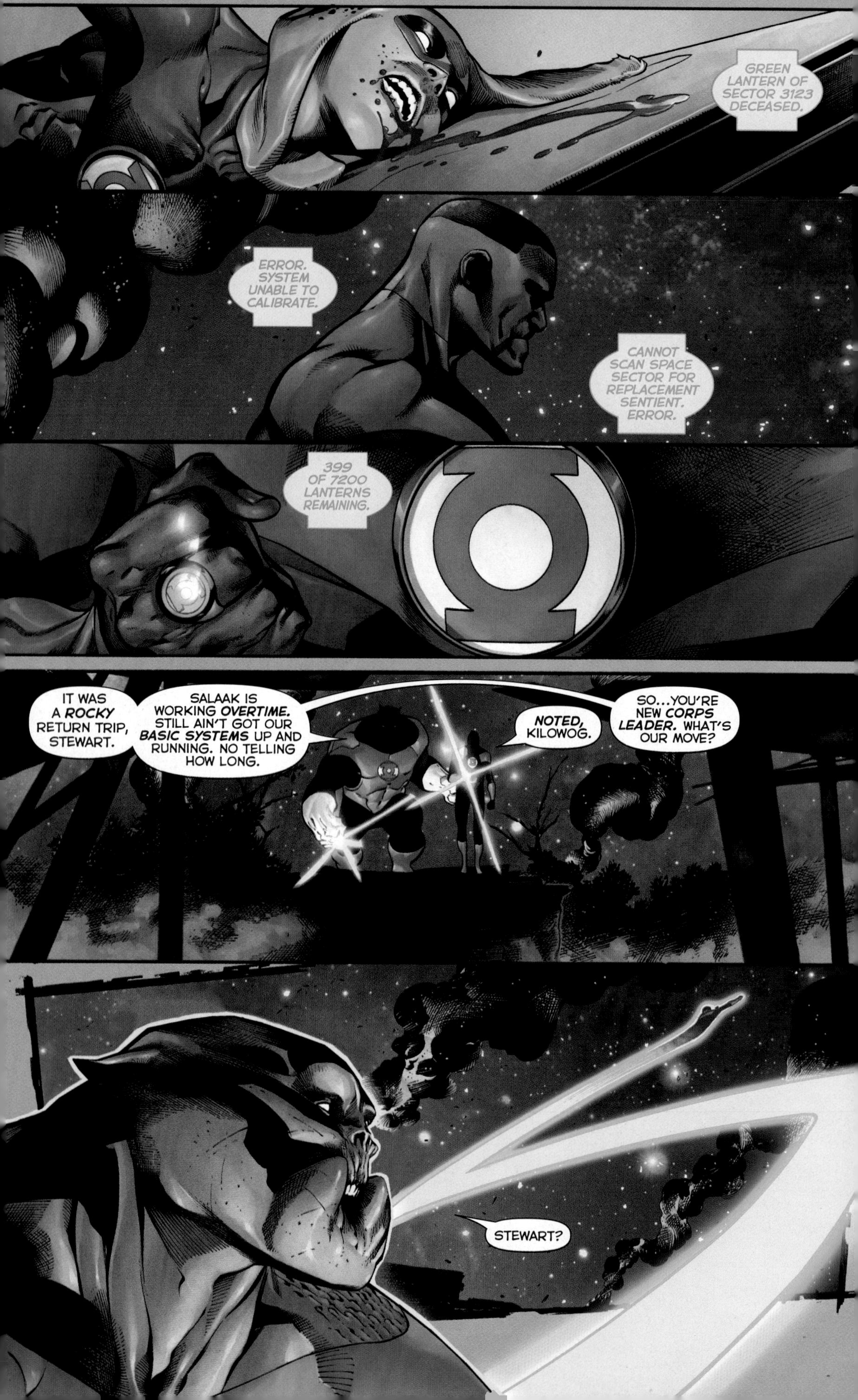
GREEN LANTERN OF SECTOR 3123 DECEASED.
ERROR. SYSTEM UNABLE TO CALIBRATE.
CANNOT SCAN SPACE SECTOR FOR REPLACEMENT SENTIENT. ERROR.
399 OF 7200 LANTERNS REMAINING.
IT WAS A ROCKY RETURN TRIP, STEWART.
SALAAK IS WORKING OVERTIME. STILL AIN'T GOT OUR BASIC SYSTEMS UP AND RUNNING. NO TELLING HOW LONG.
NOTED, KILOWOG.
SO...YOU'RE NEW CORPS LEADER. WHAT'S OUR MOVE?
STEWART?

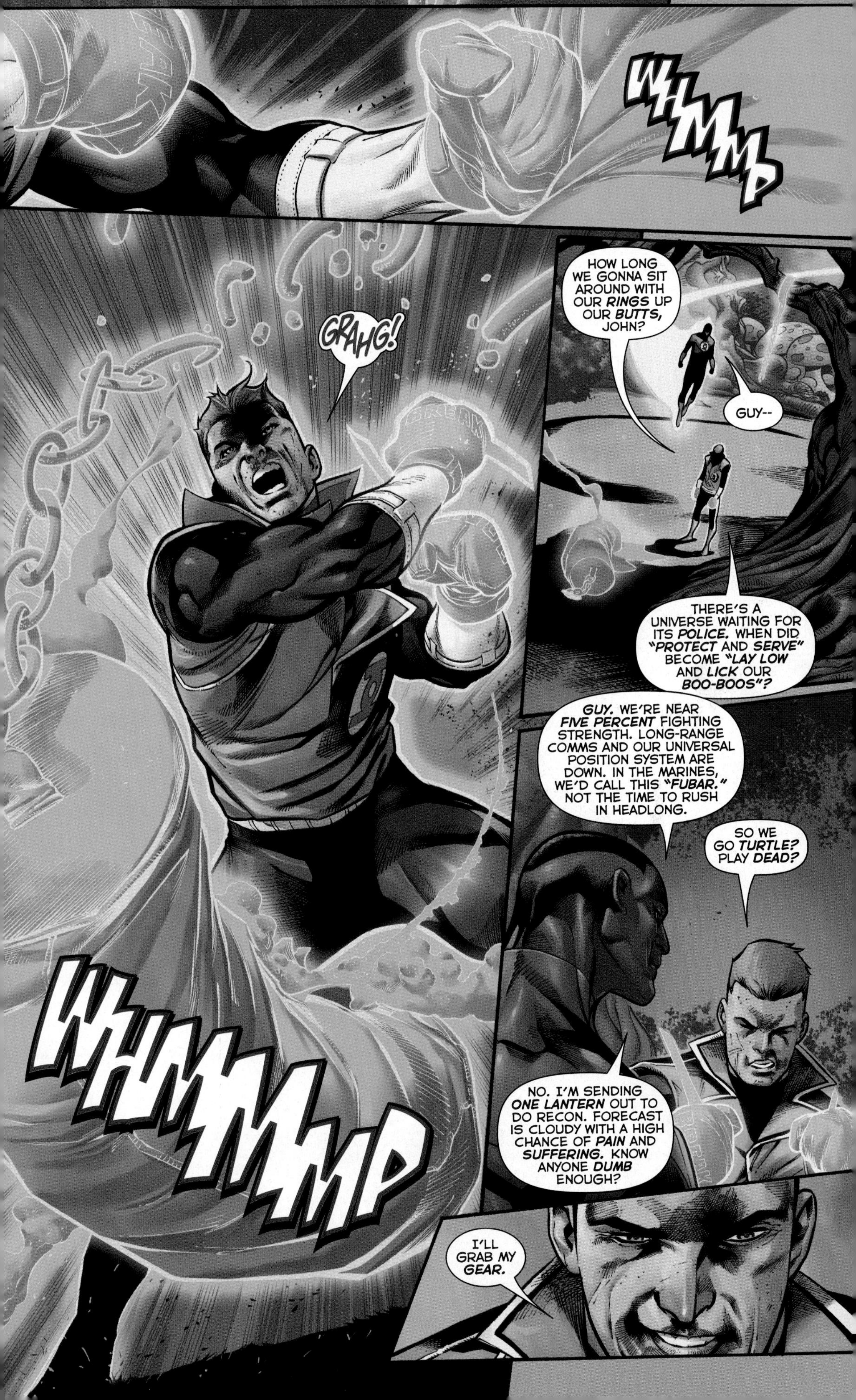
WHMMP
GRAHG!
WHMMMMP
HOW LONG WE GONNA SIT AROUND WITH OUR RINGS UP OUR BUTTS, JOHN?
GUY--
THERE'S A UNIVERSE WAITING FOR ITS POLICE. WHEN DID "PROTECT AND SERVE" BECOME "LAY LOW AND LICK OUR BOO-BOOS"?
GUY. WE'RE NEAR FIVE PERCENT FIGHTING STRENGTH. LONG-RANGE COMMS AND OUR UNIVERSAL POSITION SYSTEM ARE DOWN. IN THE MARINES, WE'D CALL THIS "FUBAR." NOT THE TIME TO RUSH IN HEADLONG.
SO WE GO TURTLE? PLAY DEAD?
NO. I'M SENDING ONE LANTERN OUT TO DO RECON. FORECAST IS CLOUDY WITH A HIGH CHANCE OF PAIN AND SUFFERING. KNOW ANYONE DUMB ENOUGH?
I'LL GRAB MY GEAR.

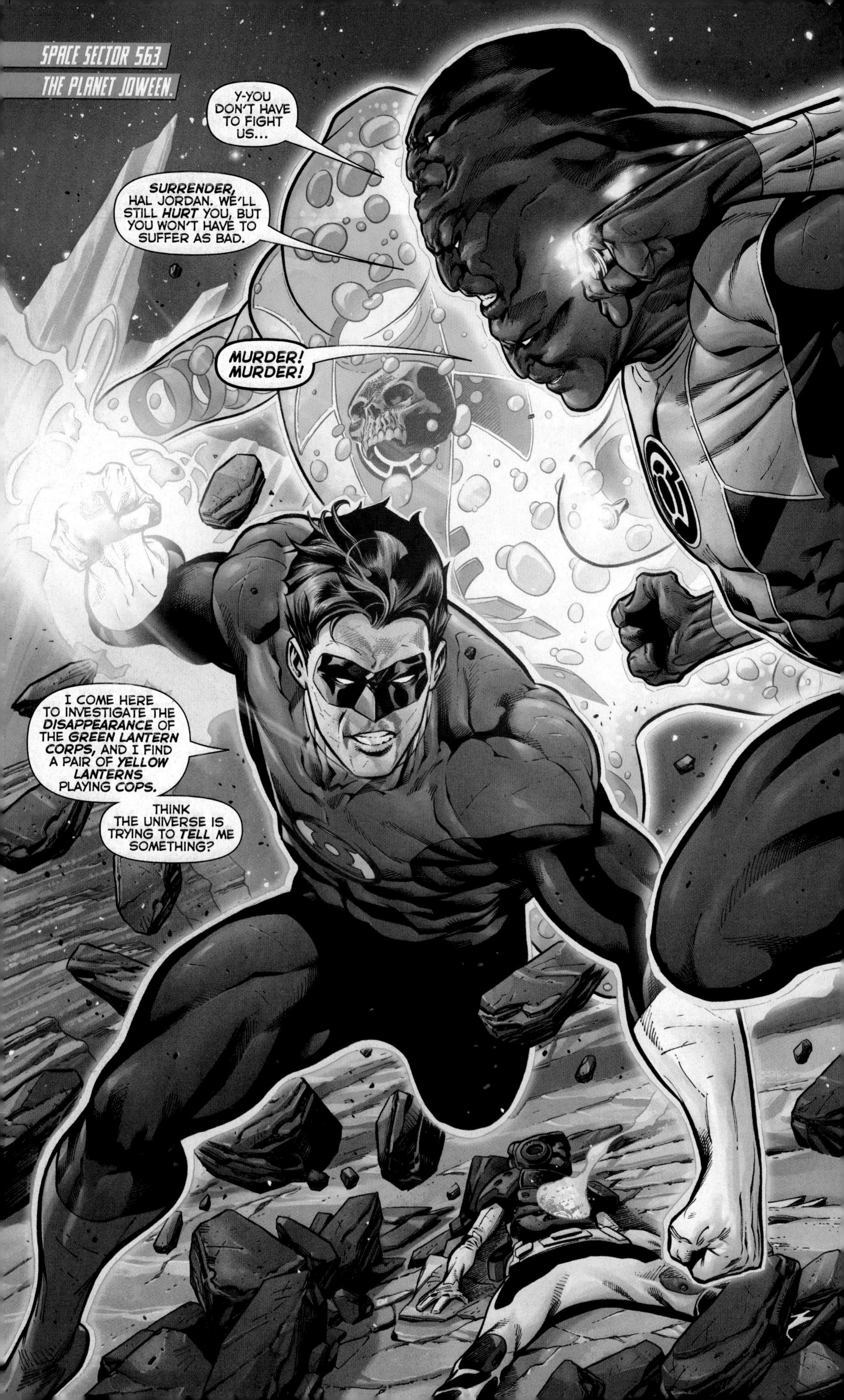
SPACE SECTOR 563.
THE PLANET JOWEEN.
Y-YOU DON'T HAVE TO FIGHT US...
SURRENDER, HAL JORDAN. WE'LL STILL HURT YOU, BUT YOU WON'T HAVE TO SUFFER AS BAD.
MURDER! MURDER!
I COME HERE TO INVESTIGATE THE DISAPPEARANCE OF THE GREEN LANTERN CORPS, AND I FIND A PAIR OF YELLOW LANTERNS PLAYING COPS.
THINK THE UNIVERSE IS TRYING TO TELL ME SOMETHING?

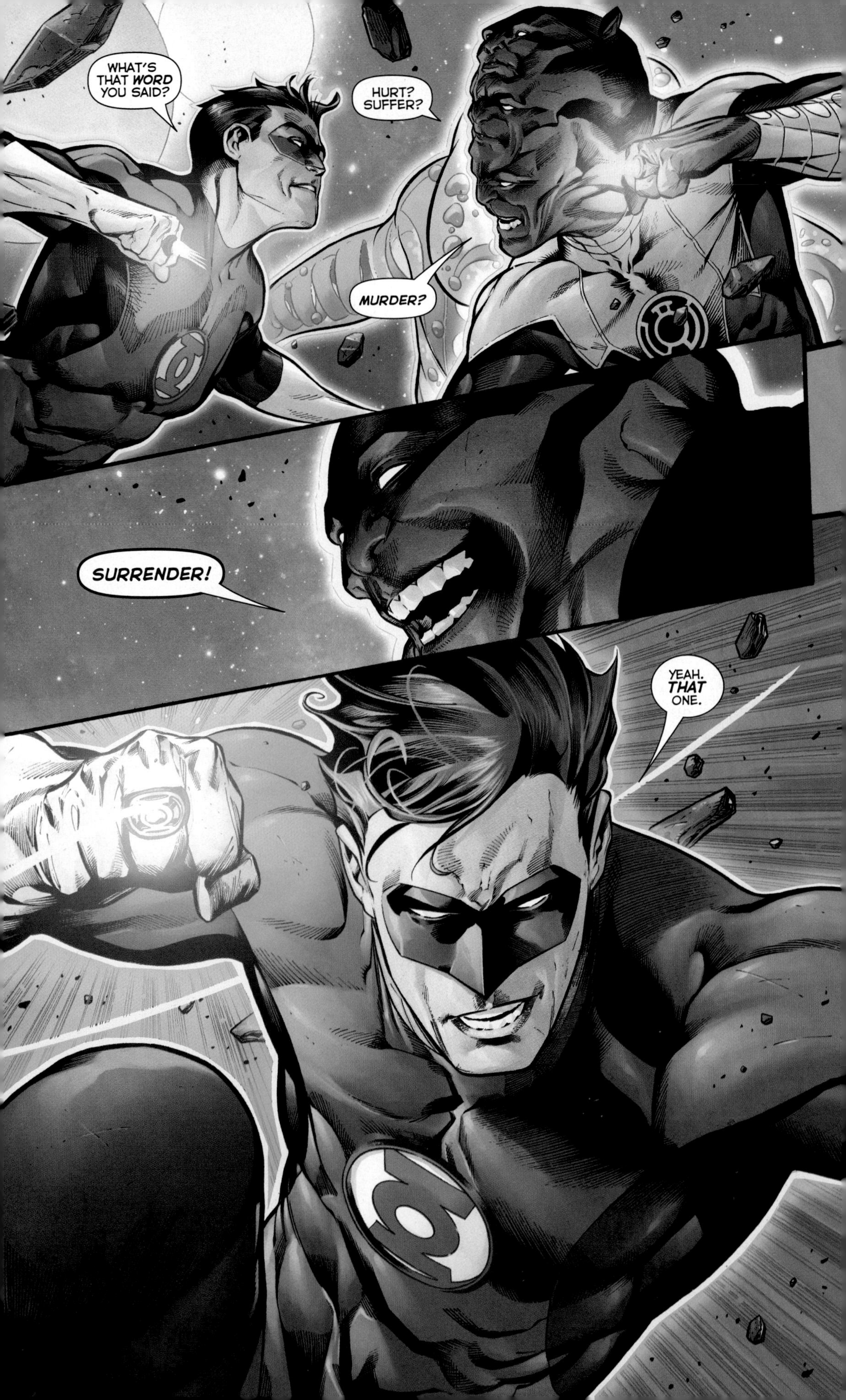
WHAT'S THAT WORD YOU SAID?
HURT? SUFFER?
MURDER?
SURRENDER!
YEAH. THAT ONE.

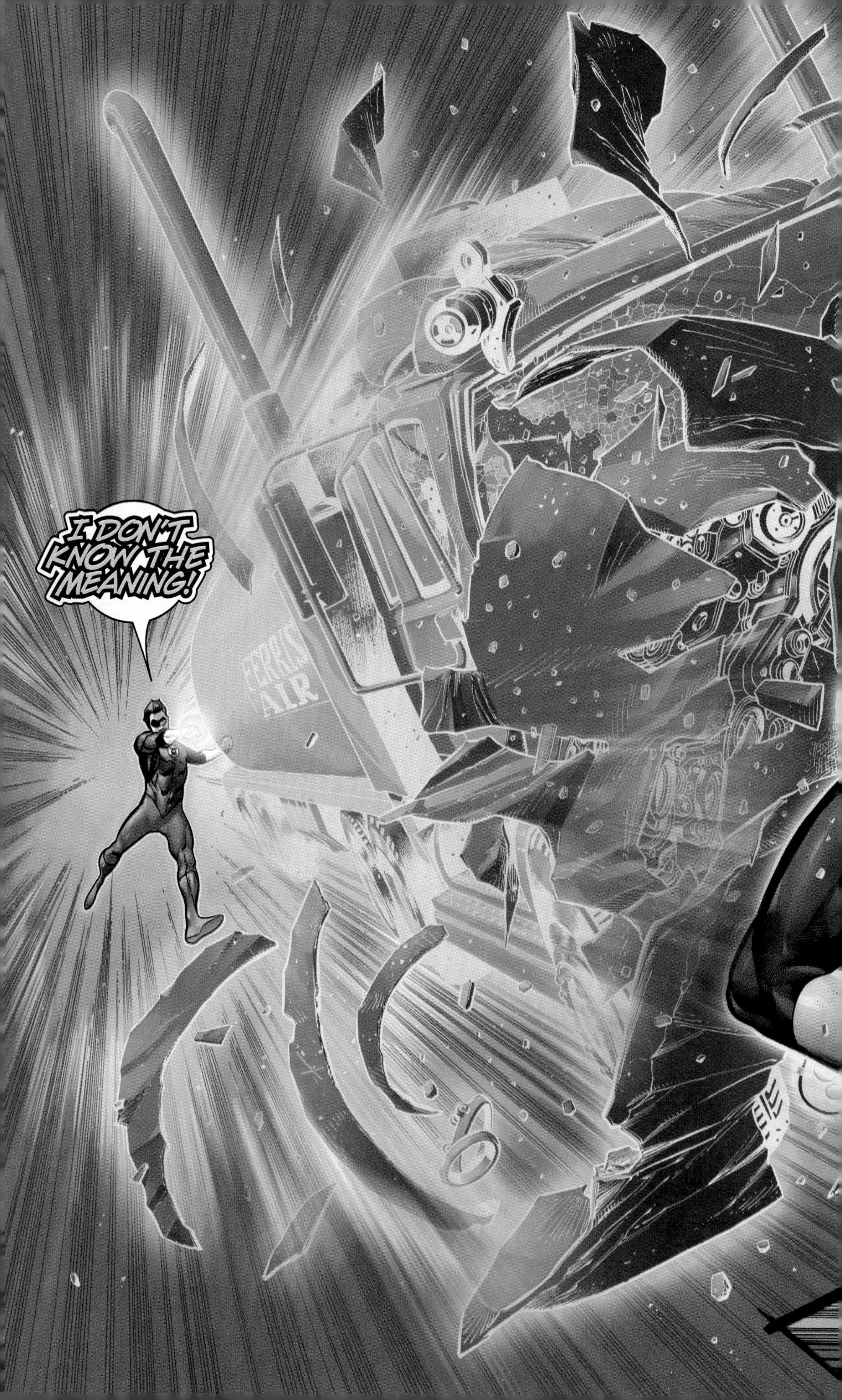

I DON'T KNOW THE MEANING!
FERRIS AIR

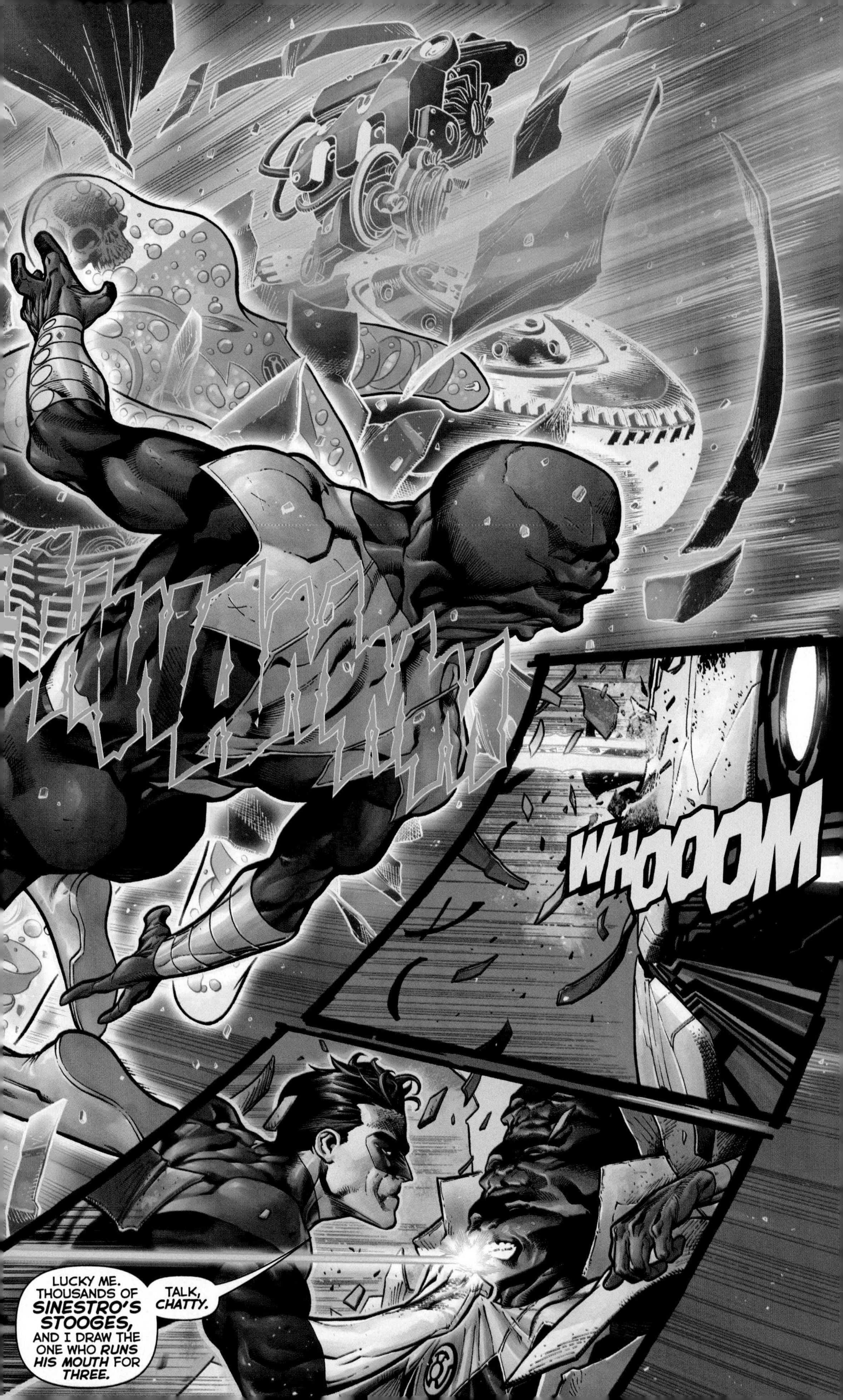
WHOOOM
LUCKY ME. THOUSANDS OF SINESTRO'S STOOGES, AND I DRAW THE ONE WHO RUNS HIS MOUTH FOR THREE.
TALK, CHATTY.

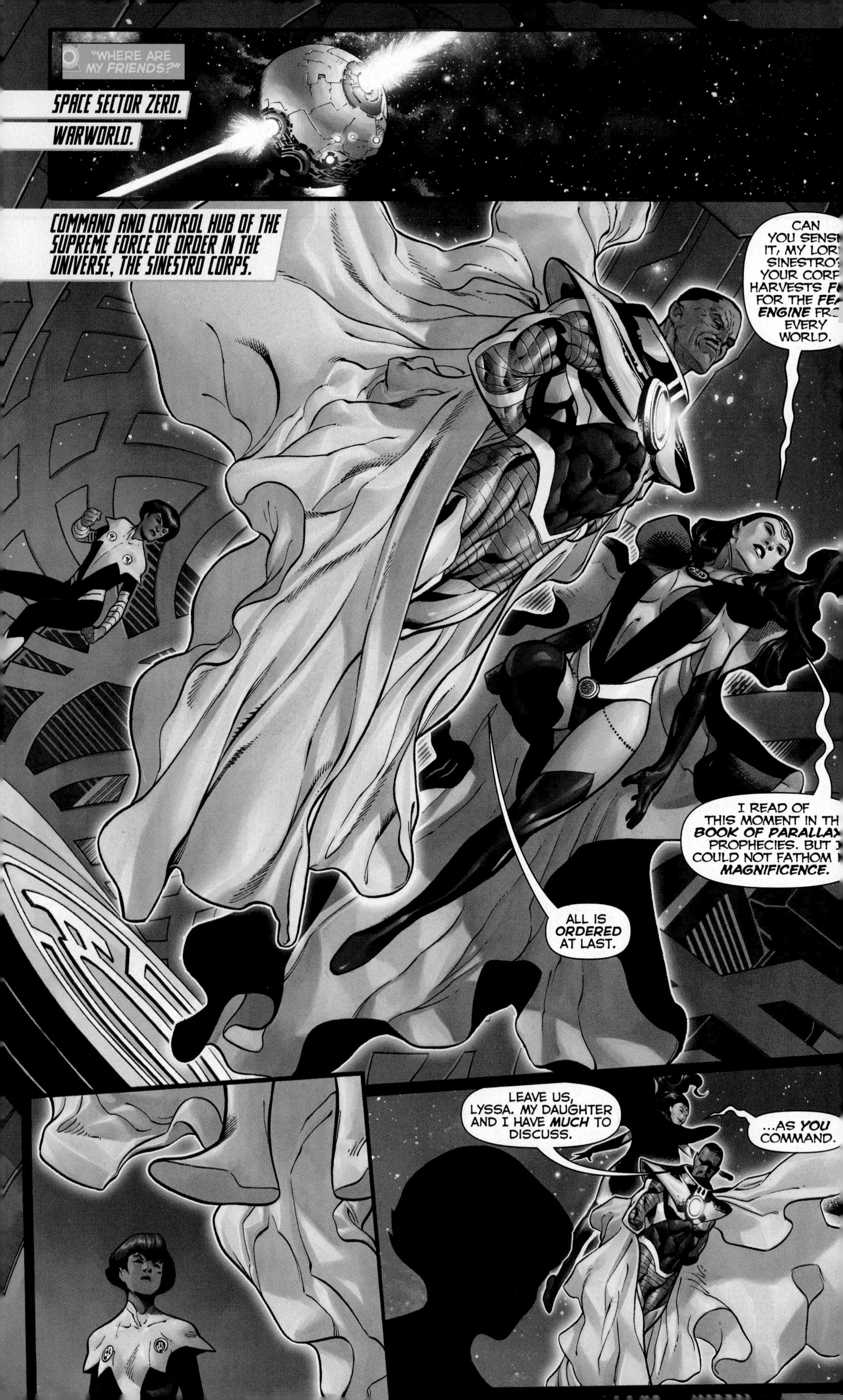
"WHERE ARE MY FRIENDS?"
SPACE SECTOR ZERO.
WARWORLD.
COMMAND AND CONTROL HUB OF THE SUPREME FORCE OF ORDER IN THE UNIVERSE, THE SINESTRO CORPS.
ALL IS ORDERED AT LAST.
LEAVE US, LYSSA. MY DAUGHTER AND I HAVE MUCH TO DISCUSS.
...AS YOU COMMAND.

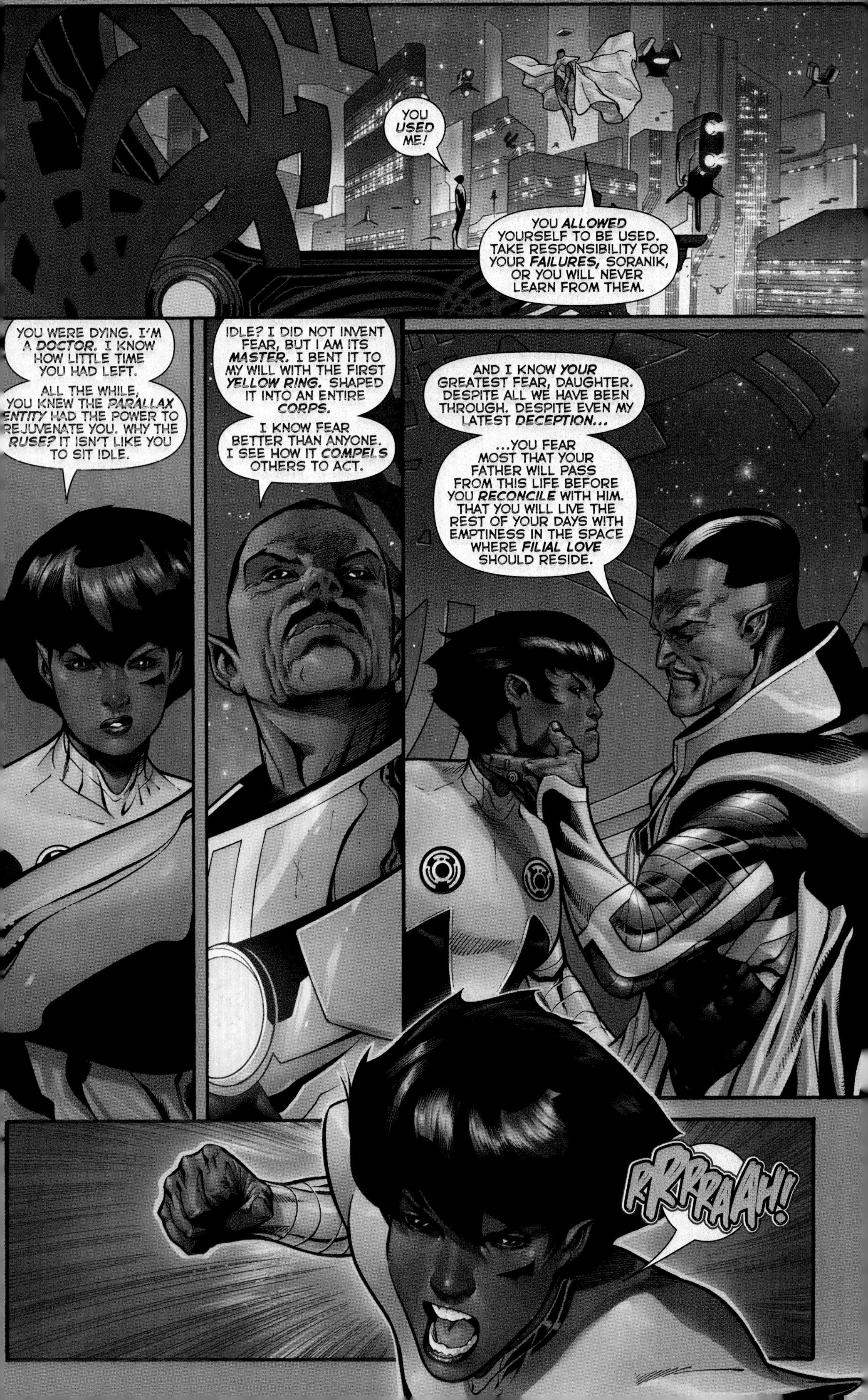
YOU USED ME!
YOU ALLOWED YOURSELF TO BE USED. TAKE RESPONSIBILITY FOR YOUR FAILURES, SORANIK, OR YOU WILL NEVER LEARN FROM THEM.
YOU WERE DYING. I'M A DOCTOR. I KNOW HOW LITTLE TIME YOU HAD LEFT.
ALL THE WHILE, YOU KNEW THE PARALLAX ENTITY HAD THE POWER TO REJUVENATE YOU. WHY THE RUSE? IT ISN'T LIKE YOU TO SIT IDLE.
IDLE? I DID NOT INVENT FEAR, BUT I AM ITS MASTER. I BENT IT TO MY WILL WITH THE FIRST YELLOW RING. SHAPED IT INTO AN ENTIRE CORPS.
I KNOW FEAR BETTER THAN ANYONE. I SEE HOW IT COMPELS OTHERS TO ACT.
AND I KNOW YOUR GREATEST FEAR, DAUGHTER. DESPITE ALL WE HAVE BEEN THROUGH. DESPITE EVEN MY LATEST DECEPTION...
...YOU FEAR MOST THAT YOUR FATHER WILL PASS FROM THIS LIFE BEFORE YOU RECONCILE WITH HIM. THAT YOU WILL LIVE THE REST OF YOUR DAYS WITH EMPTINESS IN THE SPACE WHERE FILIAL LOVE SHOULD RESIDE.
RRRRAAAH!

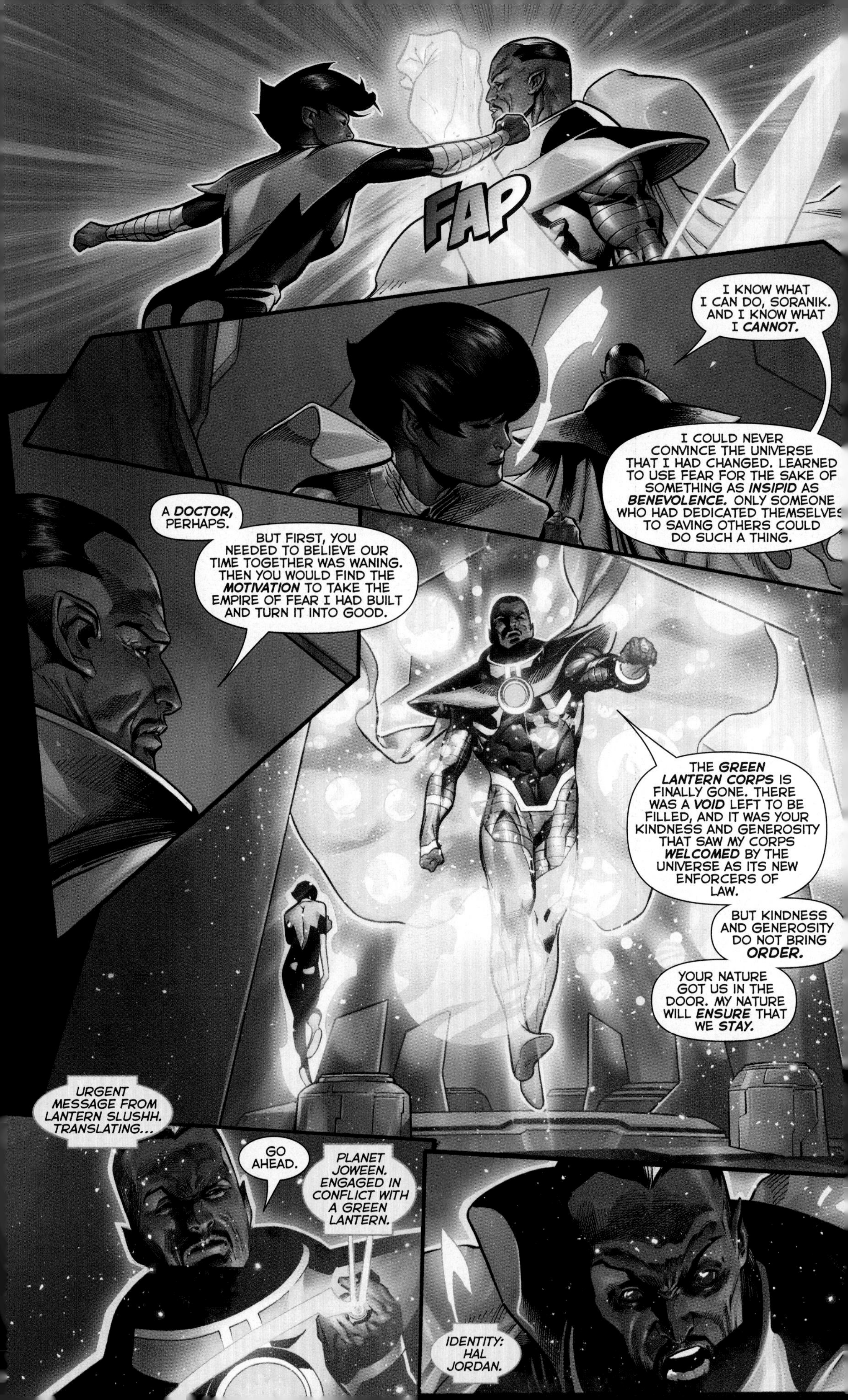
FAP
I KNOW WHAT I CAN DO, SORANIK. AND I KNOW WHAT I CANNOT.
I COULD NEVER CONVINCE THE UNIVERSE THAT I HAD CHANGED. LEARNED TO USE FEAR FOR THE SAKE OF SOMETHING AS INSIPID AS BENEVOLENCE. ONLY SOMEONE WHO HAD DEDICATED THEMSELVES TO SAVING OTHERS COULD DO SUCH A THING.
A DOCTOR, PERHAPS.
BUT FIRST, YOU NEEDED TO BELIEVE OUR TIME TOGETHER WAS WANING. THEN YOU WOULD FIND THE MOTIVATION TO TAKE THE EMPIRE OF FEAR I HAD BUILT AND TURN IT INTO GOOD.
THE GREEN LANTERN CORPS IS FINALLY GONE. THERE WAS A VOID LEFT TO BE FILLED, AND IT WAS YOUR KINDNESS AND GENEROSITY THAT SAW MY CORPS WELCOMED BY THE UNIVERSE AS ITS NEW ENFORCERS OF LAW.
BUT KINDNESS AND GENEROSITY DO NOT BRING ORDER.
YOUR NATURE GOT US IN THE DOOR. MY NATURE WILL ENSURE THAT WE STAY.
URGENT MESSAGE FROM LANTERN SLUSHH. TRANSLATING...
GO AHEAD.
PLANET JOWEEN. ENGAGED IN CONFLICT WITH A GREEN LANTERN.
IDENTITY: HAL JORDAN.

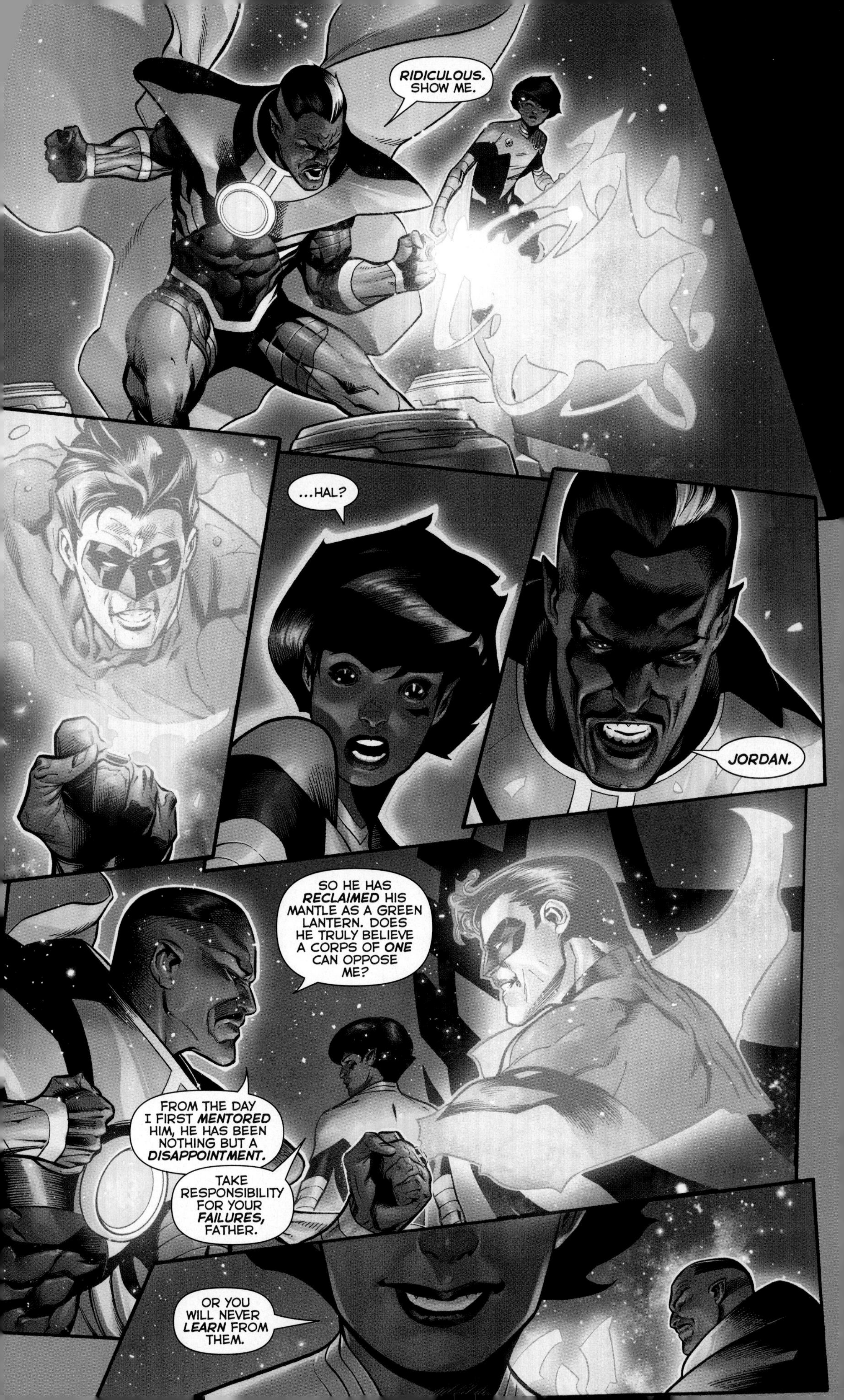
RIDICULOUS. SHOW ME.
...HAL?
JORDAN.
SO HE HAS RECLAIMED HIS MANTLE AS A GREEN LANTERN. DOES HE TRULY BELIEVE A CORPS OF ONE CAN OPPOSE ME?
FROM THE DAY I FIRST MENTORED HIM, HE HAS BEEN NOTHING BUT A DISAPPOINTMENT.
TAKE RESPONSIBILITY FOR YOUR FAILURES, FATHER.
OR YOU WILL NEVER LEARN FROM THEM.

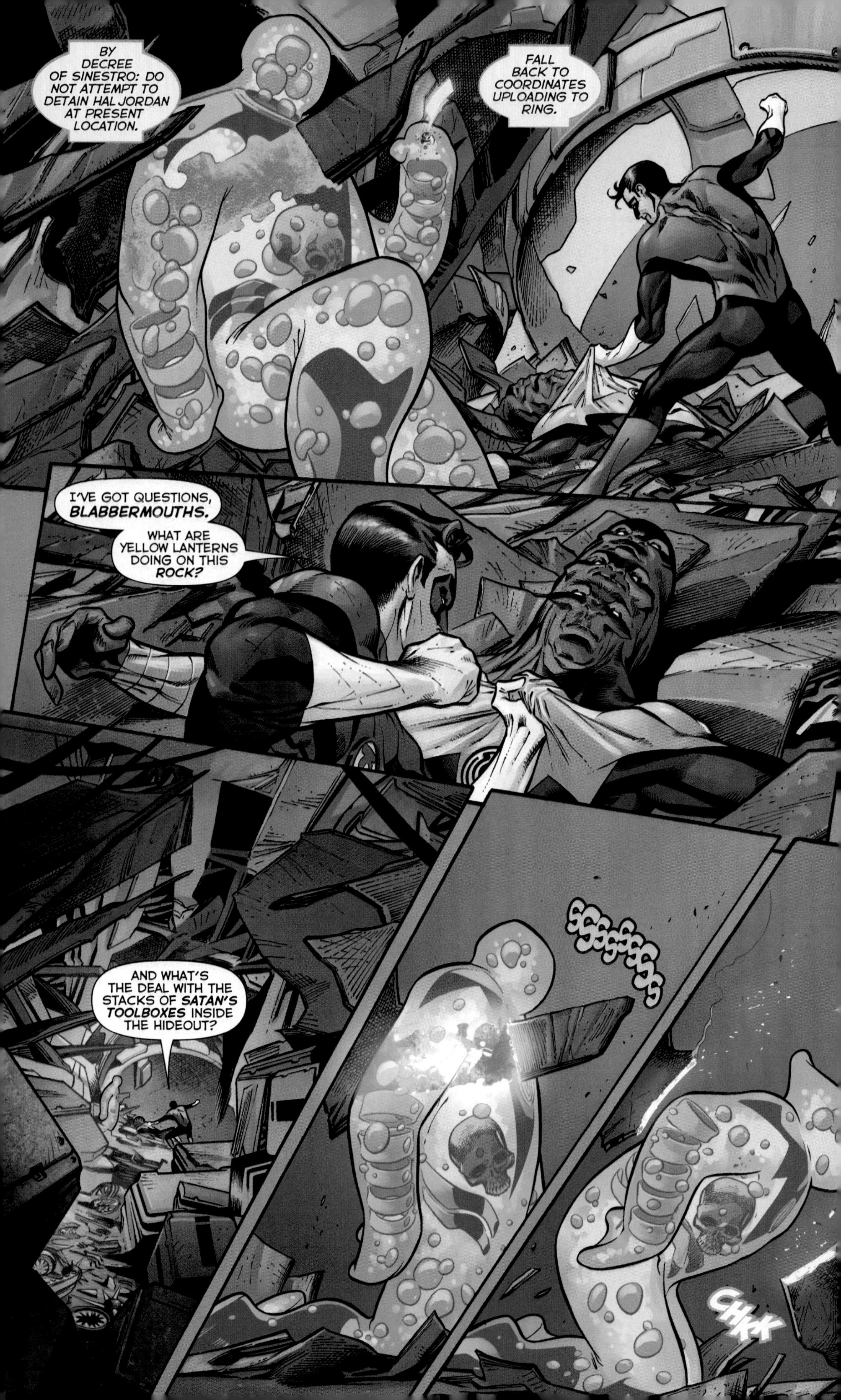
BY DECREE OF SINESTRO: DO NOT ATTEMPT TO DETAIN HAL JORDAN AT PRESENT LOCATION.
FALL BACK TO COORDINATES UPLOADING TO RING.
I'VE GOT QUESTIONS, BLABBERMOUTHS.
WHAT ARE YELLOW LANTERNS DOING ON THIS ROCK?
AND WHAT'S THE DEAL WITH THE STACKS OF SATAN'S TOOLBOXES INSIDE THE HIDEOUT?
SSSSSSSS
CHKK

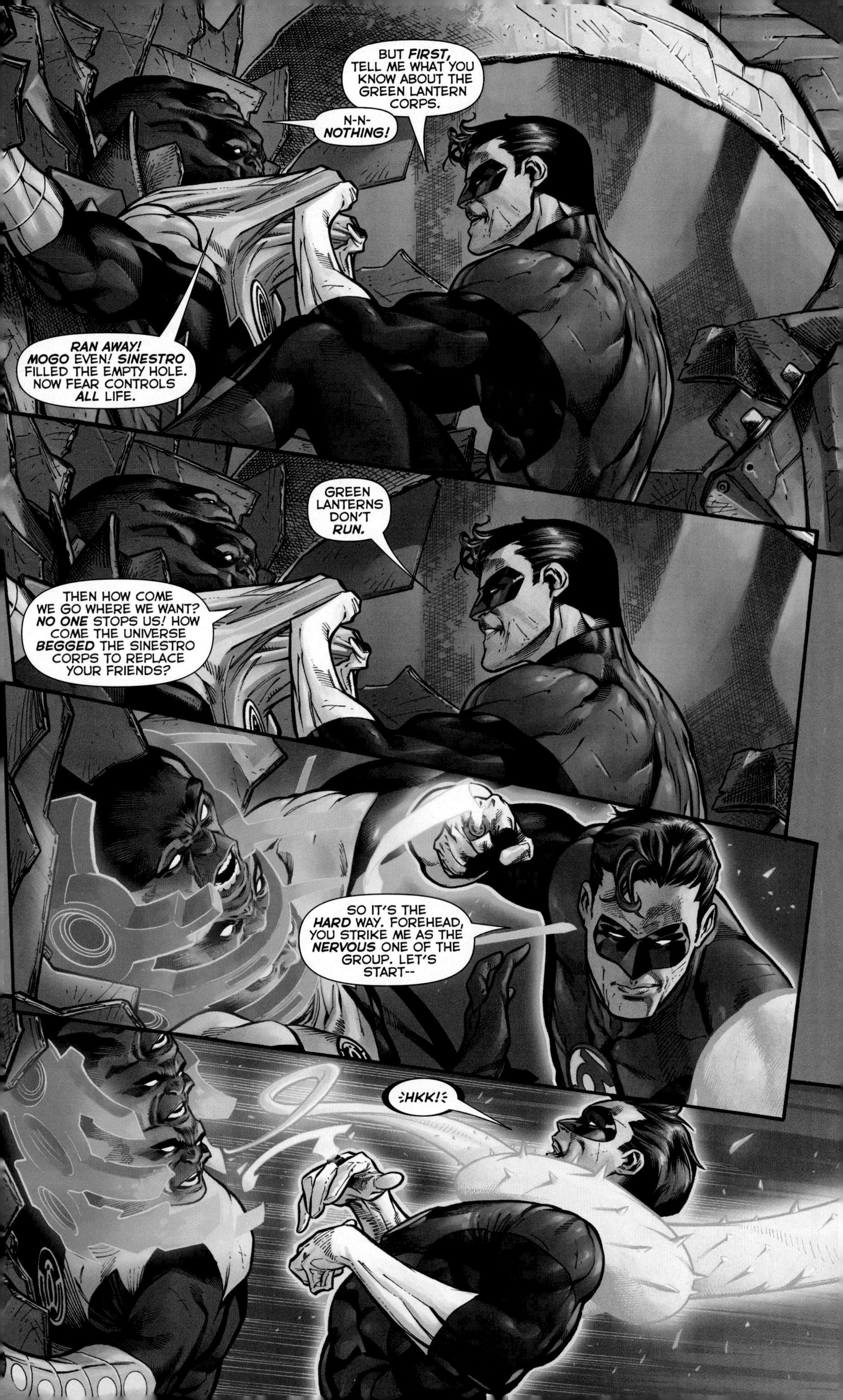
BUT FIRST, TELL ME WHAT YOU KNOW ABOUT THE GREEN LANTERN CORPS.
N-N-NOTHING!
RAN AWAY! MOGO EVEN! SINESTRO FILLED THE EMPTY HOLE. NOW FEAR CONTROLS ALL LIFE.
GREEN LANTERNS DON'T RUN.
THEN HOW COME WE GO WHERE WE WANT? NO ONE STOPS US! HOW COME THE UNIVERSE BEGGED THE SINESTRO CORPS TO REPLACE YOUR FRIENDS?
SO IT'S THE HARD WAY. FOREHEAD, YOU STRIKE ME AS THE NERVOUS ONE OF THE GROUP. LET'S START--
HKK!

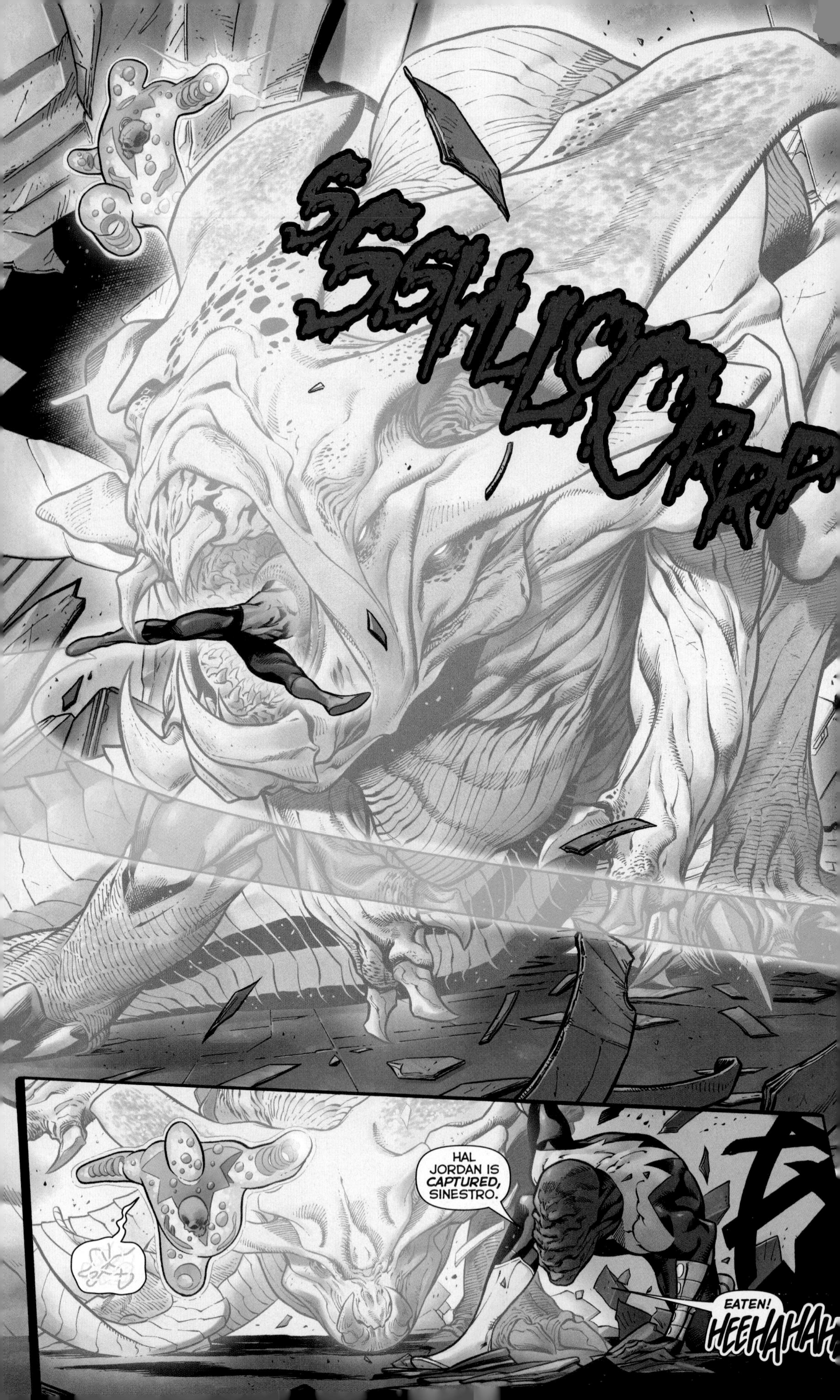

SSSHLLOORRP
HAL JORDAN IS CAPTURED, SINESTRO.
EATEN! HEEHAHAH

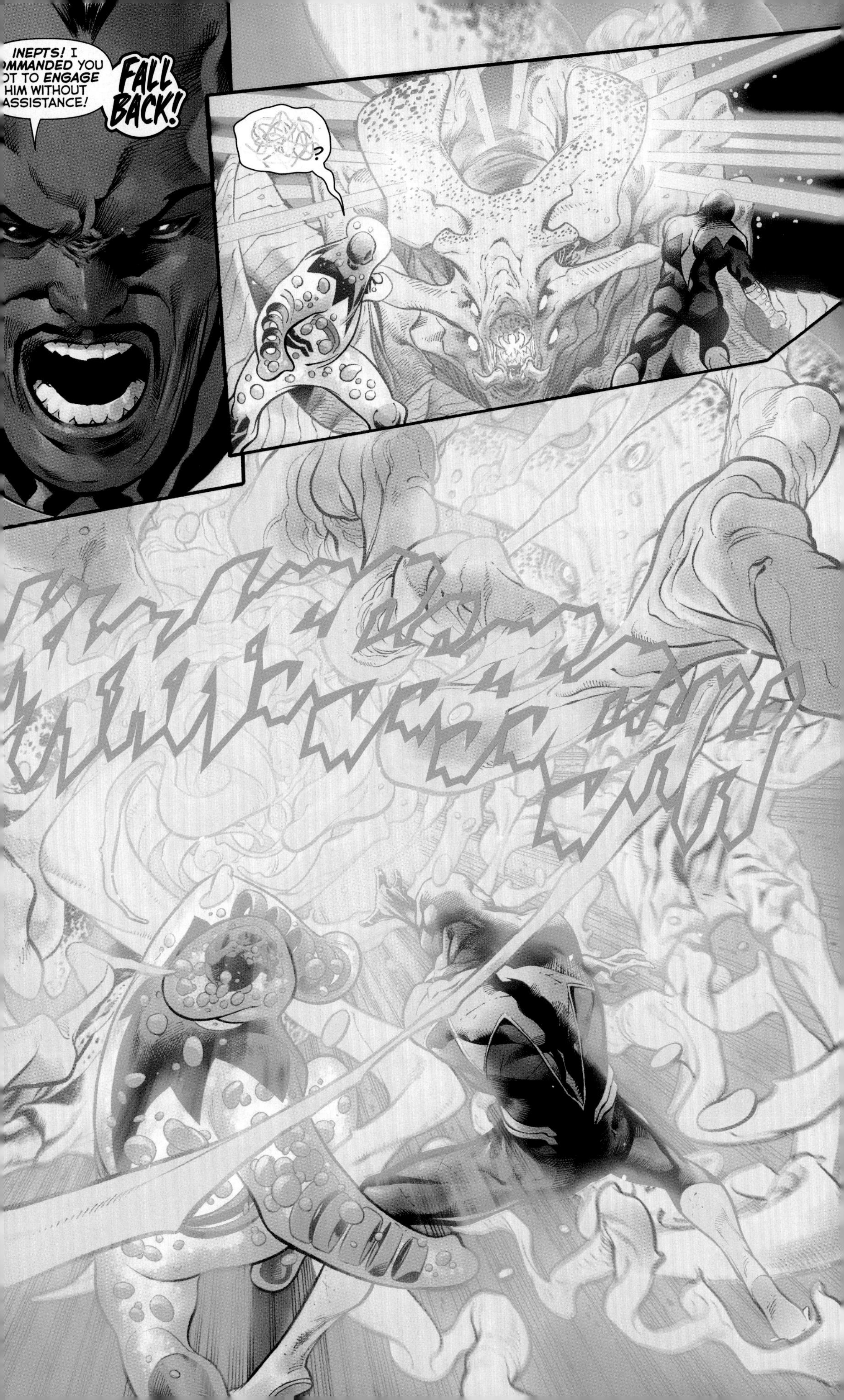
INEPTS! I OMMANDED YOU OT TO ENGAGE HIM WITHOUT ASSISTANCE!
FALL BACK!
?

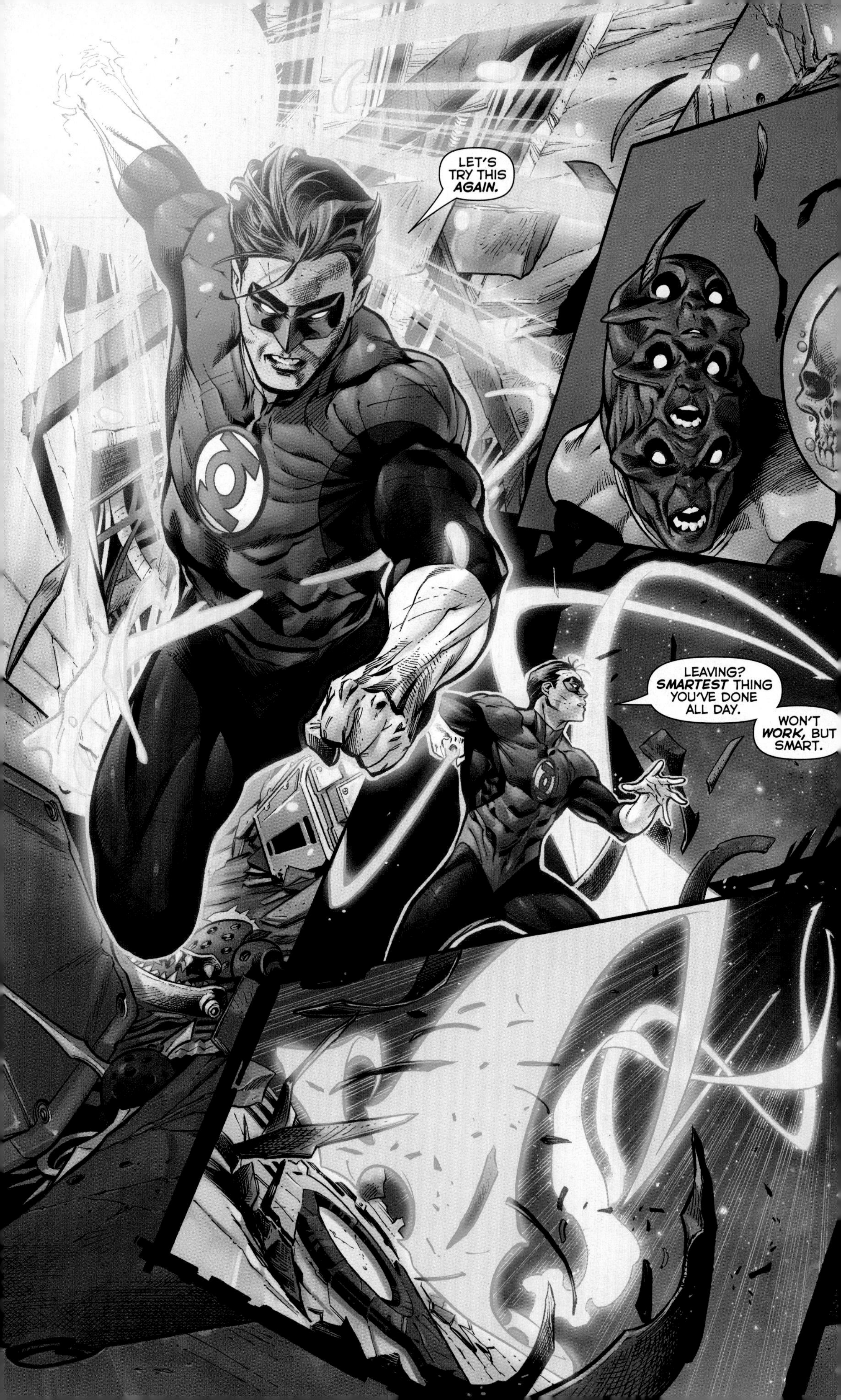
LET'S TRY THIS AGAIN.
LEAVING? SMARTEST THING YOU'VE DONE ALL DAY.
WON'T WORK, BUT SMART.

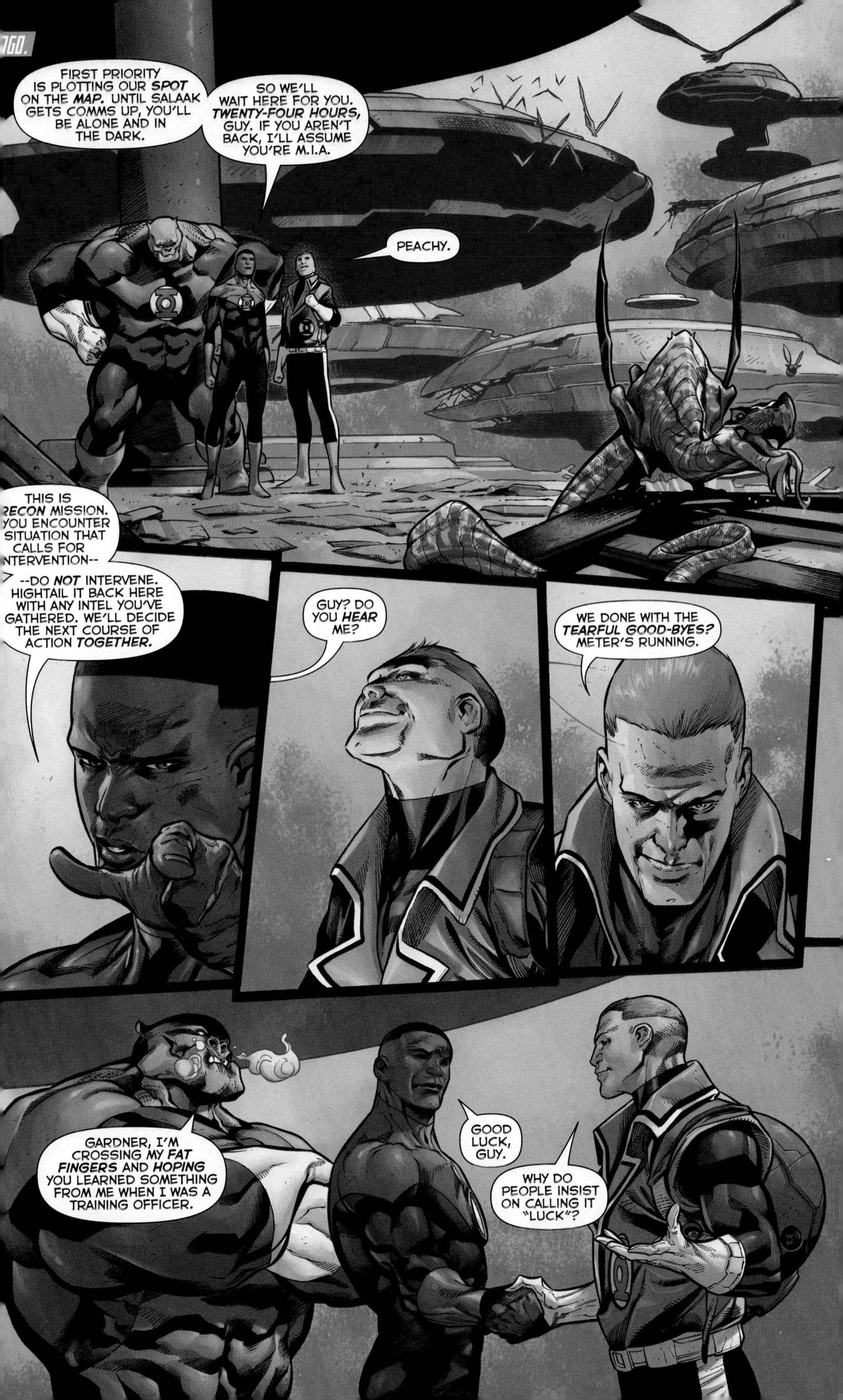

FIRST PRIORITY IS PLOTTING OUR SPOT ON THE MAP. UNTIL SALAAK GETS COMMS UP, YOU'LL BE ALONE AND IN THE DARK.
SO WE'LL WAIT HERE FOR YOU. TWENTY-FOUR HOURS, GUY. IF YOU AREN'T BACK, I'LL ASSUME YOU'RE M.I.A.
PEACHY.
THIS IS RECON MISSION. YOU ENCOUNTER SITUATION THAT CALLS FOR INTERVENTION--
--DO NOT INTERVENE. HIGHTAIL IT BACK HERE WITH ANY INTEL YOU'VE GATHERED. WE'LL DECIDE THE NEXT COURSE OF ACTION TOGETHER.
GUY? DO YOU HEAR ME?
WE DONE WITH THE TEARFUL GOOD-BYES? METER'S RUNNING.
GARDNER, I'M CROSSING MY FAT FINGERS AND HOPING YOU LEARNED SOMETHING FROM ME WHEN I WAS A TRAINING OFFICER.
GOOD LUCK, GUY.
WHY DO PEOPLE INSIST ON CALLING IT "LUCK"?

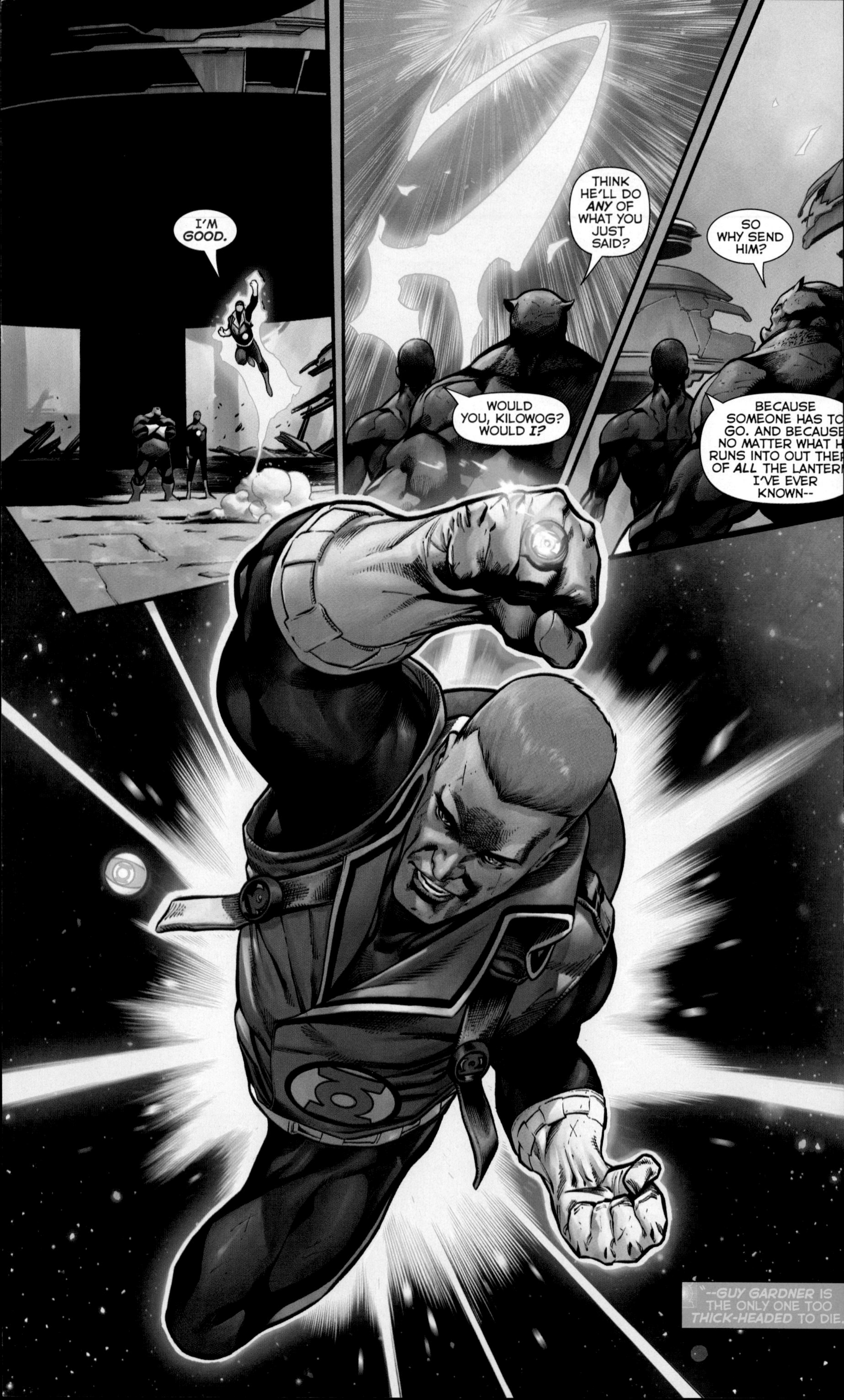
I'M GOOD.
THINK HE'LL DO ANY OF WHAT YOU JUST SAID?
WOULD YOU, KILOWOG? WOULD I?
SO WHY SEND HIM?
BECAUSE SOMEONE HAS TO GO. AND BECAUSE NO MATTER WHAT H RUNS INTO OUT THER OF ALL THE LANTER I'VE EVER KNOWN--
"--GUY GARDNER IS THE ONLY ONE TOO THICK-HEADED TO DIE.

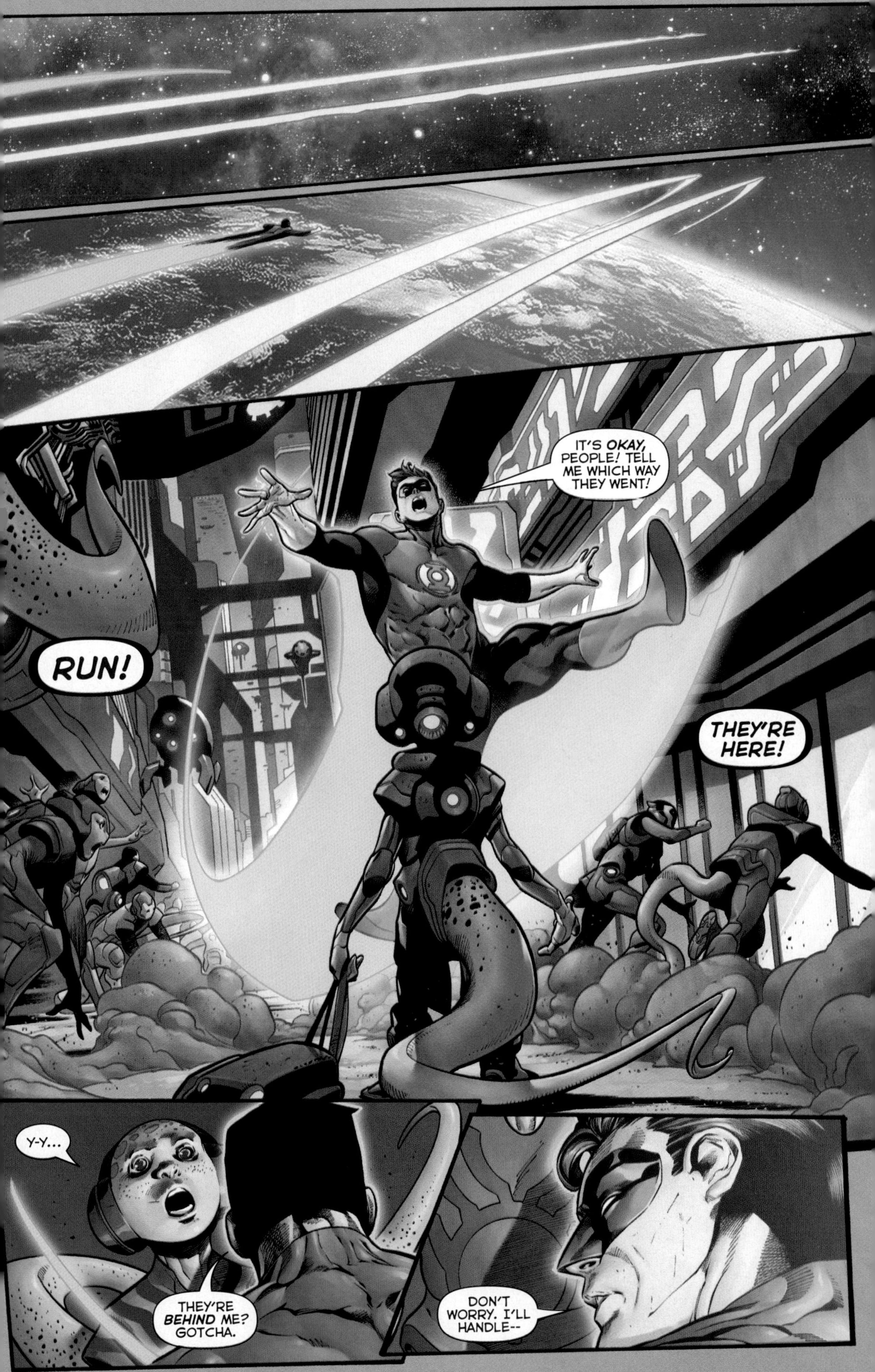
IT'S OKAY, PEOPLE! TELL ME WHICH WAY THEY WENT!
RUN!
THEY'RE HERE!
Y-Y...
THEY'RE BEHIND ME? GOTCHA.
DON'T WORRY. I'LL HANDLE--

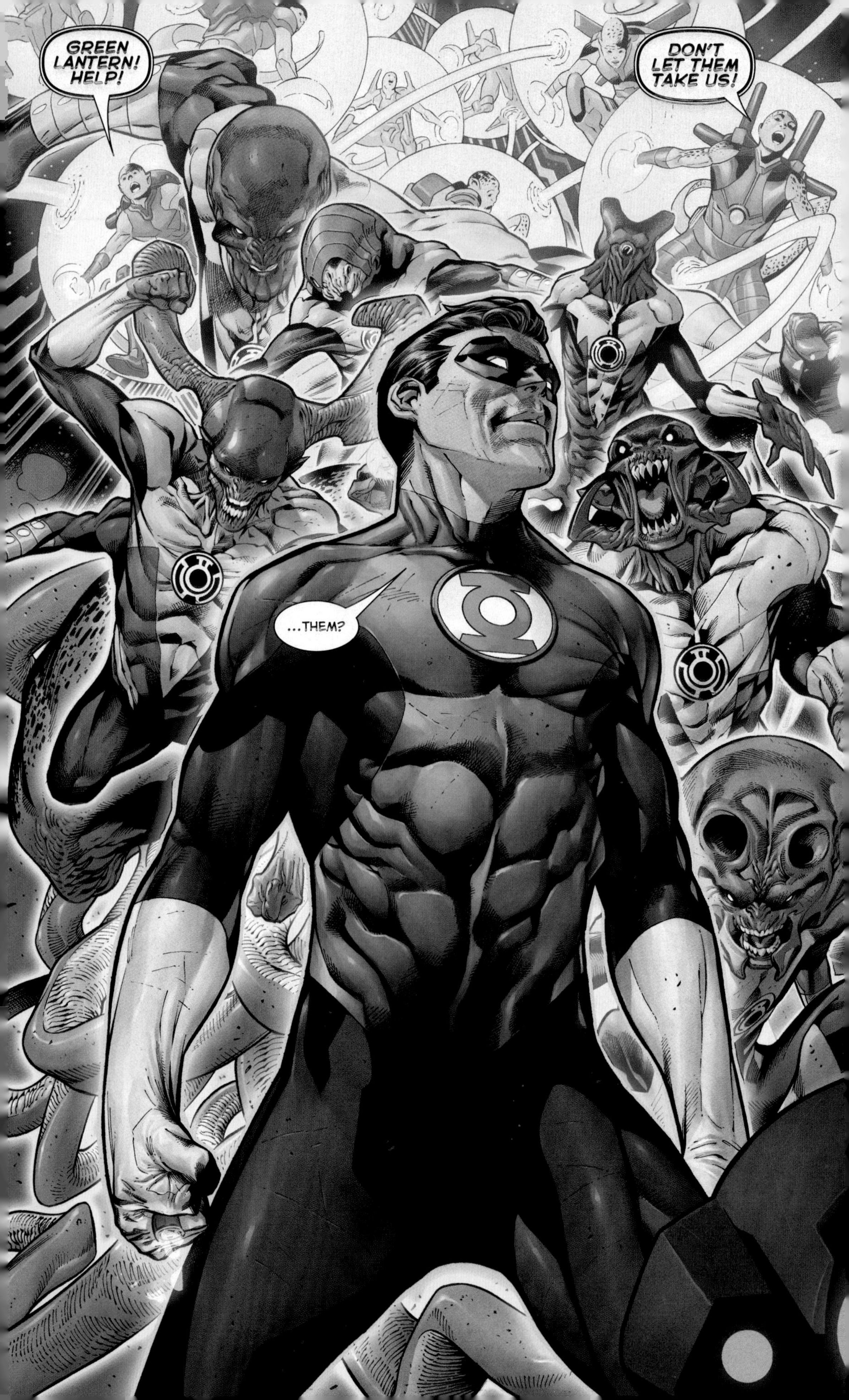
GREEN LANTERN! HELP!
DON'T LET THEM TAKE US!
...THEM?

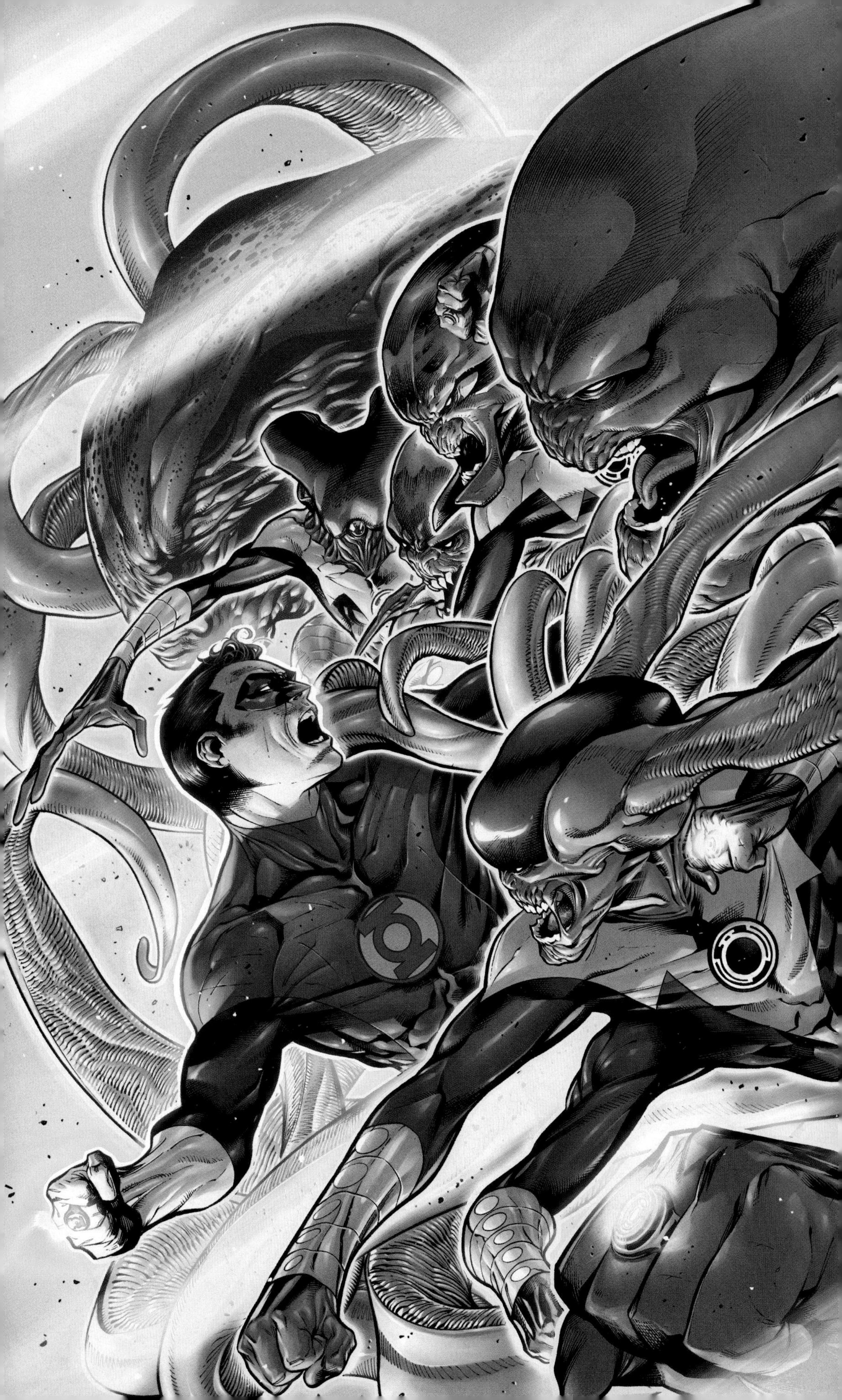

SINESTRO'S LAW PART 3: INNOCENTS LOST

RAFA SANDOVAL penciller * JORDI TARRAGONA inker * TOMEU MOREY colorist
RAFA SANDOVAL, JORDI TARRAGONA and TOMEU MOREY cover artists

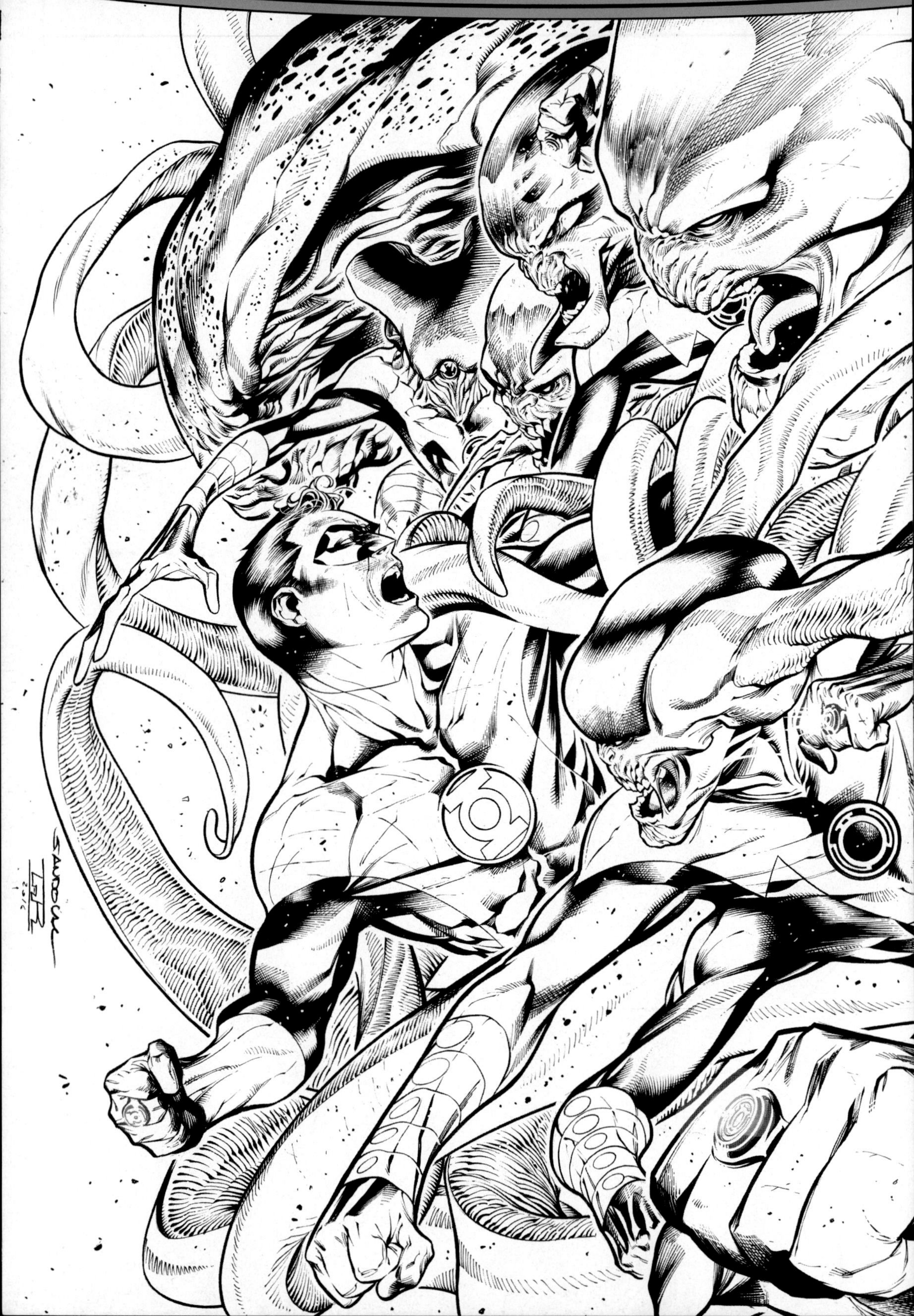

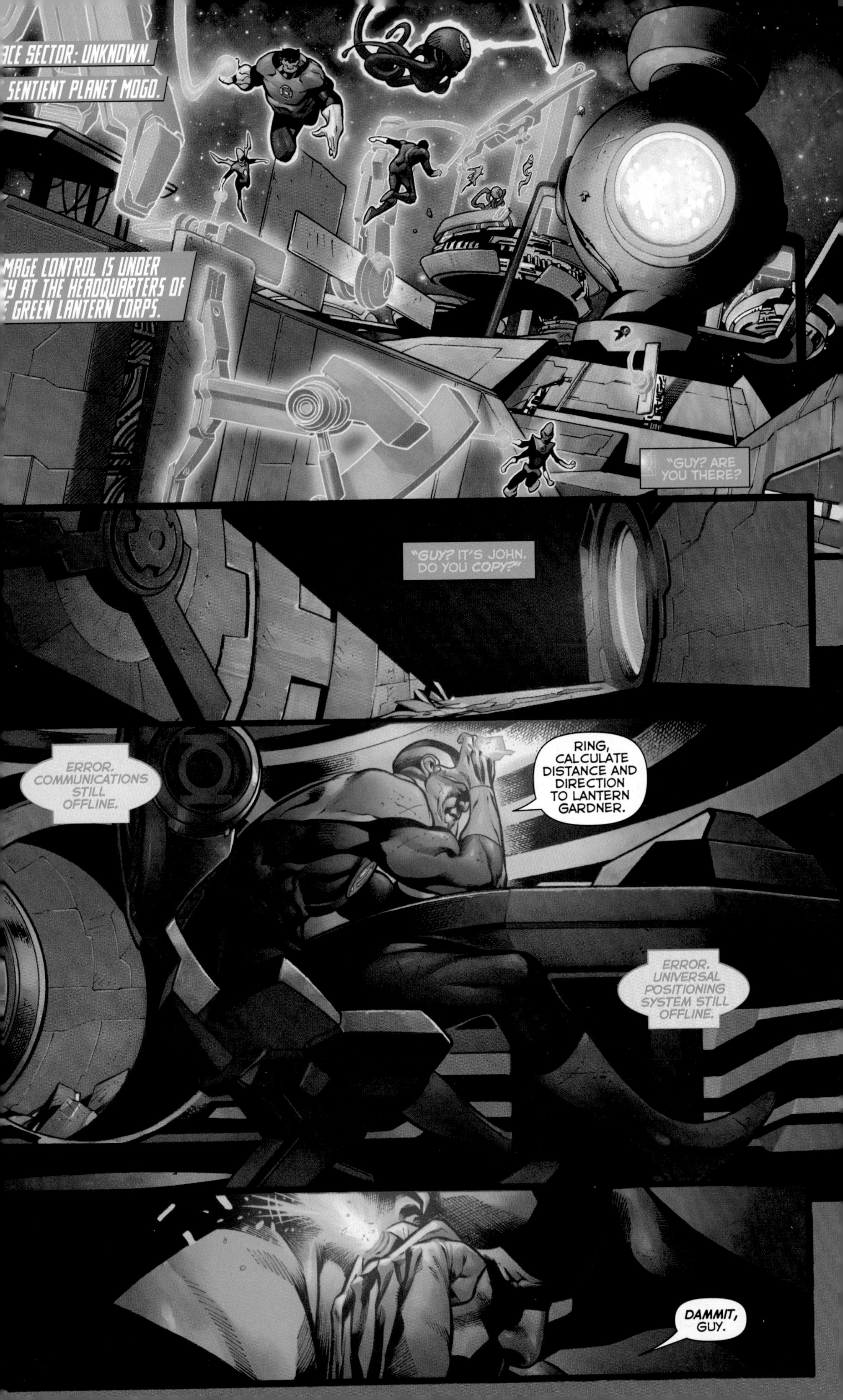
ACE SECTOR: UNKNOWN.
SENTIENT PLANET MOGO.
MAGE CONTROL IS UNDER
Y AT THE HEADQUARTERS OF
GREEN LANTERN CORPS.
"GUY? ARE YOU THERE?
"GUY? IT'S JOHN. DO YOU COPY?"
ERROR. COMMUNICATIONS STILL OFFLINE.
RING, CALCULATE DISTANCE AND DIRECTION TO LANTERN GARDNER.
ERROR. UNIVERSAL POSITIONING SYSTEM STILL OFFLINE.
DAMMIT, GUY.

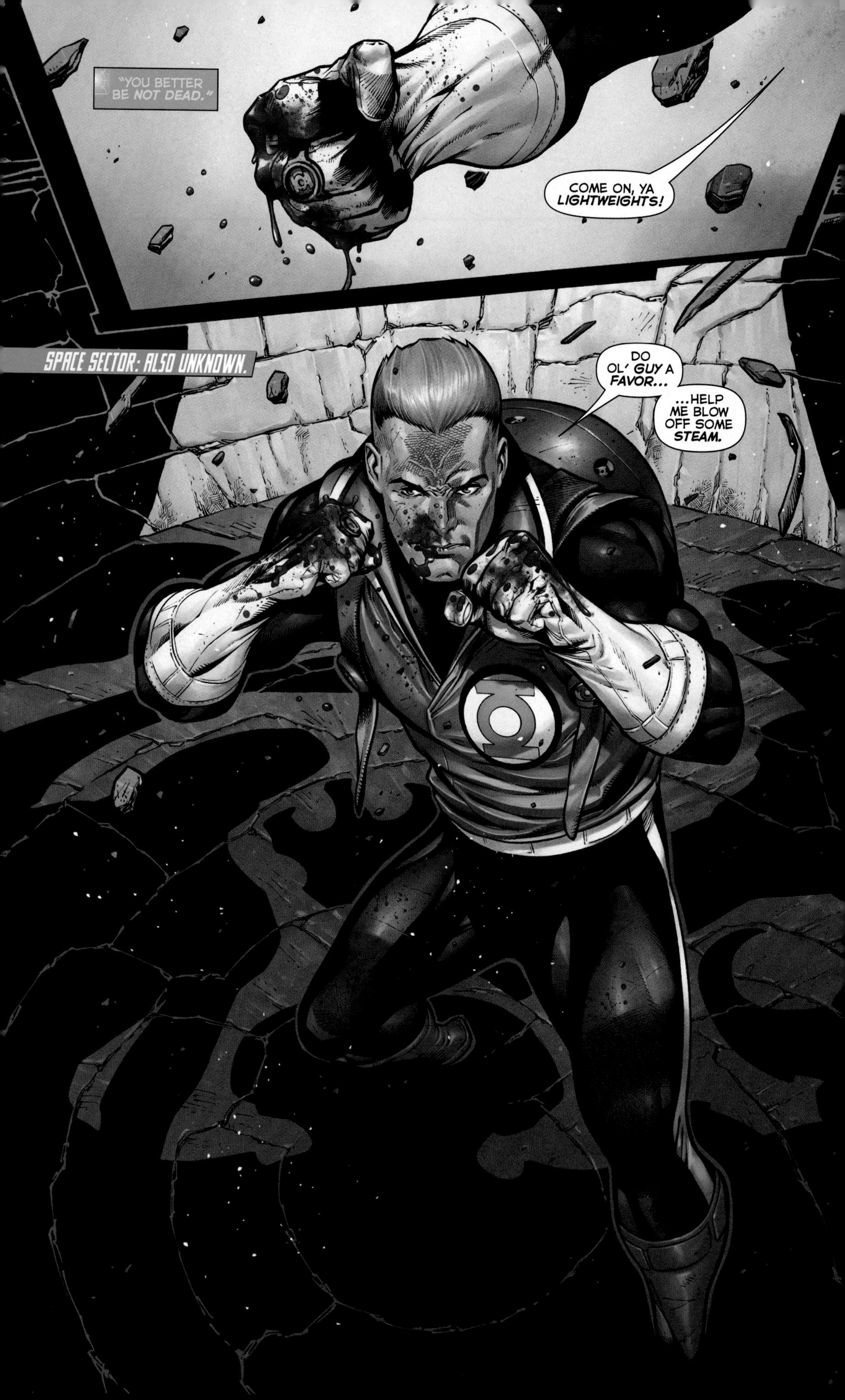
"YOU BETTER
BE NOT DEAD."
COME ON, YA LIGHTWEIGHTS!
SPACE SECTOR: ALSO UNKNOWN.
DO OL' GUY A FAVOR...
...HELP ME BLOW OFF SOME STEAM.

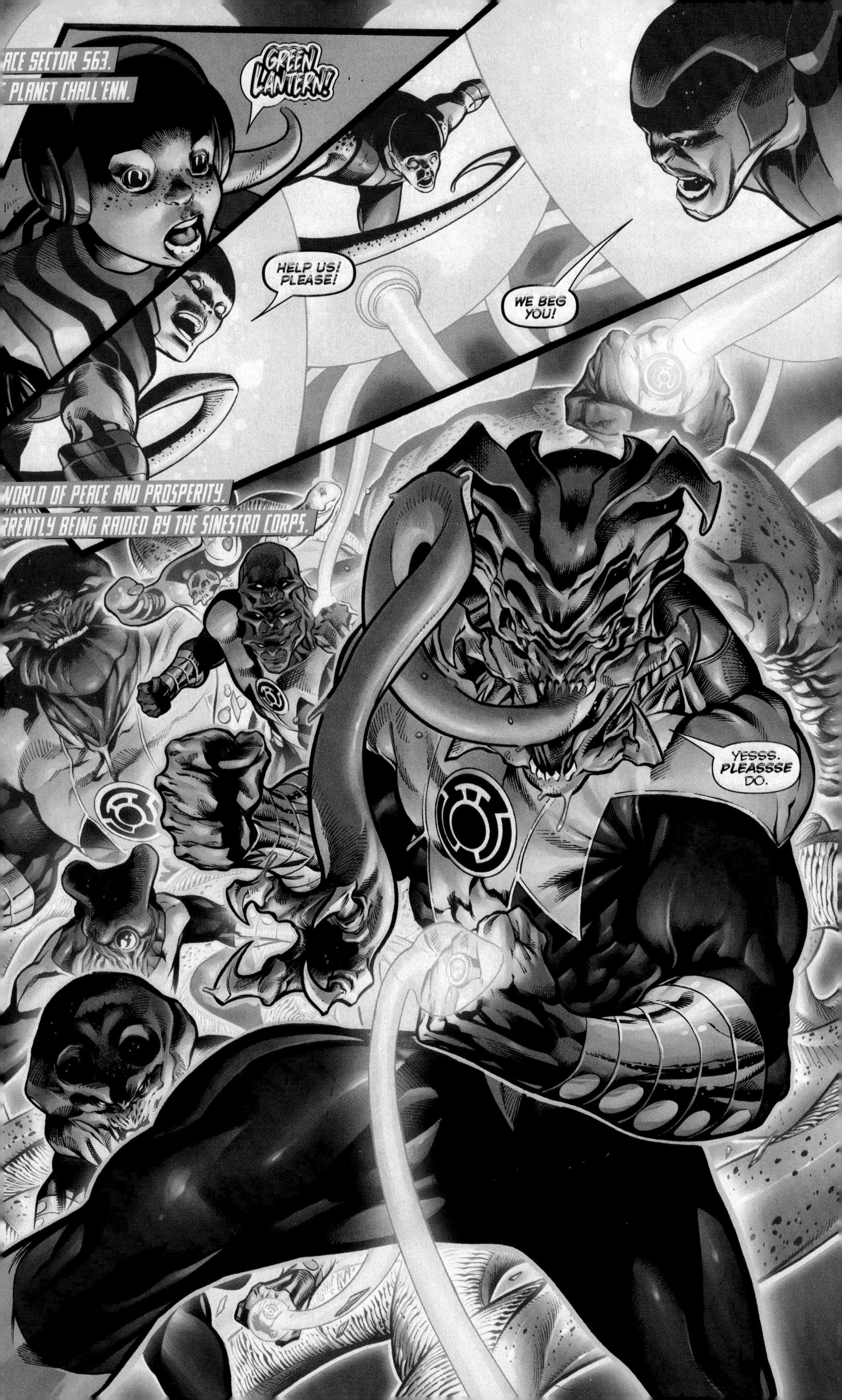

ACE SECTOR 563.
PLANET CHALL'ENN.
GREEN LANTERN!
HELP US! PLEASE!
WE BEG YOU!
WORLD OF PEACE AND PROSPERITY.
RRENTLY BEING RAIDED BY THE SINESTRO CORPS.
YESSS. PLEASSSE DO.

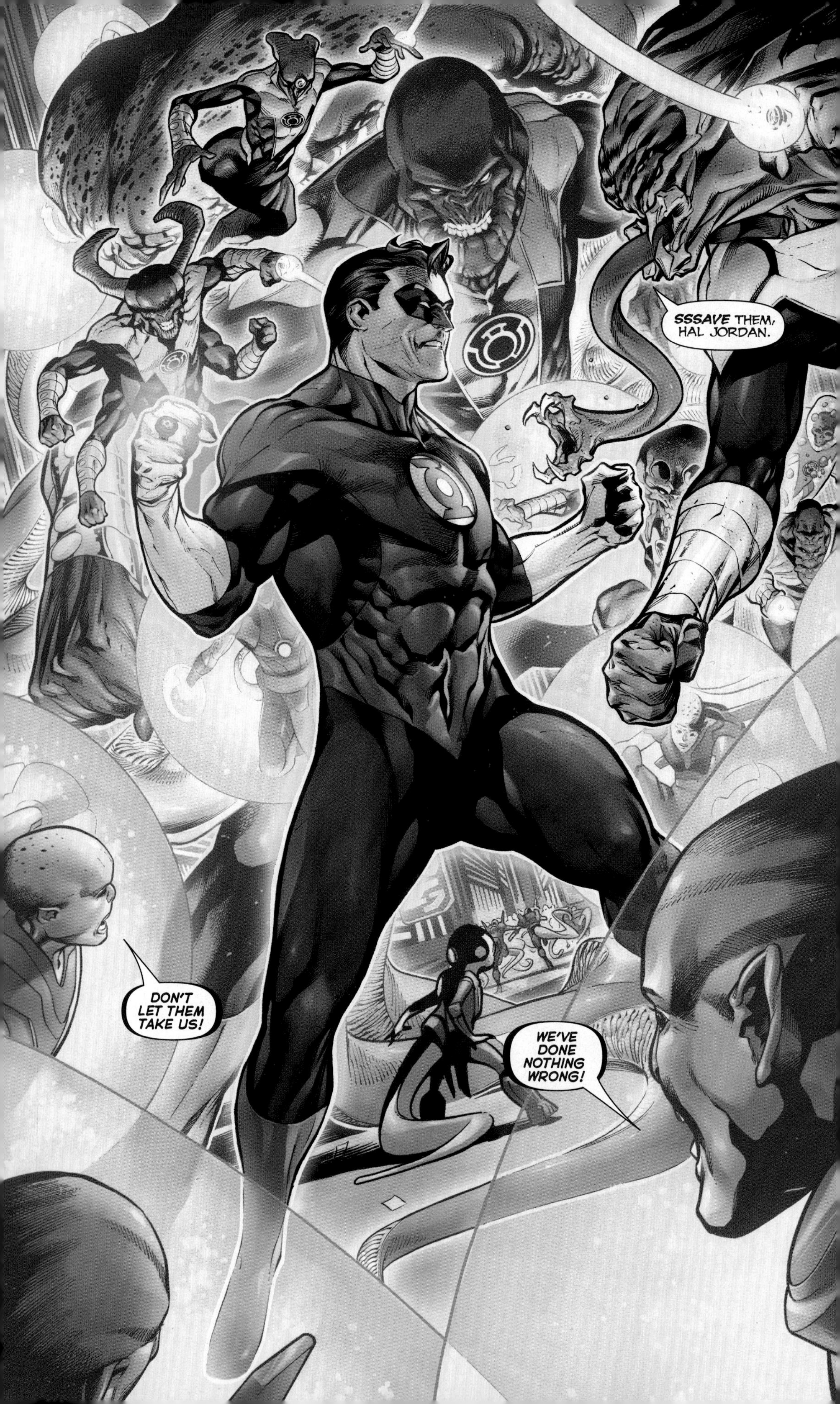
SSSAVE THEM, HAL JORDAN.
DON'T LET THEM TAKE US!
WE'VE DONE NOTHING WRONG!

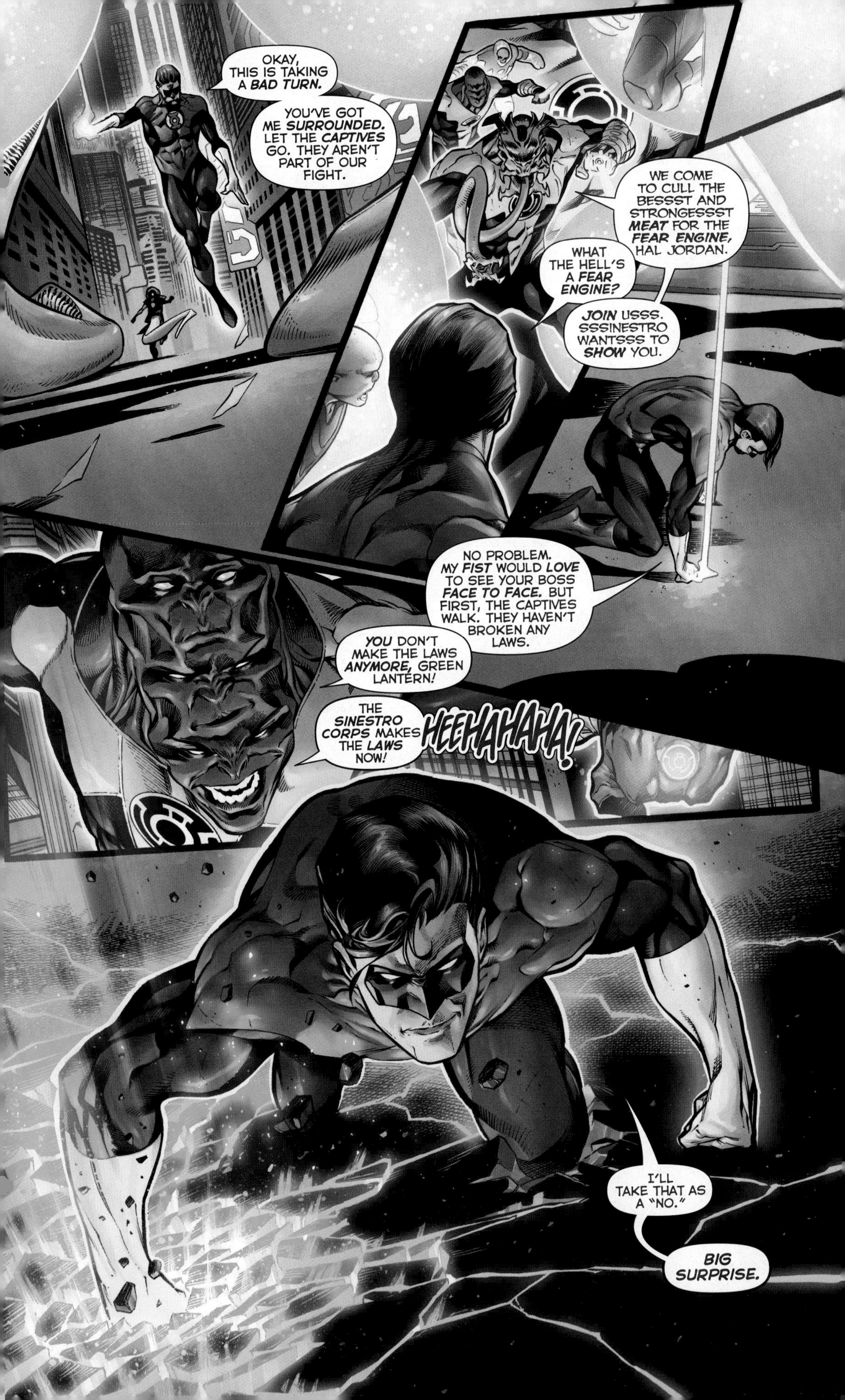
OKAY, THIS IS TAKING A BAD TURN.
YOU'VE GOT ME SURROUNDED. LET THE CAPTIVES GO. THEY AREN'T PART OF OUR FIGHT.
WE COME TO CULL THE BESSST AND STRONGESSST MEAT FOR THE FEAR ENGINE, HAL JORDAN.
WHAT THE HELL'S A FEAR ENGINE?
JOIN USSS. SSSINESTRO WANTSSS TO SHOW YOU.
NO PROBLEM. MY FIST WOULD LOVE TO SEE YOUR BOSS FACE TO FACE. BUT FIRST, THE CAPTIVES WALK. THEY HAVEN'T BROKEN ANY LAWS.
YOU DON'T MAKE THE LAWS ANYMORE, GREEN LANTERN!
THE SINESTRO CORPS MAKES THE LAWS NOW!
HEEHAHAHA!
I'LL TAKE THAT AS A "NO."
BIG SURPRISE.

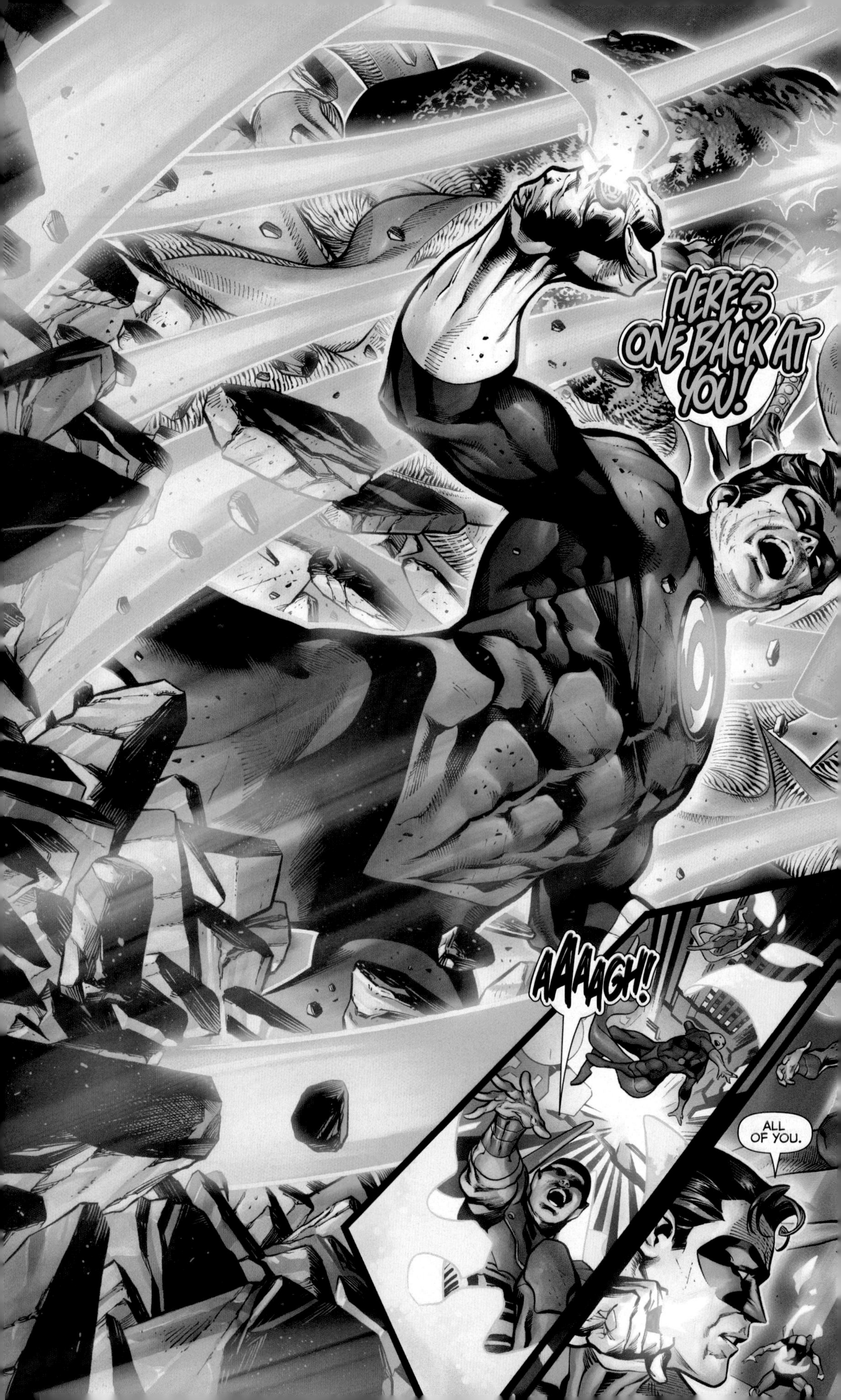
HERE'S ONE BACK AT YOU!
AAAAGH!!
ALL OF YOU.

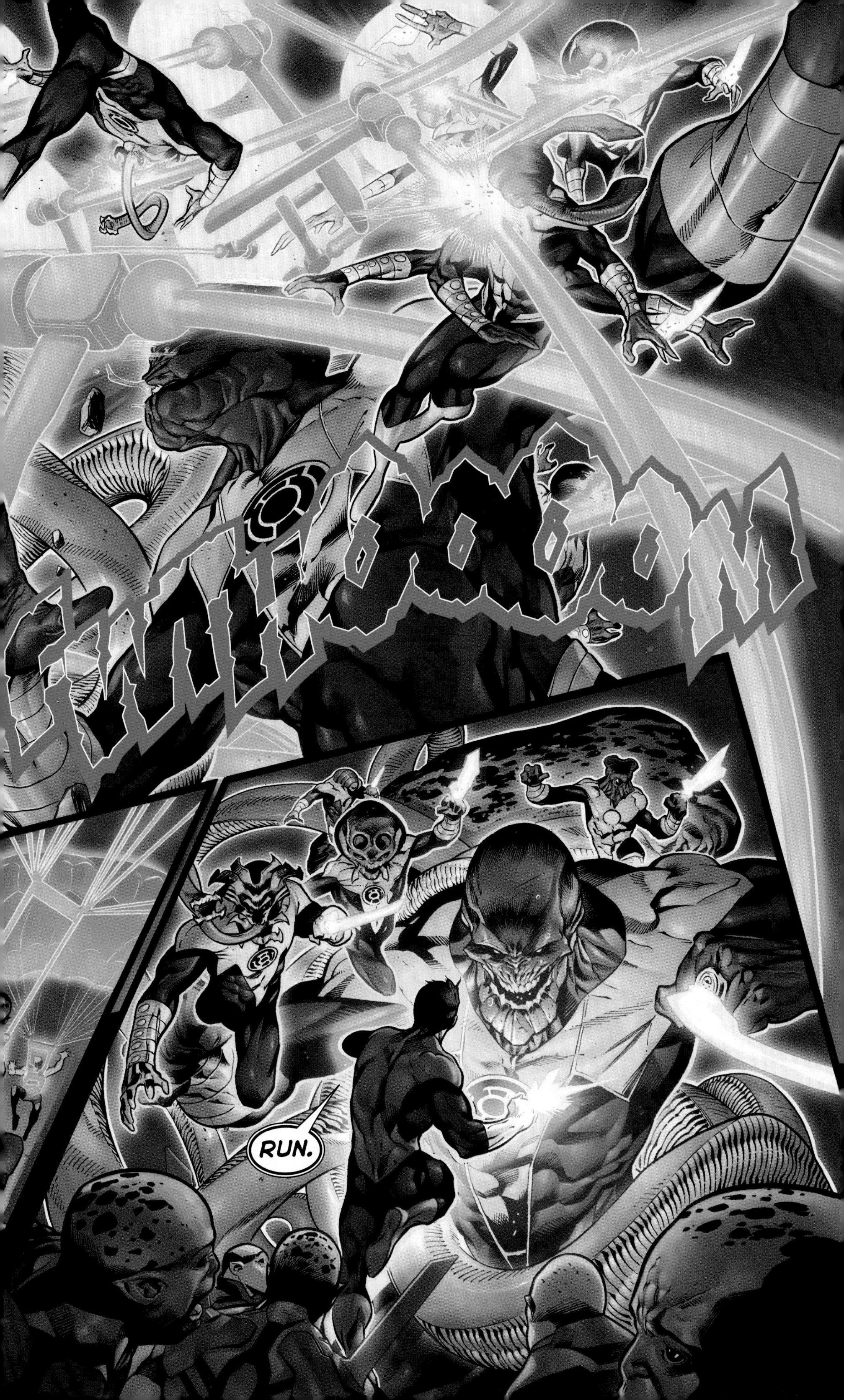
RUN.

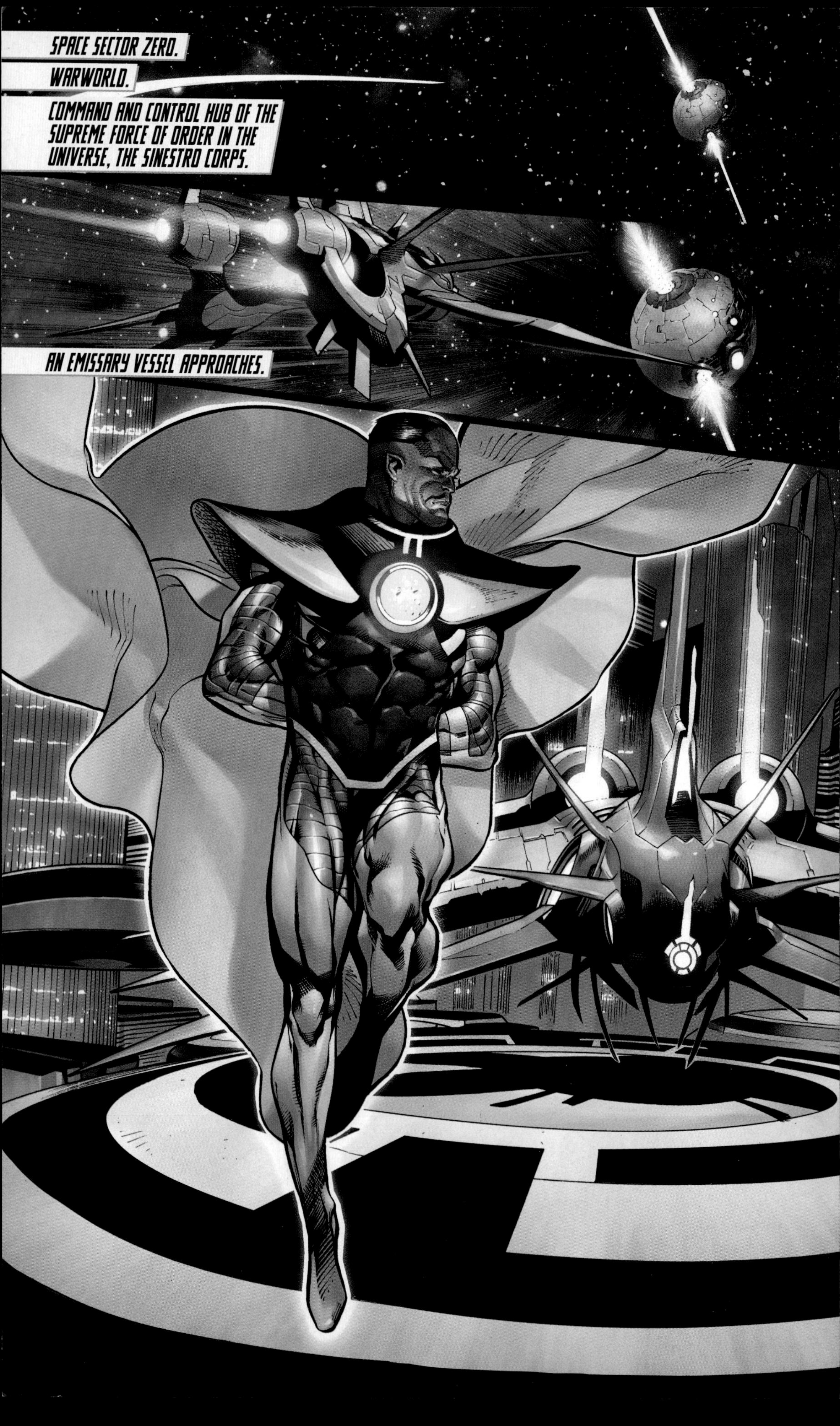
SPACE SECTOR ZERO.
WARWORLD.
COMMAND AND CONTROL HUB OF THE SUPREME FORCE OF ORDER IN THE UNIVERSE, THE SINESTRO CORPS.
AN EMISSARY VESSEL APPROACHES.

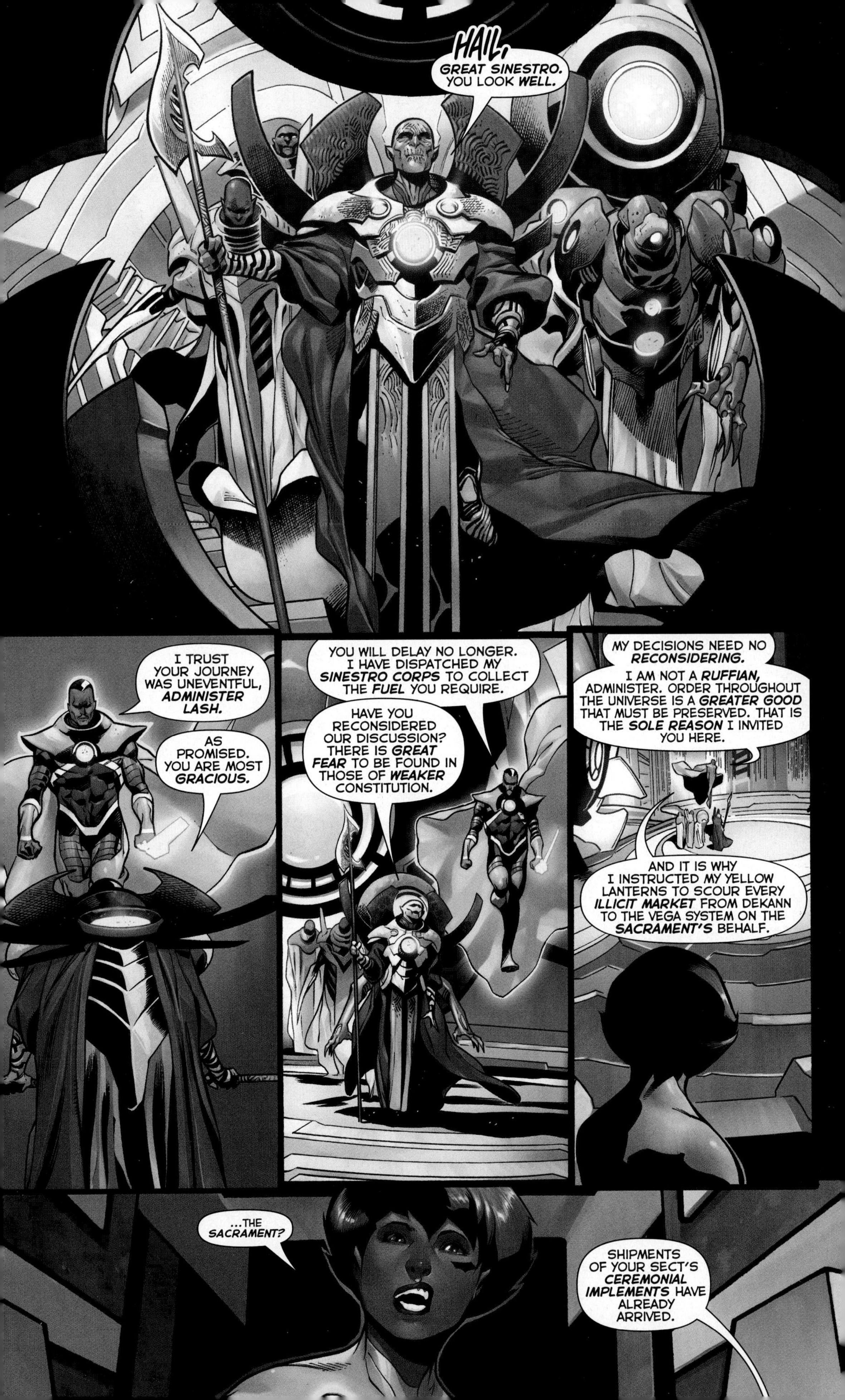
HAIL, GREAT SINESTRO. YOU LOOK WELL.
I TRUST YOUR JOURNEY WAS UNEVENTFUL, ADMINISTER LASH.
AS PROMISED. YOU ARE MOST GRACIOUS.
YOU WILL DELAY NO LONGER. I HAVE DISPATCHED MY SINESTRO CORPS TO COLLECT THE FUEL YOU REQUIRE.
HAVE YOU RECONSIDERED OUR DISCUSSION? THERE IS GREAT FEAR TO BE FOUND IN THOSE OF WEAKER CONSTITUTION.
MY DECISIONS NEED NO RECONSIDERING.
I AM NOT A RUFFIAN, ADMINISTER. ORDER THROUGHOUT THE UNIVERSE IS A GREATER GOOD THAT MUST BE PRESERVED. THAT IS THE SOLE REASON I INVITED YOU HERE.
AND IT IS WHY I INSTRUCTED MY YELLOW LANTERNS TO SCOUR EVERY ILLICIT MARKET FROM DEKANN TO THE VEGA SYSTEM ON THE SACRAMENT'S BEHALF.
...THE SACRAMENT?
SHIPMENTS OF YOUR SECT'S CEREMONIAL IMPLEMENTS HAVE ALREADY ARRIVED.

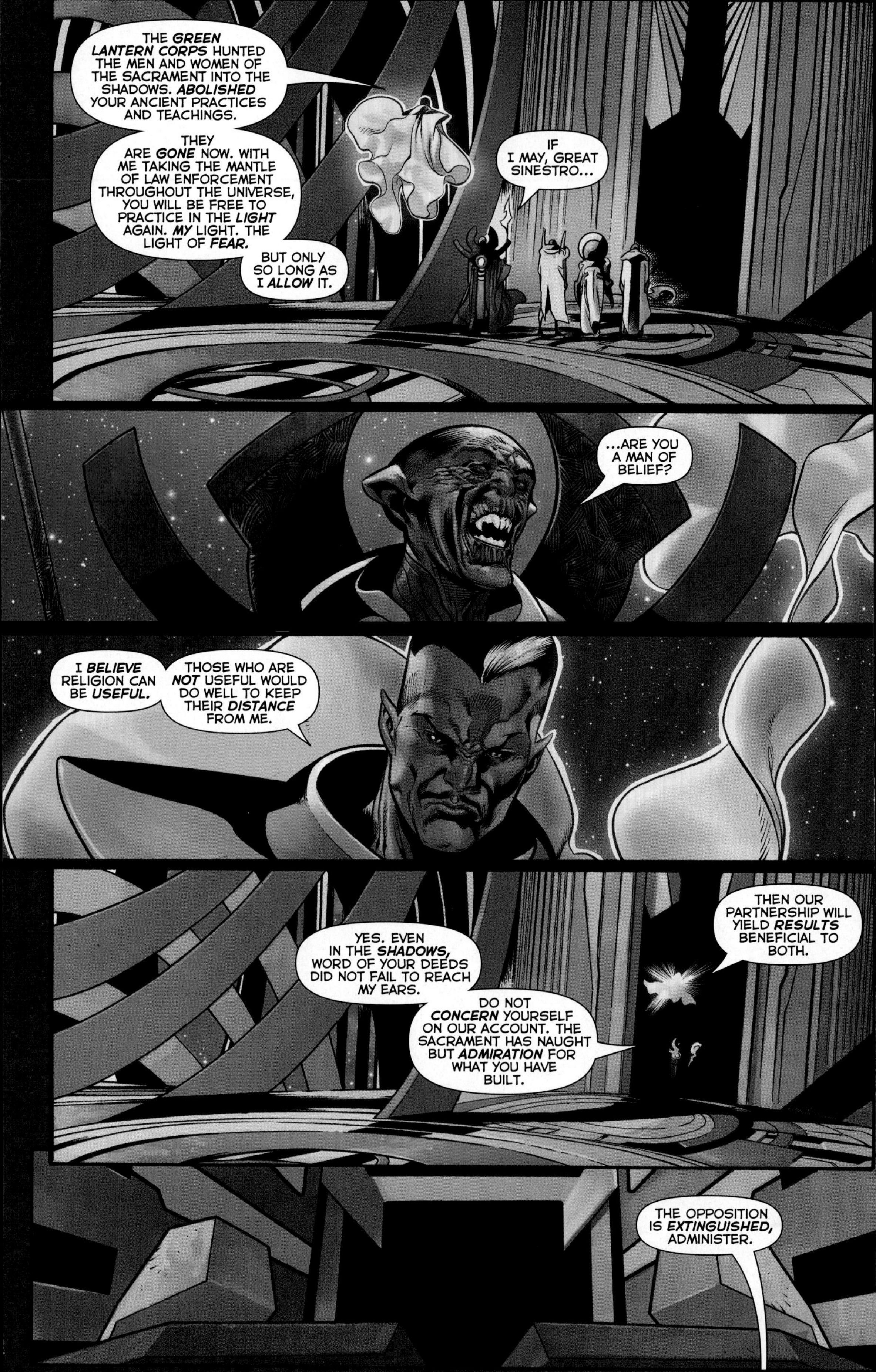
THE GREEN LANTERN CORPS HUNTED THE MEN AND WOMEN OF THE SACRAMENT INTO THE SHADOWS. ABOLISHED YOUR ANCIENT PRACTICES AND TEACHINGS.
THEY ARE GONE NOW. WITH ME TAKING THE MANTLE OF LAW ENFORCEMENT THROUGHOUT THE UNIVERSE, YOU WILL BE FREE TO PRACTICE IN THE LIGHT AGAIN. MY LIGHT. THE LIGHT OF FEAR.
BUT ONLY SO LONG AS I ALLOW IT.
IF I MAY, GREAT SINESTRO...
...ARE YOU A MAN OF BELIEF?
I BELIEVE RELIGION CAN BE USEFUL.
THOSE WHO ARE NOT USEFUL WOULD DO WELL TO KEEP THEIR DISTANCE FROM ME.
YES. EVEN IN THE SHADOWS, WORD OF YOUR DEEDS DID NOT FAIL TO REACH MY EARS.
DO NOT CONCERN YOURSELF ON OUR ACCOUNT. THE SACRAMENT HAS NAUGHT BUT ADMIRATION FOR WHAT YOU HAVE BUILT.
THEN OUR PARTNERSHIP WILL YIELD RESULTS BENEFICIAL TO BOTH.
THE OPPOSITION IS EXTINGUISHED, ADMINISTER.

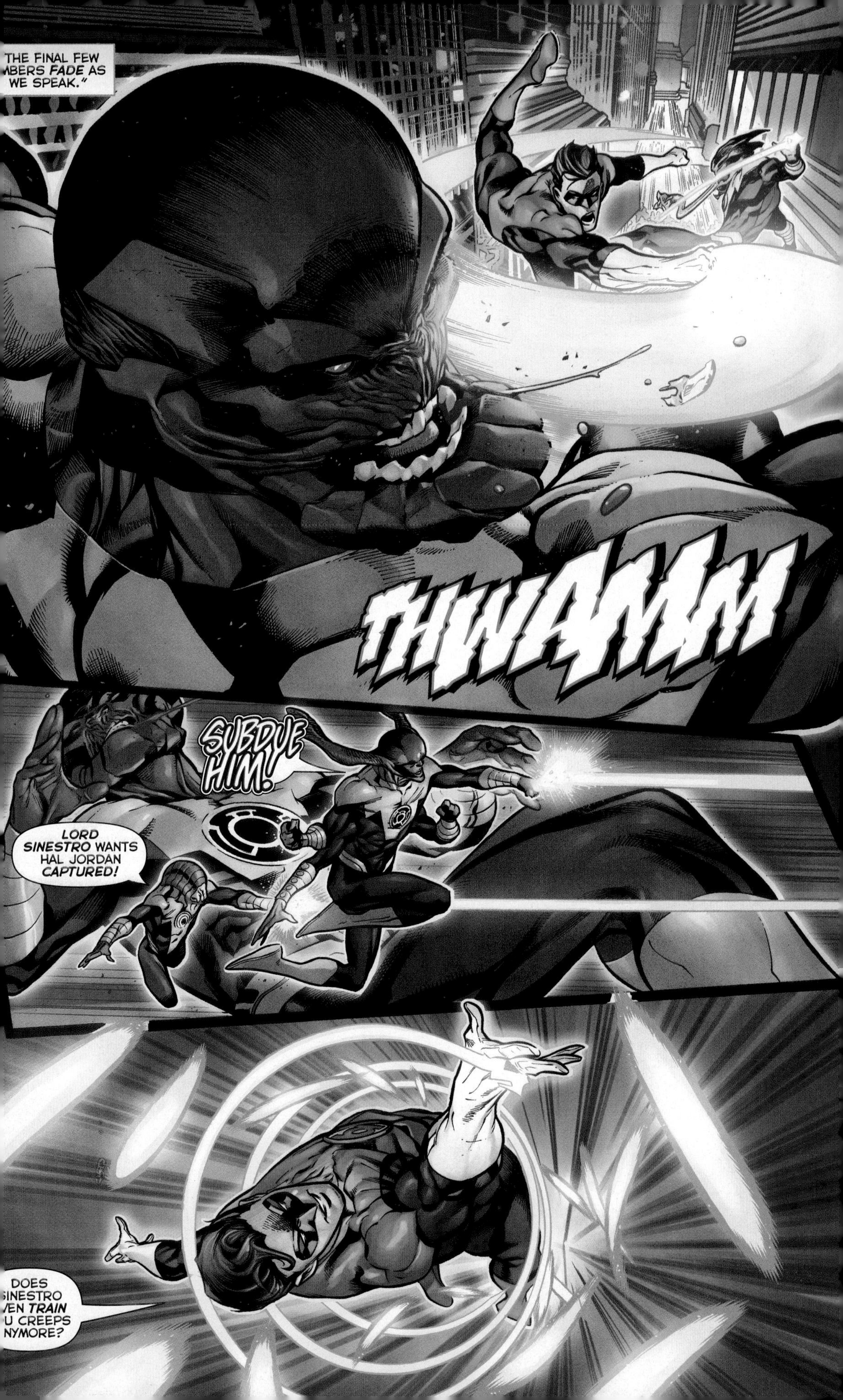
THE FINAL FEW
MBERS FADE AS
WE SPEAK."
THWAMM
SUBDUE HIM!
LORD SINESTRO WANTS HAL JORDAN CAPTURED!
DOES
SINESTRO
VEN TRAIN
U CREEPS
NYMORE?

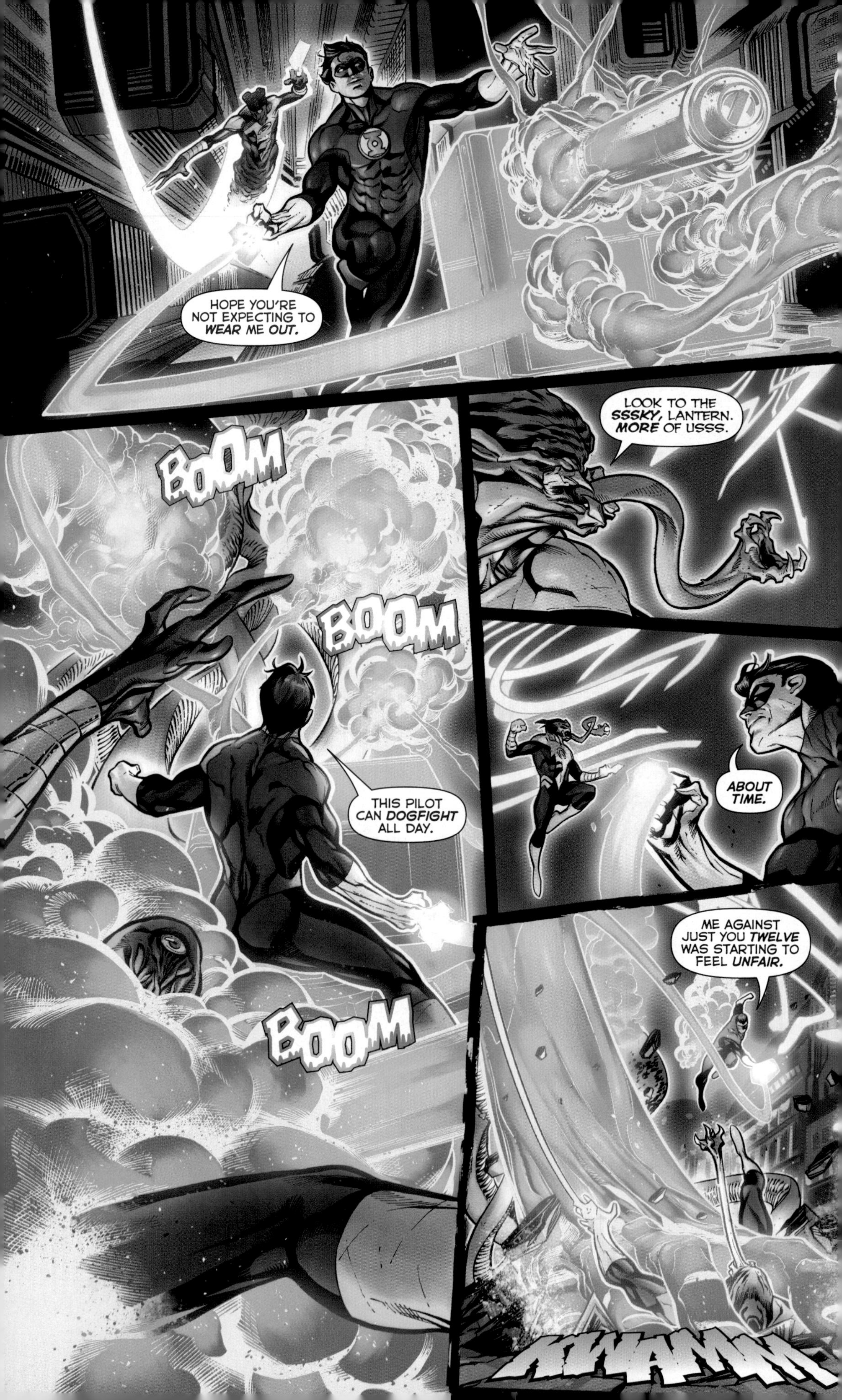
HOPE YOU'RE NOT EXPECTING TO WEAR ME OUT.
BOOM
LOOK TO THE SSSKY, LANTERN. MORE OF USSS.
BOOM
THIS PILOT CAN DOGFIGHT ALL DAY.
ABOUT TIME.
BOOM
ME AGAINST JUST YOU TWELVE WAS STARTING TO FEEL UNFAIR.

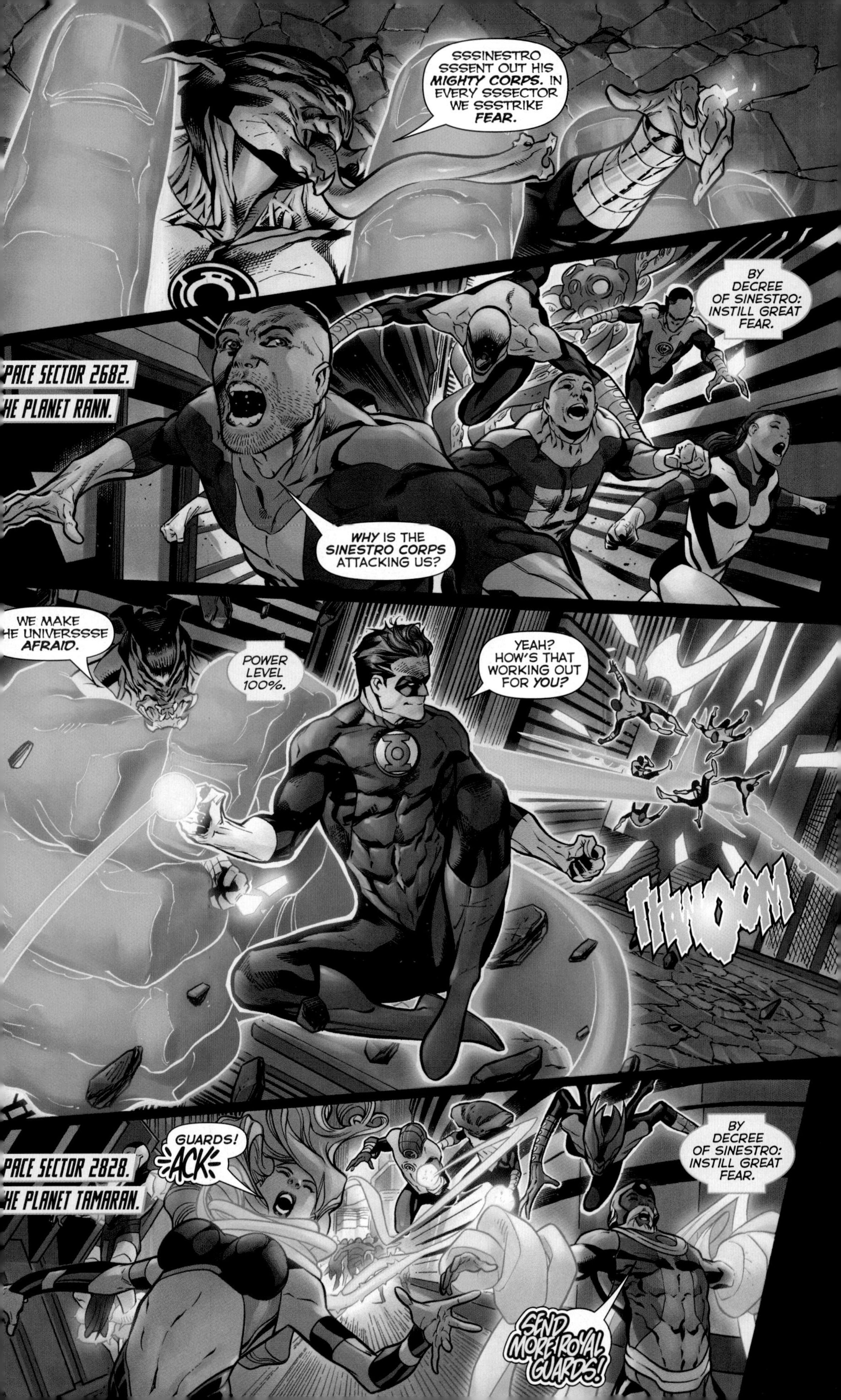

SSSINESTRO SSSENT OUT HIS MIGHTY CORPS. IN EVERY SSSECTOR WE SSSTRIKE FEAR.
BY DECREE OF SINESTRO: INSTILL GREAT FEAR.
PACE SECTOR 2682.
HE PLANET RANN.
WHY IS THE SINESTRO CORPS ATTACKING US?
WE MAKE HE UNIVERSSSE AFRAID.
POWER LEVEL 100%.
YEAH? HOW'S THAT WORKING OUT FOR YOU?
THHOOM
PACE SECTOR 2828.
HE PLANET TAMARAN.
GUARDS!
ACK
BY DECREE OF SINESTRO: INSTILL GREAT FEAR.
SEND MORE ROYAL GUARDS!

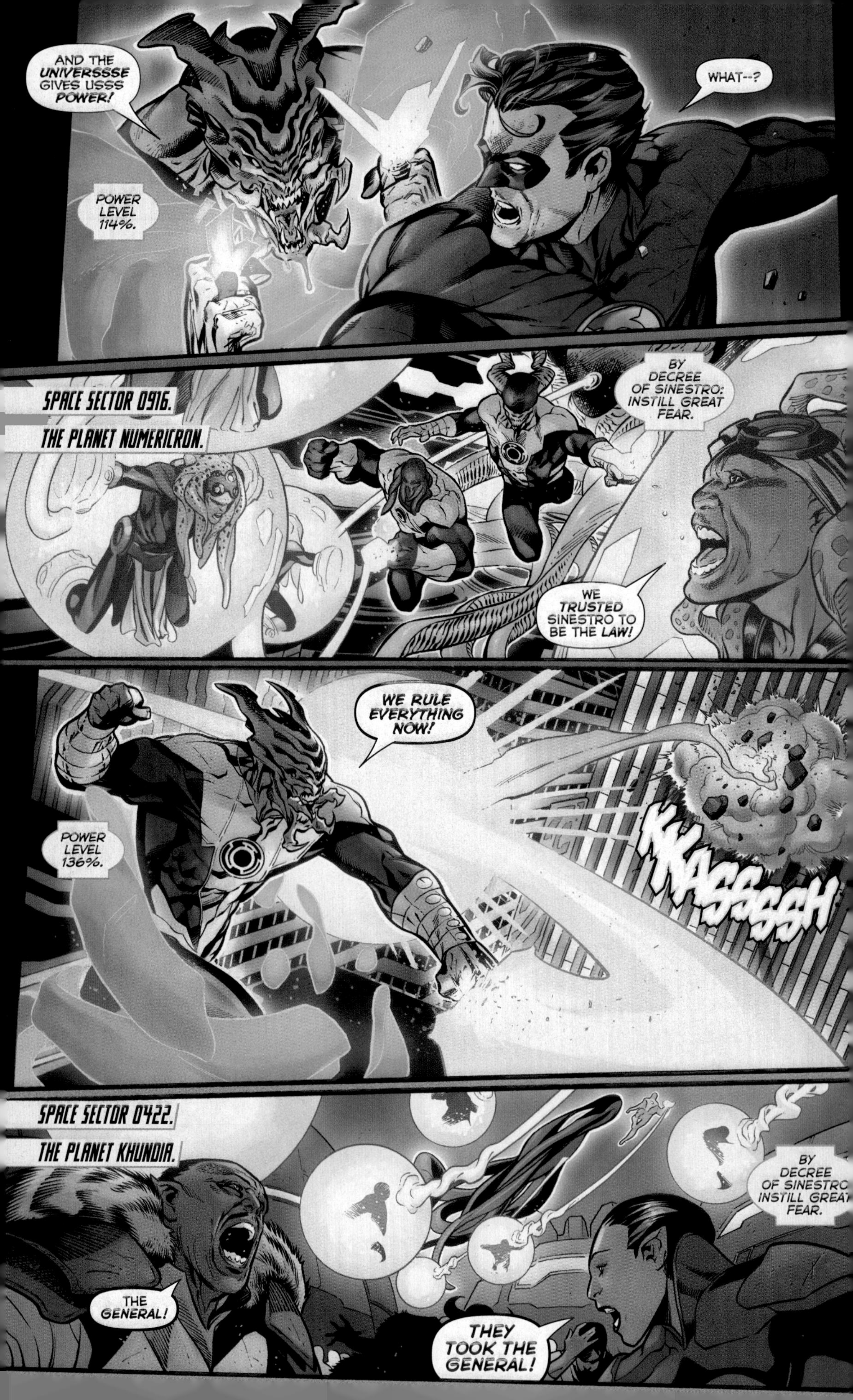

AND THE UNIVERSSSE GIVES USSS POWER!
WHAT--?
POWER LEVEL 114%.
SPACE SECTOR 0916.
THE PLANET NUMERICRON.
BY DECREE OF SINESTRO: INSTILL GREAT FEAR.
WE TRUSTED SINESTRO TO BE THE LAW!
WE RULE EVERYTHING NOW!
POWER LEVEL 136%.
KKASSSSH
SPACE SECTOR 0422.
THE PLANET KHUNDIA.
BY DECREE OF SINESTRO INSTILL GREAT FEAR.
THE GENERAL!
THEY TOOK THE GENERAL!

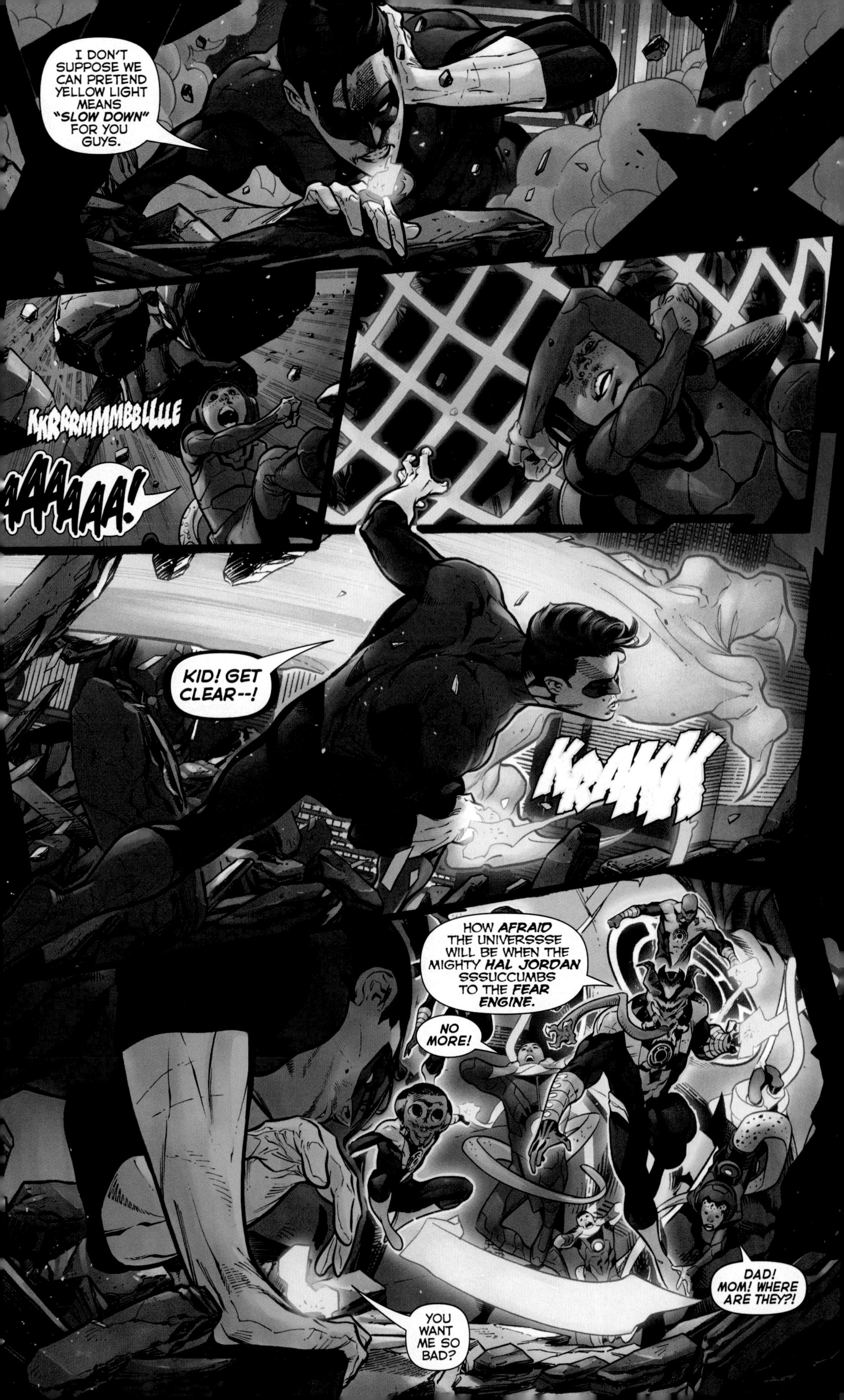
I DON'T SUPPOSE WE CAN PRETEND YELLOW LIGHT MEANS "SLOW DOWN" FOR YOU GUYS.
KKRRRMMMBBLLLE
AAAAAAAA!
KID! GET CLEAR--!
KRAKK
HOW AFRAID THE UNIVERSSSE WILL BE WHEN THE MIGHTY HAL JORDAN SSSUCCUMBS TO THE FEAR ENGINE.
NO MORE!
YOU WANT ME SO BAD?
DAD! MOM! WHERE ARE THEY?!

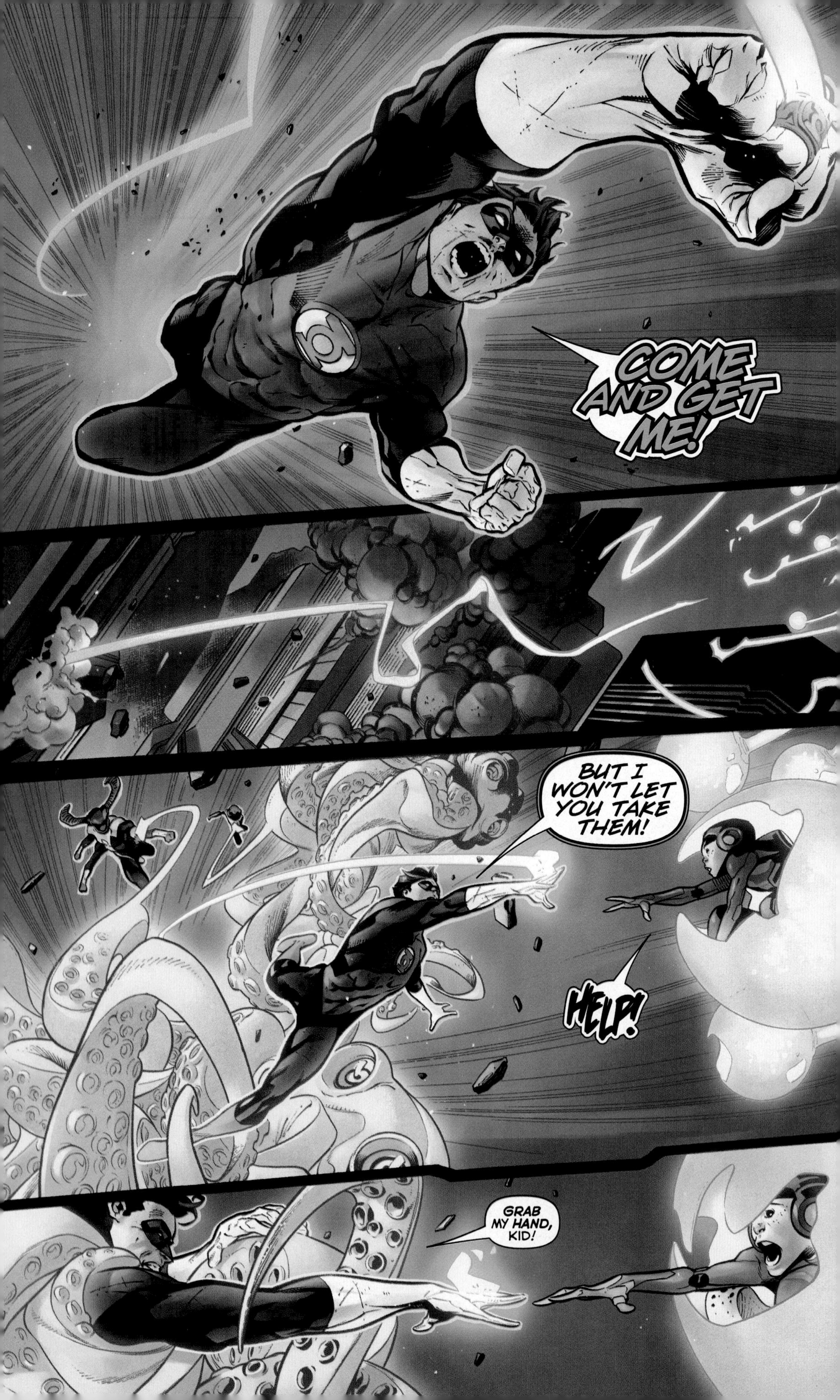
COME AND GET ME!
BUT I WON'T LET YOU TAKE THEM!
HELP!
GRAB MY HAND, KID!

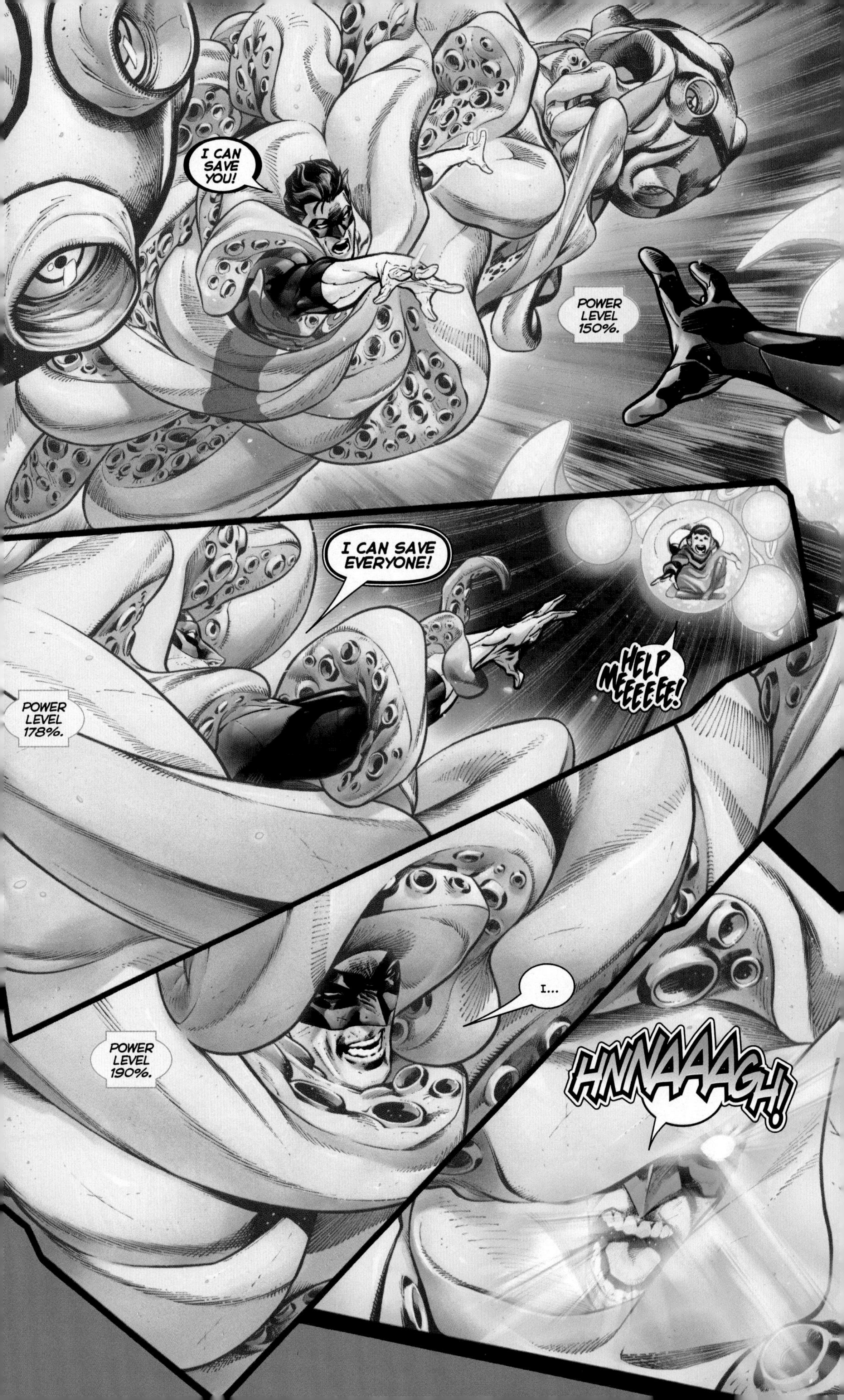
I CAN SAVE YOU!
POWER LEVEL 150%.
I CAN SAVE EVERYONE!
HELP MEEEEEE!
POWER LEVEL 178%.
I...
POWER LEVEL 190%.
HNNAAAGH!

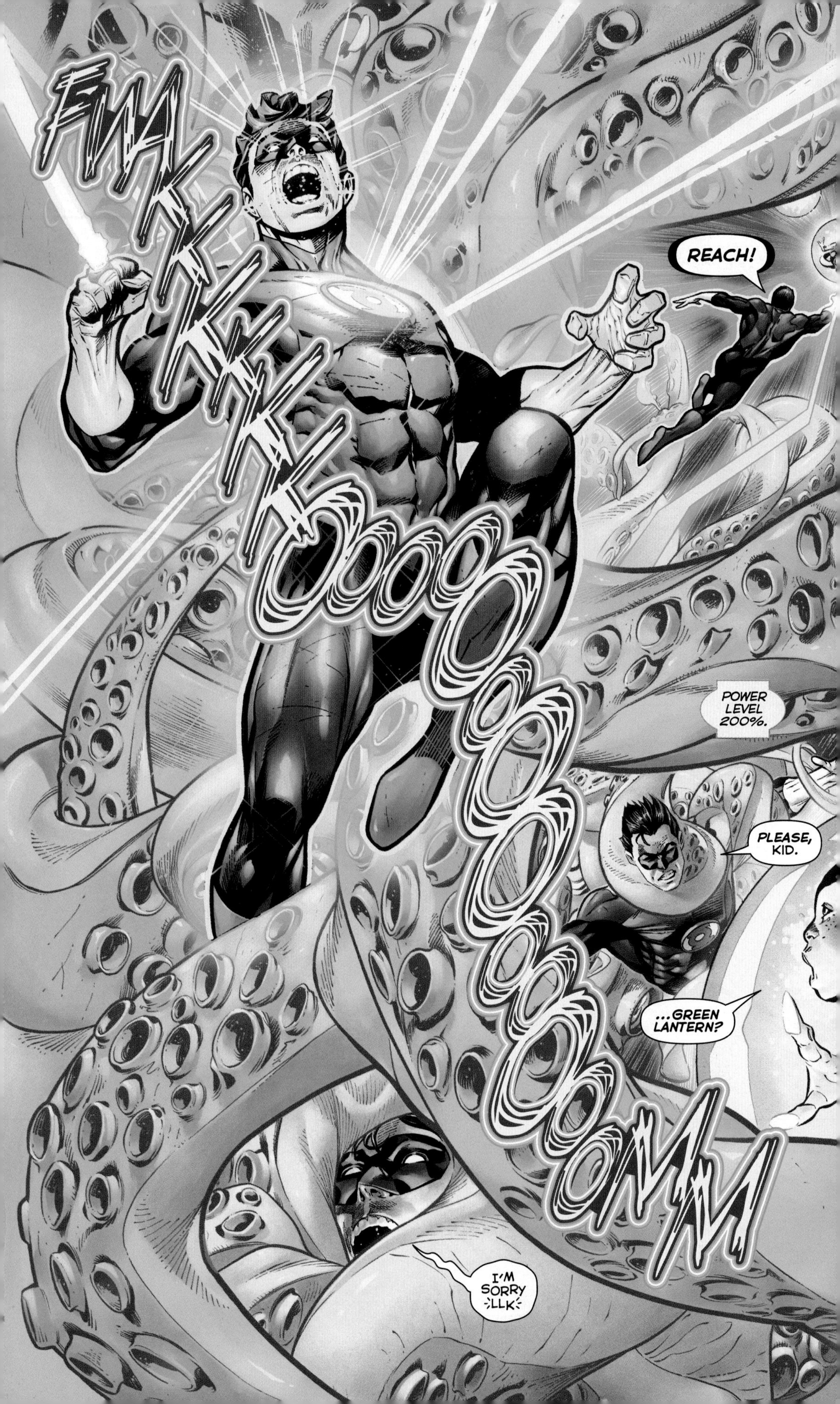
FWKKKKOOOOOOOOOOOOOOOOOOOOM
REACH!
POWER LEVEL 200%.
PLEASE, KID.
...GREEN LANTERN?
I'M SORRY -LLK-

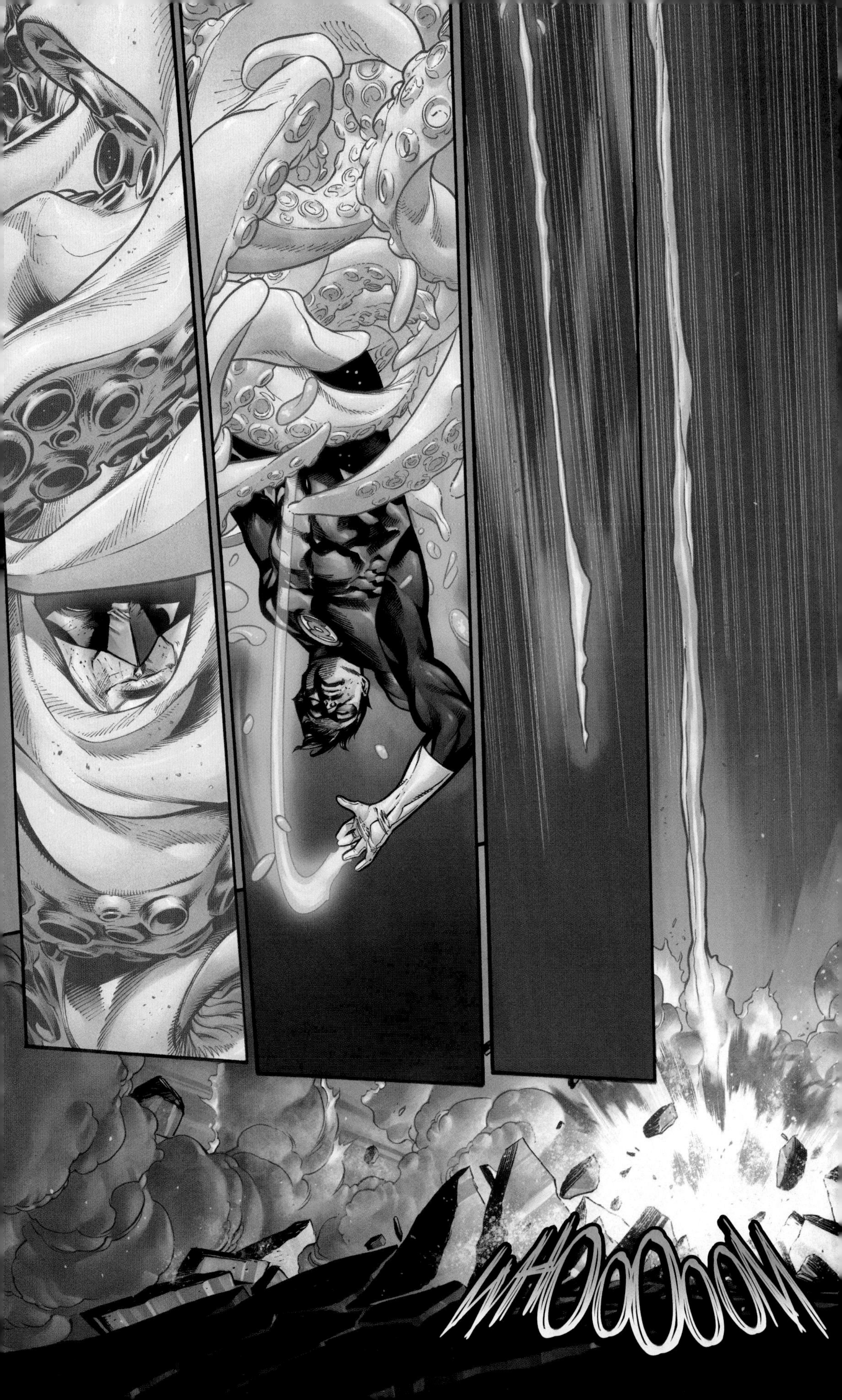
WHOOOOOM

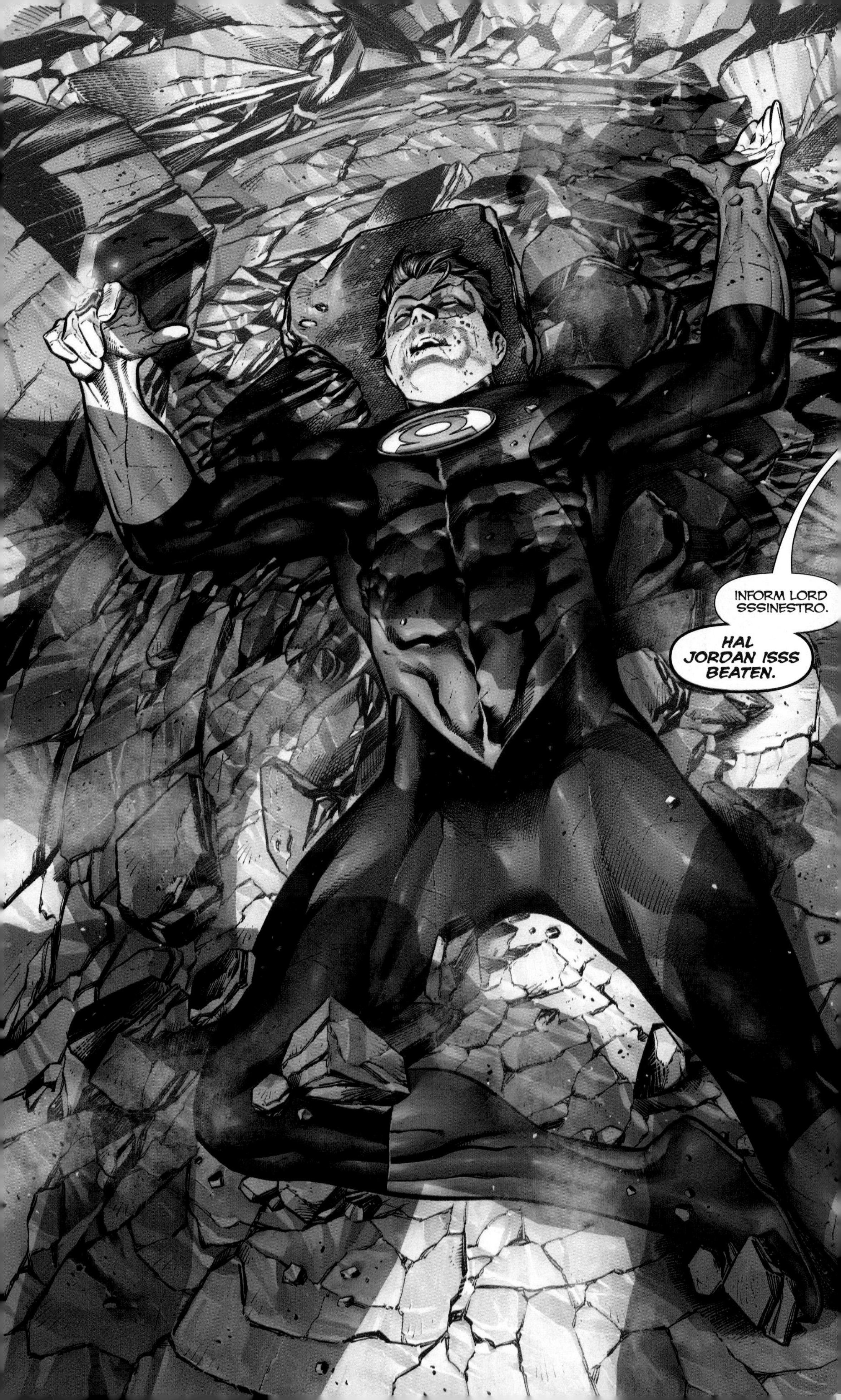
INFORM LORD SSSINESTRO.
HAL JORDAN ISSS BEATEN.

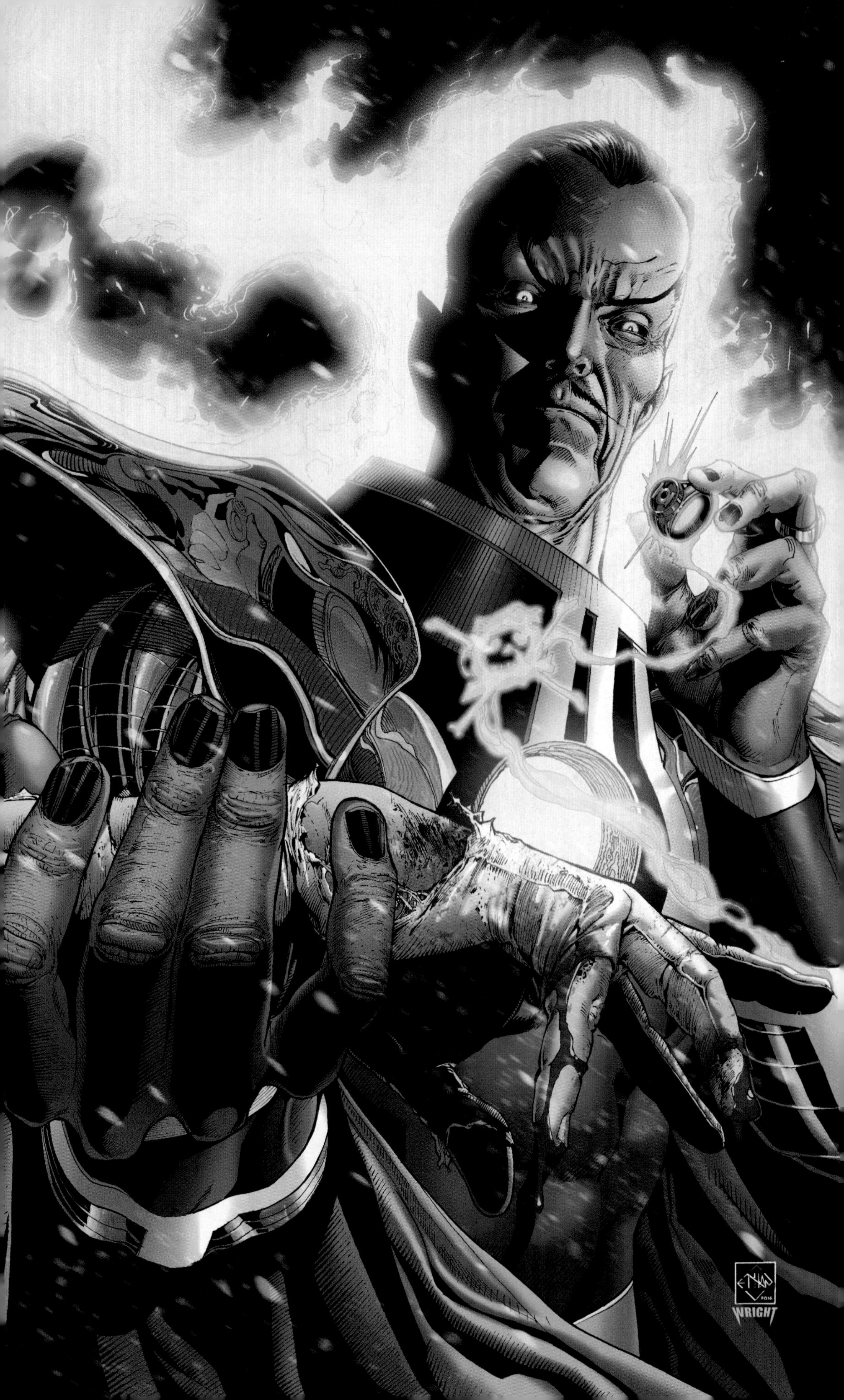
WRIGHT

SINESTRO'S LAW PART 4: THE FEAR ENGINE

ETHAN VAN SCIVER artist * JASON WRIGHT colorist * ETHAN VAN SCIVER and JASON WRIGHT cover artists

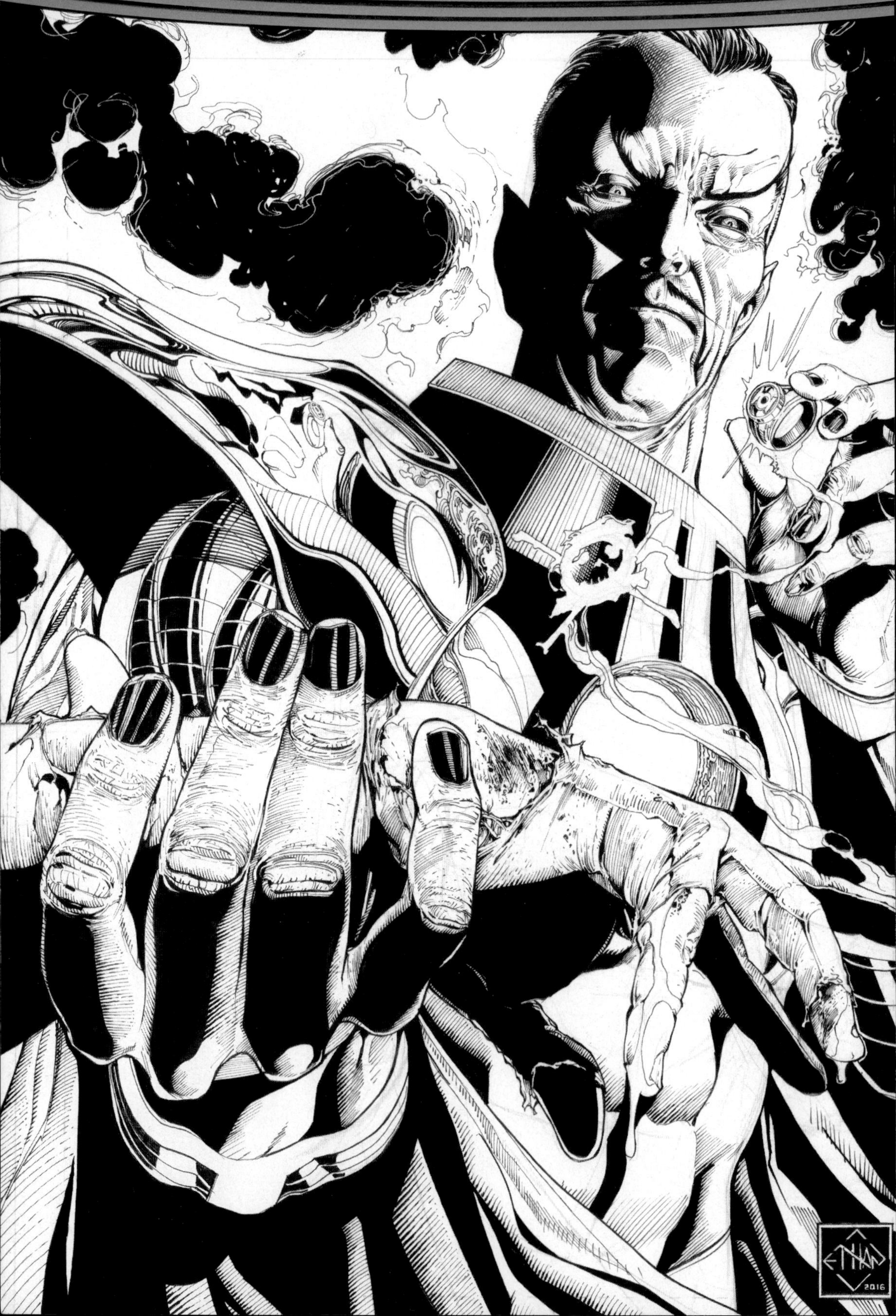

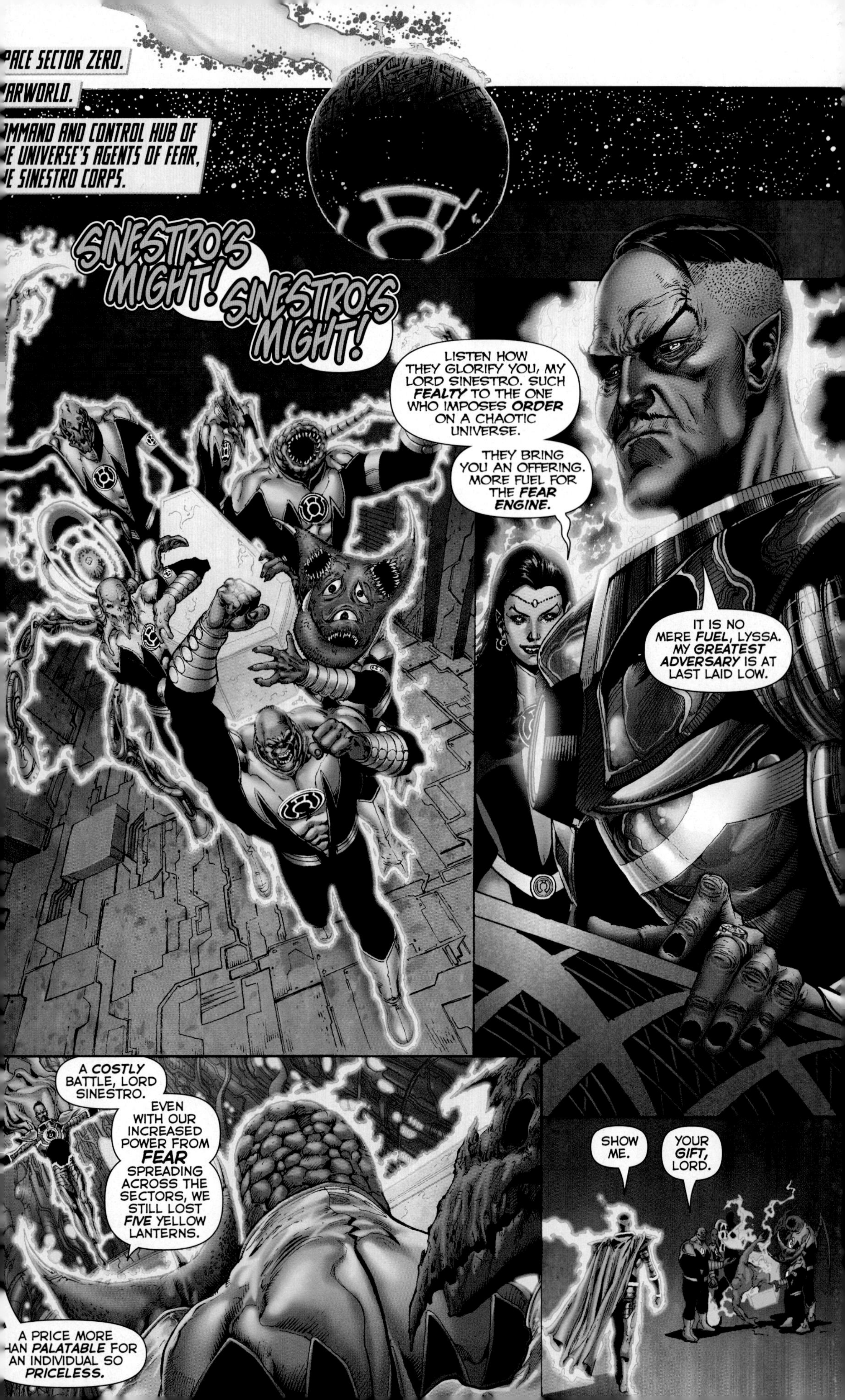
PACE SECTOR ZERO.
ARWORLD.
MMAND AND CONTROL HUB OF E UNIVERSE'S AGENTS OF FEAR, E SINESTRO CORPS.
SINESTRO'S MIGHT!
SINESTRO'S MIGHT!
LISTEN HOW THEY GLORIFY YOU, MY LORD SINESTRO. SUCH FEALTY TO THE ONE WHO IMPOSES ORDER ON A CHAOTIC UNIVERSE.
THEY BRING YOU AN OFFERING. MORE FUEL FOR THE FEAR ENGINE.
IT IS NO MERE FUEL, LYSSA. MY GREATEST ADVERSARY IS AT LAST LAID LOW.
A COSTLY BATTLE, LORD SINESTRO.
EVEN WITH OUR INCREASED POWER FROM FEAR SPREADING ACROSS THE SECTORS, WE STILL LOST FIVE YELLOW LANTERNS.
A PRICE MORE HAN PALATABLE FOR AN INDIVIDUAL SO PRICELESS.
SHOW ME.
YOUR GIFT, LORD.

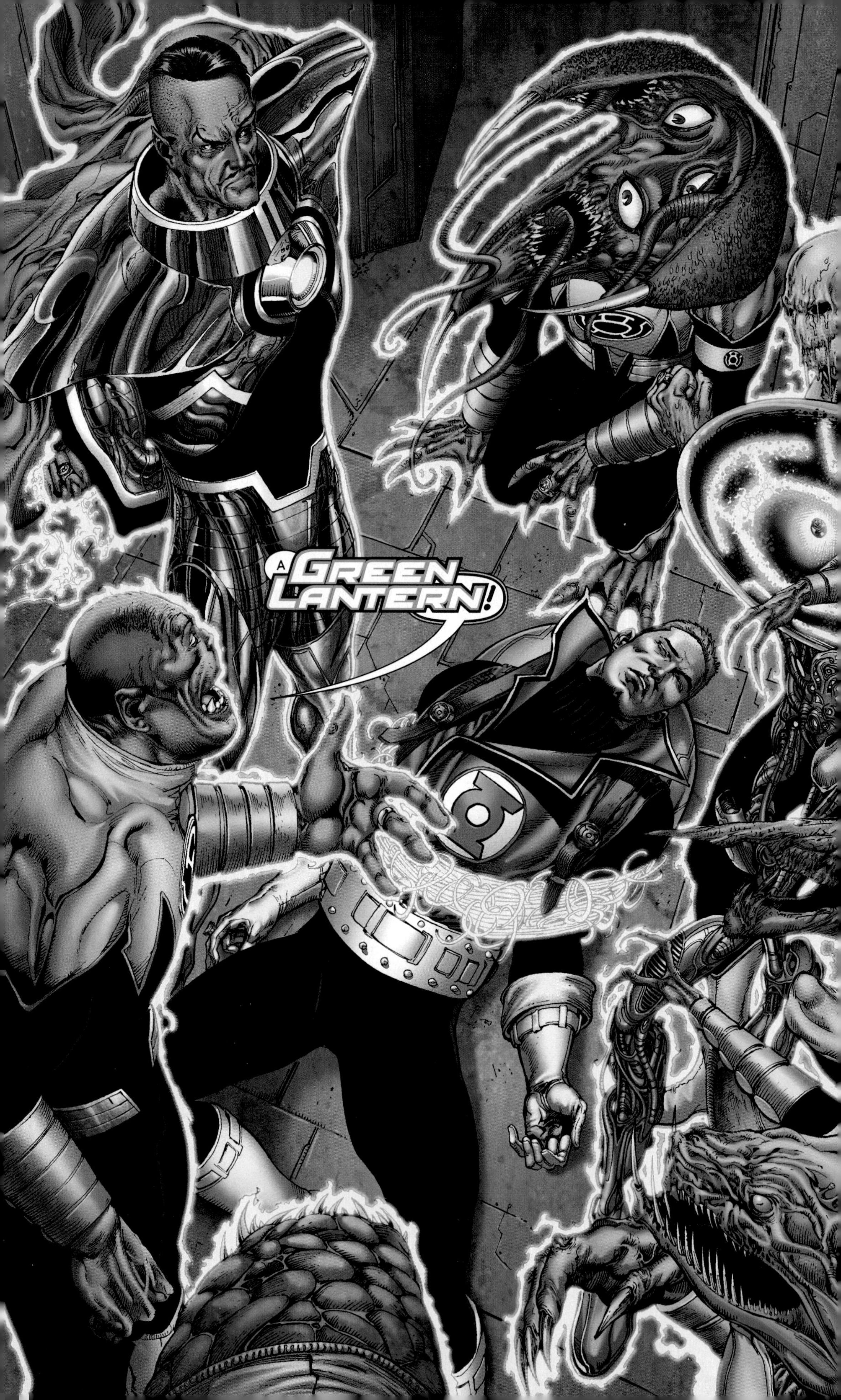
A GREEN LANTERN!

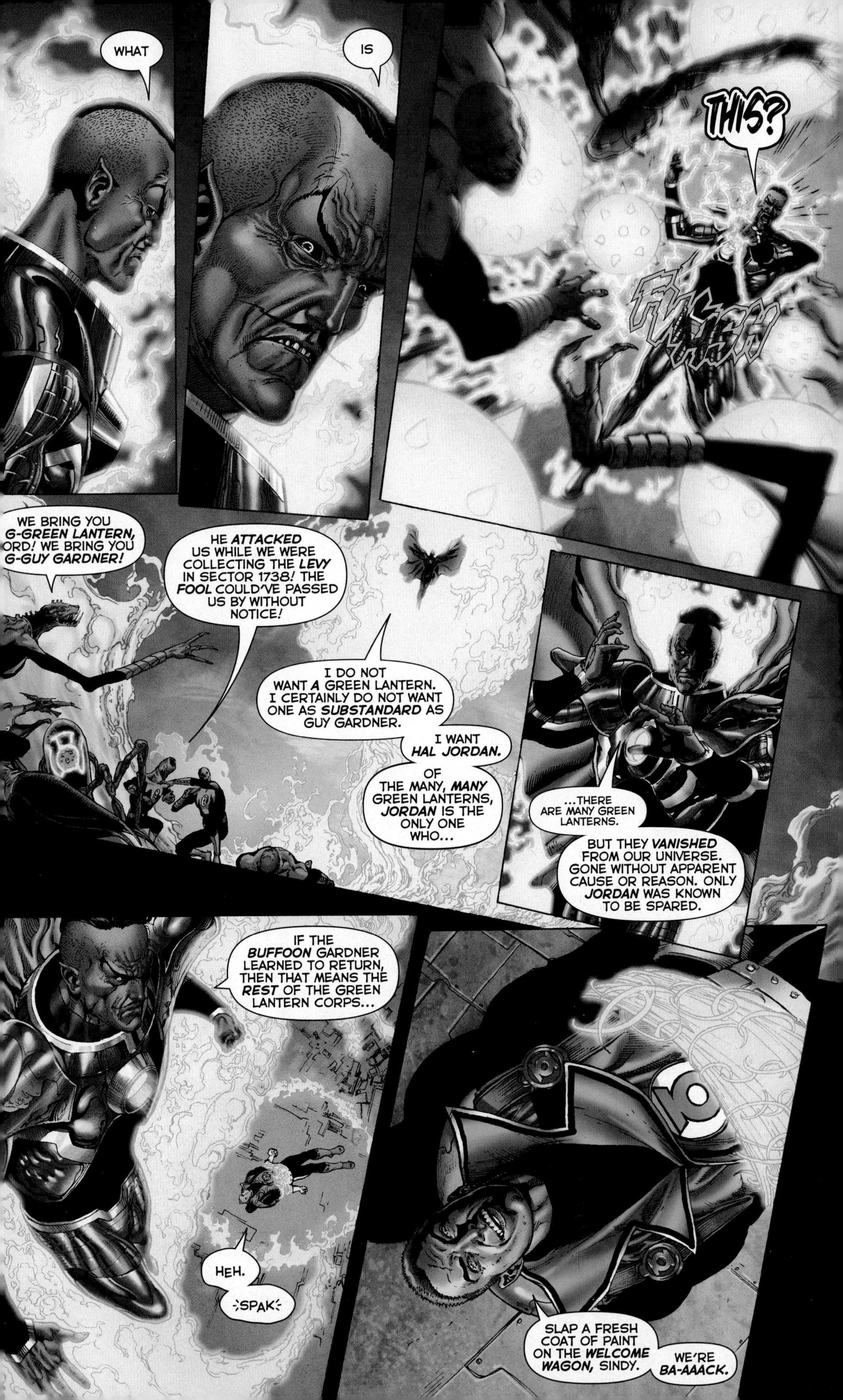
WHAT
IS
THIS?
FZZZSH
WE BRING YOU G-GREEN LANTERN, ORD! WE BRING YOU G-GUY GARDNER!
HE ATTACKED US WHILE WE WERE COLLECTING THE LEVY IN SECTOR 1738! THE FOOL COULD'VE PASSED US BY WITHOUT NOTICE!
I DO NOT WANT A GREEN LANTERN. I CERTAINLY DO NOT WANT ONE AS SUBSTANDARD AS GUY GARDNER.
I WANT HAL JORDAN.
OF THE MANY, MANY GREEN LANTERNS, JORDAN IS THE ONLY ONE WHO...
...THERE ARE MANY GREEN LANTERNS.
BUT THEY VANISHED FROM OUR UNIVERSE. GONE WITHOUT APPARENT CAUSE OR REASON. ONLY JORDAN WAS KNOWN TO BE SPARED.
IF THE BUFFOON GARDNER LEARNED TO RETURN, THEN THAT MEANS THE REST OF THE GREEN LANTERN CORPS...
HEH.
SPAK
SLAP A FRESH COAT OF PAINT ON THE WELCOME WAGON, SINDY.
WE'RE BA-AAACK.

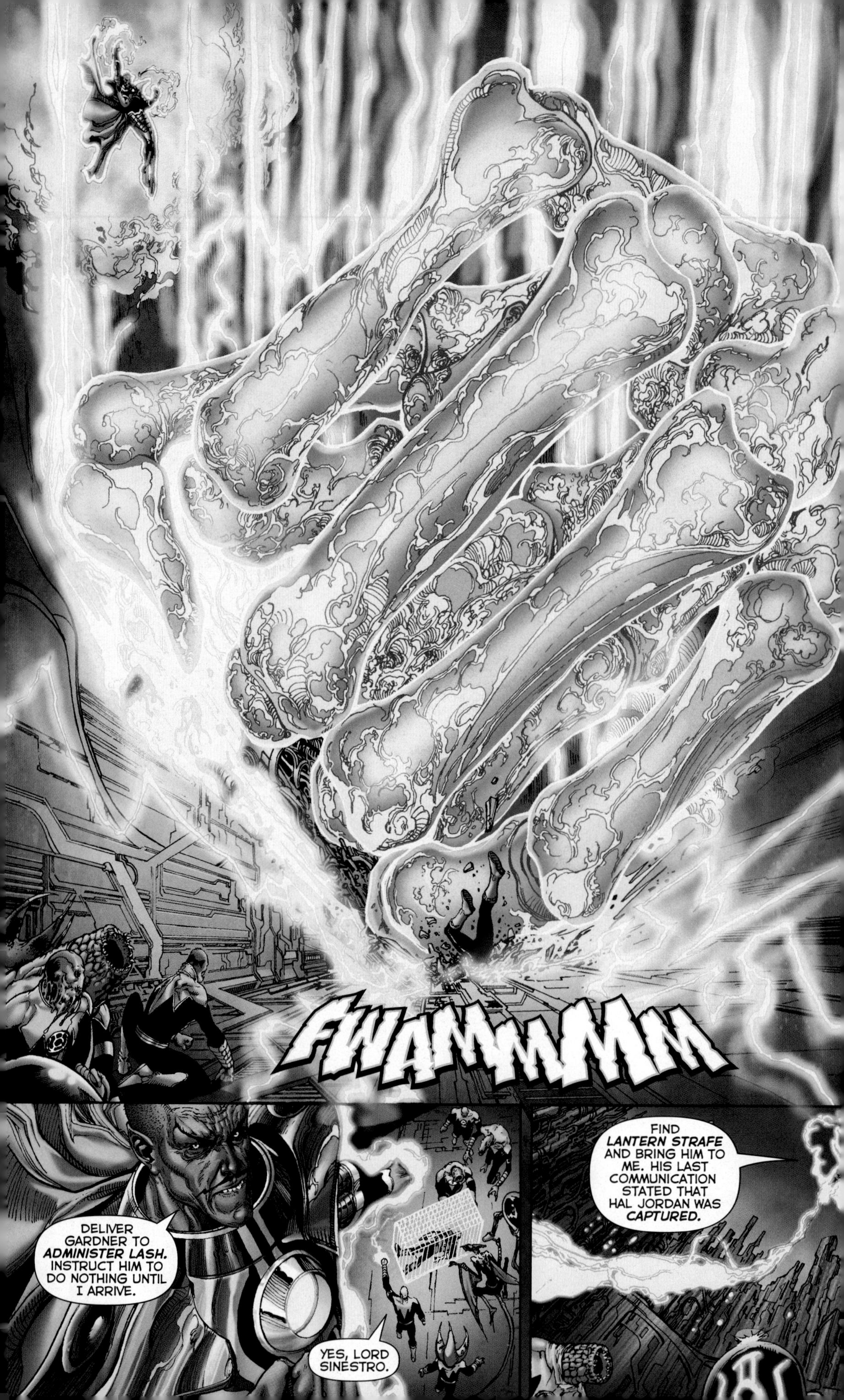
FWAMMMM
DELIVER GARDNER TO **ADMINISTER LASH.** INSTRUCT HIM TO DO NOTHING UNTIL I ARRIVE.
YES, LORD SINESTRO.
FIND ***LANTERN STRAFE*** AND BRING HIM TO ME. HIS LAST COMMUNICATION STATED THAT HAL JORDAN WAS ***CAPTURED.***

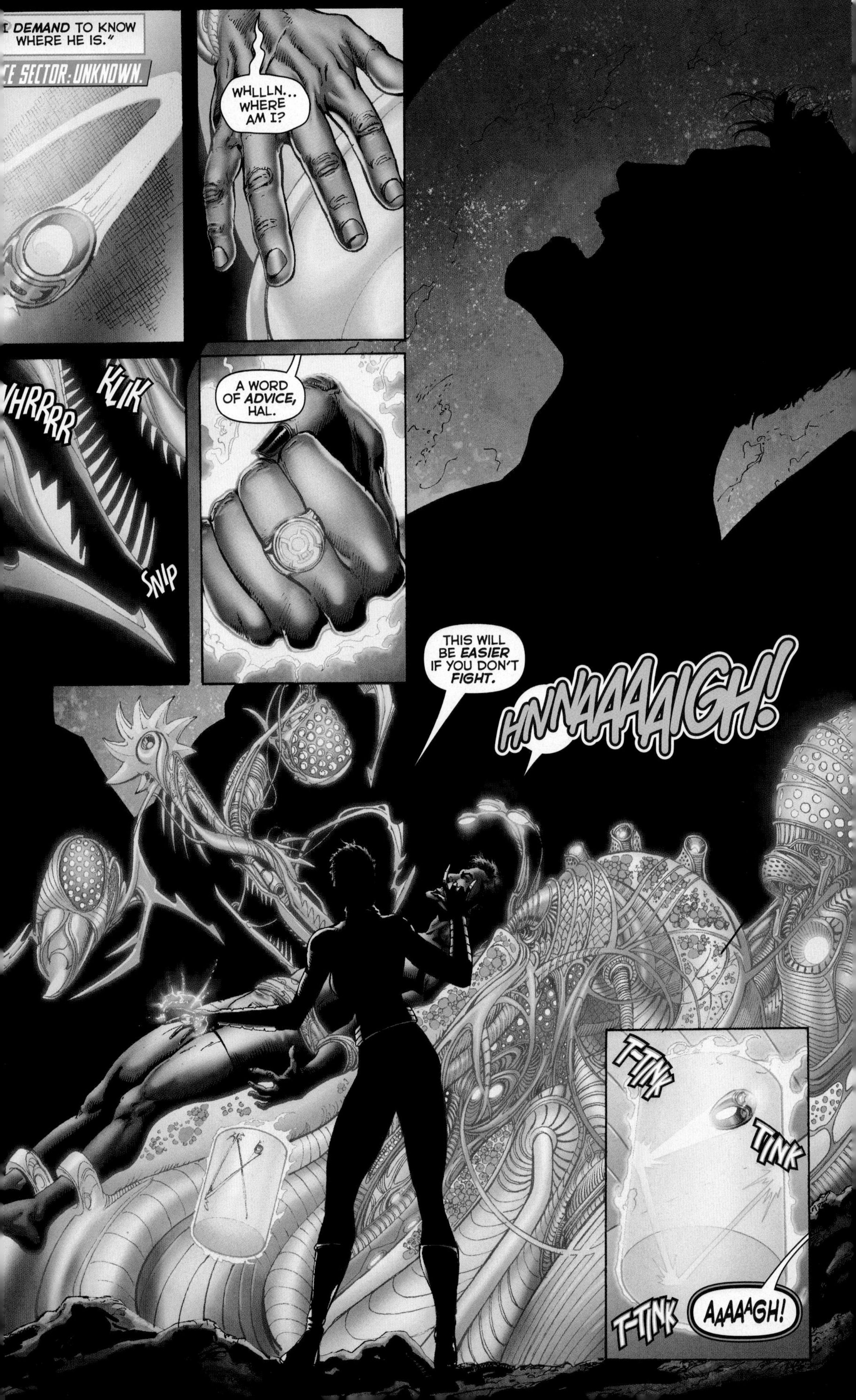

"I DEMAND TO KNOW WHERE HE IS."
CE SECTOR: UNKNOWN.
WHLLLN... WHERE AM I?
WHRRRR
KLIK
SNIP
A WORD OF ADVICE, HAL.
THIS WILL BE EASIER IF YOU DON'T FIGHT.
HNNAAAAIGH!
T-TINK
TINK
T-TINK
AAAAAGH!

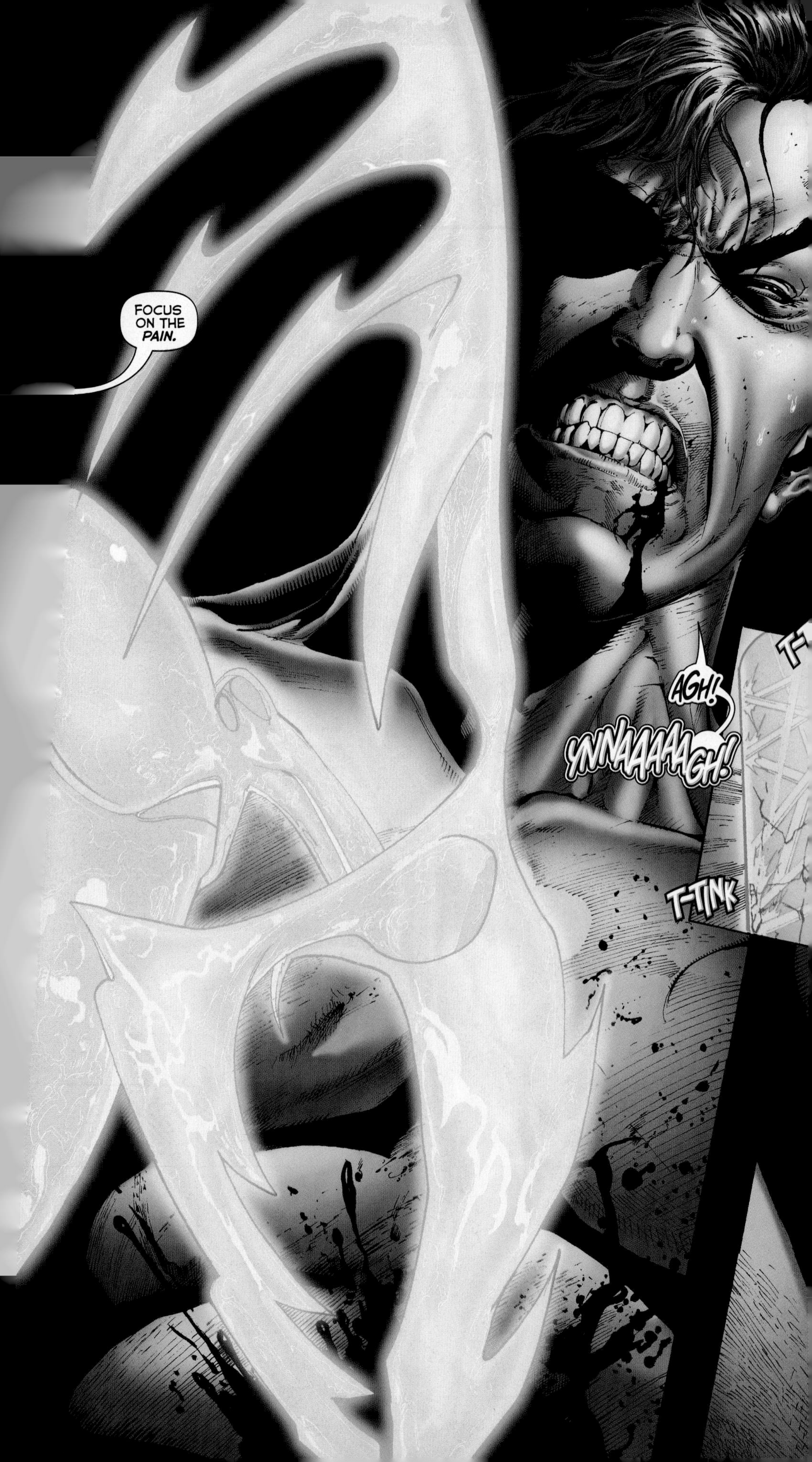
FOCUS ON THE PAIN.
AGH!
YNNAAAAAAGH!
T-TINK

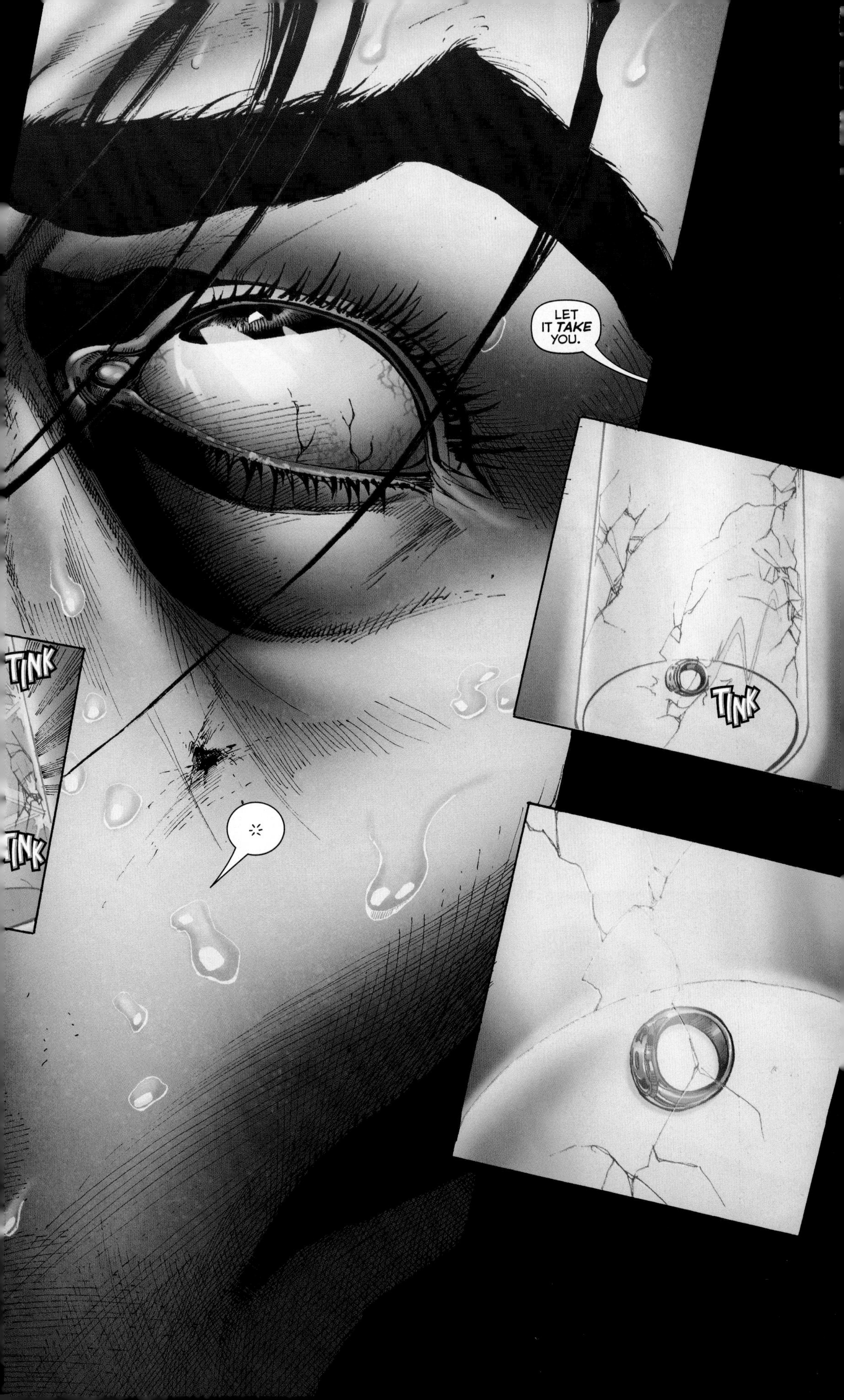

LET IT TAKE YOU.
TINK
TINK
TINK

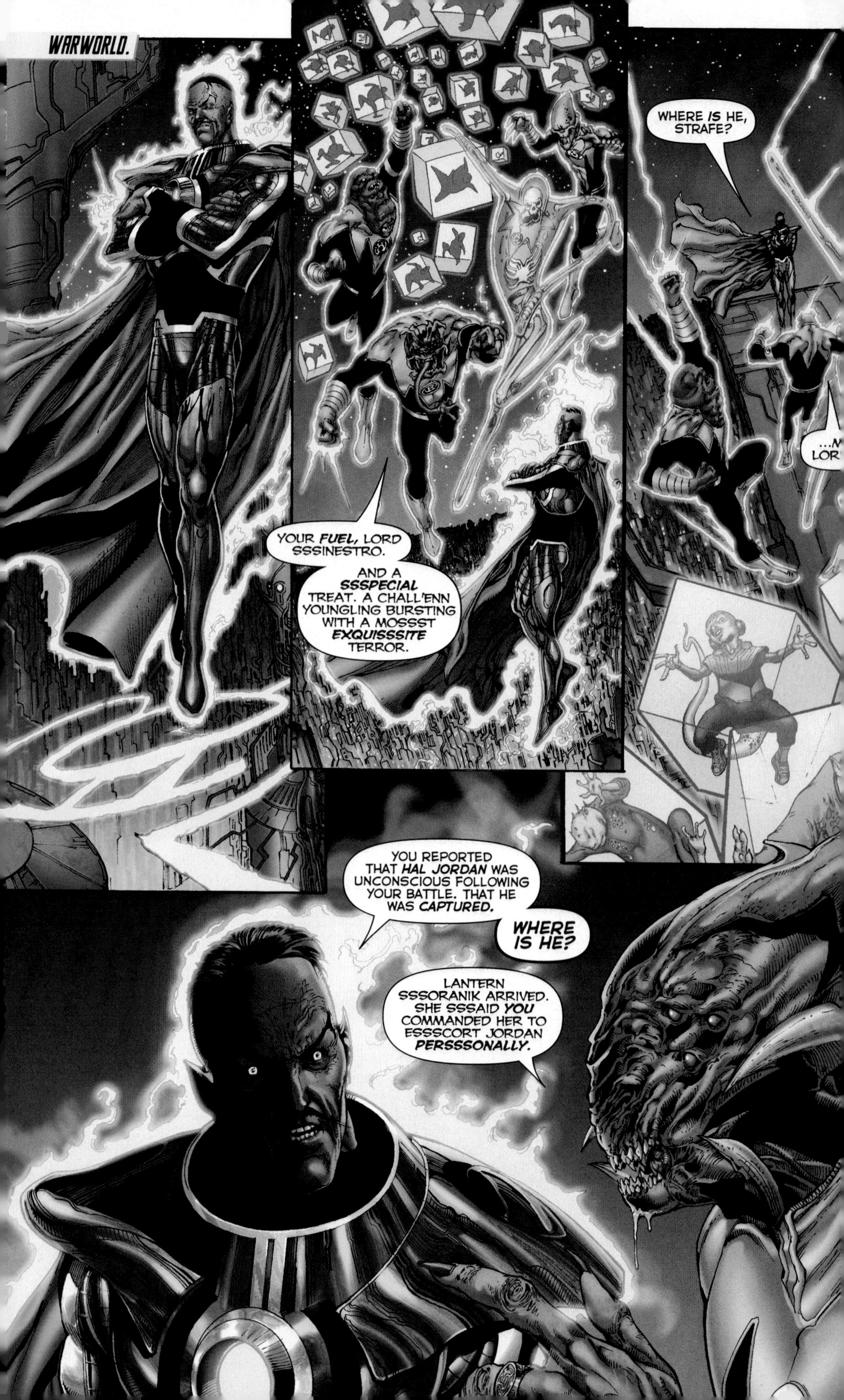
WARWORLD.
YOUR FUEL, LORD SSSINESTRO.
AND A SSSPECIAL TREAT. A CHALL'ENN YOUNGLING BURSTING WITH A MOSSST EXQUISSSITE TERROR.
WHERE IS HE, STRAFE?
YOU REPORTED THAT HAL JORDAN WAS UNCONSCIOUS FOLLOWING YOUR BATTLE. THAT HE WAS CAPTURED.
WHERE IS HE?
LANTERN SSSORANIK ARRIVED. SHE SSSAID YOU COMMANDED HER TO ESSSCORT JORDAN PERSSSONALLY.

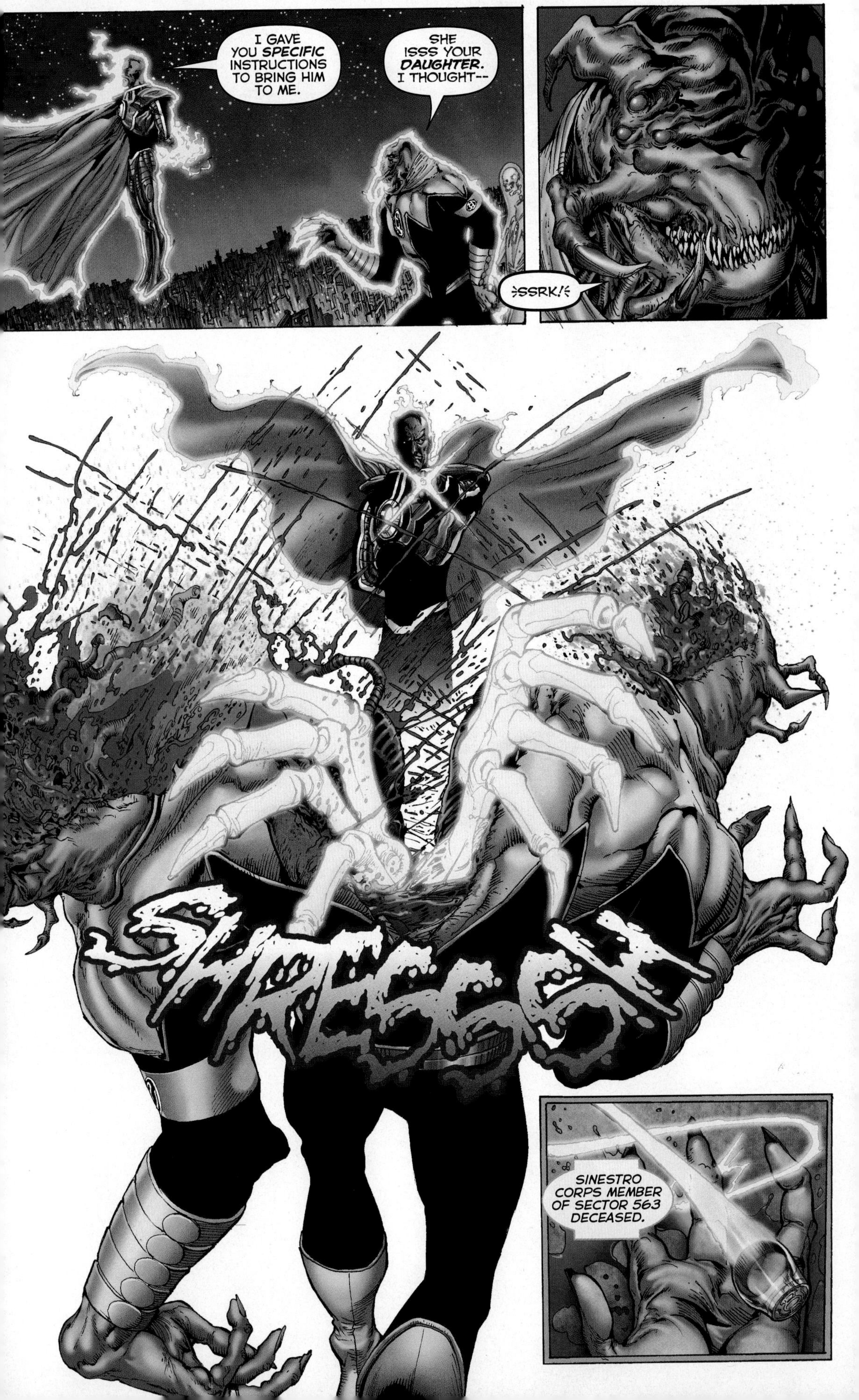
I GAVE YOU SPECIFIC INSTRUCTIONS TO BRING HIM TO ME.
SHE ISSS YOUR DAUGHTER. I THOUGHT--
SSRK!
SHRESSH
SINESTRO CORPS MEMBER OF SECTOR 563 DECEASED.

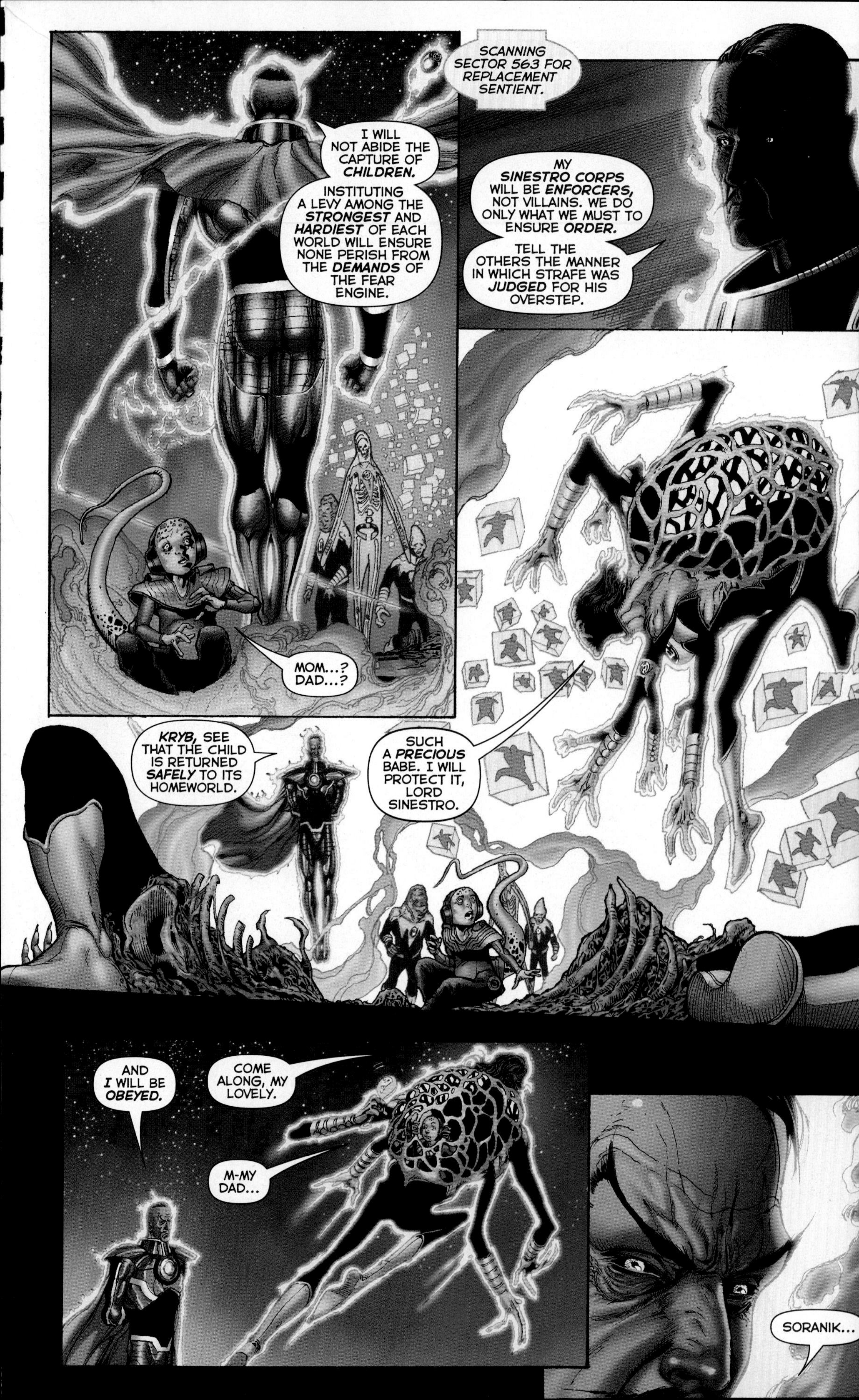
SCANNING SECTOR 563 FOR REPLACEMENT SENTIENT.
I WILL NOT ABIDE THE CAPTURE OF CHILDREN.
INSTITUTING A LEVY AMONG THE STRONGEST AND HARDIEST OF EACH WORLD WILL ENSURE NONE PERISH FROM THE DEMANDS OF THE FEAR ENGINE.
MY SINESTRO CORPS WILL BE ENFORCERS, NOT VILLAINS. WE DO ONLY WHAT WE MUST TO ENSURE ORDER.
TELL THE OTHERS THE MANNER IN WHICH STRAFE WAS JUDGED FOR HIS OVERSTEP.
MOM...? DAD...?
KRYB, SEE THAT THE CHILD IS RETURNED SAFELY TO ITS HOMEWORLD.
SUCH A PRECIOUS BABE. I WILL PROTECT IT, LORD SINESTRO.
AND I WILL BE OBEYED.
COME ALONG, MY LOVELY.
M-MY DAD...
SORANIK...

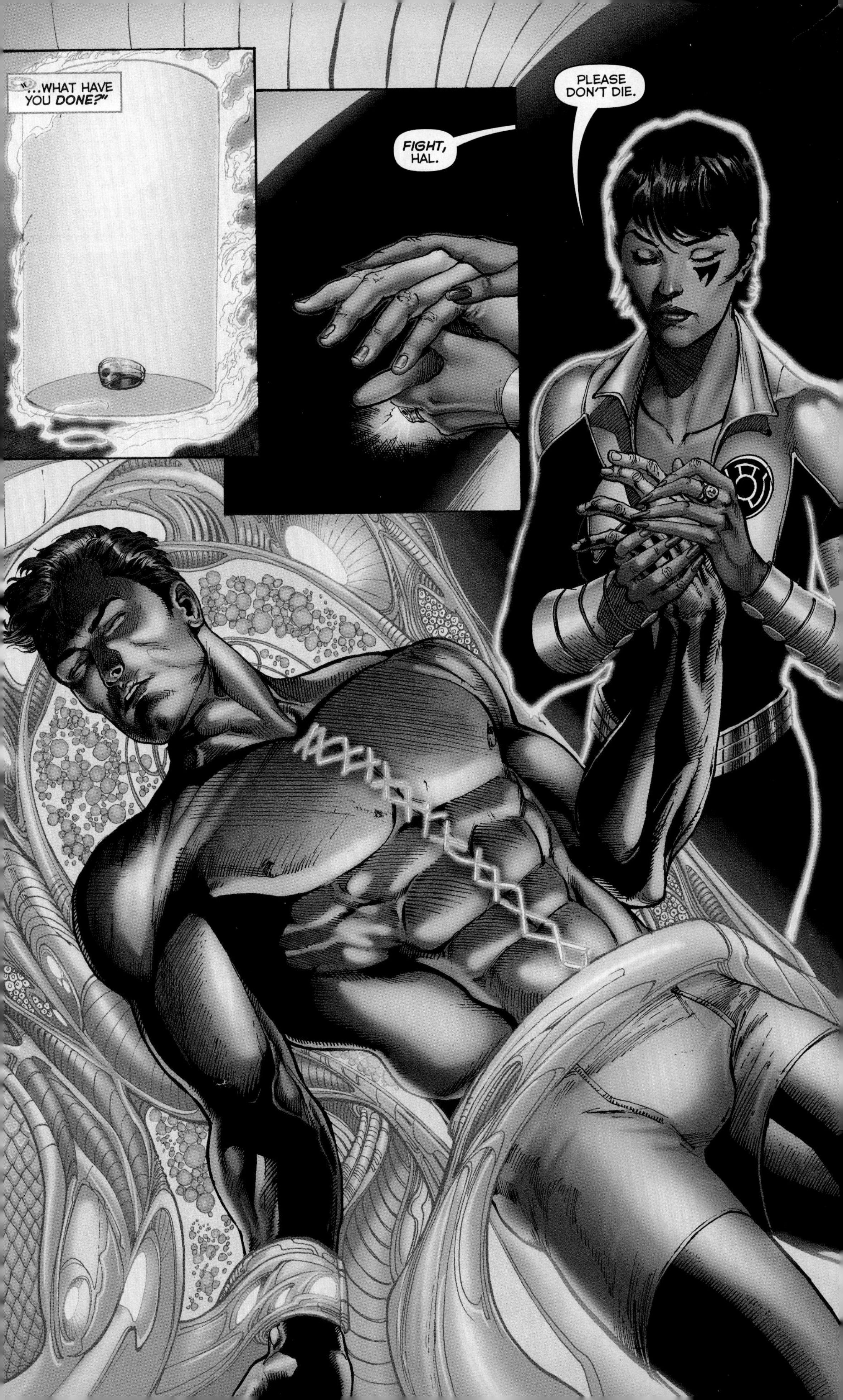
"...WHAT HAVE YOU *DONE?*"
FIGHT, HAL.
PLEASE DON'T DIE.

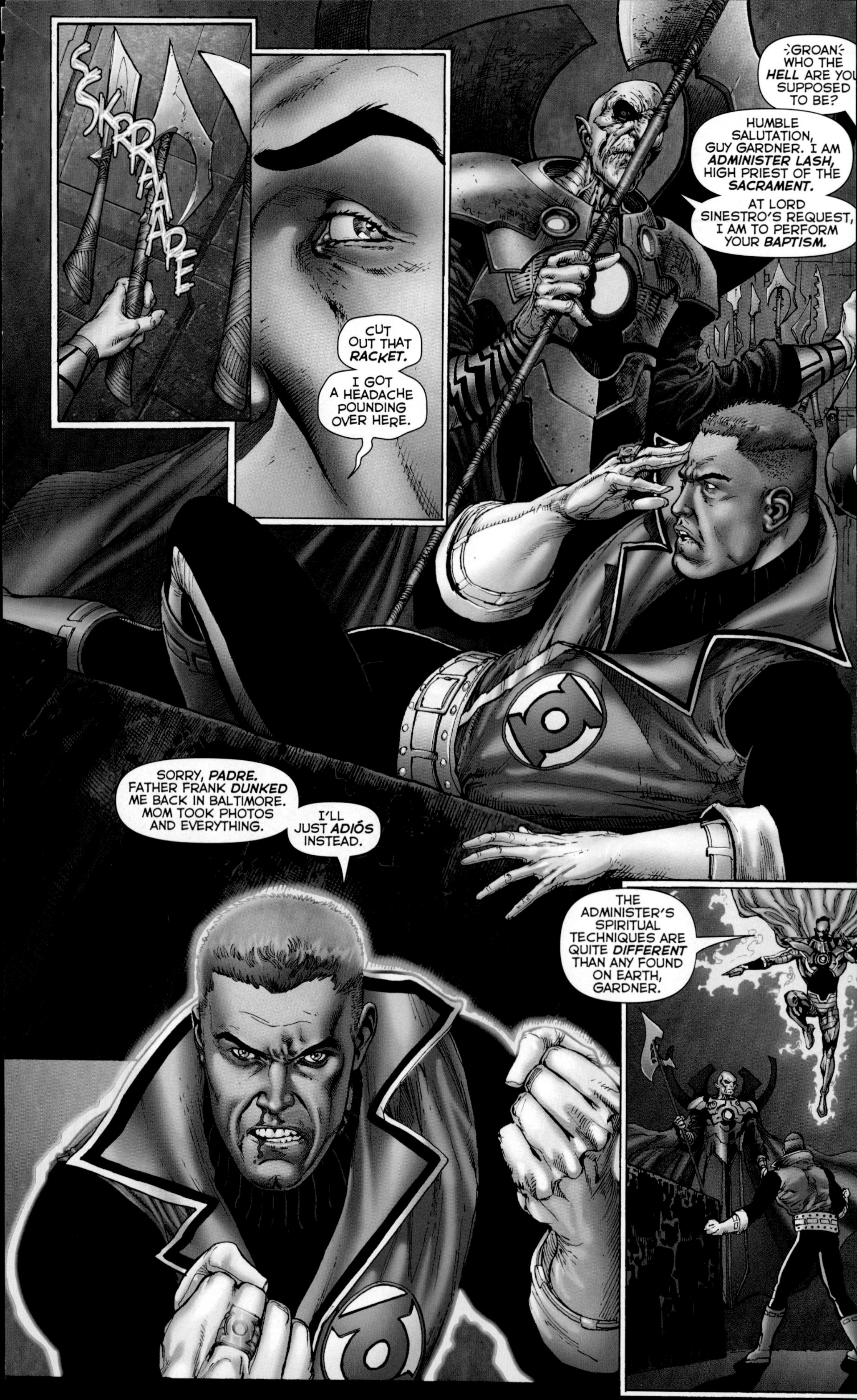
SKRRAAAPE
-GROAN- WHO THE HELL ARE YOU SUPPOSED TO BE?
HUMBLE SALUTATION, GUY GARDNER. I AM ADMINISTER LASH, HIGH PRIEST OF THE SACRAMENT.
AT LORD SINESTRO'S REQUEST, I AM TO PERFORM YOUR BAPTISM.
CUT OUT THAT RACKET.
I GOT A HEADACHE POUNDING OVER HERE.
SORRY, PADRE. FATHER FRANK DUNKED ME BACK IN BALTIMORE. MOM TOOK PHOTOS AND EVERYTHING.
I'LL JUST ADIÓS INSTEAD.
THE ADMINISTER'S SPIRITUAL TECHNIQUES ARE QUITE DIFFERENT THAN ANY FOUND ON EARTH, GARDNER.

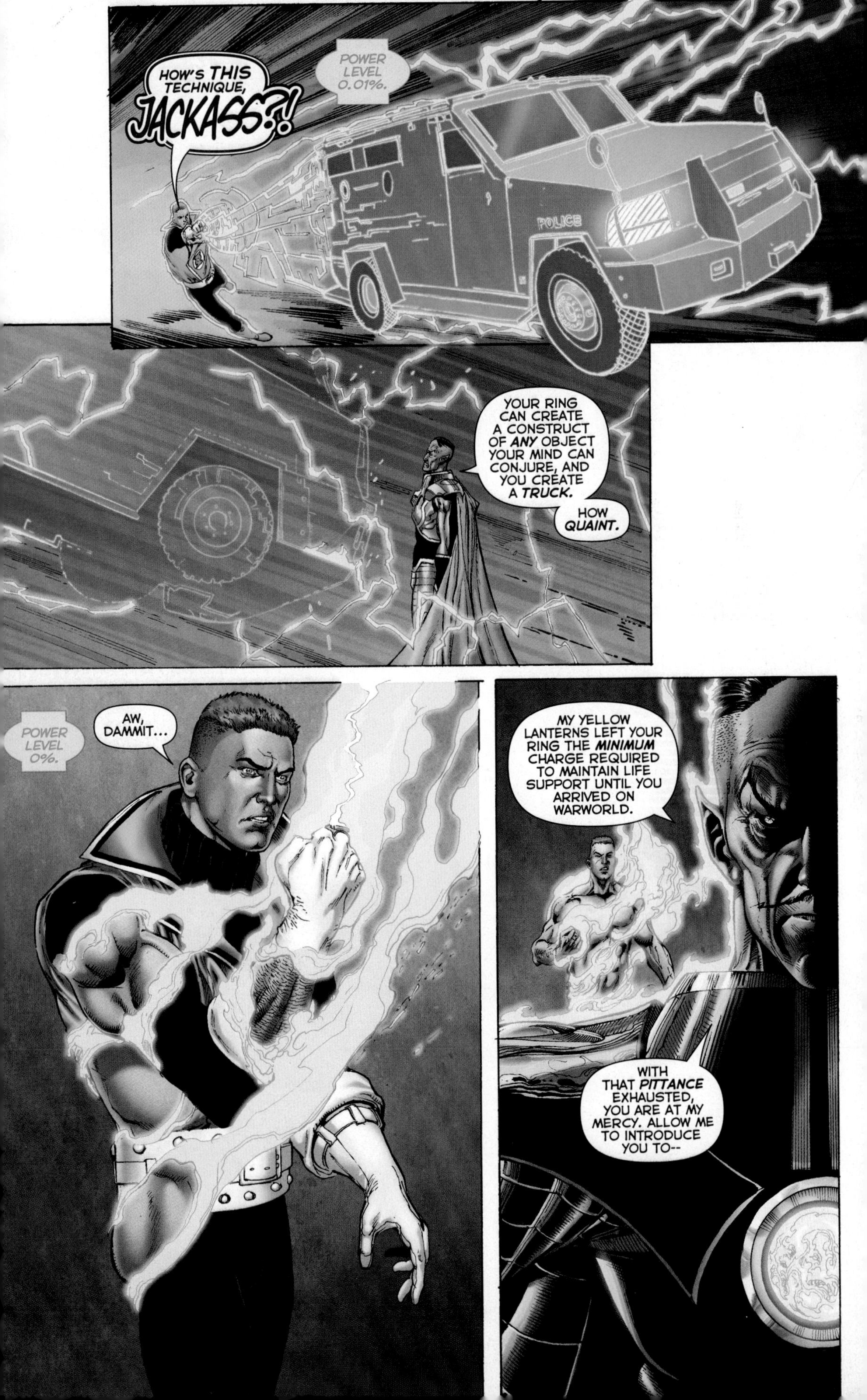
POWER LEVEL 0.01%.
HOW'S THIS TECHNIQUE, JACKASS?!
POLICE
YOUR RING CAN CREATE A CONSTRUCT OF ANY OBJECT YOUR MIND CAN CONJURE, AND YOU CREATE A TRUCK.
HOW QUAINT.
POWER LEVEL 0%.
AW, DAMMIT...
MY YELLOW LANTERNS LEFT YOUR RING THE MINIMUM CHARGE REQUIRED TO MAINTAIN LIFE SUPPORT UNTIL YOU ARRIVED ON WARWORLD.
WITH THAT PITTANCE EXHAUSTED, YOU ARE AT MY MERCY. ALLOW ME TO INTRODUCE YOU TO--

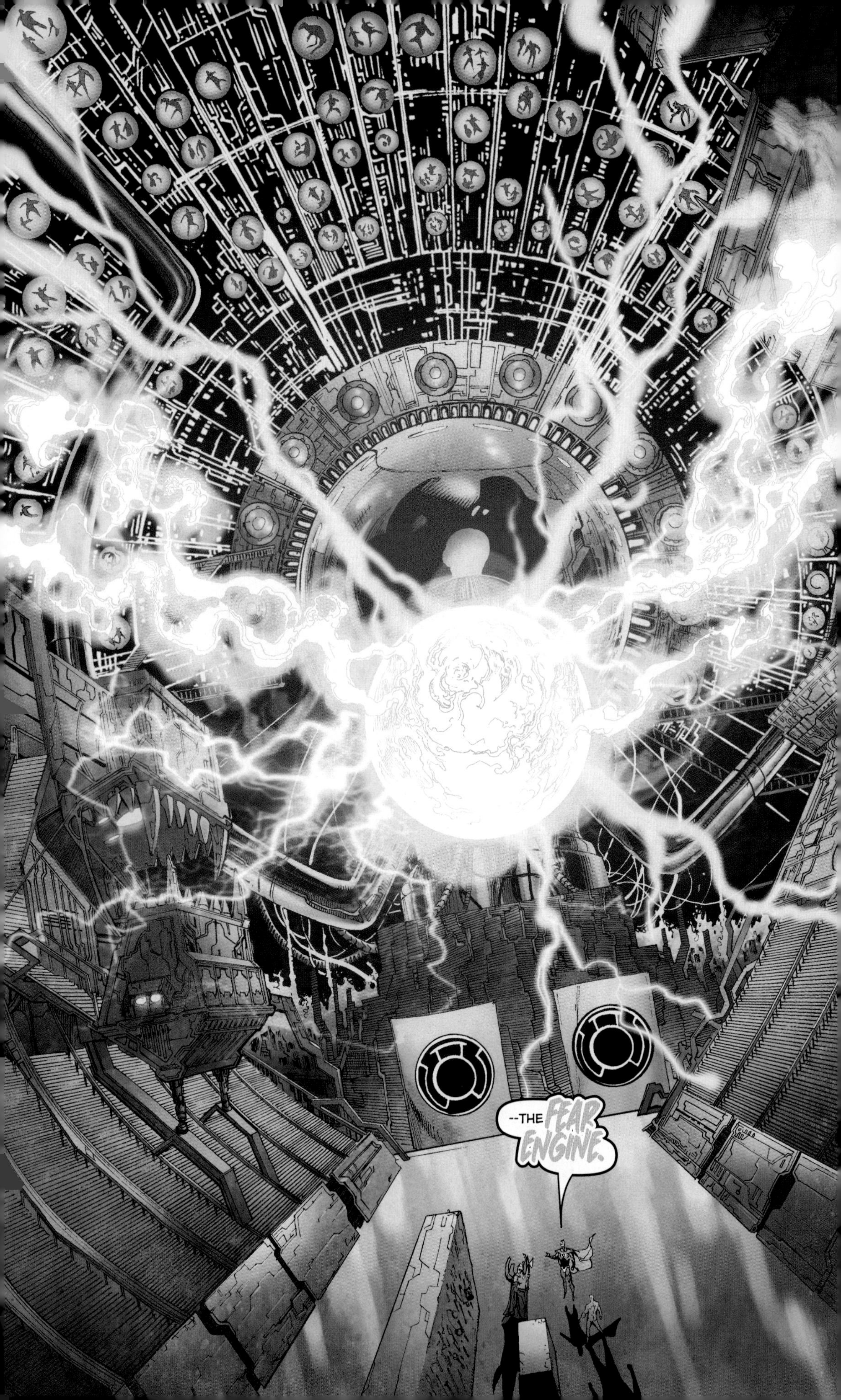
--THE FEAR ENGINE.

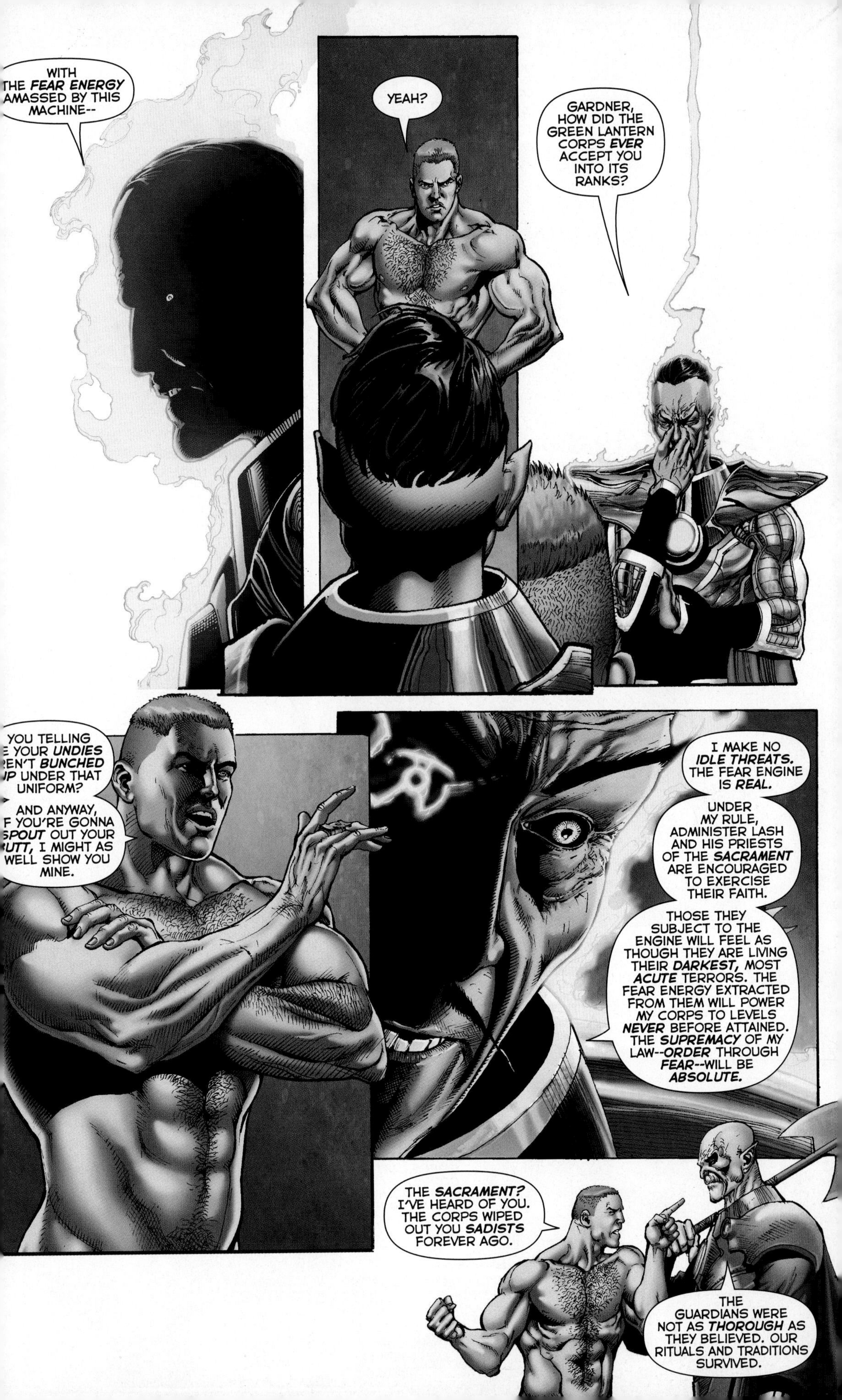

WITH THE FEAR ENERGY AMASSED BY THIS MACHINE--
YEAH?
GARDNER, HOW DID THE GREEN LANTERN CORPS EVER ACCEPT YOU INTO ITS RANKS?
YOU TELLING E YOUR UNDIES REN'T BUNCHED UP UNDER THAT UNIFORM?
AND ANYWAY, F YOU'RE GONNA SPOUT OUT YOUR UTT, I MIGHT AS WELL SHOW YOU MINE.
I MAKE NO IDLE THREATS. THE FEAR ENGINE IS REAL.
UNDER MY RULE, ADMINISTER LASH AND HIS PRIESTS OF THE SACRAMENT ARE ENCOURAGED TO EXERCISE THEIR FAITH.
THOSE THEY SUBJECT TO THE ENGINE WILL FEEL AS THOUGH THEY ARE LIVING THEIR DARKEST, MOST ACUTE TERRORS. THE FEAR ENERGY EXTRACTED FROM THEM WILL POWER MY CORPS TO LEVELS NEVER BEFORE ATTAINED. THE SUPREMACY OF MY LAW--ORDER THROUGH FEAR--WILL BE ABSOLUTE.
THE SACRAMENT? I'VE HEARD OF YOU. THE CORPS WIPED OUT YOU SADISTS FOREVER AGO.
THE GUARDIANS WERE NOT AS THOROUGH AS THEY BELIEVED. OUR RITUALS AND TRADITIONS SURVIVED.

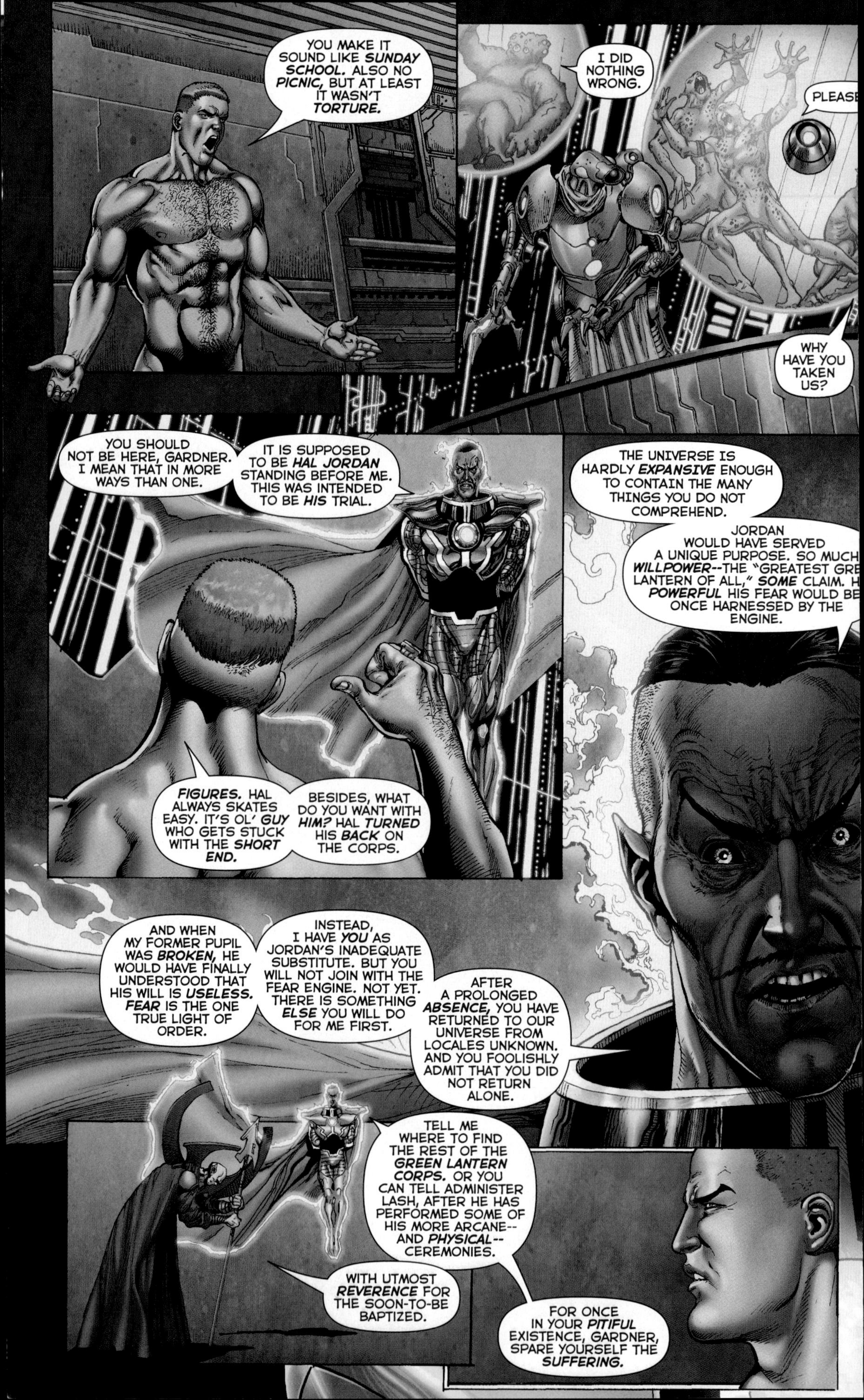
YOU MAKE IT SOUND LIKE SUNDAY SCHOOL. ALSO NO PICNIC, BUT AT LEAST IT WASN'T TORTURE.
I DID NOTHING WRONG.
PLEASE
WHY HAVE YOU TAKEN US?
YOU SHOULD NOT BE HERE, GARDNER. I MEAN THAT IN MORE WAYS THAN ONE.
IT IS SUPPOSED TO BE HAL JORDAN STANDING BEFORE ME. THIS WAS INTENDED TO BE HIS TRIAL.
FIGURES. HAL ALWAYS SKATES EASY. IT'S OL' GUY WHO GETS STUCK WITH THE SHORT END.
BESIDES, WHAT DO YOU WANT WITH HIM? HAL TURNED HIS BACK ON THE CORPS.
THE UNIVERSE IS HARDLY EXPANSIVE ENOUGH TO CONTAIN THE MANY THINGS YOU DO NOT COMPREHEND.
JORDAN WOULD HAVE SERVED A UNIQUE PURPOSE. SO MUCH WILLPOWER--THE "GREATEST GRE LANTERN OF ALL," SOME CLAIM. H POWERFUL HIS FEAR WOULD BE ONCE HARNESSED BY THE ENGINE.
AND WHEN MY FORMER PUPIL WAS BROKEN, HE WOULD HAVE FINALLY UNDERSTOOD THAT HIS WILL IS USELESS. FEAR IS THE ONE TRUE LIGHT OF ORDER.
INSTEAD, I HAVE YOU AS JORDAN'S INADEQUATE SUBSTITUTE. BUT YOU WILL NOT JOIN WITH THE FEAR ENGINE. NOT YET. THERE IS SOMETHING ELSE YOU WILL DO FOR ME FIRST.
AFTER A PROLONGED ABSENCE, YOU HAVE RETURNED TO OUR UNIVERSE FROM LOCALES UNKNOWN. AND YOU FOOLISHLY ADMIT THAT YOU DID NOT RETURN ALONE.
TELL ME WHERE TO FIND THE REST OF THE GREEN LANTERN CORPS. OR YOU CAN TELL ADMINISTER LASH, AFTER HE HAS PERFORMED SOME OF HIS MORE ARCANE-- AND PHYSICAL-- CEREMONIES.
WITH UTMOST REVERENCE FOR THE SOON-TO-BE BAPTIZED.
FOR ONCE IN YOUR PITIFUL EXISTENCE, GARDNER, SPARE YOURSELF THE SUFFERING.

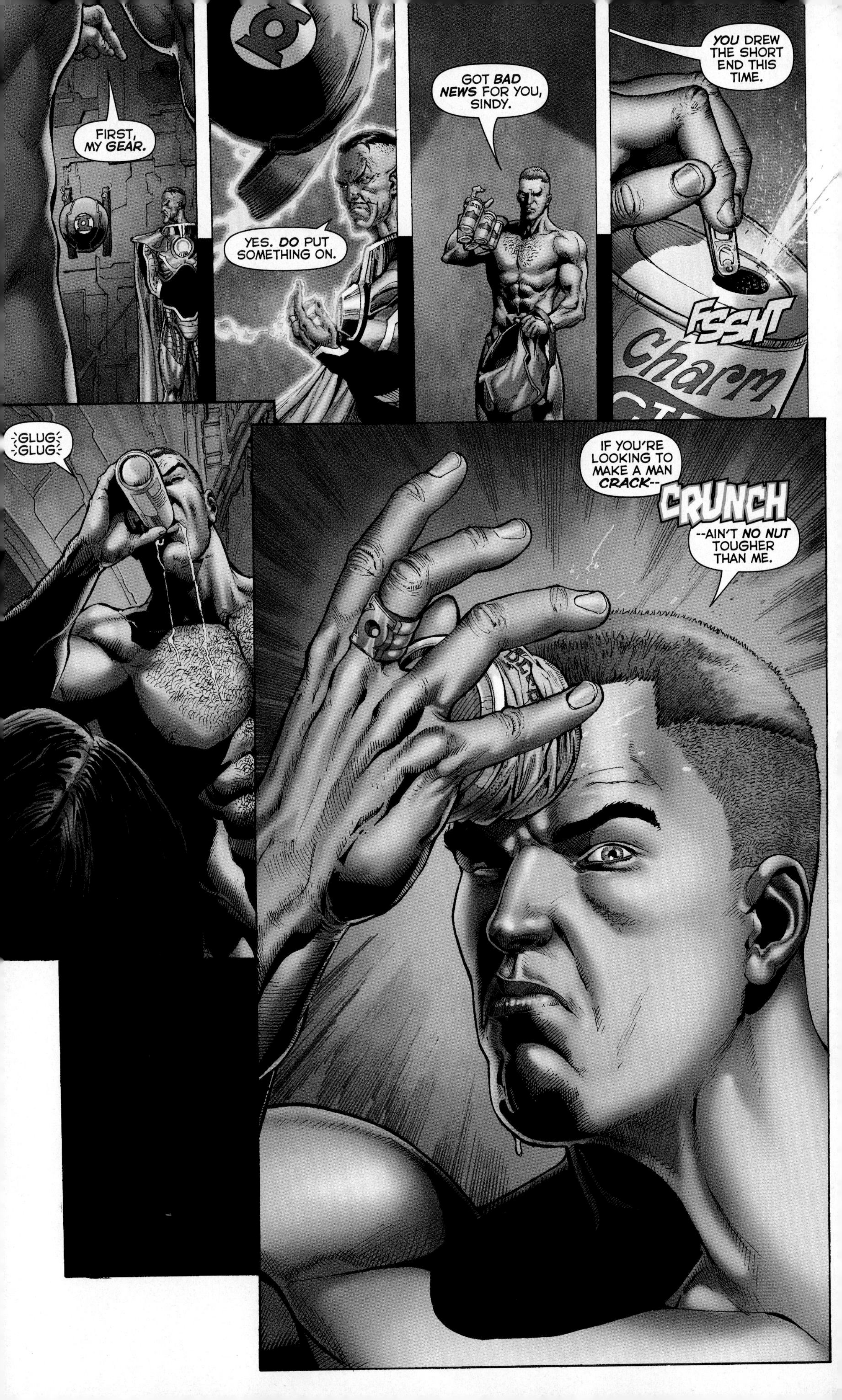
FIRST, MY GEAR.
YES. DO PUT SOMETHING ON.
GOT BAD NEWS FOR YOU, SINDY.
YOU DREW THE SHORT END THIS TIME.
FSSHT
Charm
GLUG GLUG
IF YOU'RE LOOKING TO MAKE A MAN CRACK--
CRUNCH
--AIN'T NO NUT TOUGHER THAN ME.

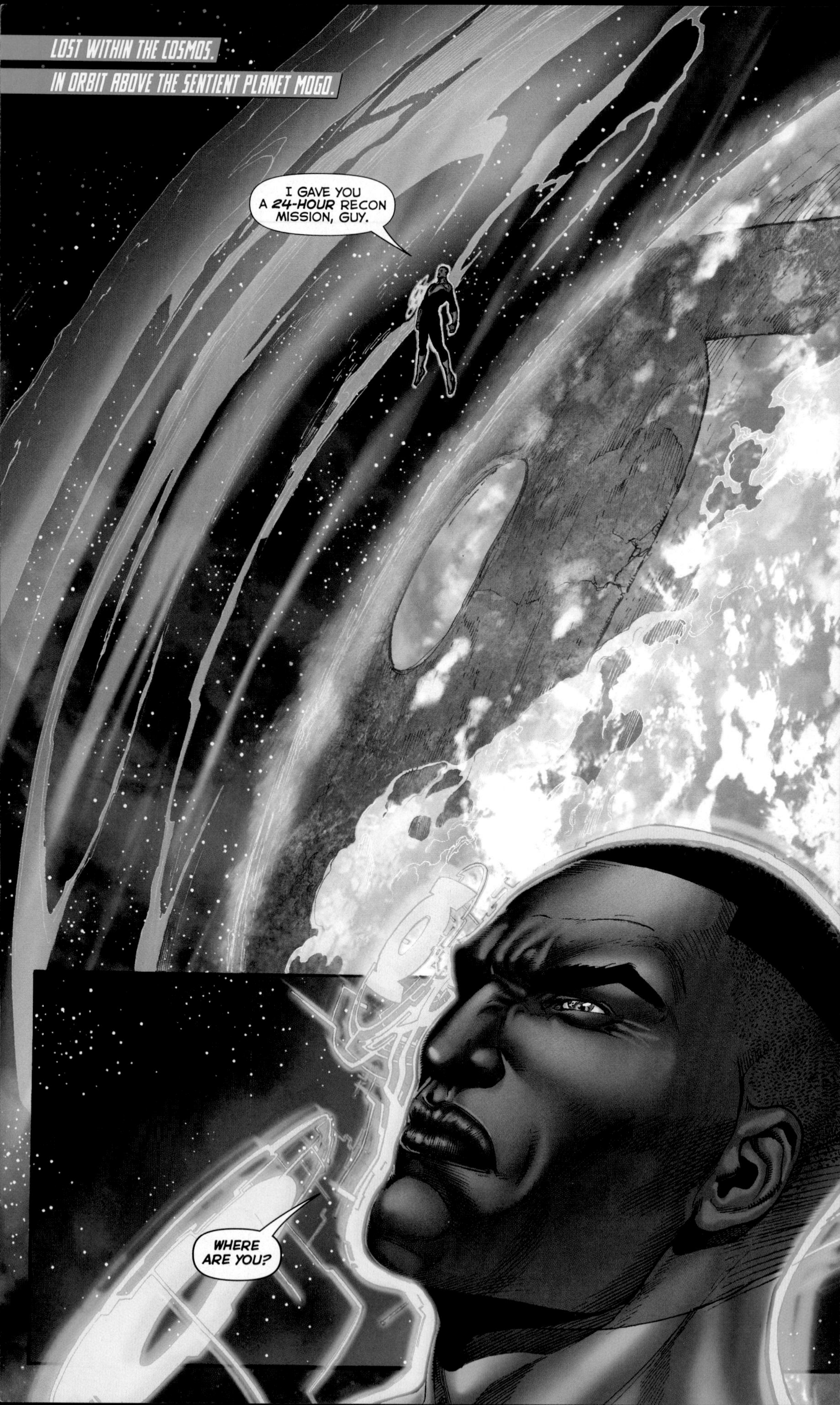

LOST WITHIN THE COSMOS.
IN ORBIT ABOVE THE SENTIENT PLANET MOGO.
I GAVE YOU A 24-HOUR RECON MISSION, GUY.
WHERE ARE YOU?

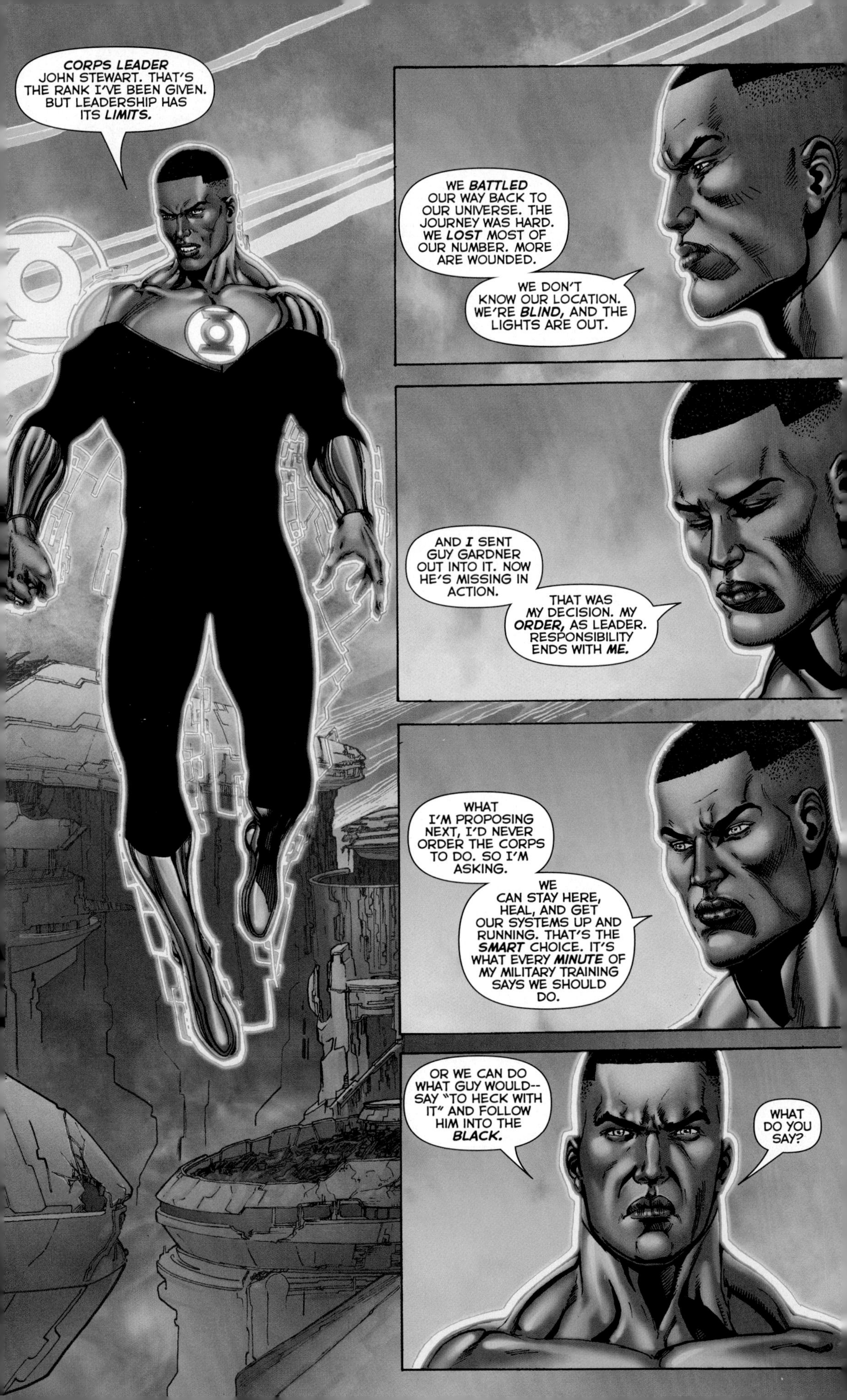
CORPS LEADER JOHN STEWART. THAT'S THE RANK I'VE BEEN GIVEN. BUT LEADERSHIP HAS ITS LIMITS.
WE BATTLED OUR WAY BACK TO OUR UNIVERSE. THE JOURNEY WAS HARD. WE LOST MOST OF OUR NUMBER. MORE ARE WOUNDED.
WE DON'T KNOW OUR LOCATION. WE'RE BLIND, AND THE LIGHTS ARE OUT.
AND I SENT GUY GARDNER OUT INTO IT. NOW HE'S MISSING IN ACTION.
THAT WAS MY DECISION. MY ORDER, AS LEADER. RESPONSIBILITY ENDS WITH ME.
WHAT I'M PROPOSING NEXT, I'D NEVER ORDER THE CORPS TO DO. SO I'M ASKING.
WE CAN STAY HERE, HEAL, AND GET OUR SYSTEMS UP AND RUNNING. THAT'S THE SMART CHOICE. IT'S WHAT EVERY MINUTE OF MY MILITARY TRAINING SAYS WE SHOULD DO.
OR WE CAN DO WHAT GUY WOULD-- SAY "TO HECK WITH IT" AND FOLLOW HIM INTO THE BLACK.
WHAT DO YOU SAY?

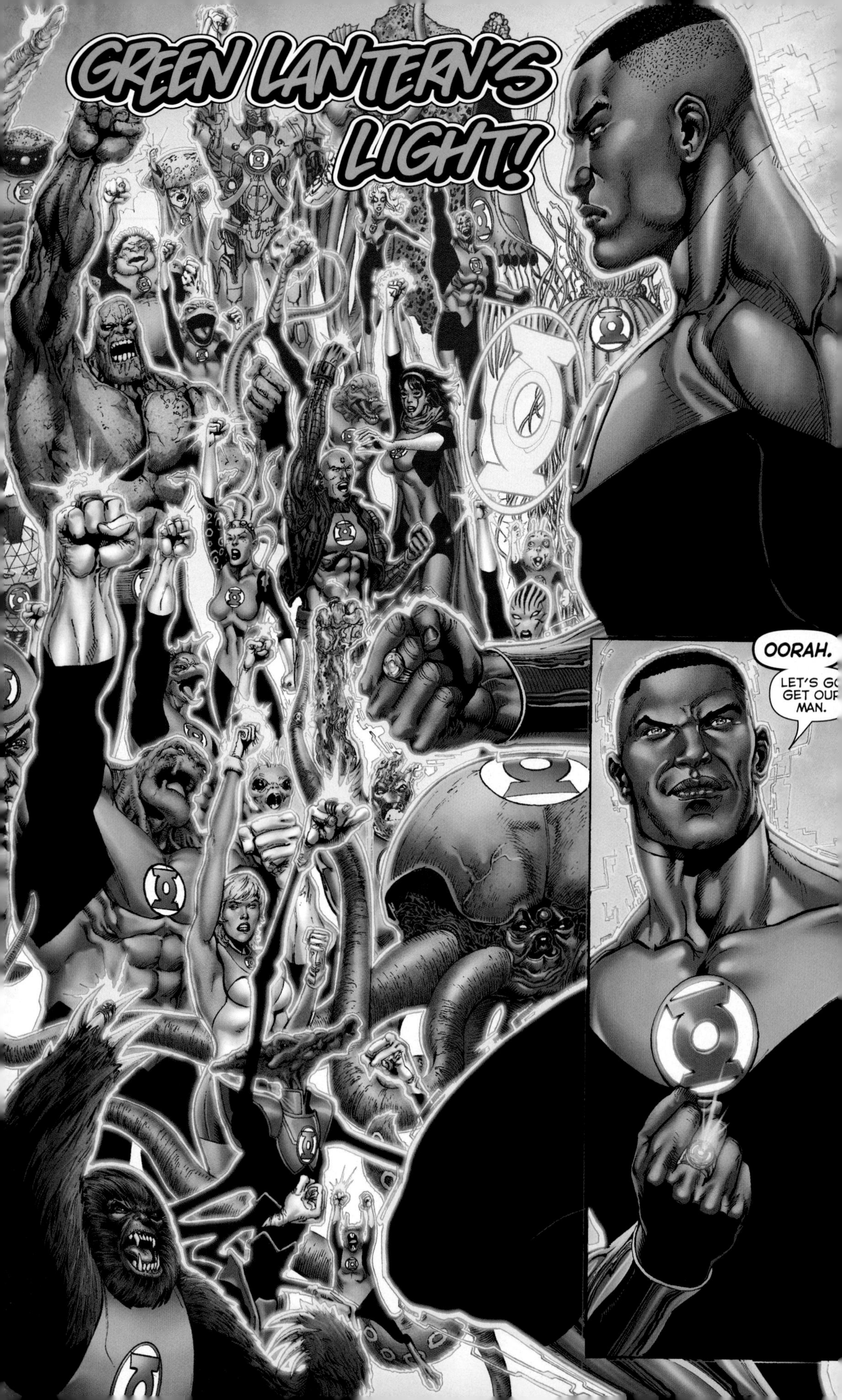
GREEN LANTERN'S LIGHT!
OORAH.
LET'S GO GET OUR MAN.

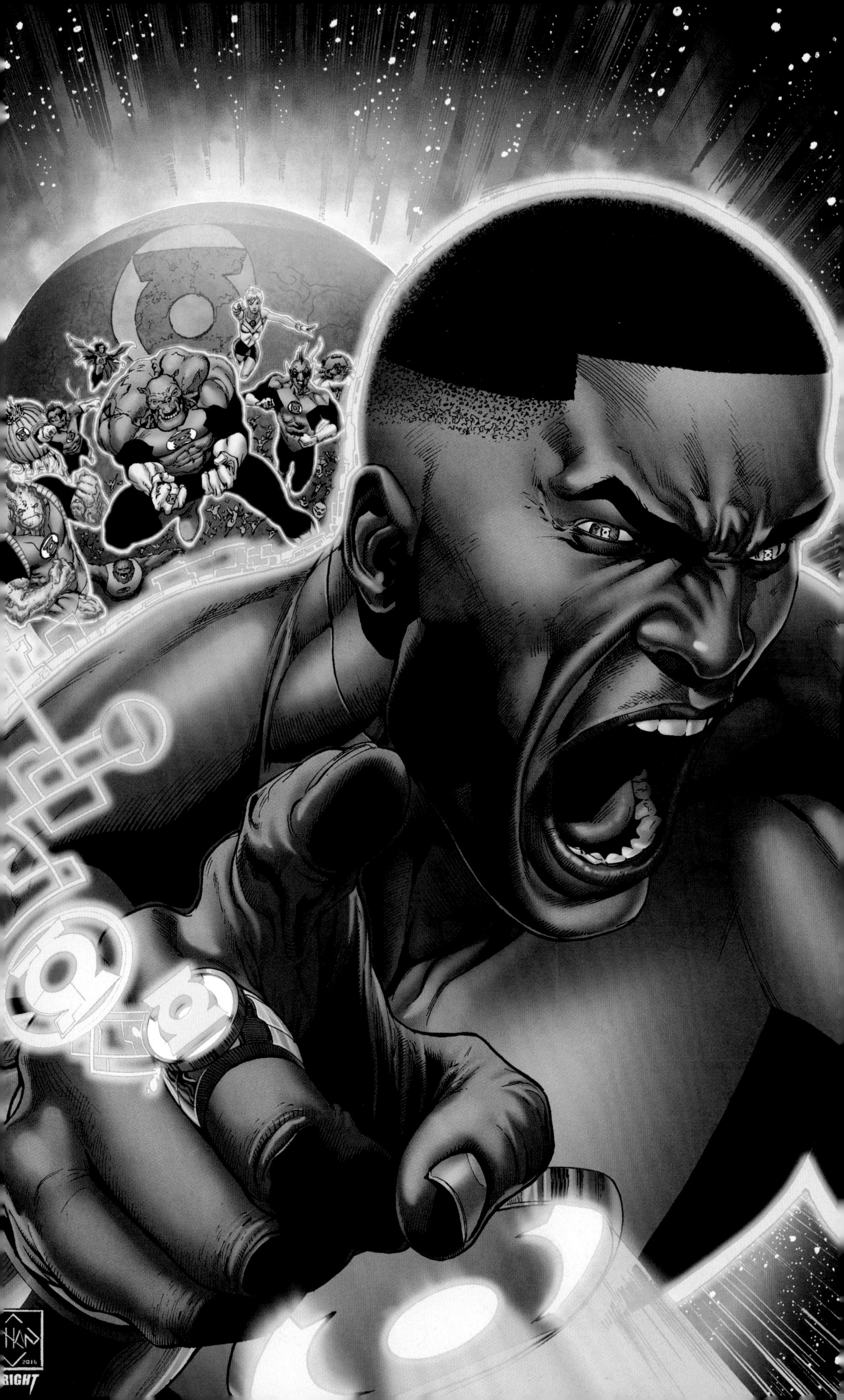

SINESTRO'S LAW PART 5: JOINING FORCES

ETHAN VAN SCIVER artist * JASON WRIGHT colorist * ETHAN VAN SCIVER and JASON WRIGHT cover artists

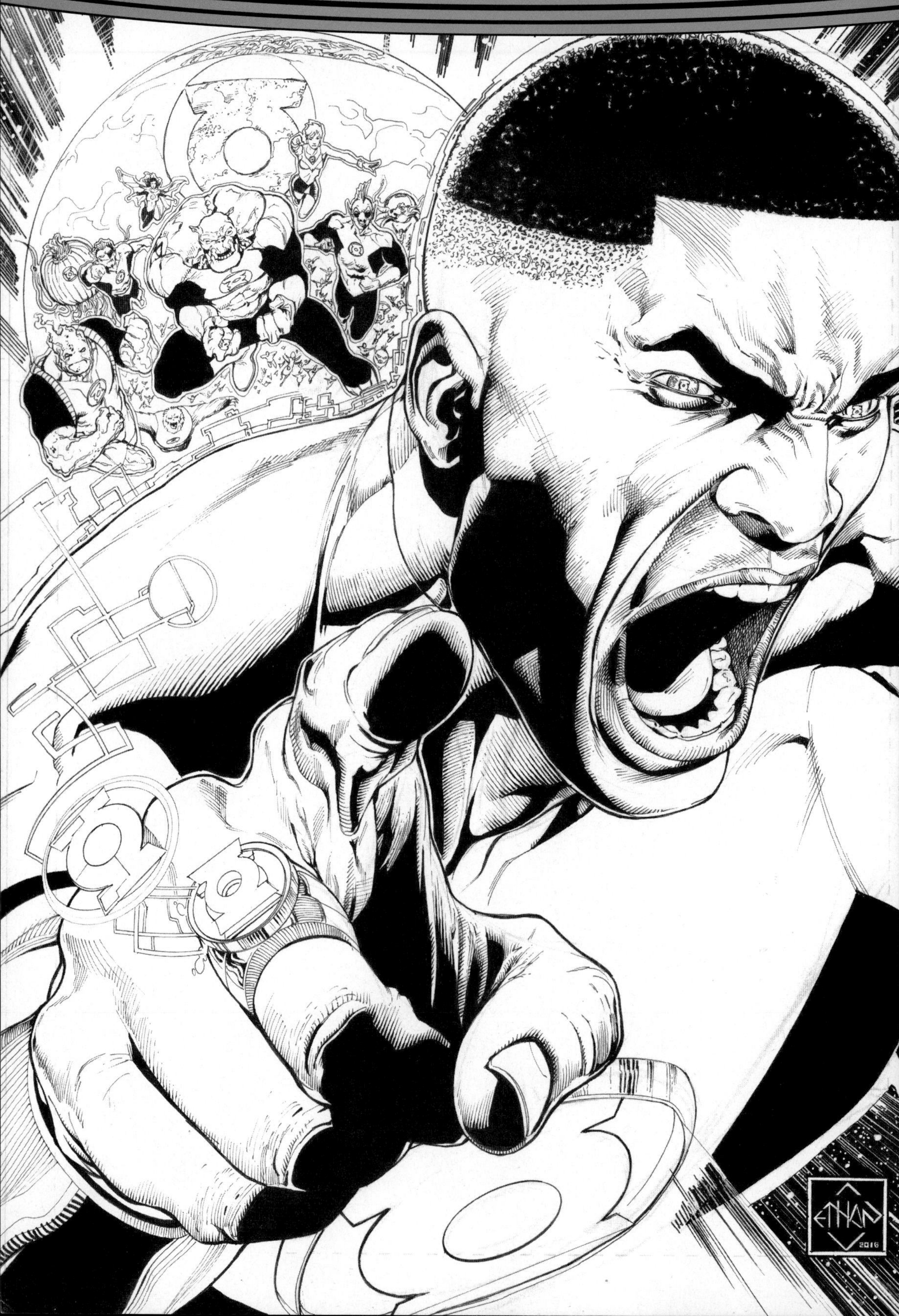

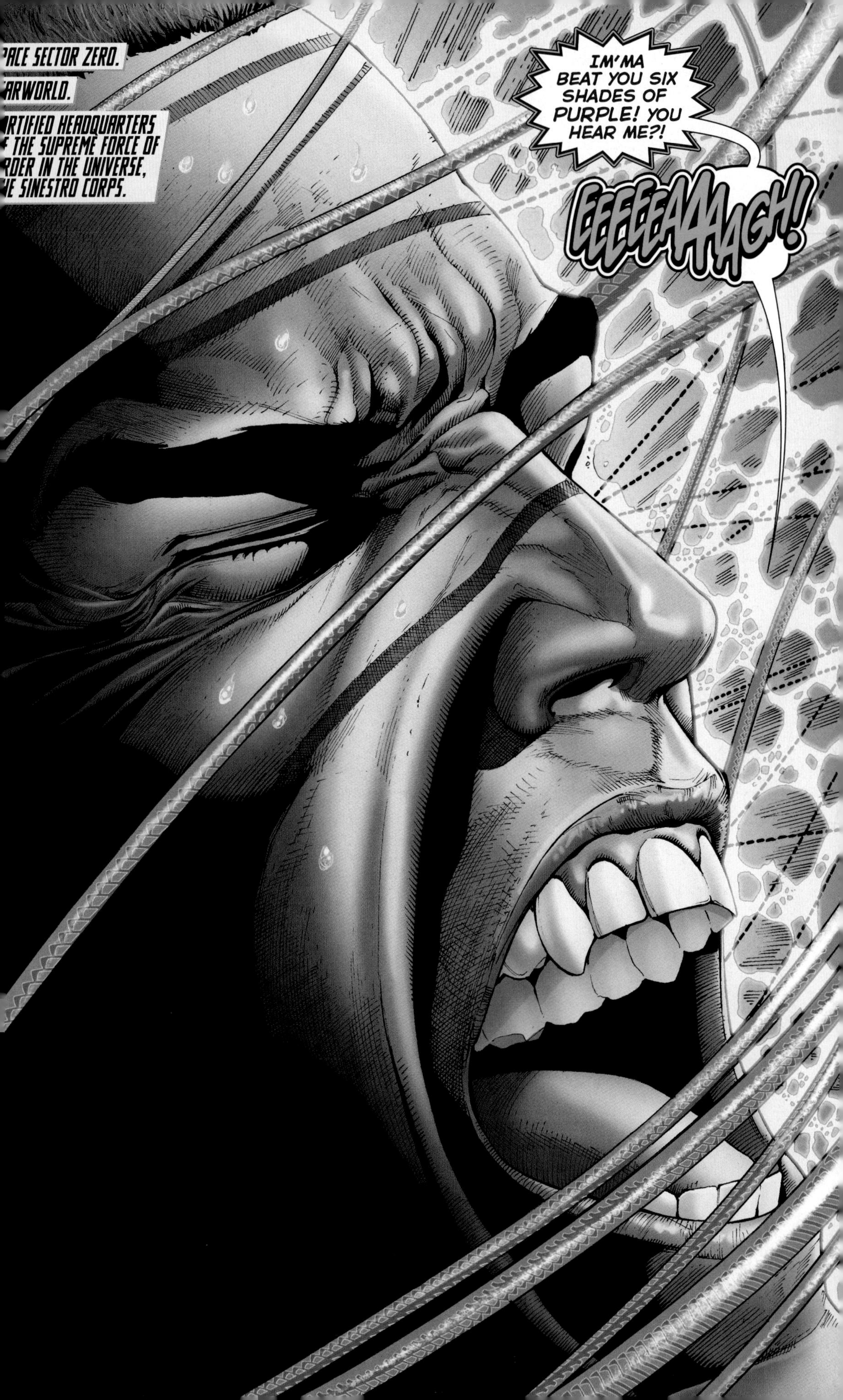
PACE SECTOR ZERO.
ARWORLD.
RTIFIED HEADQUARTERS
THE SUPREME FORCE OF
RDER IN THE UNIVERSE,
HE SINESTRO CORPS.
IM'MA BEAT YOU SIX SHADES OF PURPLE! YOU HEAR ME?!
EEEEEAAAAAGH!

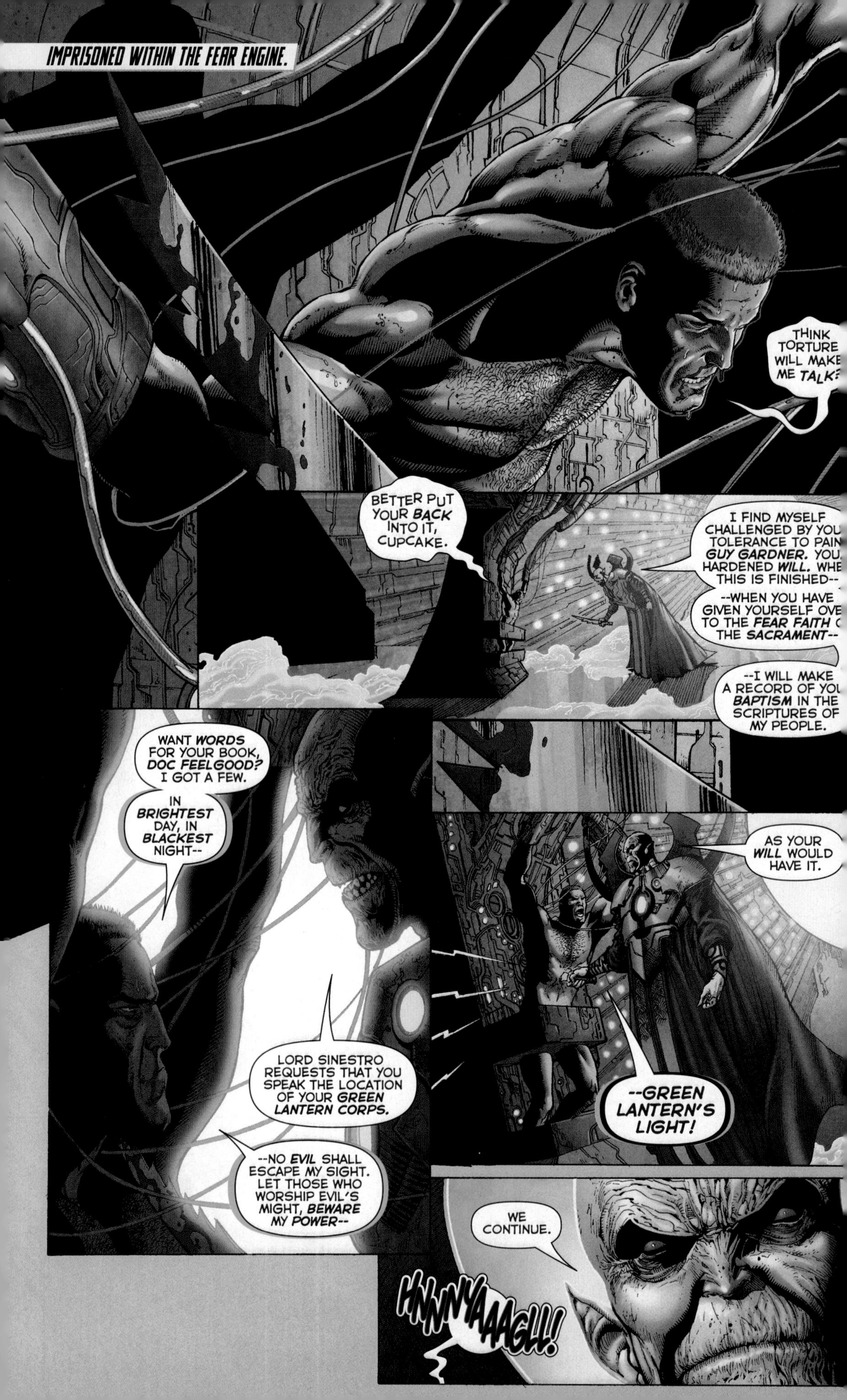
IMPRISONED WITHIN THE FEAR ENGINE.
THINK TORTURE WILL MAKE ME TALK?
BETTER PUT YOUR BACK INTO IT, CUPCAKE.
I FIND MYSELF CHALLENGED BY YOU TOLERANCE TO PAIN GUY GARDNER. YOU HARDENED WILL. WHE THIS IS FINISHED--
--WHEN YOU HAVE GIVEN YOURSELF OVE TO THE FEAR FAITH C THE SACRAMENT--
--I WILL MAKE A RECORD OF YOU BAPTISM IN THE SCRIPTURES OF MY PEOPLE.
WANT WORDS FOR YOUR BOOK, DOC FEELGOOD? I GOT A FEW.
IN BRIGHTEST DAY, IN BLACKEST NIGHT--
LORD SINESTRO REQUESTS THAT YOU SPEAK THE LOCATION OF YOUR GREEN LANTERN CORPS.
--NO EVIL SHALL ESCAPE MY SIGHT. LET THOSE WHO WORSHIP EVIL'S MIGHT, BEWARE MY POWER--
AS YOUR WILL WOULD HAVE IT.
--GREEN LANTERN'S LIGHT!
WE CONTINUE.
HNNNYAAAGLL!

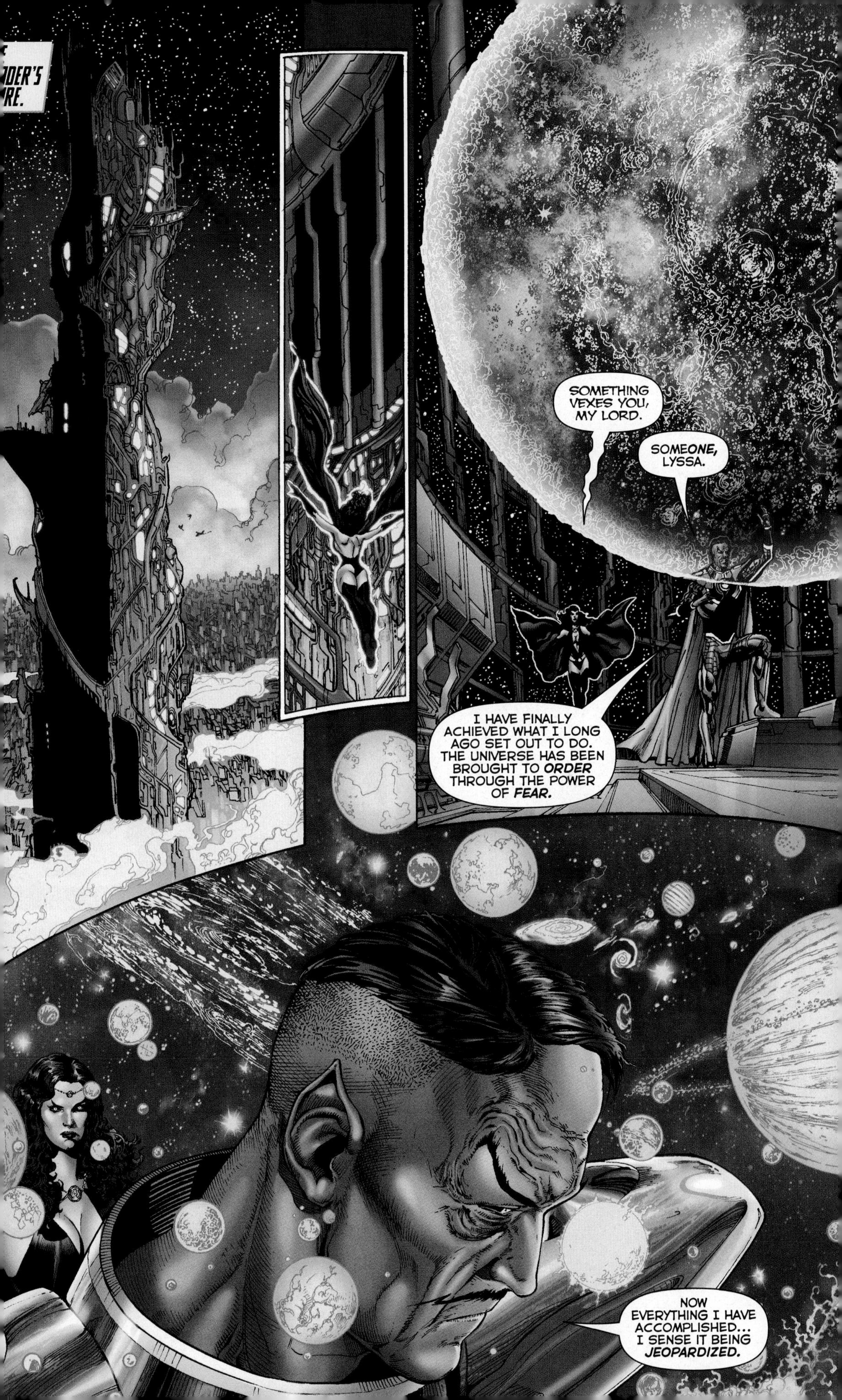
SOMETHING VEXES YOU, MY LORD.
SOMEONE, LYSSA.
I HAVE FINALLY ACHIEVED WHAT I LONG AGO SET OUT TO DO. THE UNIVERSE HAS BEEN BROUGHT TO ORDER THROUGH THE POWER OF FEAR.
NOW EVERYTHING I HAVE ACCOMPLISHED... I SENSE IT BEING JEOPARDIZED.

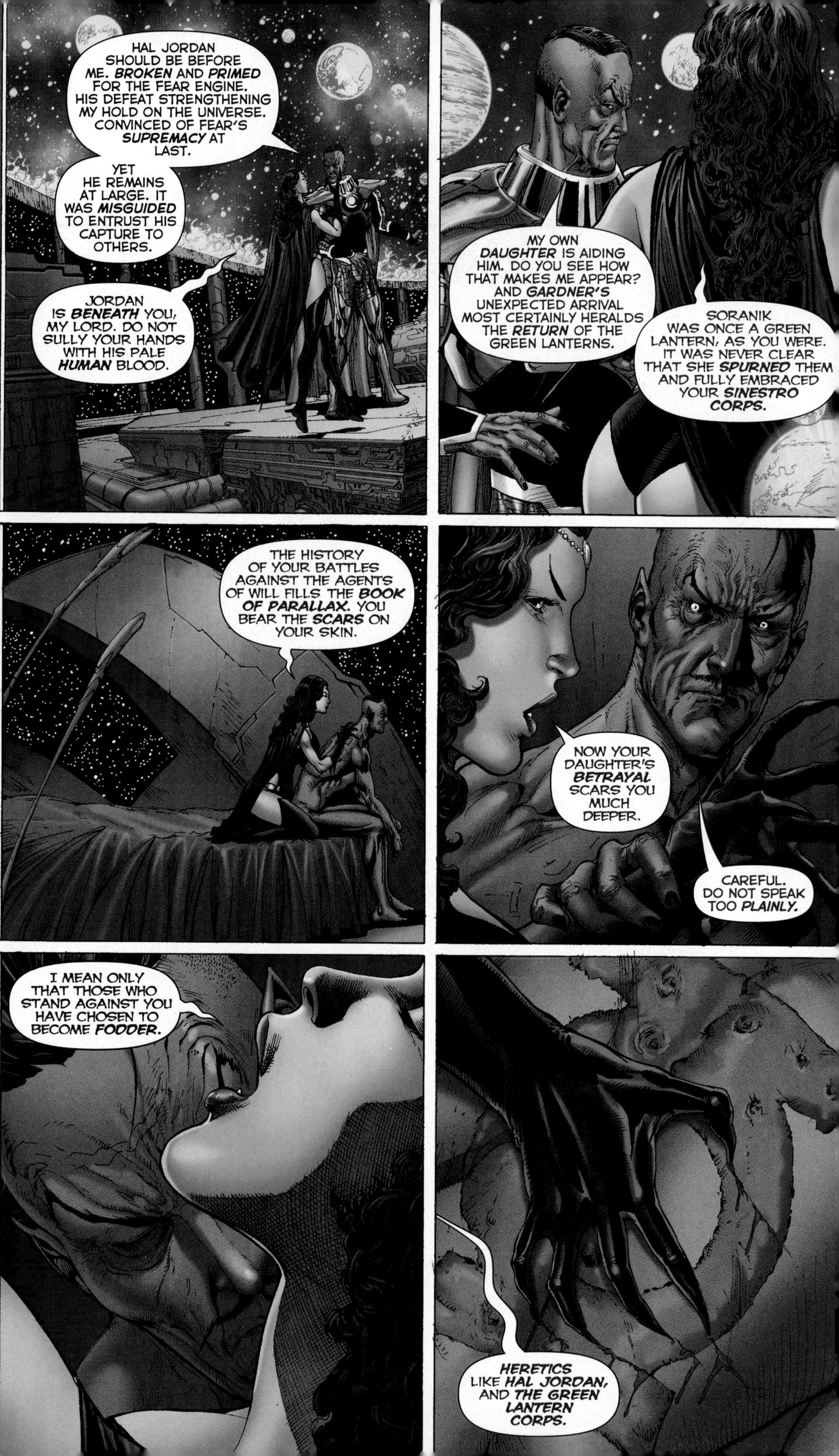
HAL JORDAN SHOULD BE BEFORE ME. BROKEN AND PRIMED FOR THE FEAR ENGINE. HIS DEFEAT STRENGTHENING MY HOLD ON THE UNIVERSE. CONVINCED OF FEAR'S SUPREMACY AT LAST.
YET HE REMAINS AT LARGE. IT WAS MISGUIDED TO ENTRUST HIS CAPTURE TO OTHERS.
JORDAN IS BENEATH YOU, MY LORD. DO NOT SULLY YOUR HANDS WITH HIS PALE HUMAN BLOOD.
MY OWN DAUGHTER IS AIDING HIM. DO YOU SEE HOW THAT MAKES ME APPEAR? AND GARDNER'S UNEXPECTED ARRIVAL MOST CERTAINLY HERALDS THE RETURN OF THE GREEN LANTERNS.
SORANIK WAS ONCE A GREEN LANTERN, AS YOU WERE. IT WAS NEVER CLEAR THAT SHE SPURNED THEM AND FULLY EMBRACED YOUR SINESTRO CORPS.
THE HISTORY OF YOUR BATTLES AGAINST THE AGENTS OF WILL FILLS THE BOOK OF PARALLAX. YOU BEAR THE SCARS ON YOUR SKIN.
NOW YOUR DAUGHTER'S BETRAYAL SCARS YOU MUCH DEEPER.
CAREFUL. DO NOT SPEAK TOO PLAINLY.
I MEAN ONLY THAT THOSE WHO STAND AGAINST YOU HAVE CHOSEN TO BECOME FODDER.
HERETICS LIKE HAL JORDAN, AND THE GREEN LANTERN CORPS.

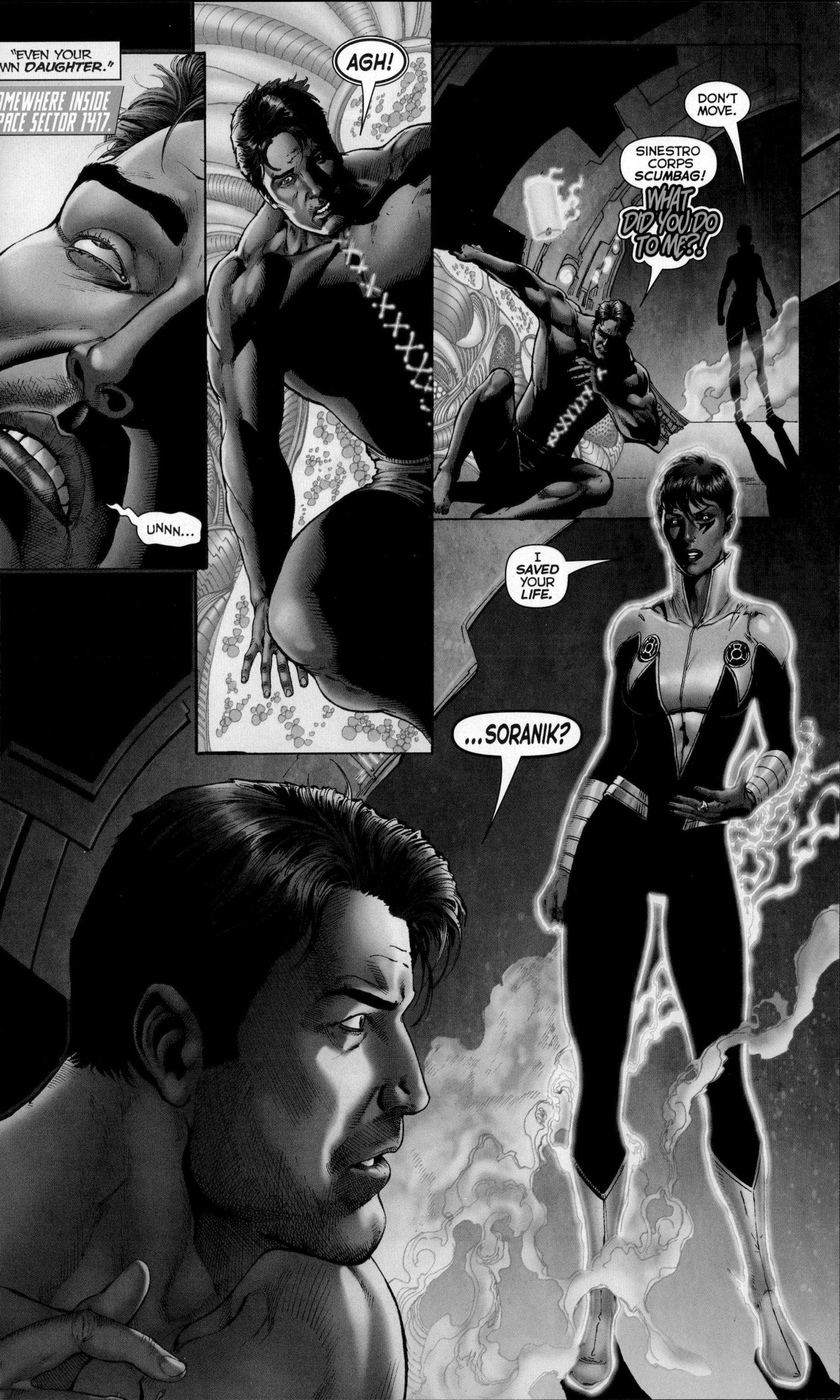
"EVEN YOUR
WN DAUGHTER."
OMEWHERE INSIDE
PACE SECTOR 1417.
UNNN...
AGH!
DON'T MOVE.
SINESTRO CORPS SCUMBAG!
WHAT DID YOU DO TO ME?!
I SAVED YOUR LIFE.
...SORANIK?

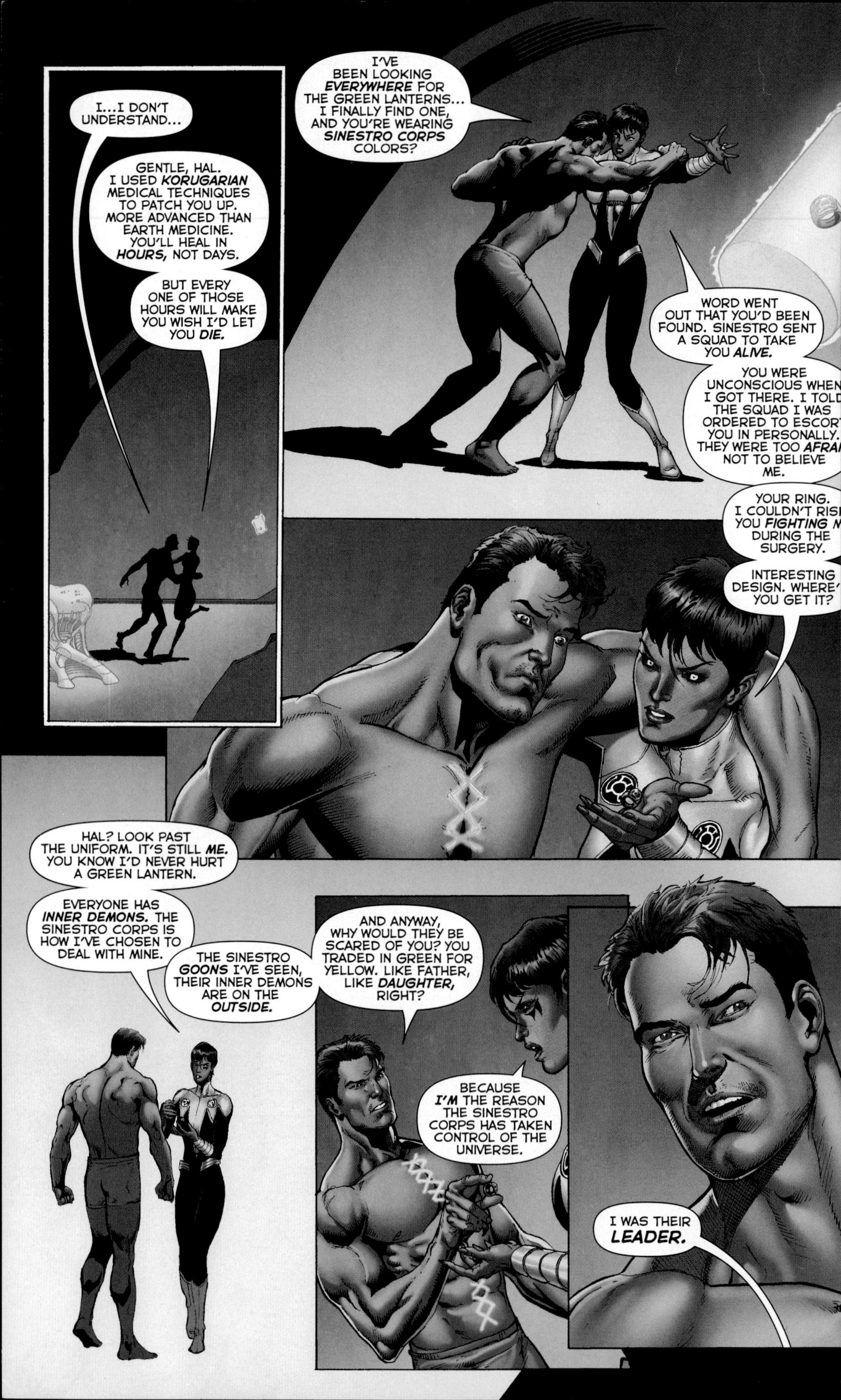

I...I DON'T UNDERSTAND...
GENTLE, HAL. I USED KORUGARIAN MEDICAL TECHNIQUES TO PATCH YOU UP. MORE ADVANCED THAN EARTH MEDICINE. YOU'LL HEAL IN HOURS, NOT DAYS.
BUT EVERY ONE OF THOSE HOURS WILL MAKE YOU WISH I'D LET YOU DIE.
I'VE BEEN LOOKING EVERYWHERE FOR THE GREEN LANTERNS... I FINALLY FIND ONE, AND YOU'RE WEARING SINESTRO CORPS COLORS?
WORD WENT OUT THAT YOU'D BEEN FOUND. SINESTRO SENT A SQUAD TO TAKE YOU ALIVE.
YOU WERE UNCONSCIOUS WHEN I GOT THERE. I TOLD THE SQUAD I WAS ORDERED TO ESCORT YOU IN PERSONALLY. THEY WERE TOO AFRAI NOT TO BELIEVE ME.
YOUR RING. I COULDN'T RISK YOU FIGHTING M DURING THE SURGERY.
INTERESTING DESIGN. WHERE' YOU GET IT?
HAL? LOOK PAST THE UNIFORM. IT'S STILL ME. YOU KNOW I'D NEVER HURT A GREEN LANTERN.
EVERYONE HAS INNER DEMONS. THE SINESTRO CORPS IS HOW I'VE CHOSEN TO DEAL WITH MINE.
THE SINESTRO GOONS I'VE SEEN, THEIR INNER DEMONS ARE ON THE OUTSIDE.
AND ANYWAY, WHY WOULD THEY BE SCARED OF YOU? YOU TRADED IN GREEN FOR YELLOW. LIKE FATHER, LIKE DAUGHTER, RIGHT?
BECAUSE I'M THE REASON THE SINESTRO CORPS HAS TAKEN CONTROL OF THE UNIVERSE.
I WAS THEIR LEADER.

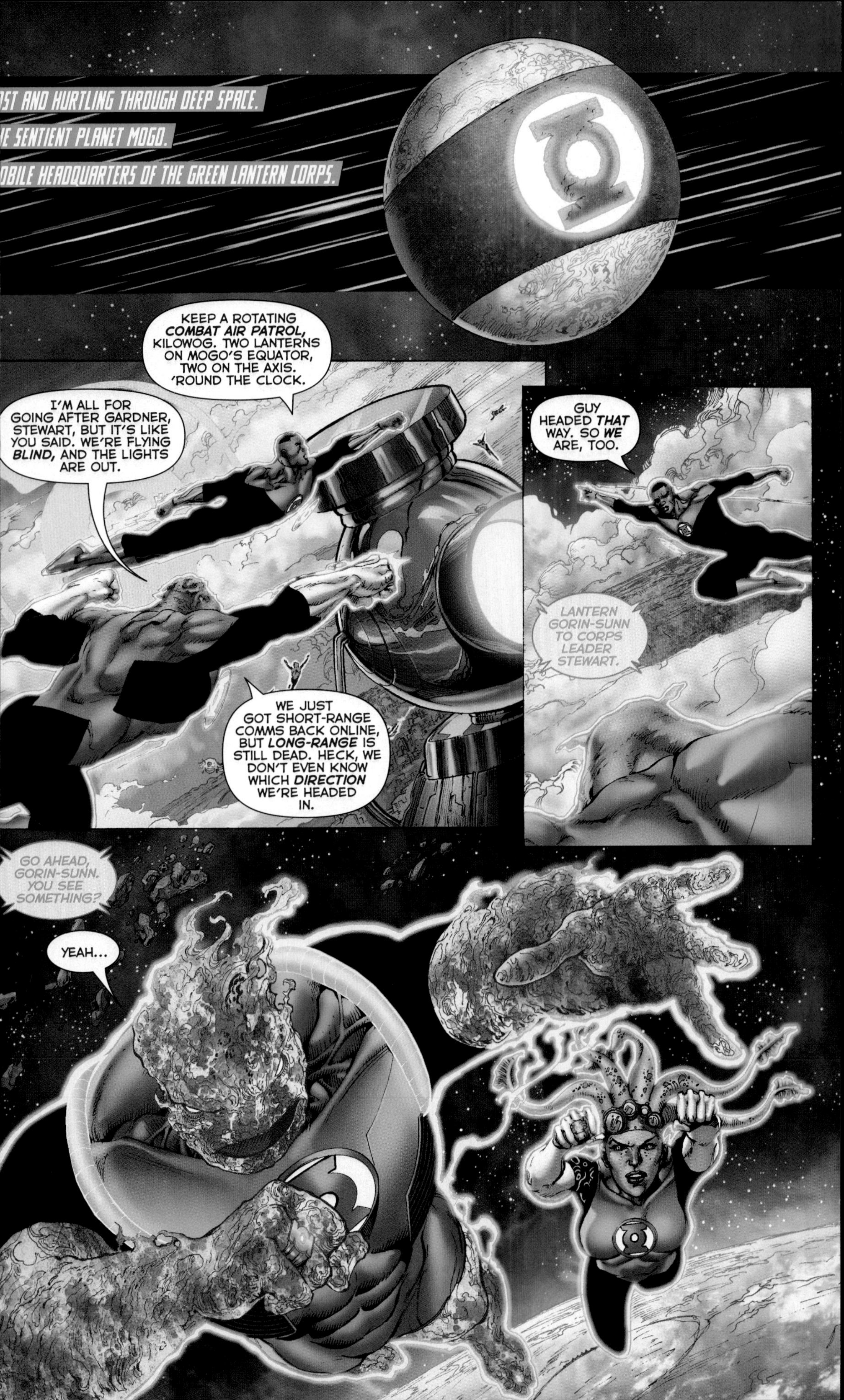
ST AND HURTLING THROUGH DEEP SPACE.
E SENTIENT PLANET MOGO.
OBILE HEADQUARTERS OF THE GREEN LANTERN CORPS.
KEEP A ROTATING COMBAT AIR PATROL, KILOWOG. TWO LANTERNS ON MOGO'S EQUATOR, TWO ON THE AXIS. 'ROUND THE CLOCK.
I'M ALL FOR GOING AFTER GARDNER, STEWART, BUT IT'S LIKE YOU SAID. WE'RE FLYING BLIND, AND THE LIGHTS ARE OUT.
WE JUST GOT SHORT-RANGE COMMS BACK ONLINE, BUT LONG-RANGE IS STILL DEAD. HECK, WE DON'T EVEN KNOW WHICH DIRECTION WE'RE HEADED IN.
GUY HEADED THAT WAY. SO WE ARE, TOO.
LANTERN GORIN-SUNN TO CORPS LEADER STEWART.
GO AHEAD, GORIN-SUNN. YOU SEE SOMETHING?
YEAH...

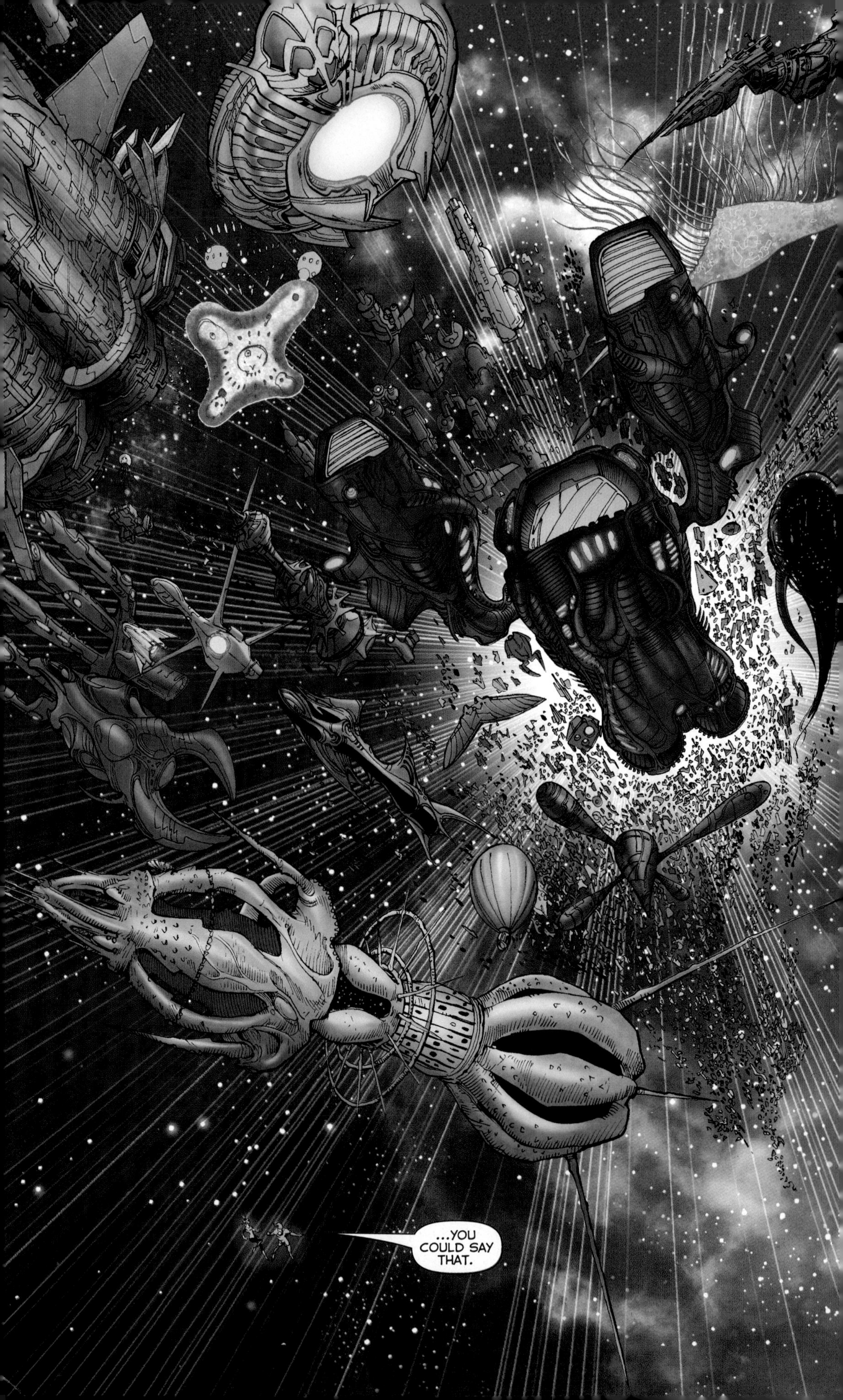
...YOU COULD SAY THAT.

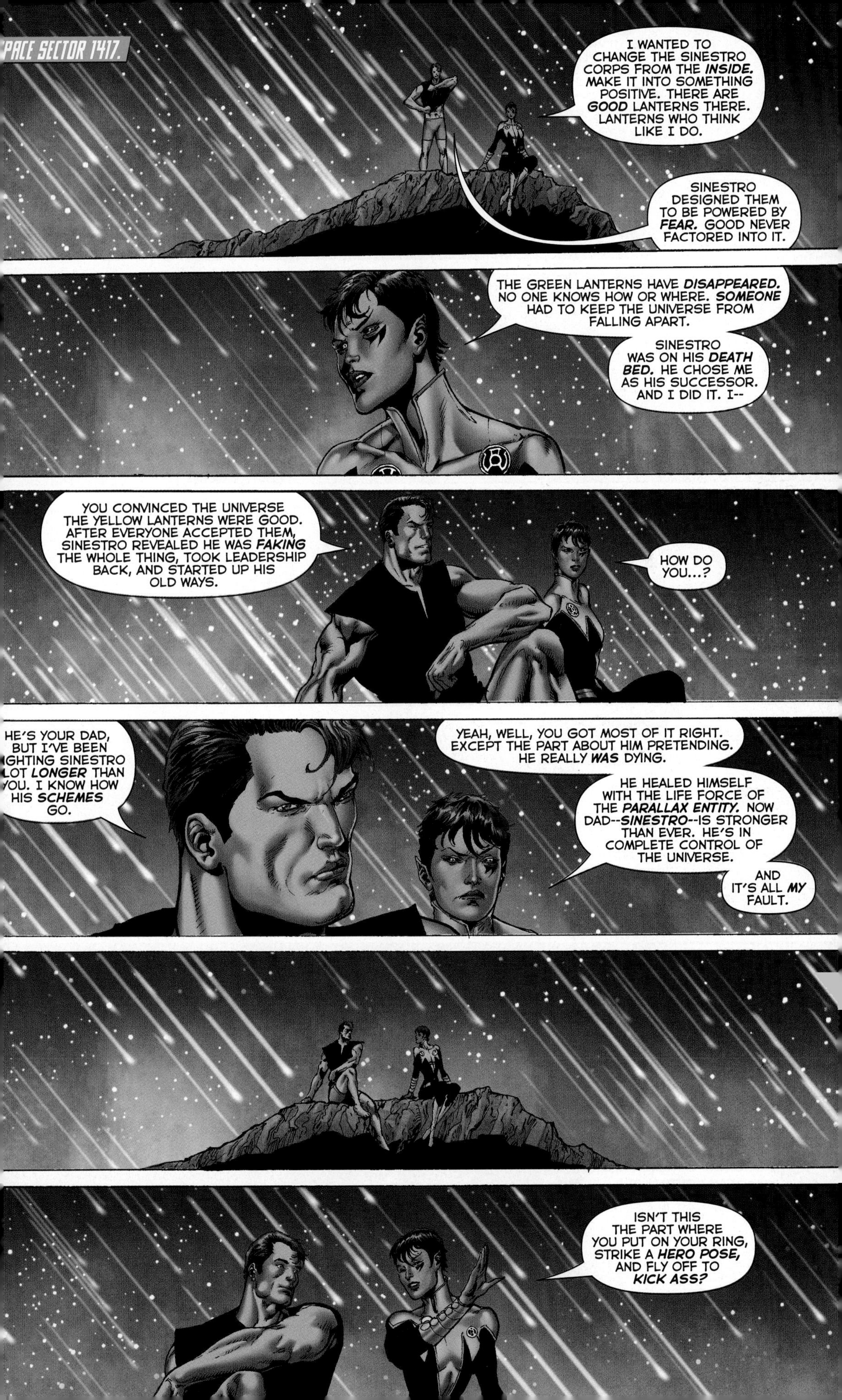
PACE SECTOR 1417.
I WANTED TO CHANGE THE SINESTRO CORPS FROM THE *INSIDE.* MAKE IT INTO SOMETHING POSITIVE. THERE ARE *GOOD* LANTERNS THERE. LANTERNS WHO THINK LIKE I DO.
SINESTRO DESIGNED THEM TO BE POWERED BY *FEAR.* GOOD NEVER FACTORED INTO IT.
THE GREEN LANTERNS HAVE *DISAPPEARED.* NO ONE KNOWS HOW OR WHERE. *SOMEONE* HAD TO KEEP THE UNIVERSE FROM FALLING APART.
SINESTRO WAS ON HIS *DEATH BED.* HE CHOSE ME AS HIS SUCCESSOR. AND I DID IT. I--
YOU CONVINCED THE UNIVERSE THE YELLOW LANTERNS WERE GOOD. AFTER EVERYONE ACCEPTED THEM, SINESTRO REVEALED HE WAS *FAKING* THE WHOLE THING, TOOK LEADERSHIP BACK, AND STARTED UP HIS OLD WAYS.
HOW DO YOU...?
HE'S YOUR DAD, BUT I'VE BEEN IGHTING SINESTRO LOT *LONGER* THAN YOU. I KNOW HOW HIS *SCHEMES* GO.
YEAH, WELL, YOU GOT MOST OF IT RIGHT. EXCEPT THE PART ABOUT HIM PRETENDING. HE REALLY *WAS* DYING.
HE HEALED HIMSELF WITH THE LIFE FORCE OF THE *PARALLAX ENTITY.* NOW DAD--*SINESTRO*--IS STRONGER THAN EVER. HE'S IN COMPLETE CONTROL OF THE UNIVERSE.
AND IT'S ALL *MY* FAULT.
ISN'T THIS THE PART WHERE YOU PUT ON YOUR RING, STRIKE A *HERO POSE,* AND FLY OFF TO *KICK ASS?*

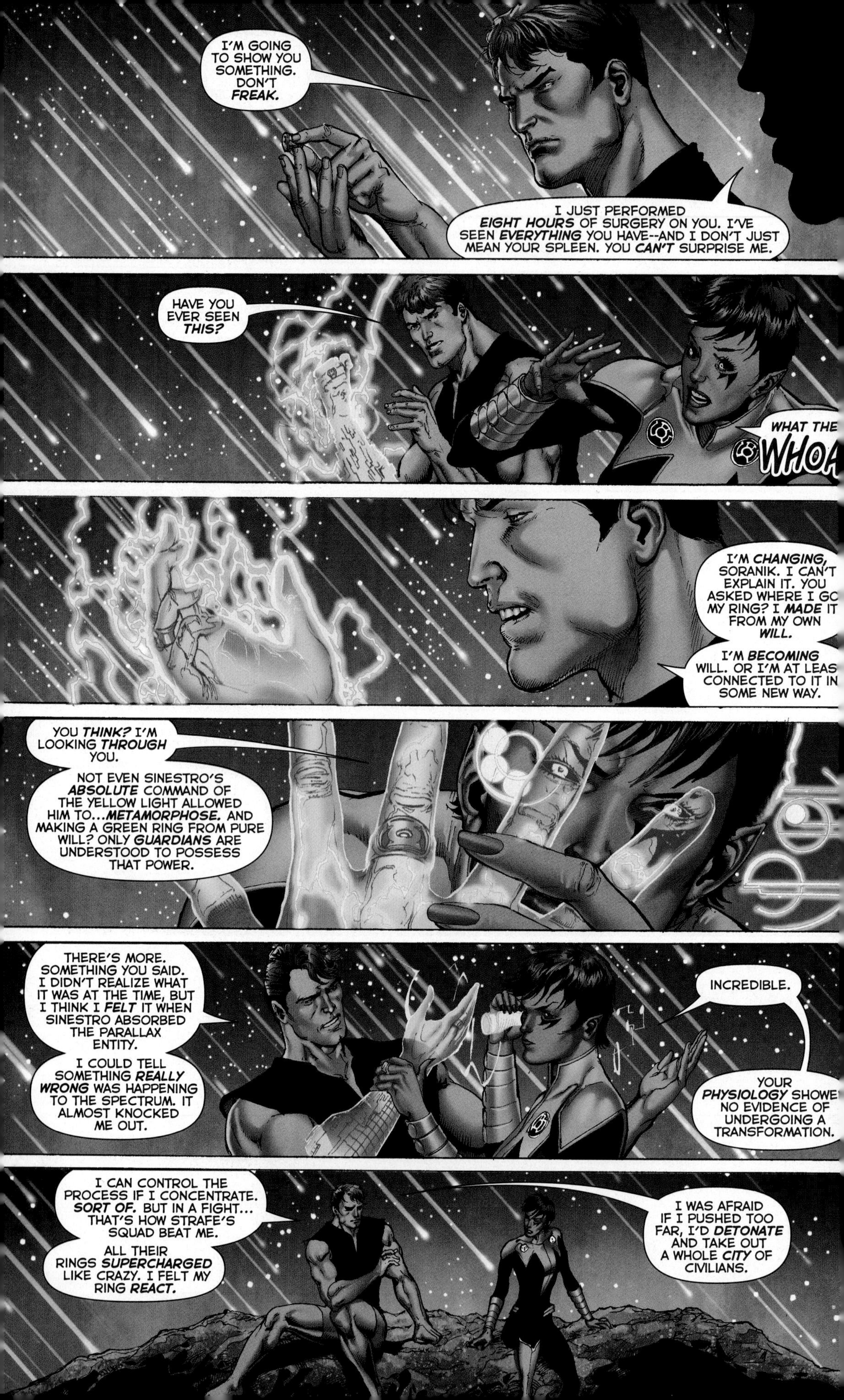
I'M GOING TO SHOW YOU SOMETHING. DON'T FREAK.
I JUST PERFORMED EIGHT HOURS OF SURGERY ON YOU. I'VE SEEN EVERYTHING YOU HAVE--AND I DON'T JUST MEAN YOUR SPLEEN. YOU CAN'T SURPRISE ME.
HAVE YOU EVER SEEN THIS?
WHAT THE
WHOA
I'M CHANGING, SORANIK. I CAN'T EXPLAIN IT. YOU ASKED WHERE I GO MY RING? I MADE IT FROM MY OWN WILL.
I'M BECOMING WILL. OR I'M AT LEAS CONNECTED TO IT IN SOME NEW WAY.
YOU THINK? I'M LOOKING THROUGH YOU.
NOT EVEN SINESTRO'S ABSOLUTE COMMAND OF THE YELLOW LIGHT ALLOWED HIM TO...METAMORPHOSE. AND MAKING A GREEN RING FROM PURE WILL? ONLY GUARDIANS ARE UNDERSTOOD TO POSSESS THAT POWER.
THERE'S MORE. SOMETHING YOU SAID. I DIDN'T REALIZE WHAT IT WAS AT THE TIME, BUT I THINK I FELT IT WHEN SINESTRO ABSORBED THE PARALLAX ENTITY.
I COULD TELL SOMETHING REALLY WRONG WAS HAPPENING TO THE SPECTRUM. IT ALMOST KNOCKED ME OUT.
INCREDIBLE.
YOUR PHYSIOLOGY SHOWE NO EVIDENCE OF UNDERGOING A TRANSFORMATION.
I CAN CONTROL THE PROCESS IF I CONCENTRATE. SORT OF. BUT IN A FIGHT... THAT'S HOW STRAFE'S SQUAD BEAT ME.
ALL THEIR RINGS SUPERCHARGED LIKE CRAZY. I FELT MY RING REACT.
I WAS AFRAID IF I PUSHED TOO FAR, I'D DETONATE AND TAKE OUT A WHOLE CITY OF CIVILIANS.

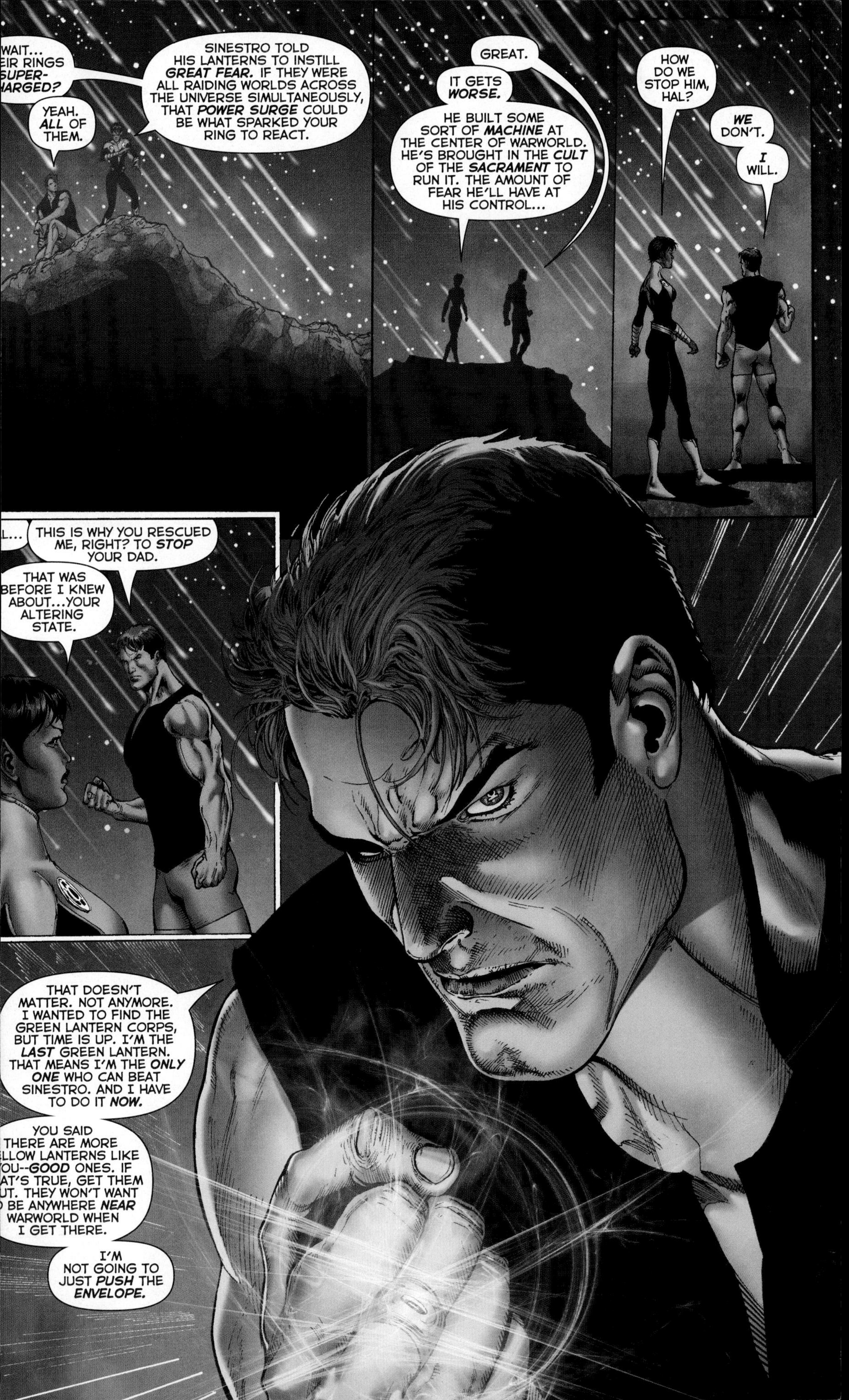
WAIT... EIR RINGS SUPER-HARGED?
SINESTRO TOLD HIS LANTERNS TO INSTILL GREAT FEAR. IF THEY WERE ALL RAIDING WORLDS ACROSS THE UNIVERSE SIMULTANEOUSLY, THAT POWER SURGE COULD BE WHAT SPARKED YOUR RING TO REACT.
YEAH. ALL OF THEM.
GREAT.
IT GETS WORSE.
HE BUILT SOME SORT OF MACHINE AT THE CENTER OF WARWORLD. HE'S BROUGHT IN THE CULT OF THE SACRAMENT TO RUN IT. THE AMOUNT OF FEAR HE'LL HAVE AT HIS CONTROL...
HOW DO WE STOP HIM, HAL?
WE DON'T.
I WILL.
L...
THIS IS WHY YOU RESCUED ME, RIGHT? TO STOP YOUR DAD.
THAT WAS BEFORE I KNEW ABOUT...YOUR ALTERING STATE.
THAT DOESN'T MATTER. NOT ANYMORE. I WANTED TO FIND THE GREEN LANTERN CORPS, BUT TIME IS UP. I'M THE LAST GREEN LANTERN. THAT MEANS I'M THE ONLY ONE WHO CAN BEAT SINESTRO. AND I HAVE TO DO IT NOW.
YOU SAID THERE ARE MORE ELLOW LANTERNS LIKE OU--GOOD ONES. IF AT'S TRUE, GET THEM UT. THEY WON'T WANT BE ANYWHERE NEAR WARWORLD WHEN I GET THERE.
I'M NOT GOING TO JUST PUSH THE ENVELOPE.

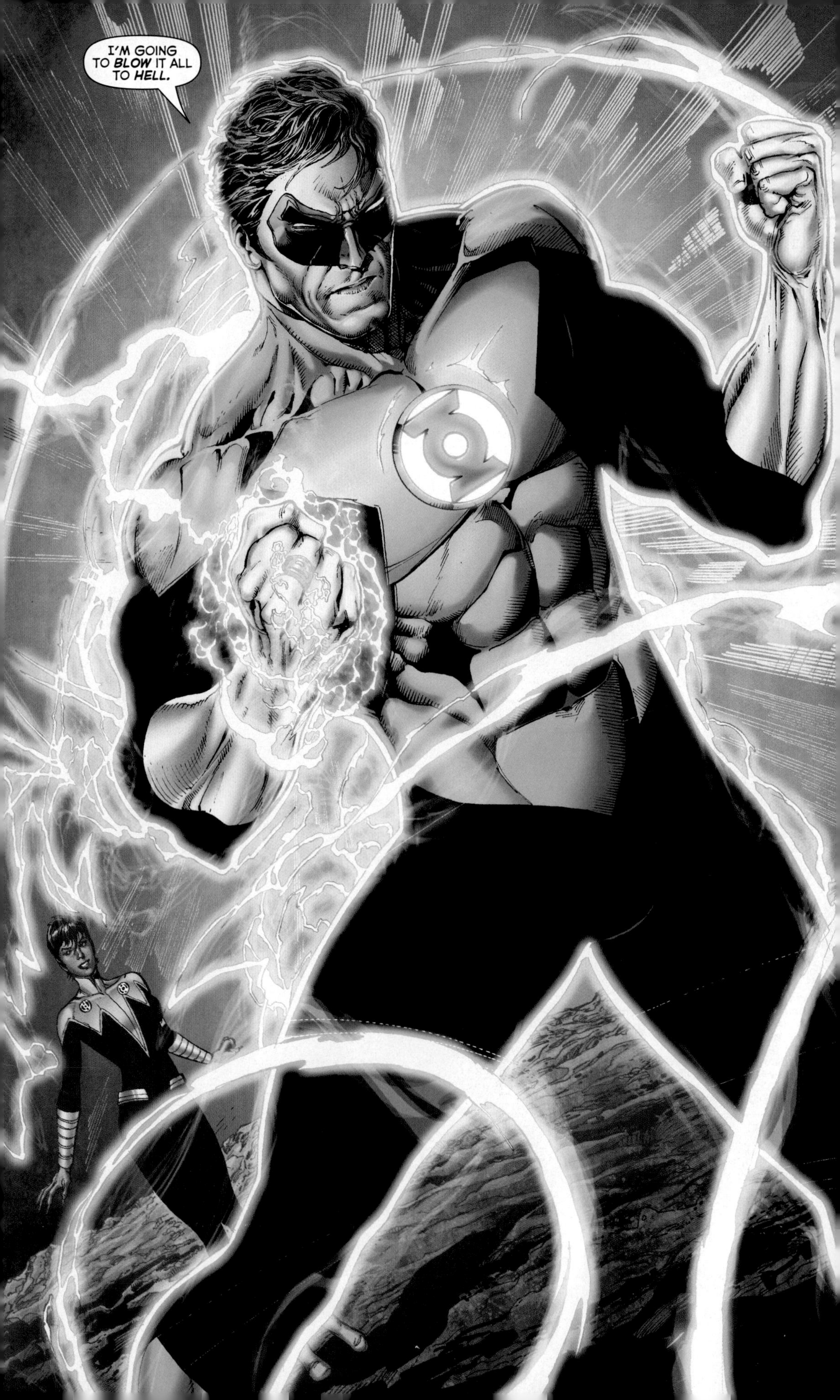
I'M GOING TO *BLOW* IT ALL TO *HELL.*

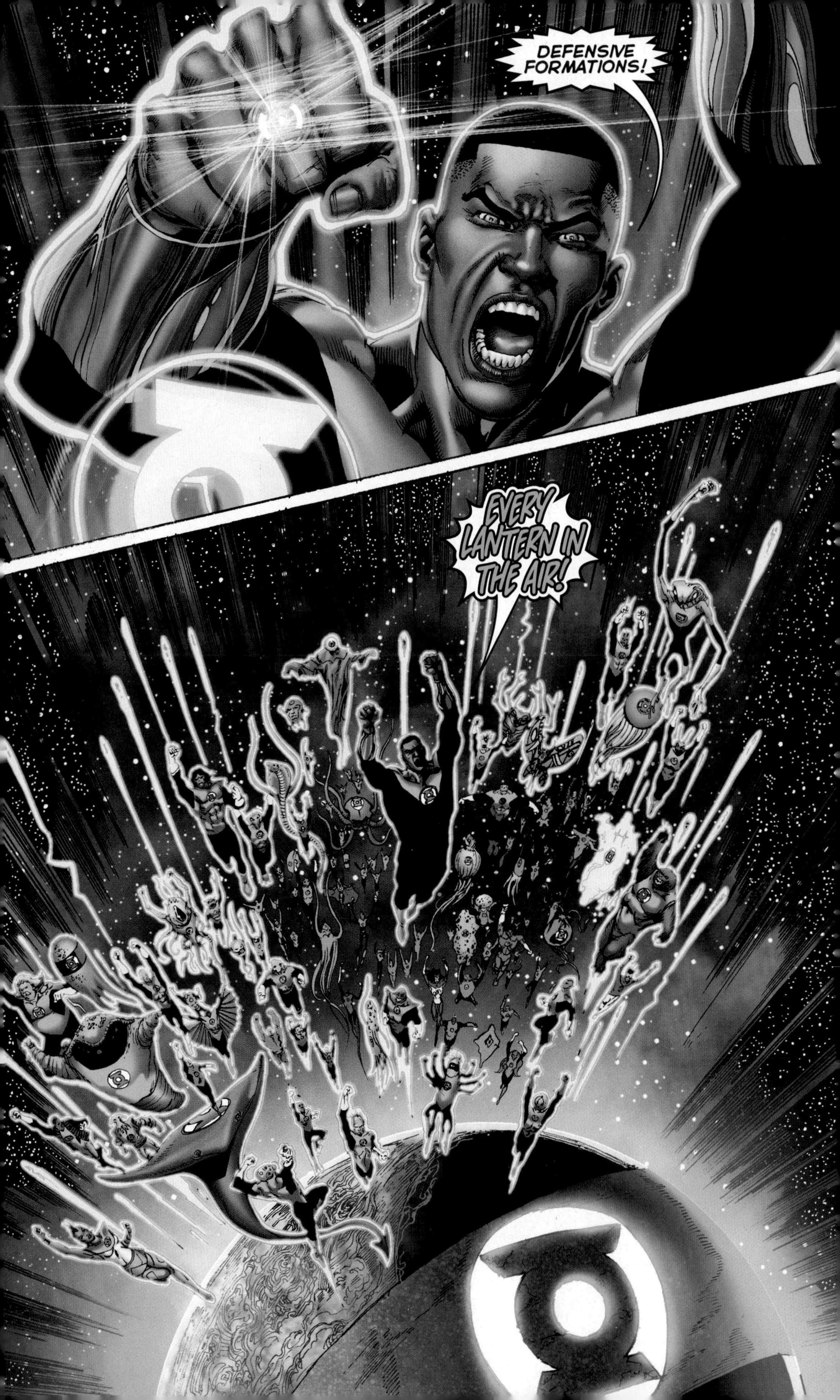
DEFENSIVE FORMATIONS!
EVERY LANTERN IN THE AIR!

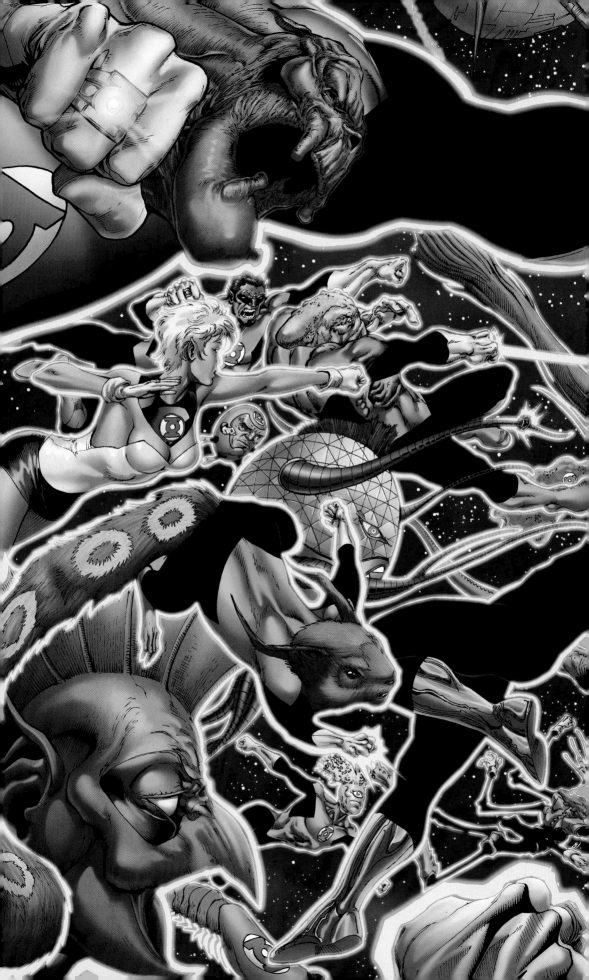

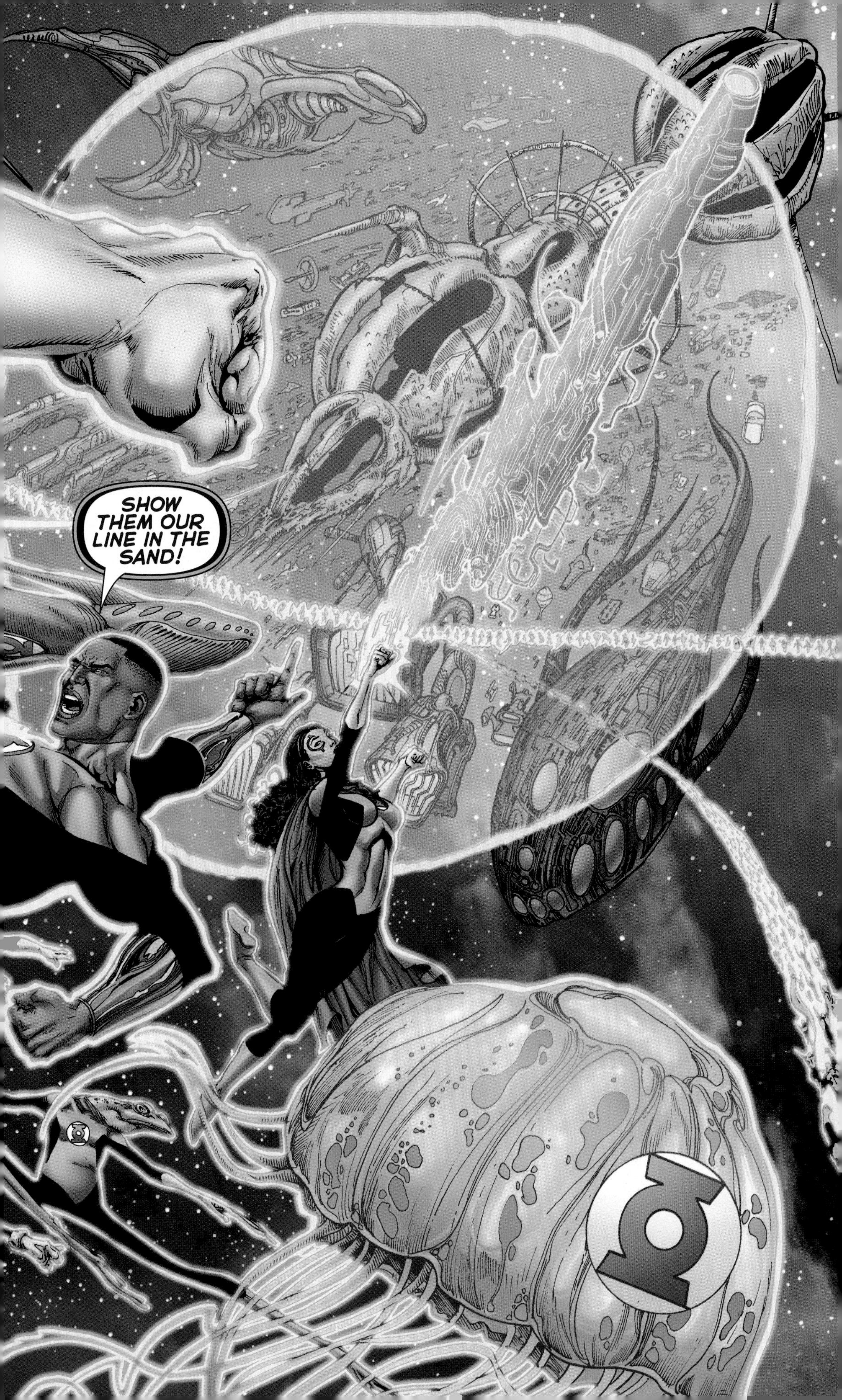
SHOW THEM OUR LINE IN THE SAND!

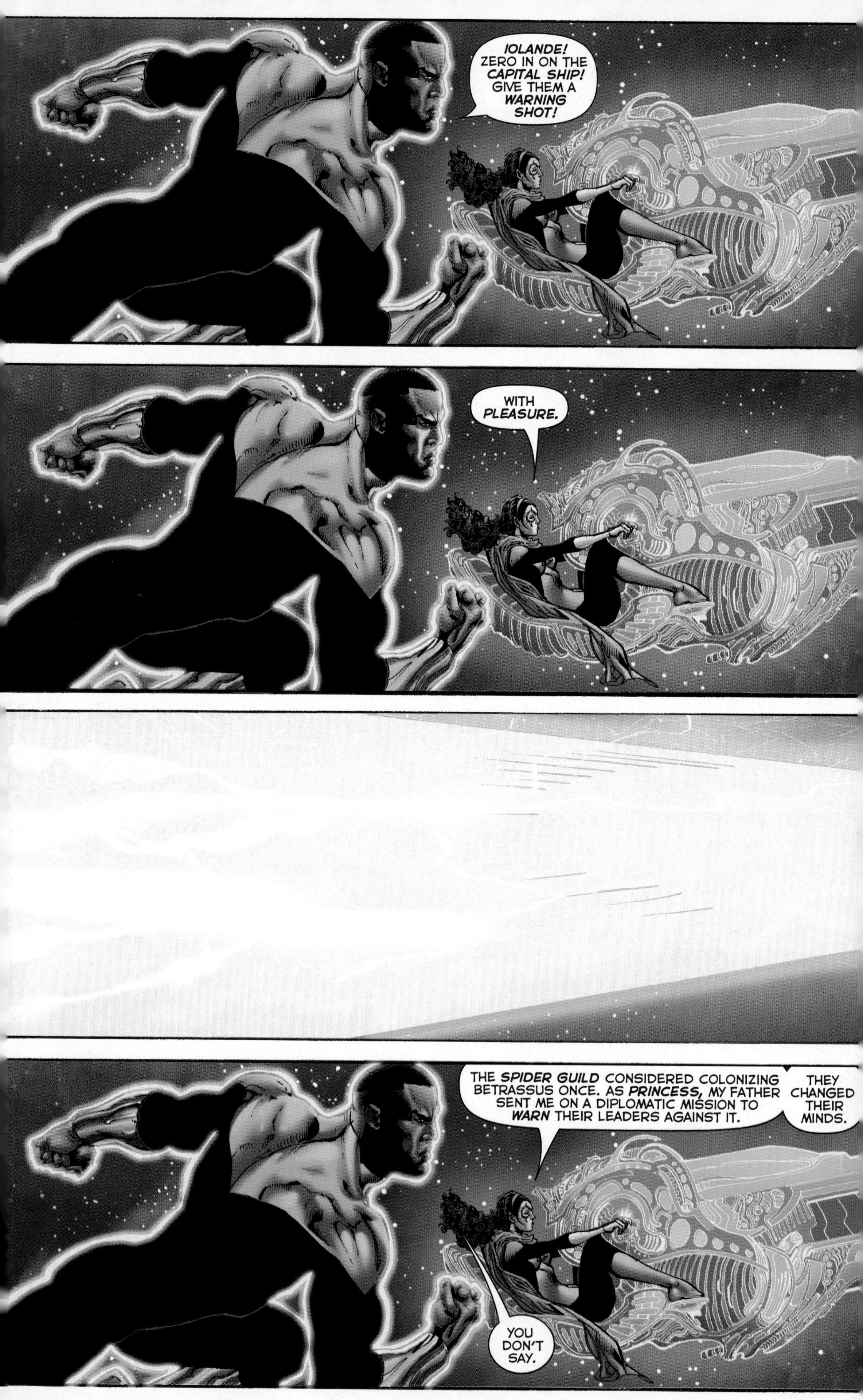
IOLANDE! ZERO IN ON THE CAPITAL SHIP! GIVE THEM A WARNING SHOT!
WITH PLEASURE.
THE SPIDER GUILD CONSIDERED COLONIZING BETRASSUS ONCE. AS PRINCESS, MY FATHER SENT ME ON A DIPLOMATIC MISSION TO WARN THEIR LEADERS AGAINST IT.
THEY CHANGED THEIR MINDS.
YOU DON'T SAY.

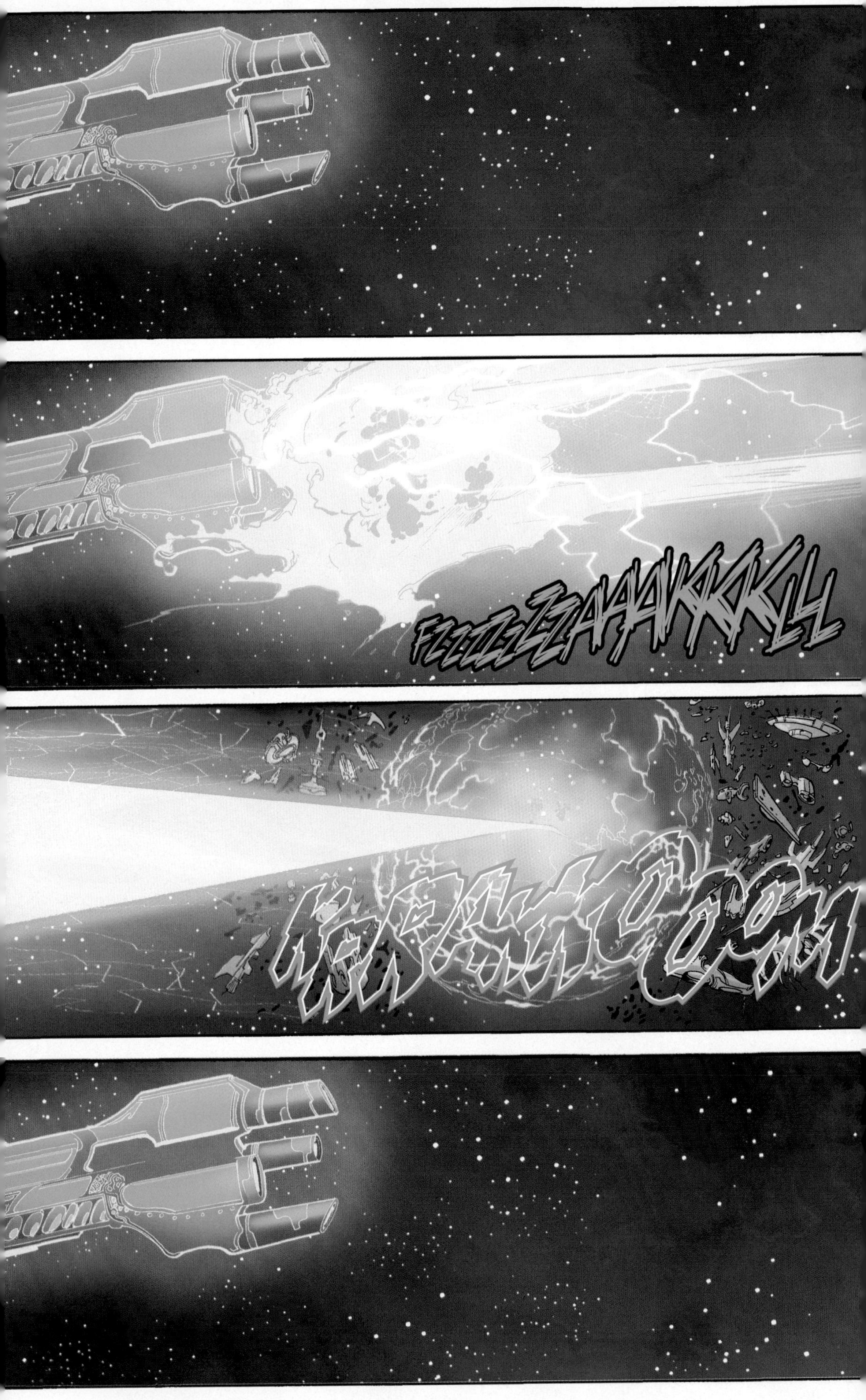
FZZZZZZZAAAKKKKLL

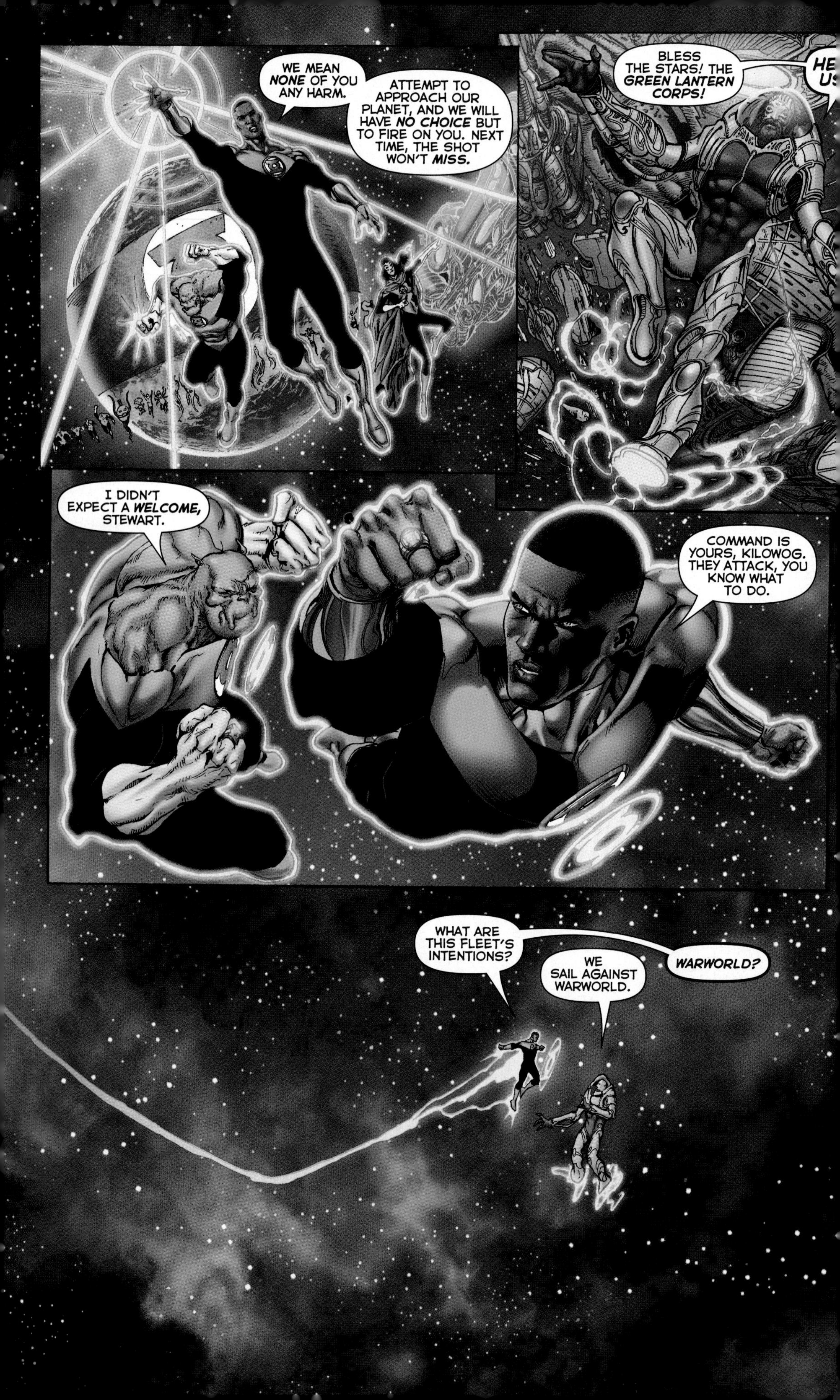
WE MEAN NONE OF YOU ANY HARM.
ATTEMPT TO APPROACH OUR PLANET, AND WE WILL HAVE NO CHOICE BUT TO FIRE ON YOU. NEXT TIME, THE SHOT WON'T MISS.
BLESS THE STARS! THE GREEN LANTERN CORPS!
I DIDN'T EXPECT A WELCOME, STEWART.
COMMAND IS YOURS, KILOWOG. THEY ATTACK, YOU KNOW WHAT TO DO.
WHAT ARE THIS FLEET'S INTENTIONS?
WE SAIL AGAINST WARWORLD.
WARWORLD?

WE THOUGHT THE GREEN LANTERNS HAD *ABANDONED* US. THE UNIVERSE WAS *UNPROTECTED.* THE *SINESTRO CORPS* IS THE POLICE NOW.

SINESTRO DISPATCHED SQUADS TO *EVERY* WORLD. THEY TOOK THE BEST AND STRONGEST. DECLARED IT A *LEVY* THAT MUST BE PAID TO MAINTAIN ORDER.

WE SAIL TO GET OUR PEOPLE BACK. BUT SINESTRO IS *MIGHTY,* AND WE HAVE NO SHIPS OF WAR. WILL YOU *HELP* US?

WE'RE SEARCHING FOR A GREEN LANTERN. *GUY GARDNER.* HE WAS ON A RECON MISSION. HE WOULD'VE PASSED BY THIS WAY.

WE SAW NO GREEN LANTERNS UNTIL YOU.

FIRST, WE DIDN'T ABANDON ANYONE. WE WERE *TAKEN.* OVER *NINETY PERCENT* OF OUR FIGHTING FORCE *DIED* GETTING BACK HERE.

SECOND, I NEED *INTEL.* MAPS. INFORMATION. YOU GIVE ME THAT, I'LL COME UP WITH A *BATTLE PLAN.*

IT'S YOURS. EVERYTHING WE HAVE.

THEN WHAT ARE WE WAITING FOR?

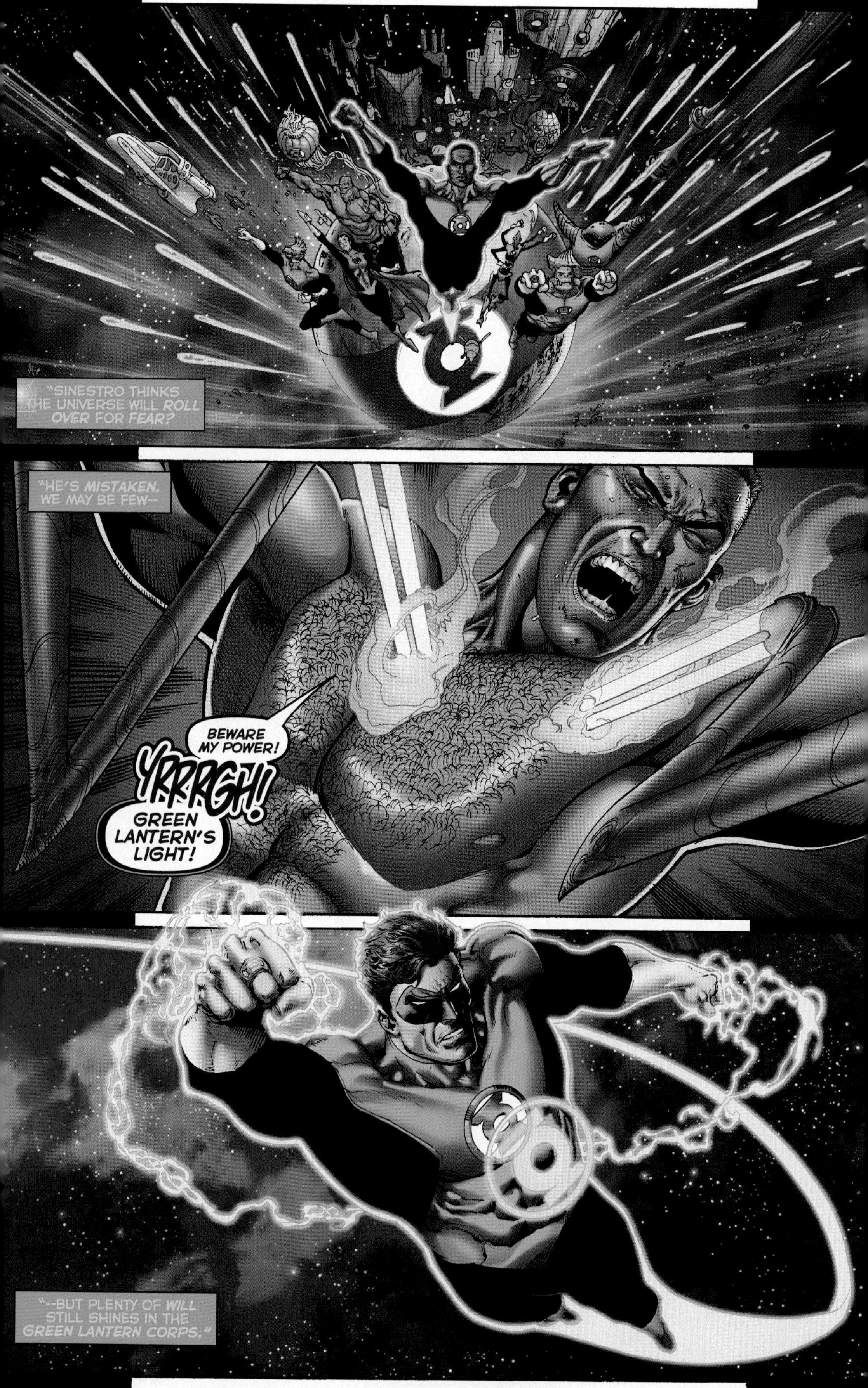
"SINESTRO THINKS THE UNIVERSE WILL ROLL OVER FOR FEAR?
"HE'S MISTAKEN. WE MAY BE FEW--
BEWARE MY POWER!
YRRRGH!
GREEN LANTERN'S LIGHT!
"--BUT PLENTY OF WILL STILL SHINES IN THE GREEN LANTERN CORPS."

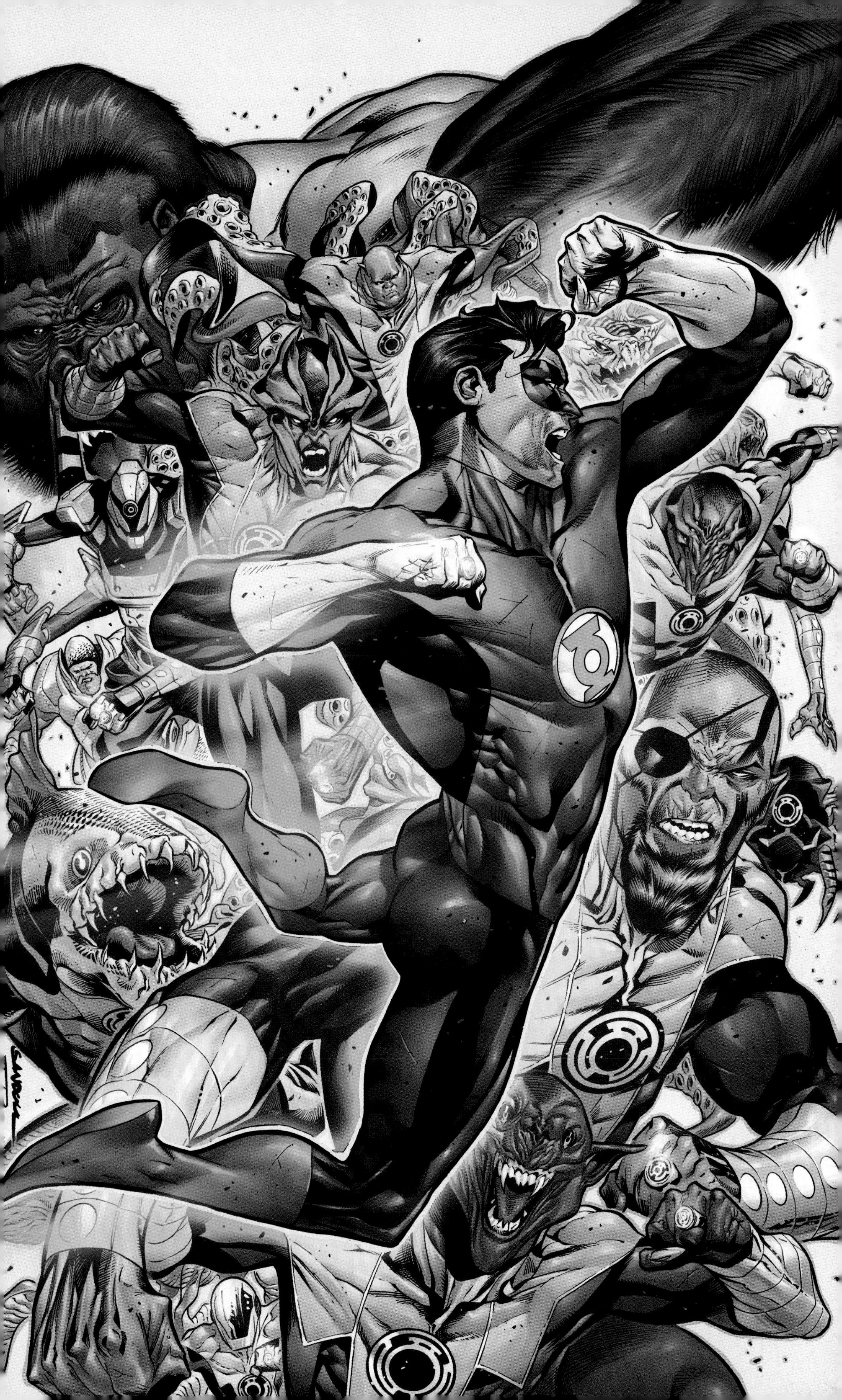

SINESTRO'S LAW PART 6: WORLD OF WAR

RAFA SANDOVAL penciller * JORDI TARRAGONA inker * TOMEU MOREY colorist

RAFA SANDOVAL, JORDI TARRAGONA and TOMEU MOREY cover artists

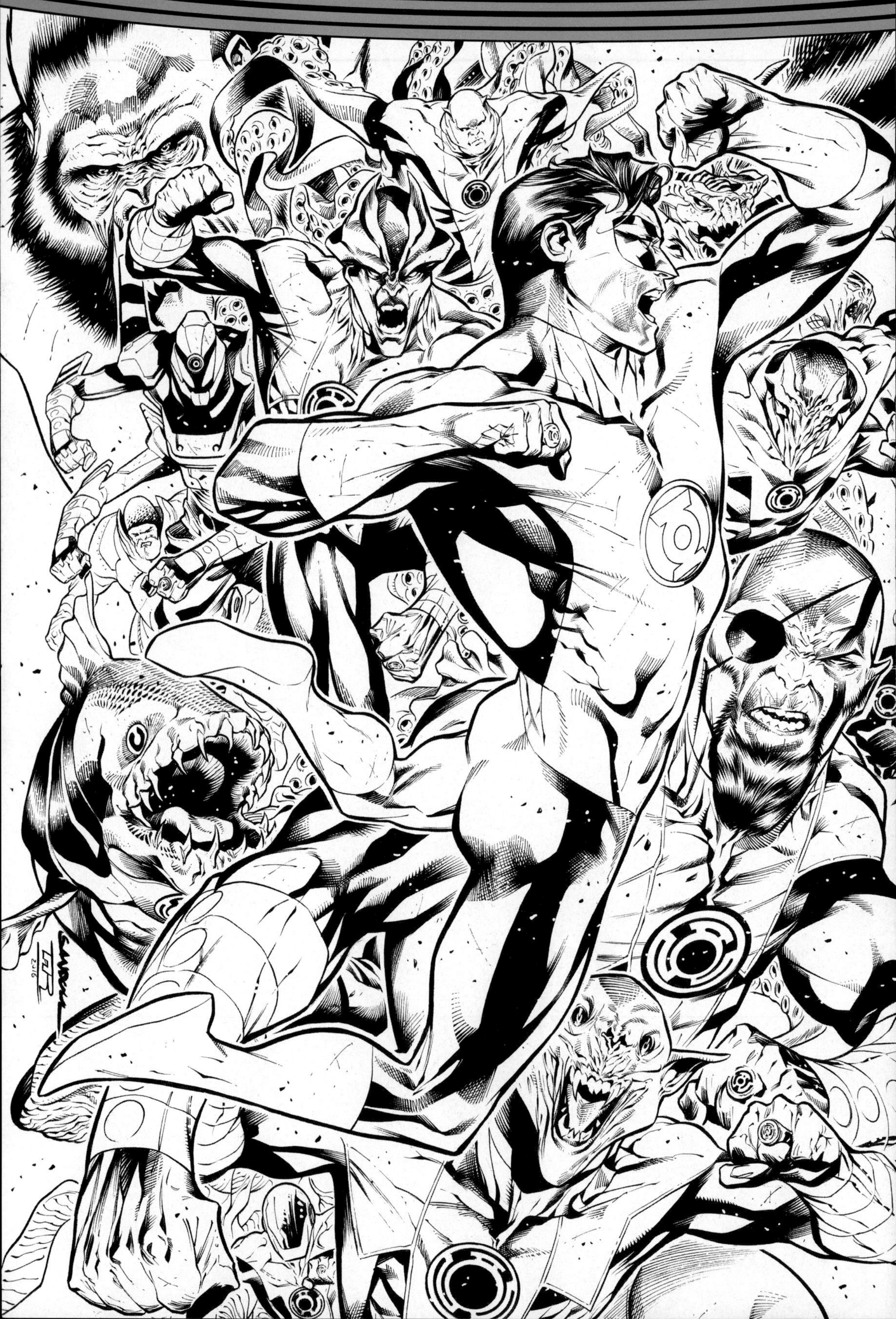

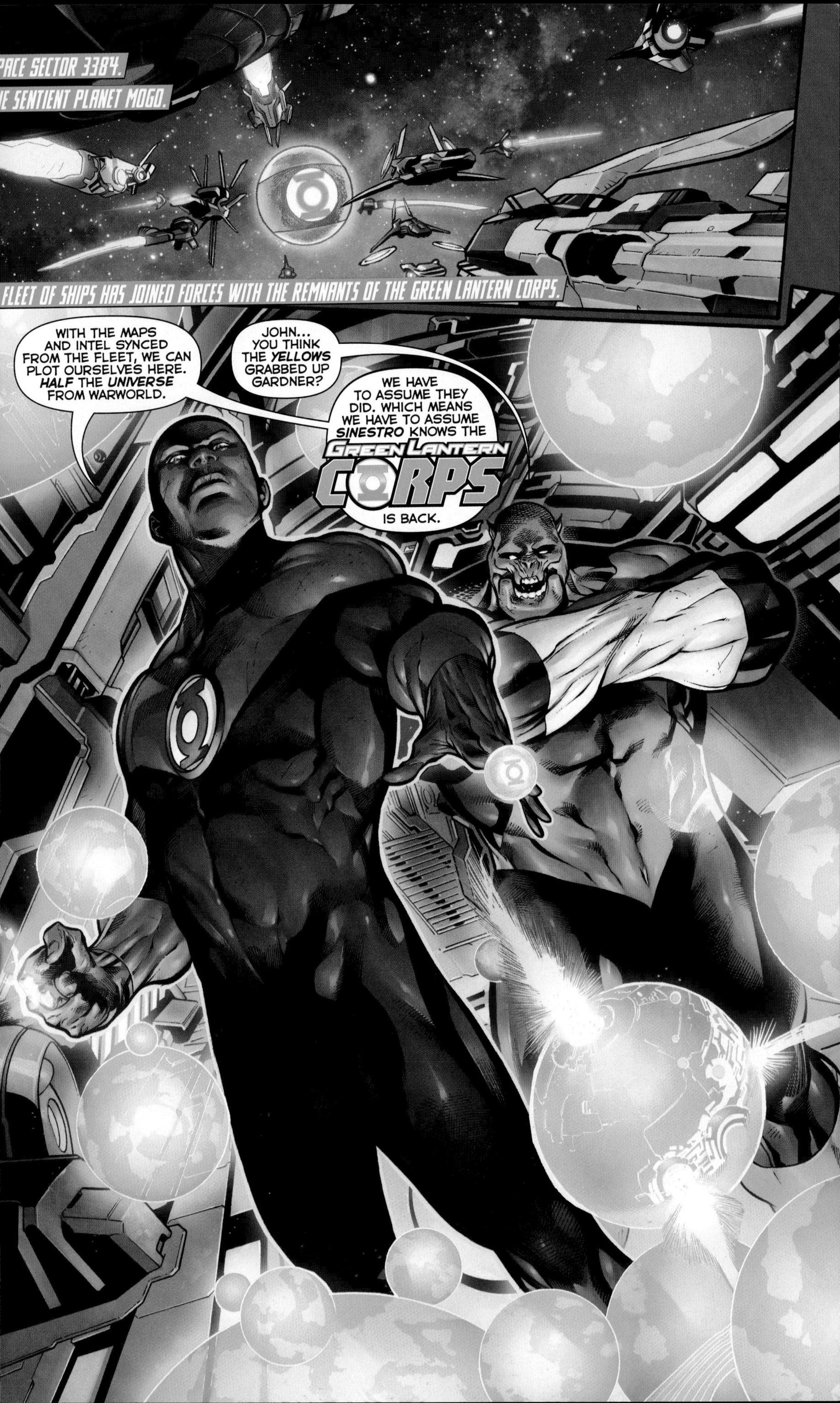

PACE SECTOR 3384.
E SENTIENT PLANET MOGO.
FLEET OF SHIPS HAS JOINED FORCES WITH THE REMNANTS OF THE GREEN LANTERN CORPS.
WITH THE MAPS AND INTEL SYNCED FROM THE FLEET, WE CAN PLOT OURSELVES HERE. HALF THE UNIVERSE FROM WARWORLD.
JOHN... YOU THINK THE YELLOWS GRABBED UP GARDNER?
WE HAVE TO ASSUME THEY DID. WHICH MEANS WE HAVE TO ASSUME SINESTRO KNOWS THE GREEN LANTERN CORPS IS BACK.

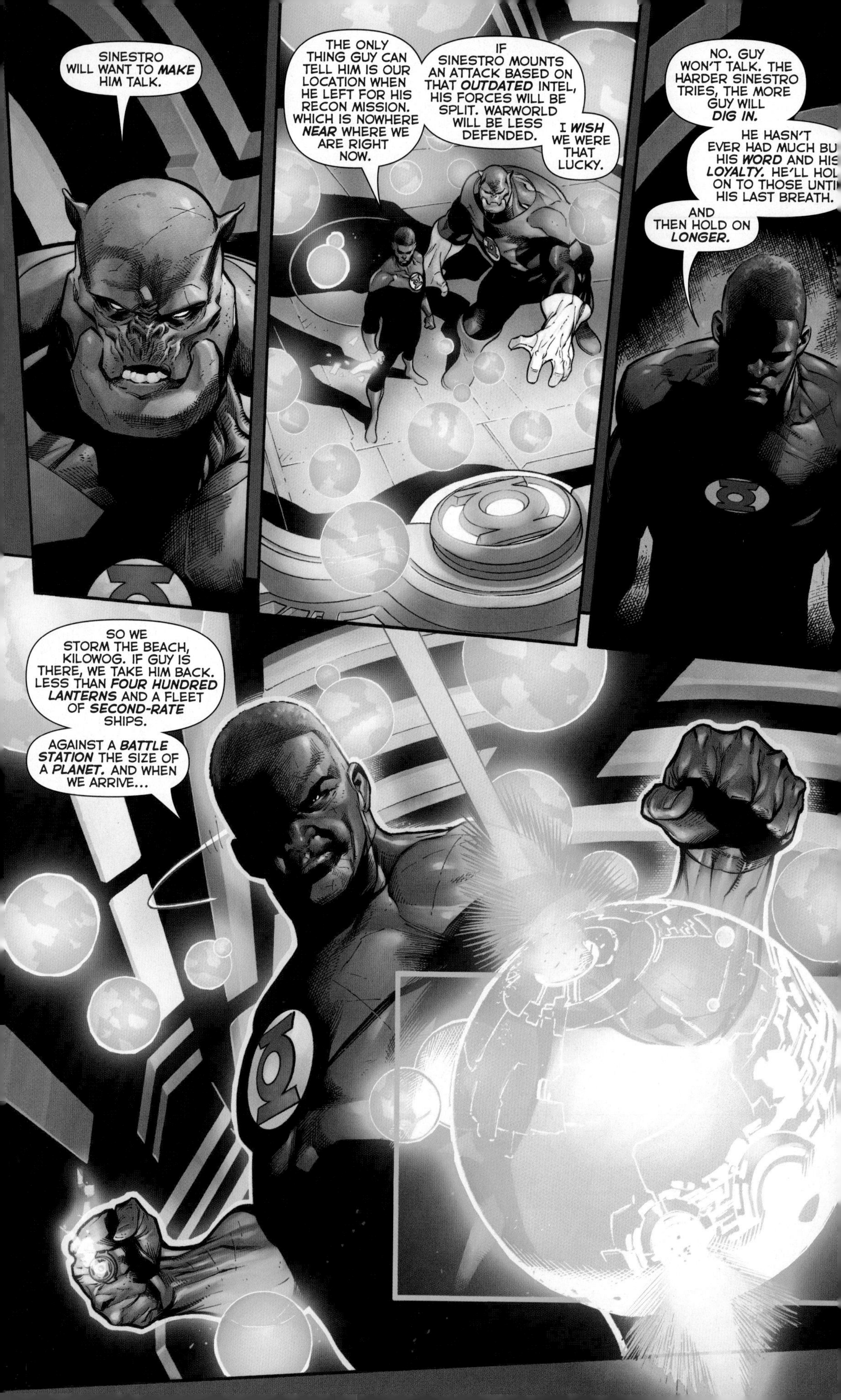
SINESTRO WILL WANT TO *MAKE* HIM TALK.
THE ONLY THING GUY CAN TELL HIM IS OUR LOCATION WHEN HE LEFT FOR HIS RECON MISSION. WHICH IS NOWHERE *NEAR* WHERE WE ARE RIGHT NOW.
IF SINESTRO MOUNTS AN ATTACK BASED ON THAT *OUTDATED* INTEL, HIS FORCES WILL BE SPLIT. WARWORLD WILL BE LESS DEFENDED.
I *WISH* WE WERE THAT LUCKY.
NO. GUY WON'T TALK. THE HARDER SINESTRO TRIES, THE MORE GUY WILL *DIG IN.*
HE HASN'T EVER HAD MUCH BU HIS *WORD* AND HIS *LOYALTY.* HE'LL HOL ON TO THOSE UNTI HIS LAST BREATH.
AND THEN HOLD ON *LONGER.*
SO WE STORM THE BEACH, KILOWOG. IF GUY IS THERE, WE TAKE HIM BACK. LESS THAN *FOUR HUNDRED LANTERNS* AND A FLEET OF *SECOND-RATE* SHIPS.
AGAINST A *BATTLE STATION* THE SIZE OF A *PLANET.* AND WHEN WE ARRIVE...

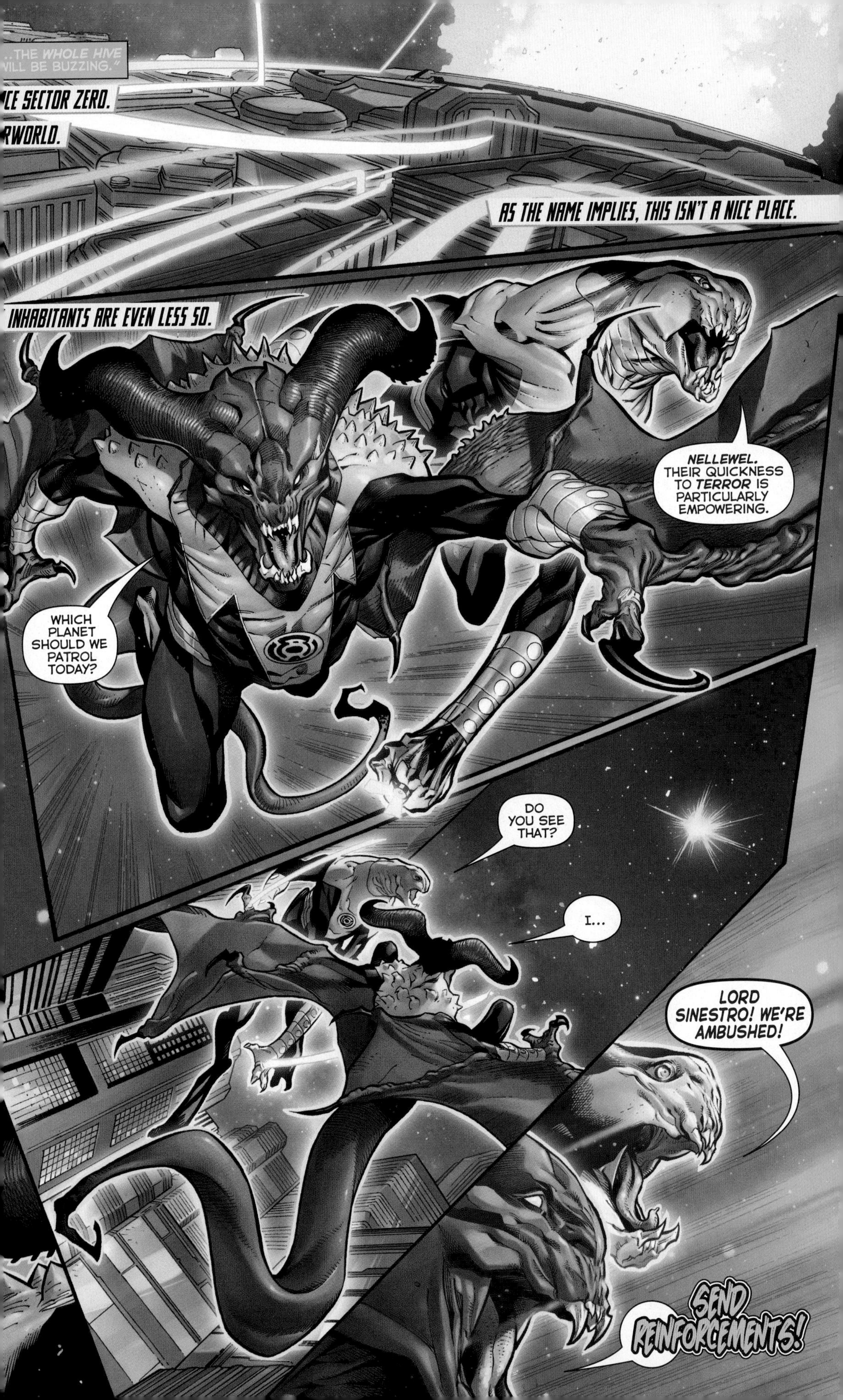
"...THE WHOLE HIVE WILL BE BUZZING."
CE SECTOR ZERO.
RWORLD.
AS THE NAME IMPLIES, THIS ISN'T A NICE PLACE.
INHABITANTS ARE EVEN LESS SO.
NELLEWEL. THEIR QUICKNESS TO TERROR IS PARTICULARLY EMPOWERING.
WHICH PLANET SHOULD WE PATROL TODAY?
DO YOU SEE THAT?
I...
LORD SINESTRO! WE'RE AMBUSHED!
SEND REINFORCEMENTS!

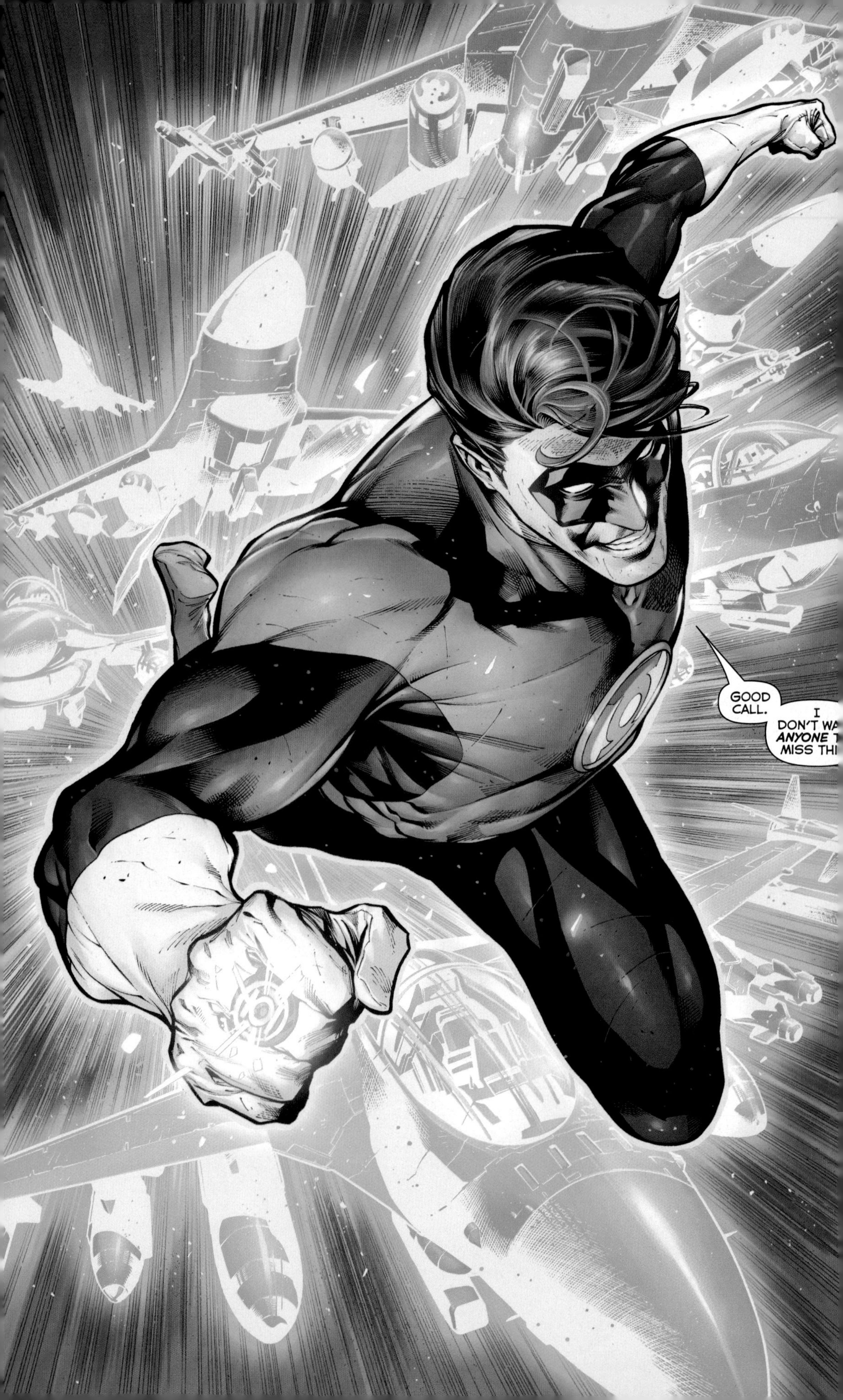
GOOD CALL.
I DON'T WA
ANYONE T
MISS THI

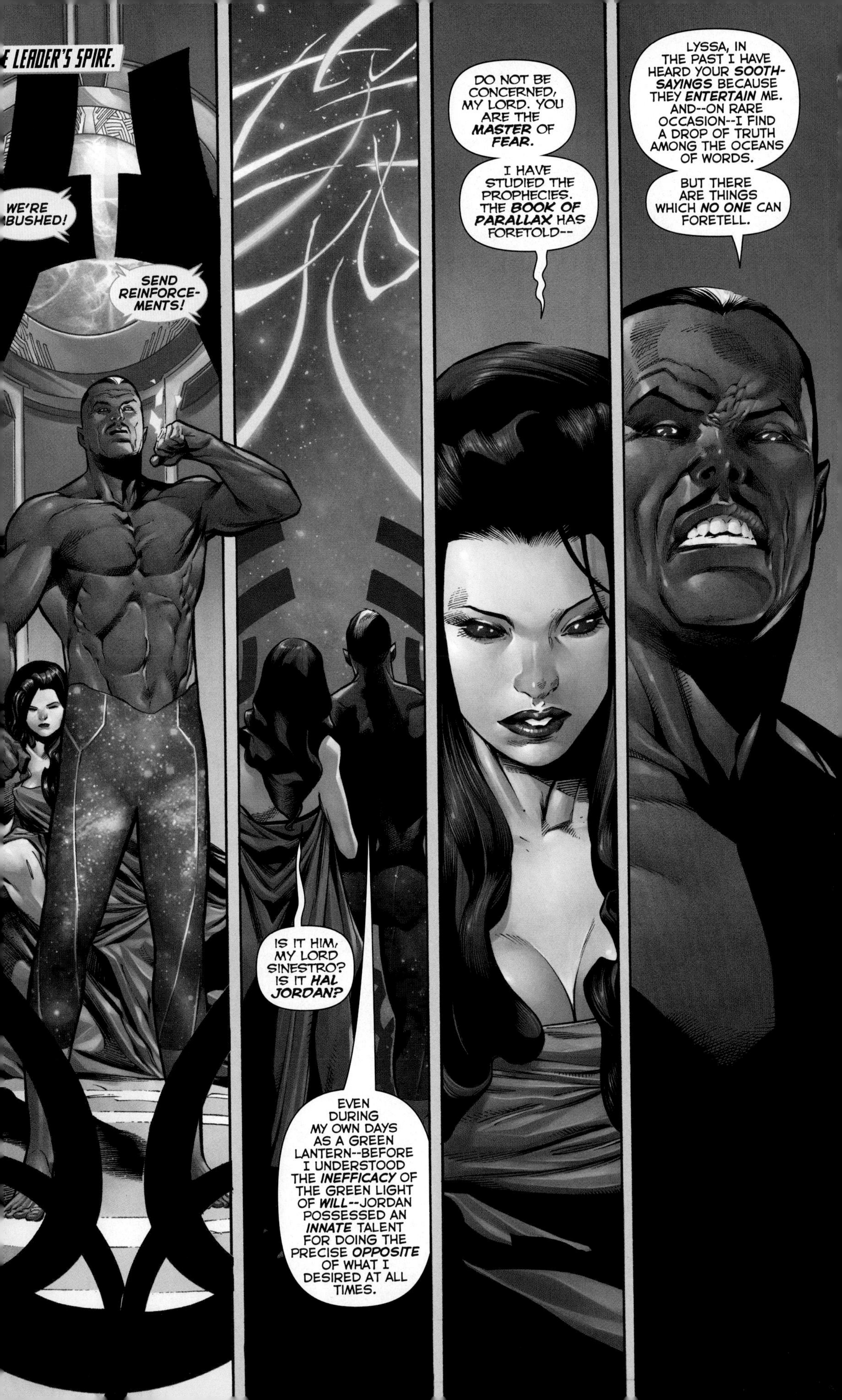

E LEADER'S SPIRE.
WE'RE
BUSHED!
SEND
REINFORCE-
MENTS!
IS IT HIM, MY LORD SINESTRO? IS IT HAL JORDAN?
EVEN DURING MY OWN DAYS AS A GREEN LANTERN--BEFORE I UNDERSTOOD THE INEFFICACY OF THE GREEN LIGHT OF WILL--JORDAN POSSESSED AN INNATE TALENT FOR DOING THE PRECISE OPPOSITE OF WHAT I DESIRED AT ALL TIMES.
DO NOT BE CONCERNED, MY LORD. YOU ARE THE MASTER OF FEAR.
I HAVE STUDIED THE PROPHECIES. THE BOOK OF PARALLAX HAS FORETOLD--
LYSSA, IN THE PAST I HAVE HEARD YOUR SOOTH-SAYINGS BECAUSE THEY ENTERTAIN ME. AND--ON RARE OCCASION--I FIND A DROP OF TRUTH AMONG THE OCEANS OF WORDS.
BUT THERE ARE THINGS WHICH NO ONE CAN FORETELL.

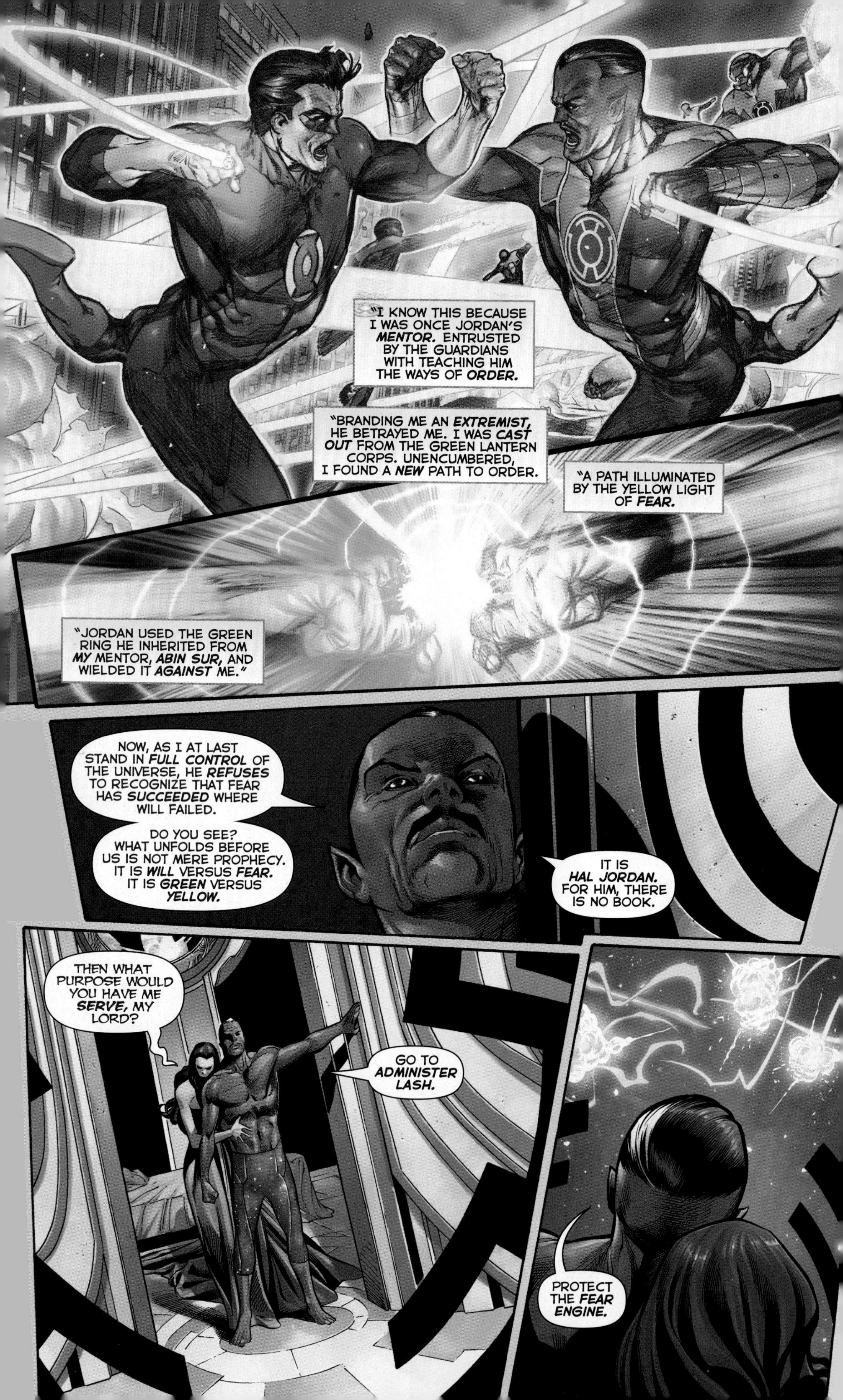
"I KNOW THIS BECAUSE I WAS ONCE JORDAN'S MENTOR. ENTRUSTED BY THE GUARDIANS WITH TEACHING HIM THE WAYS OF ORDER.
"BRANDING ME AN EXTREMIST, HE BETRAYED ME. I WAS CAST OUT FROM THE GREEN LANTERN CORPS. UNENCUMBERED, I FOUND A NEW PATH TO ORDER.
"A PATH ILLUMINATED BY THE YELLOW LIGHT OF FEAR.
"JORDAN USED THE GREEN RING HE INHERITED FROM MY MENTOR, ABIN SUR, AND WIELDED IT AGAINST ME."
NOW, AS I AT LAST STAND IN FULL CONTROL OF THE UNIVERSE, HE REFUSES TO RECOGNIZE THAT FEAR HAS SUCCEEDED WHERE WILL FAILED.
DO YOU SEE? WHAT UNFOLDS BEFORE US IS NOT MERE PROPHECY. IT IS WILL VERSUS FEAR. IT IS GREEN VERSUS YELLOW.
IT IS HAL JORDAN. FOR HIM, THERE IS NO BOOK.
THEN WHAT PURPOSE WOULD YOU HAVE ME SERVE, MY LORD?
GO TO ADMINISTER LASH.
PROTECT THE FEAR ENGINE.

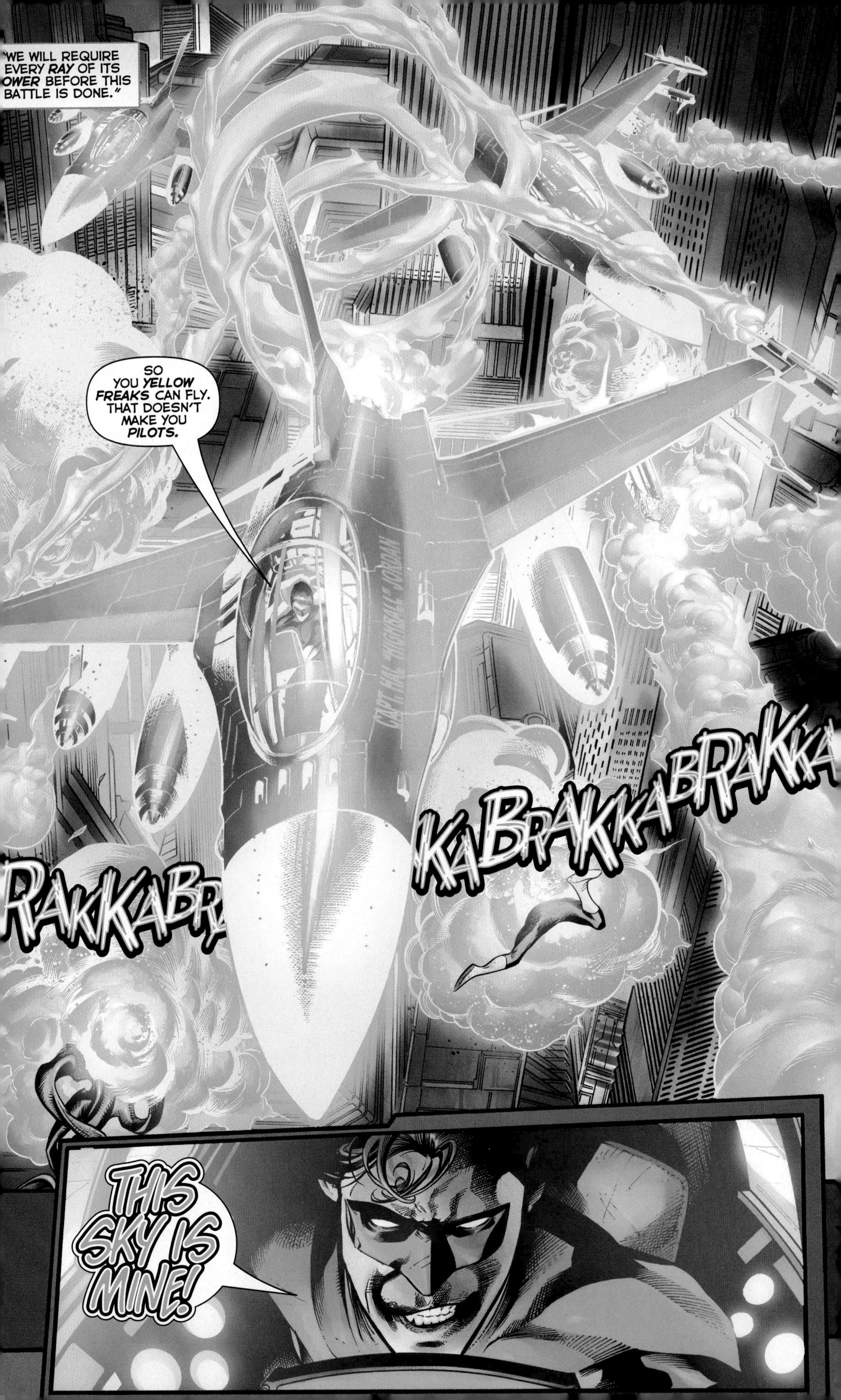
"WE WILL REQUIRE EVERY RAY OF ITS OWER BEFORE THIS BATTLE IS DONE."
SO YOU YELLOW FREAKS CAN FLY. THAT DOESN'T MAKE YOU PILOTS.
RAKKABR
KABRAKKABRAKKA
THIS SKY IS MINE!

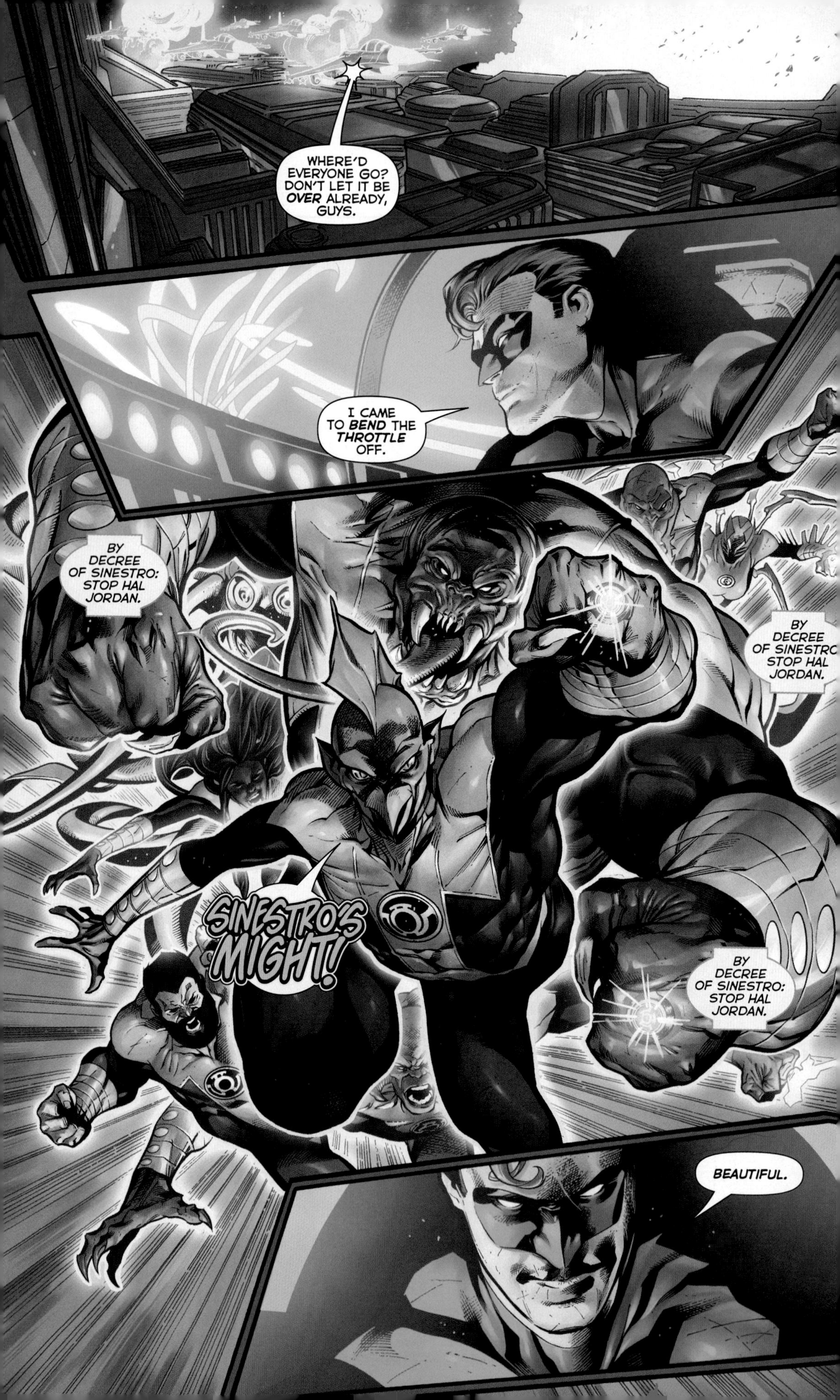
WHERE'D EVERYONE GO? DON'T LET IT BE OVER ALREADY, GUYS.
I CAME TO BEND THE THROTTLE OFF.
BY DECREE OF SINESTRO: STOP HAL JORDAN.
BY DECREE OF SINESTRO STOP HAL JORDAN.
SINESTRO'S MIGHT!
BY DECREE OF SINESTRO: STOP HAL JORDAN.
BEAUTIFUL.

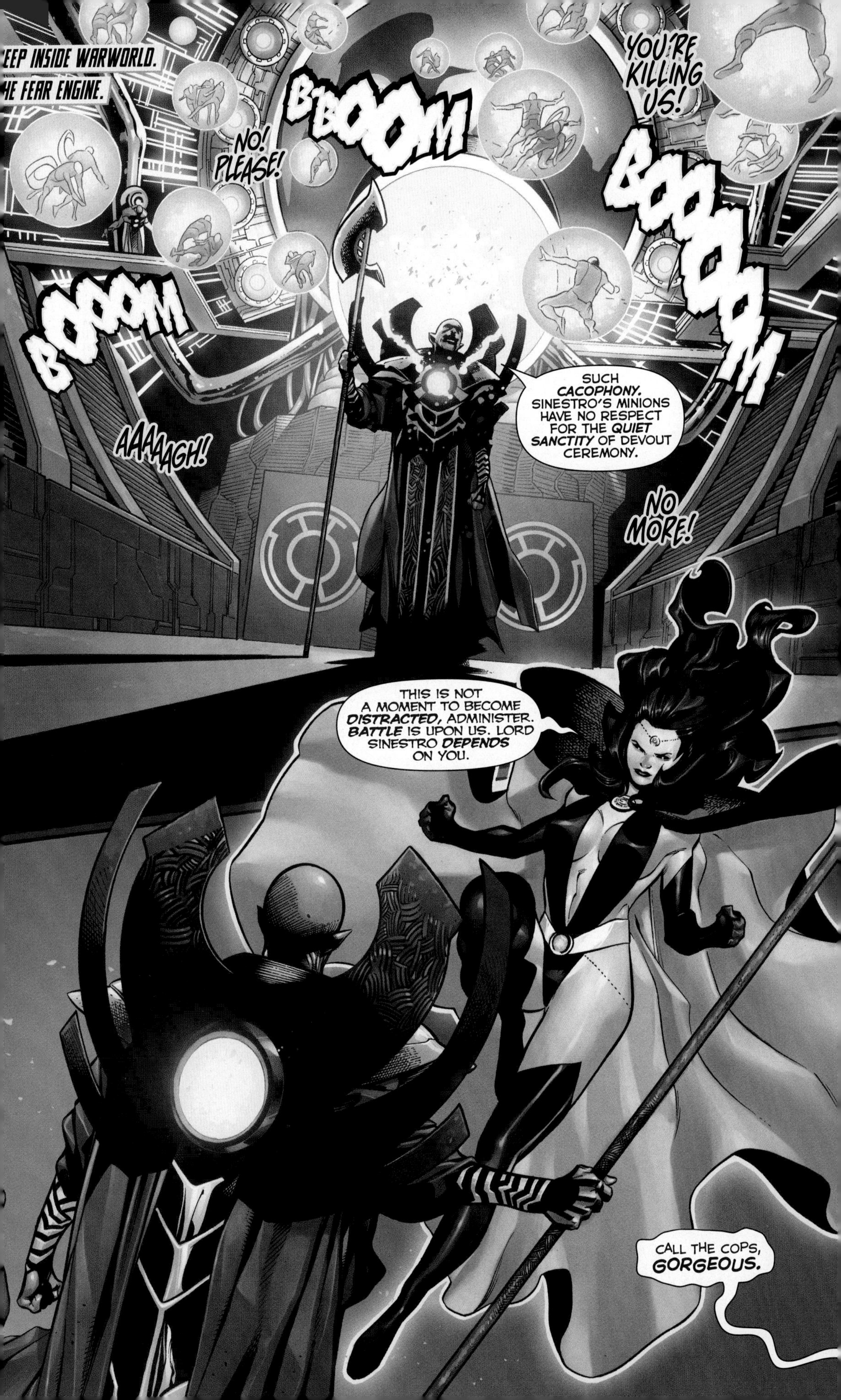
EEP INSIDE WARWORLD.
HE FEAR ENGINE.
B'BOOOM
NO! PLEASE!
YOU'RE KILLING US!
BOOOOOM
BOOOM
SUCH CACOPHONY. SINESTRO'S MINIONS HAVE NO RESPECT FOR THE QUIET SANCTITY OF DEVOUT CEREMONY.
AAAAAGH!
NO MORE!
THIS IS NOT A MOMENT TO BECOME DISTRACTED, ADMINISTER. BATTLE IS UPON US. LORD SINESTRO DEPENDS ON YOU.
CALL THE COPS, GORGEOUS.

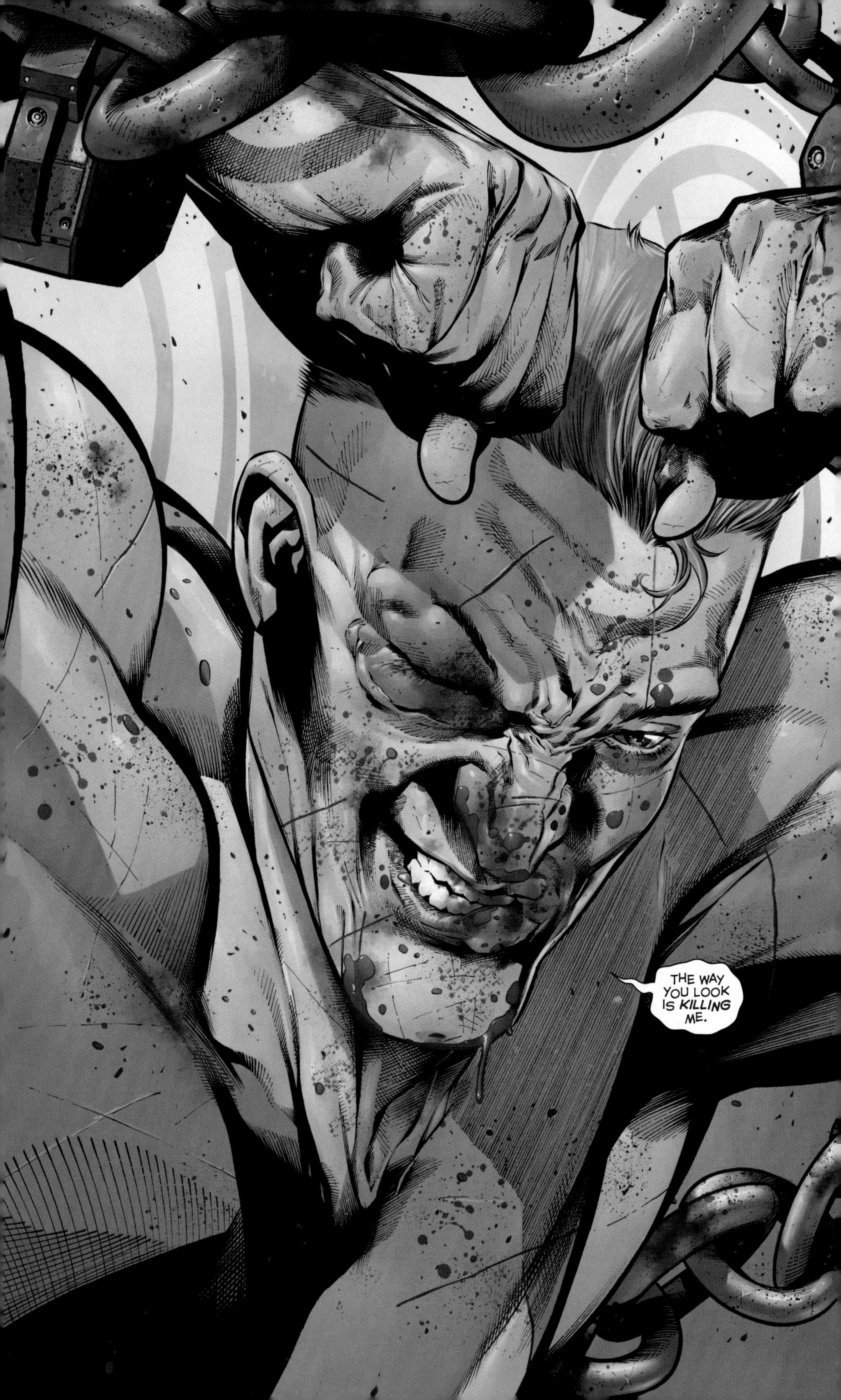
THE WAY YOU LOOK IS KILLING ME.

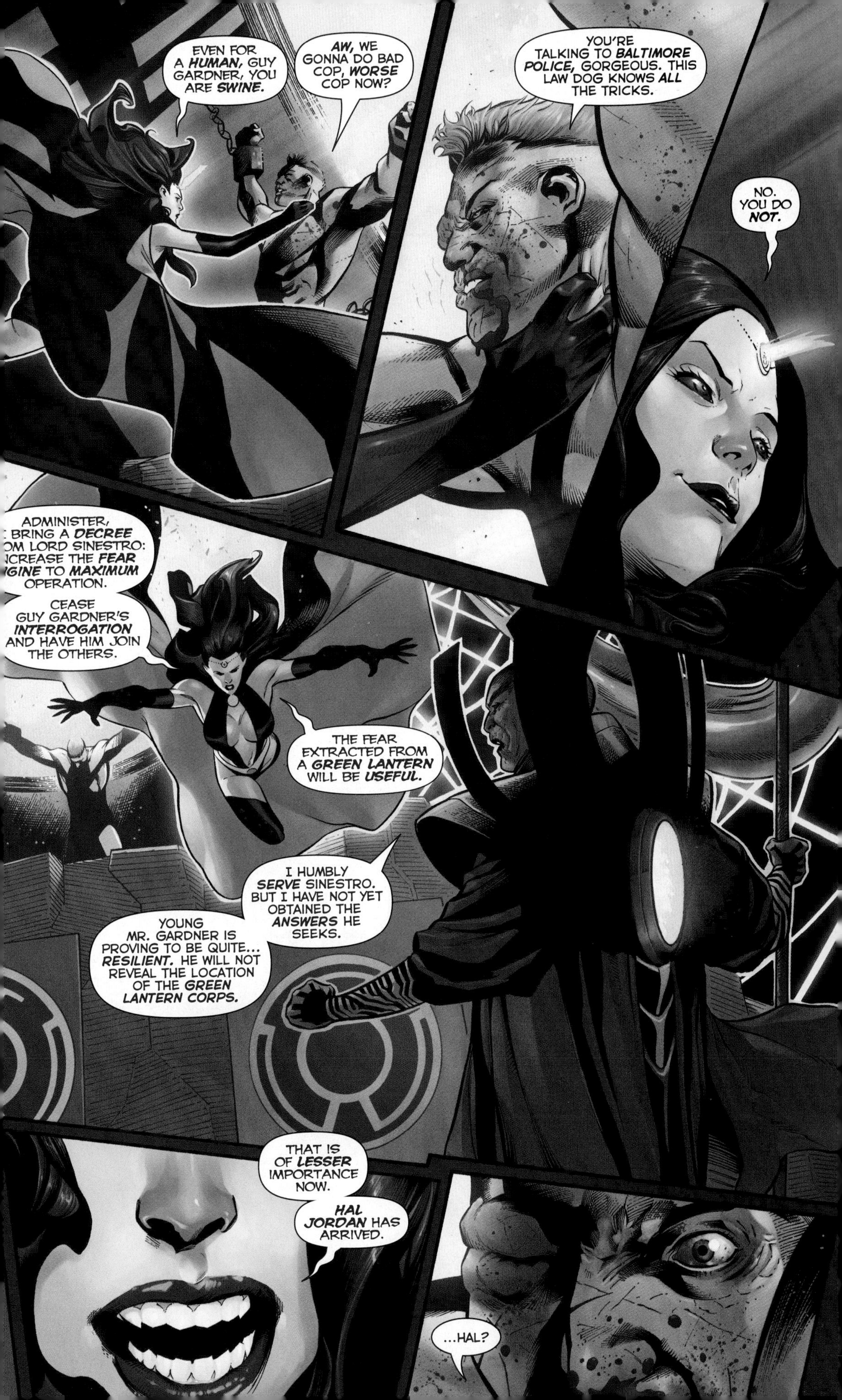

EVEN FOR A HUMAN, GUY GARDNER, YOU ARE SWINE.
AW, WE GONNA DO BAD COP, WORSE COP NOW?
YOU'RE TALKING TO BALTIMORE POLICE, GORGEOUS. THIS LAW DOG KNOWS ALL THE TRICKS.
NO. YOU DO NOT.
ADMINISTER, I BRING A DECREE FROM LORD SINESTRO: INCREASE THE FEAR ENGINE TO MAXIMUM OPERATION.
CEASE GUY GARDNER'S INTERROGATION AND HAVE HIM JOIN THE OTHERS.
THE FEAR EXTRACTED FROM A GREEN LANTERN WILL BE USEFUL.
I HUMBLY SERVE SINESTRO. BUT I HAVE NOT YET OBTAINED THE ANSWERS HE SEEKS.
YOUNG MR. GARDNER IS PROVING TO BE QUITE... RESILIENT. HE WILL NOT REVEAL THE LOCATION OF THE GREEN LANTERN CORPS.
THAT IS OF LESSER IMPORTANCE NOW.
HAL JORDAN HAS ARRIVED.
...HAL?

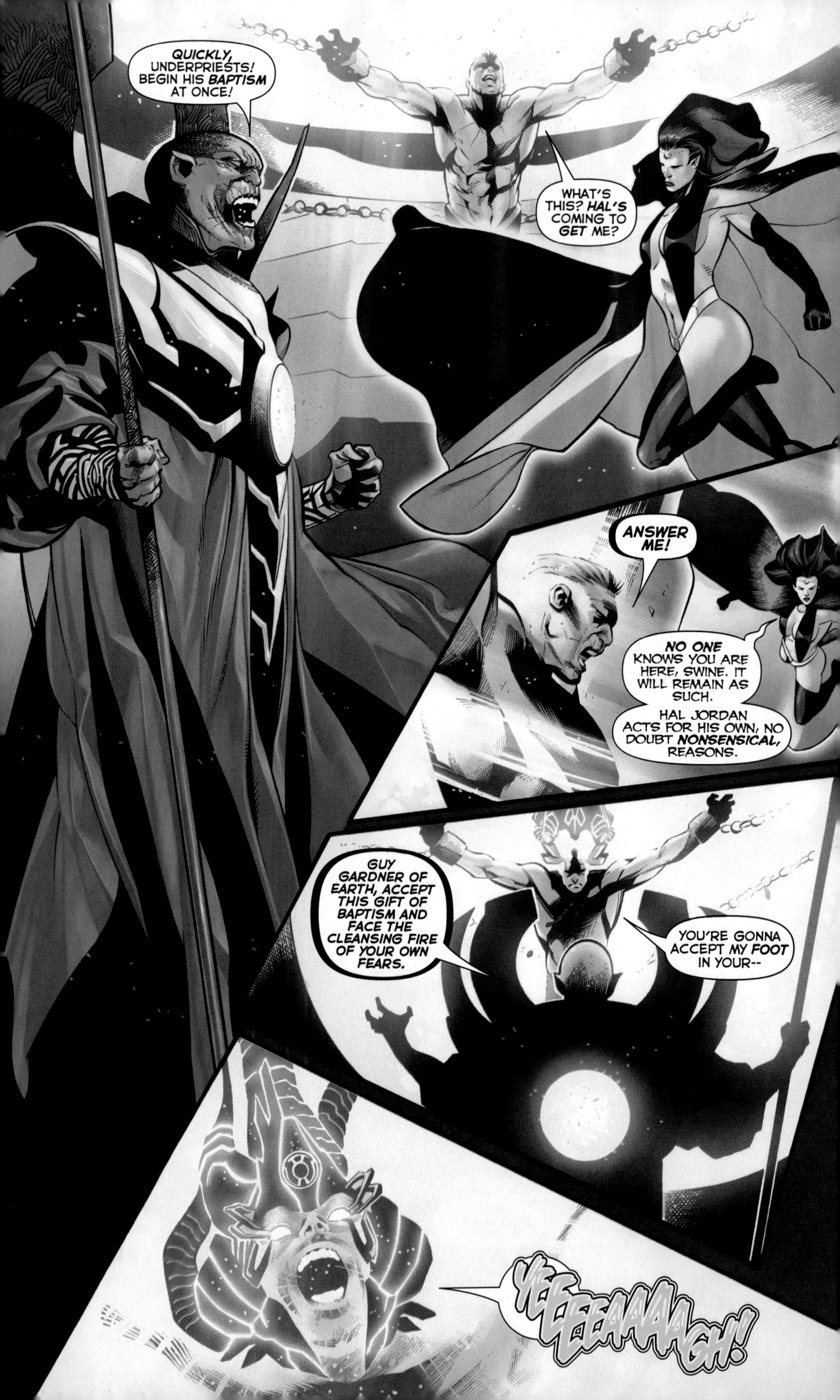
QUICKLY, UNDERPRIESTS! BEGIN HIS BAPTISM AT ONCE!
WHAT'S THIS? HAL'S COMING TO GET ME?
ANSWER ME!
NO ONE KNOWS YOU ARE HERE, SWINE. IT WILL REMAIN AS SUCH.
HAL JORDAN ACTS FOR HIS OWN, NO DOUBT NONSENSICAL, REASONS.
GUY GARDNER OF EARTH, ACCEPT THIS GIFT OF BAPTISM AND FACE THE CLEANSING FIRE OF YOUR OWN FEARS.
YOU'RE GONNA ACCEPT MY FOOT IN YOUR--
YEEEEEAAAAAAGH!

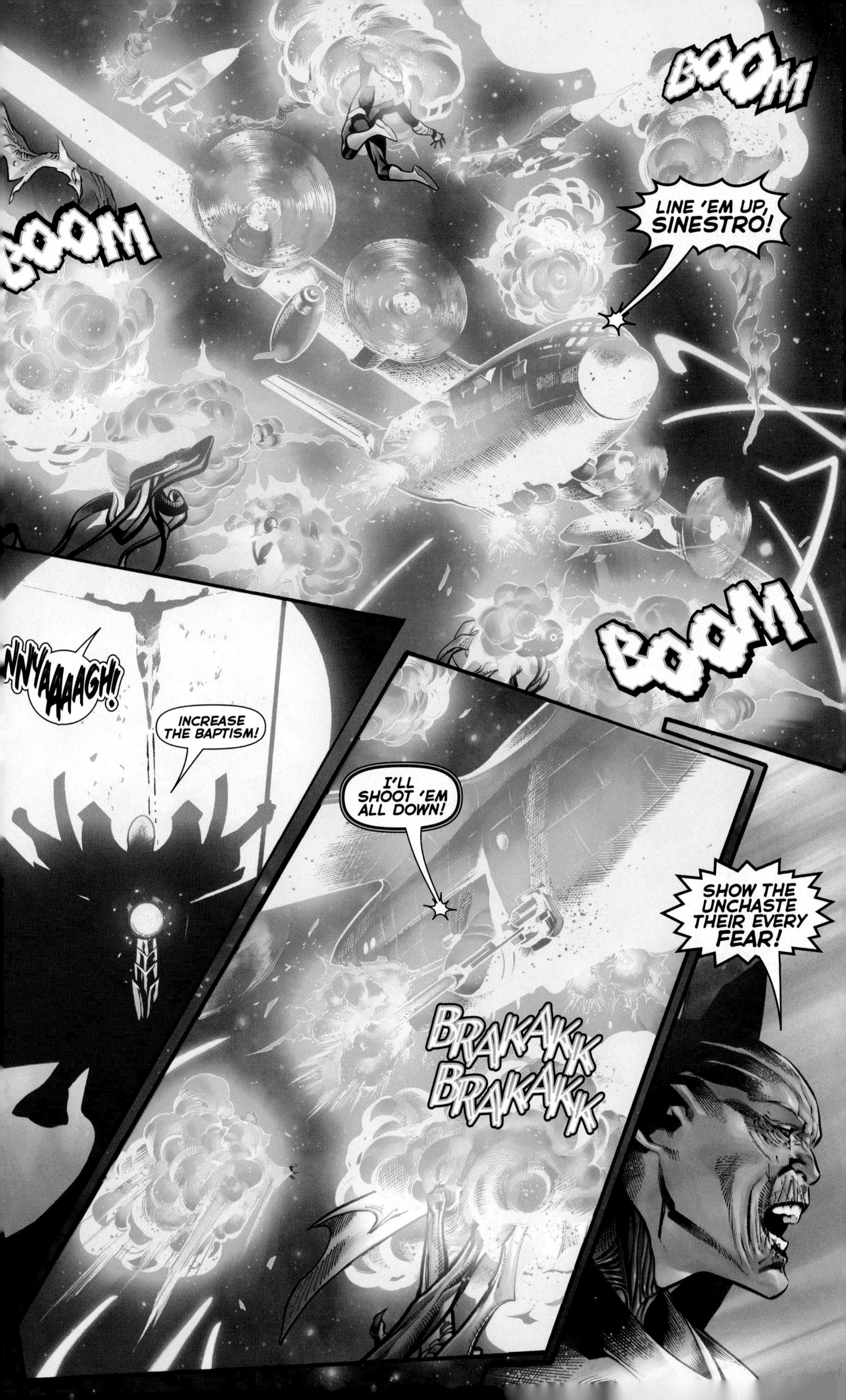
BOOM
BOOM
LINE 'EM UP, SINESTRO!
BOOM
NNYAAAAAGH!
INCREASE THE BAPTISM!
I'LL SHOOT 'EM ALL DOWN!
SHOW THE UNCHASTE THEIR EVERY FEAR!
BRAKAKKK
BRAKAKKK

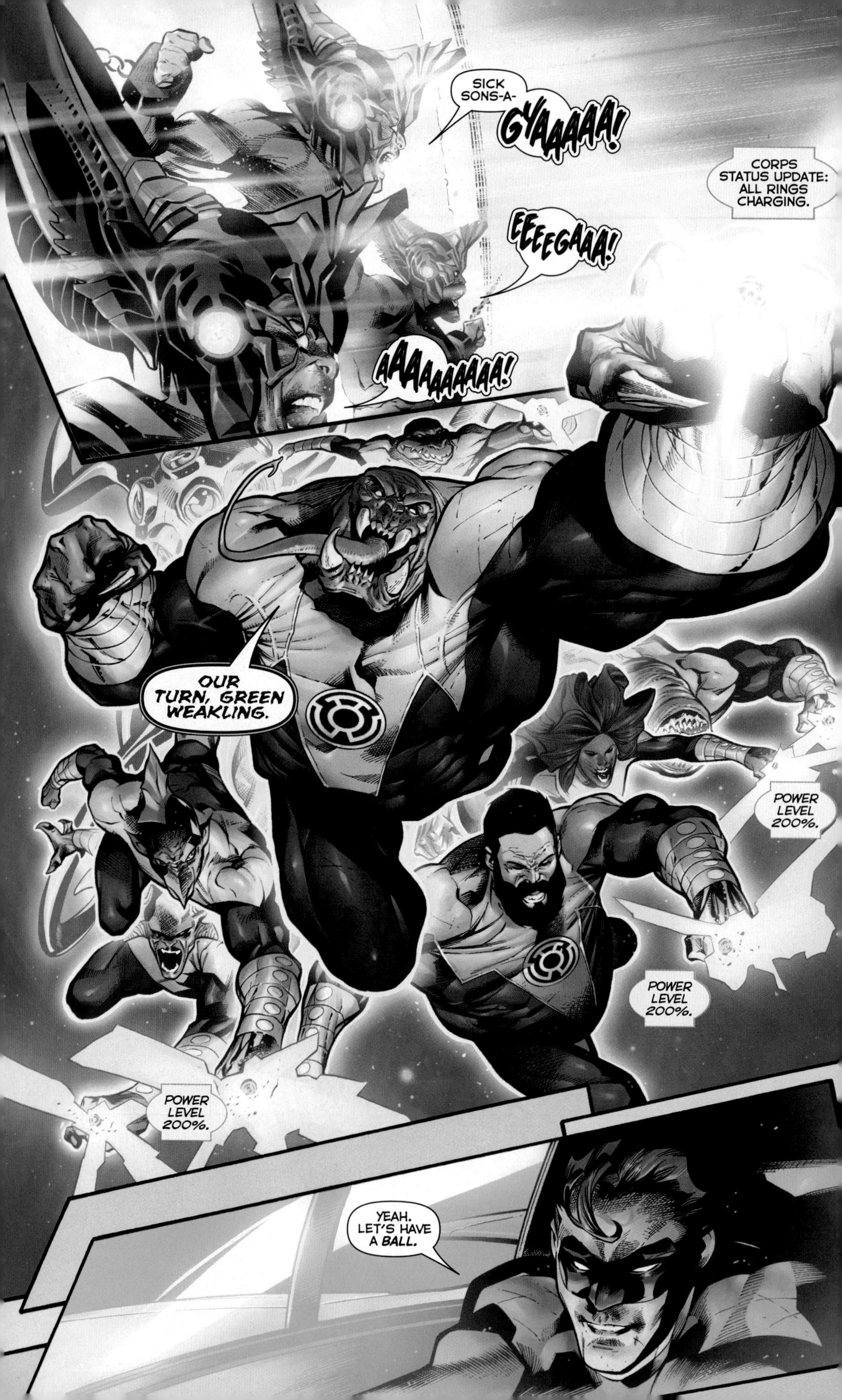
SICK SONS-A-
GYAAAAAA!
CORPS STATUS UPDATE: ALL RINGS CHARGING.
EEEEGAAA!
AAAAAAAAAA!
OUR TURN, GREEN WEAKLING.
POWER LEVEL 200%.
POWER LEVEL 200%.
POWER LEVEL 200%.
YEAH. LET'S HAVE A BALL.

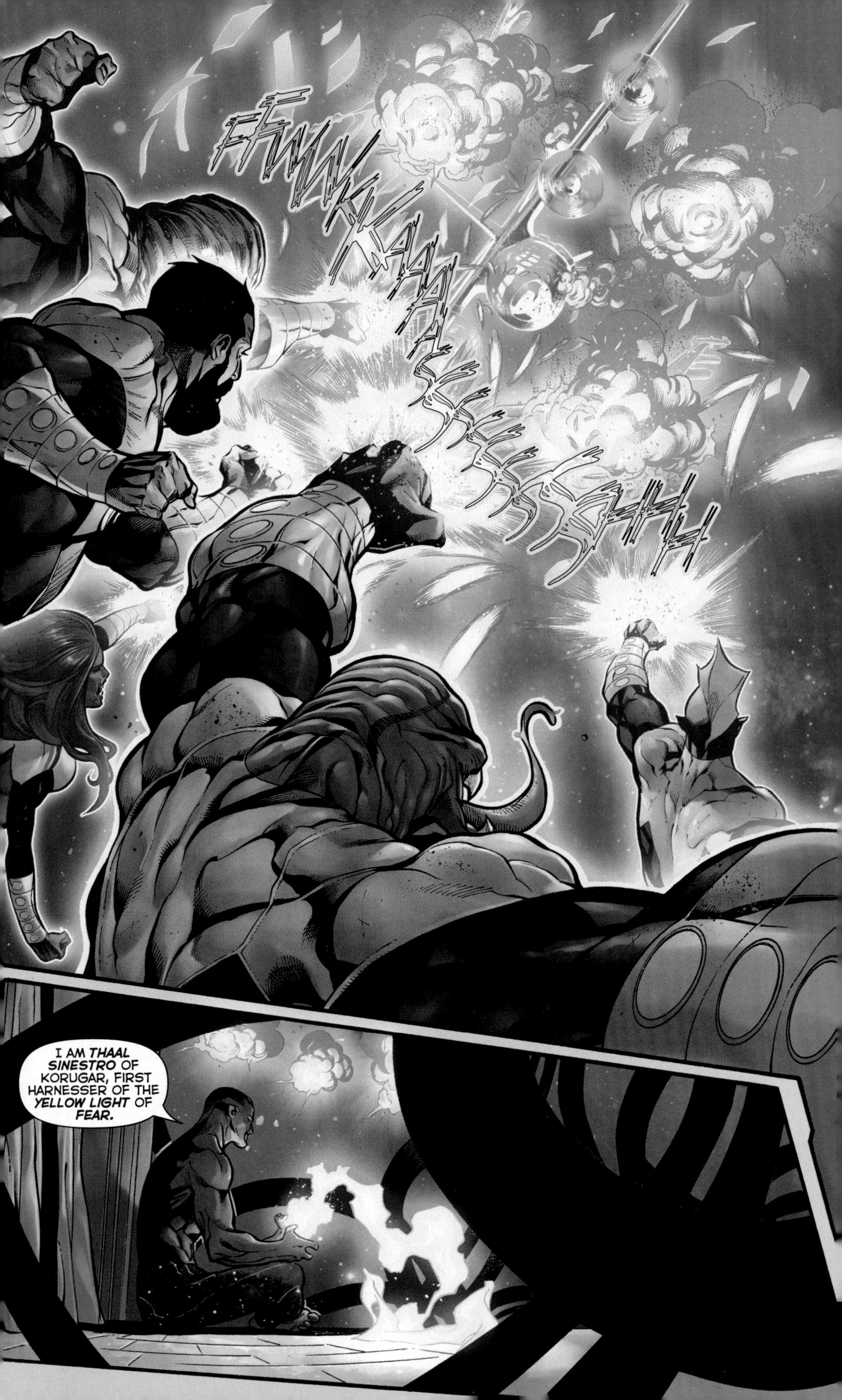
FFWWKAAAASSSSHHH
I AM THAAL SINESTRO OF KORUGAR, FIRST HARNESSER OF THE YELLOW LIGHT OF FEAR.

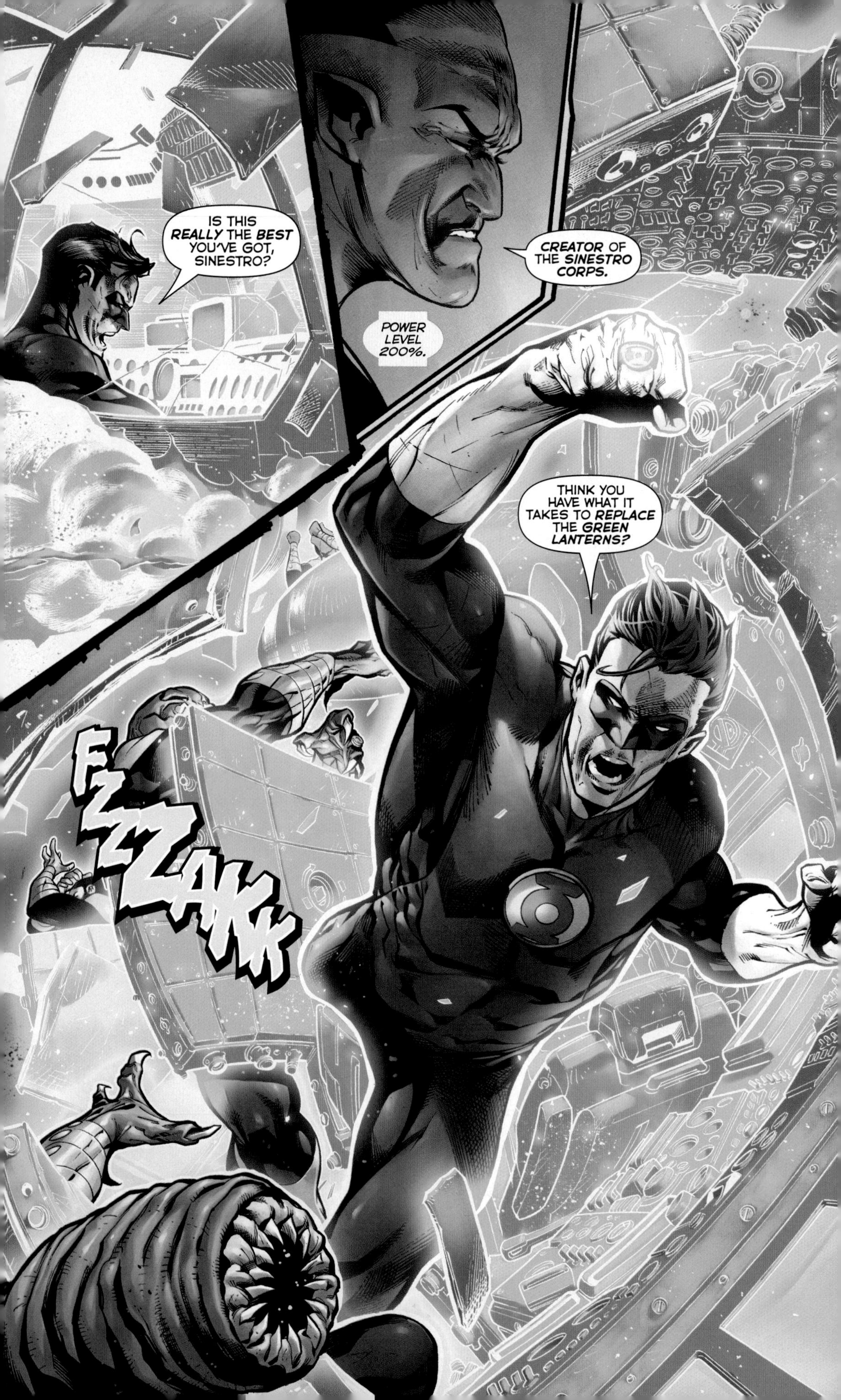
IS THIS REALLY THE BEST YOU'VE GOT, SINESTRO?
CREATOR OF THE SINESTRO CORPS.
POWER LEVEL 200%.
THINK YOU HAVE WHAT IT TAKES TO REPLACE THE GREEN LANTERNS?
FZZZAKK

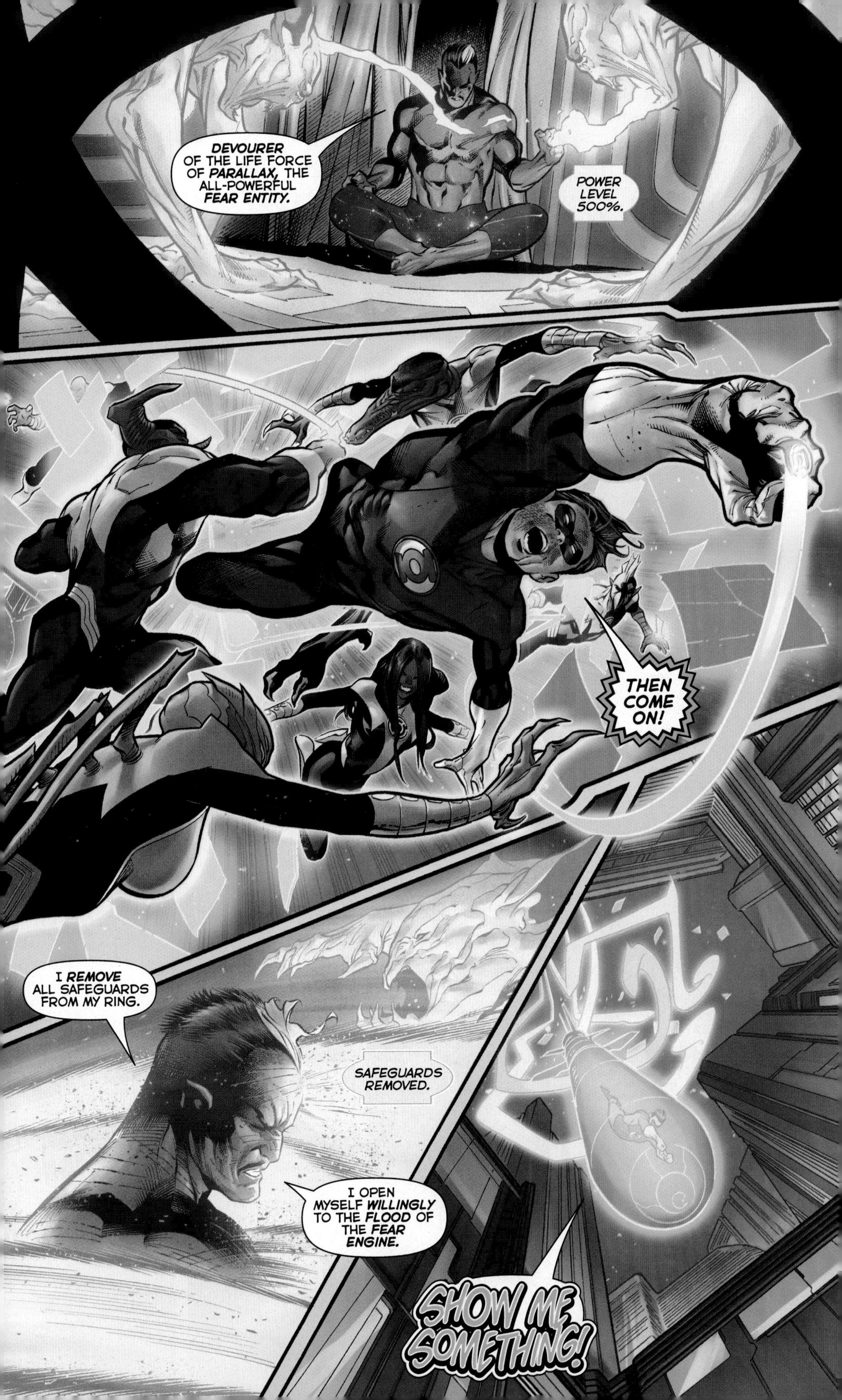

DEVOURER OF THE LIFE FORCE OF PARALLAX, THE ALL-POWERFUL FEAR ENTITY.
POWER LEVEL 500%.
THEN COME ON!
I REMOVE ALL SAFEGUARDS FROM MY RING.
SAFEGUARDS REMOVED.
I OPEN MYSELF WILLINGLY TO THE FLOOD OF THE FEAR ENGINE.
SHOW ME SOMETHING!

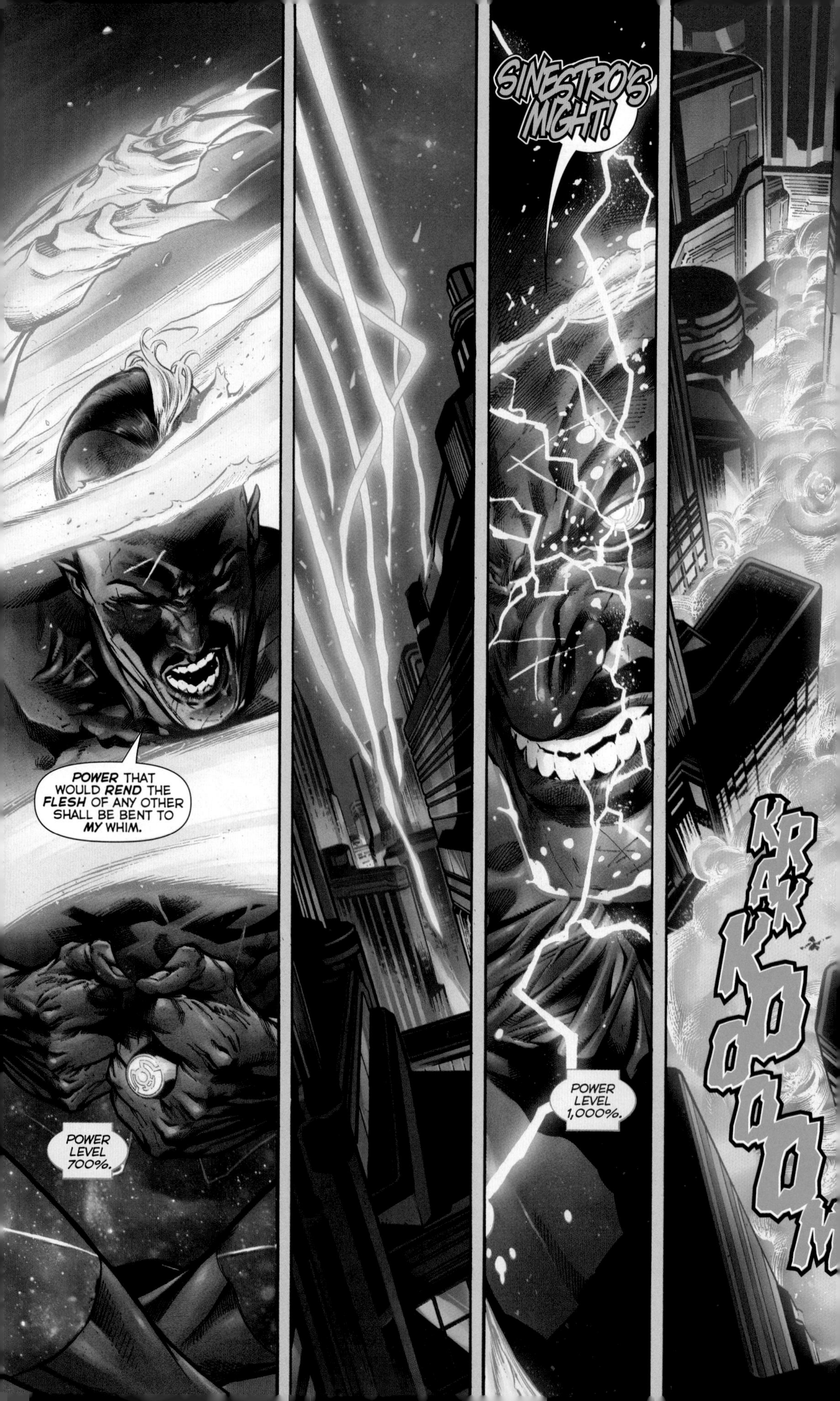

POWER THAT WOULD REND THE FLESH OF ANY OTHER SHALL BE BENT TO MY WHIM.
POWER LEVEL 700%.
SINESTRO'S MIGHT!
POWER LEVEL 1,000%.
KRAKKOOOOM

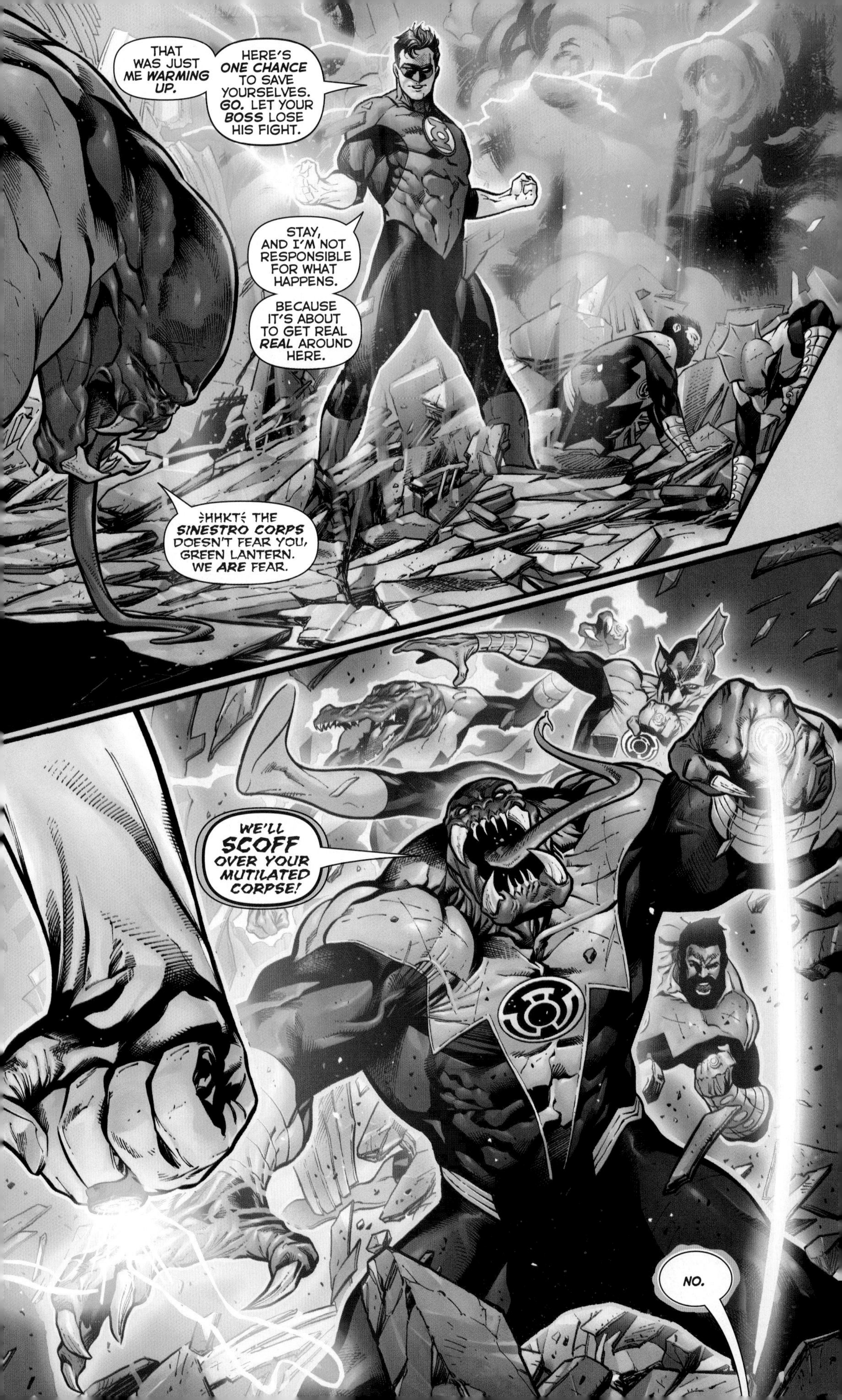
THAT WAS JUST ME WARMING UP.
HERE'S ONE CHANCE TO SAVE YOURSELVES. GO. LET YOUR BOSS LOSE HIS FIGHT.
STAY, AND I'M NOT RESPONSIBLE FOR WHAT HAPPENS.
BECAUSE IT'S ABOUT TO GET REAL REAL AROUND HERE.
HHKT THE SINESTRO CORPS DOESN'T FEAR YOU, GREEN LANTERN. WE ARE FEAR.
WE'LL SCOFF OVER YOUR MUTILATED CORPSE!
NO.

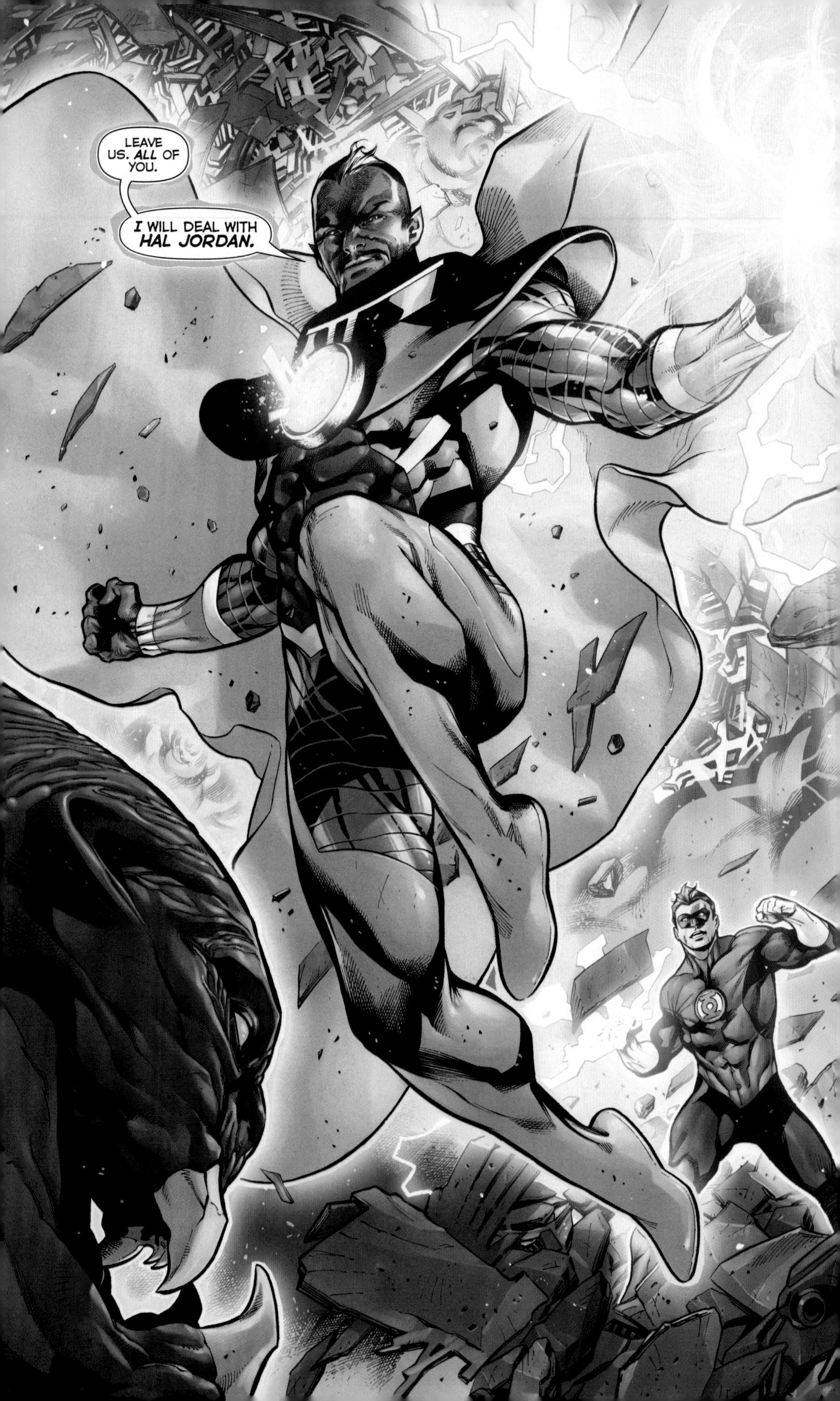
LEAVE US. ALL OF YOU.
I WILL DEAL WITH HAL JORDAN.

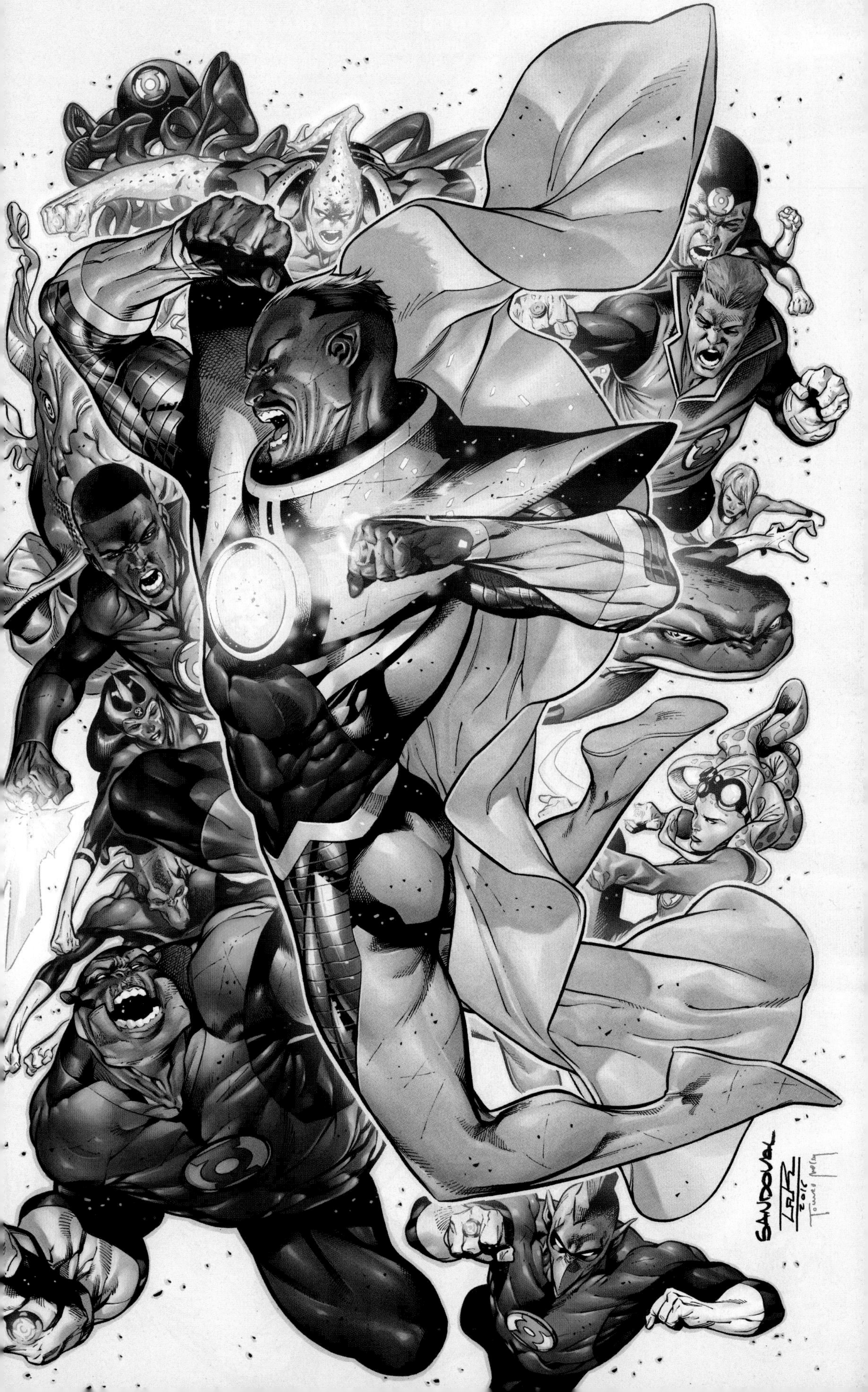
SANDOVAL

SINESTRO'S LAW CONCLUSION: FINAL FLIGHT

RAFA SANDOVAL penciller * JORDI TARRAGONA inker * TOMEU MOREY colorist

RAFA SANDOVAL, JORDI TARRAGONA and TOMEU MOREY cover artists

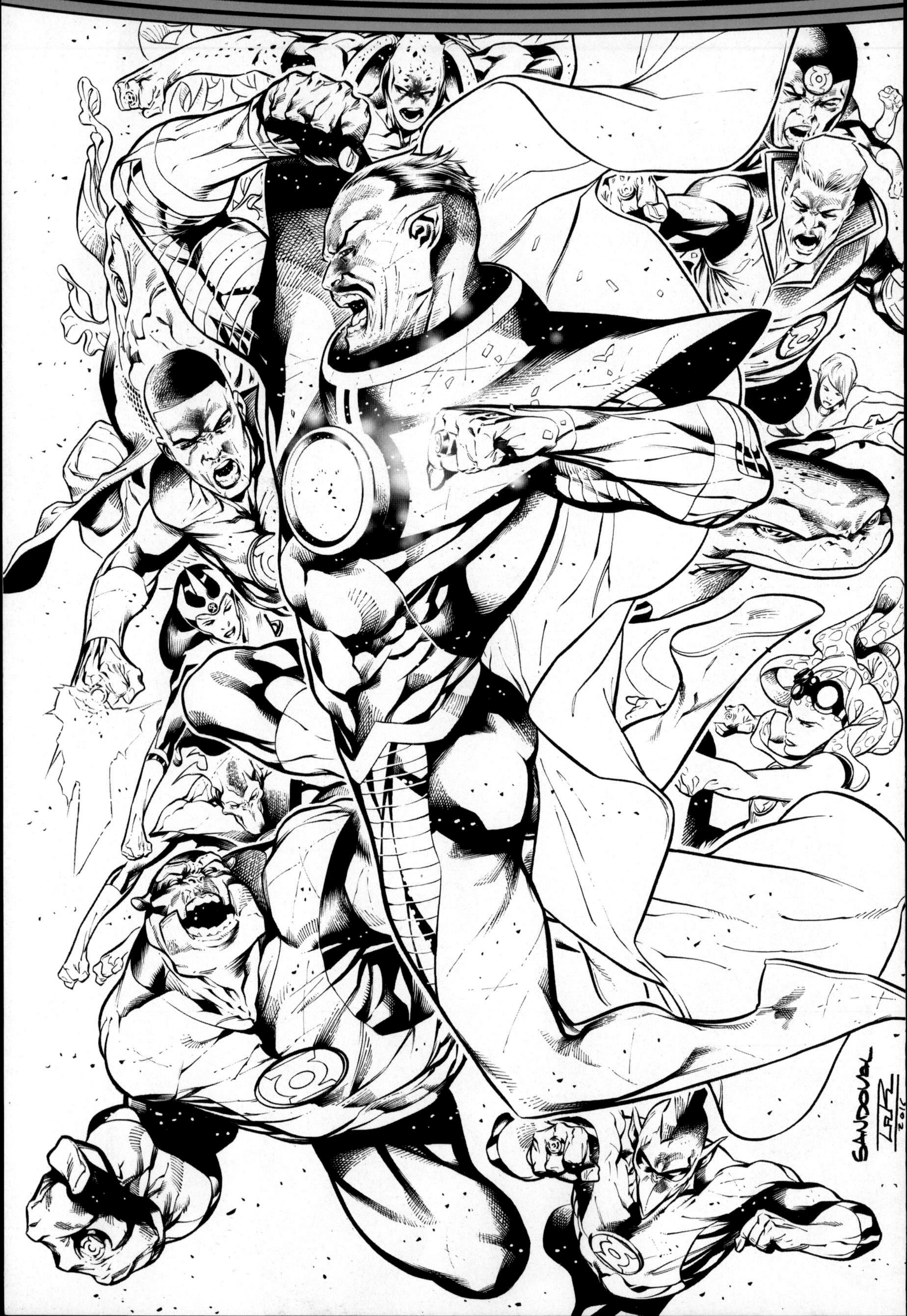
SANDOVAL

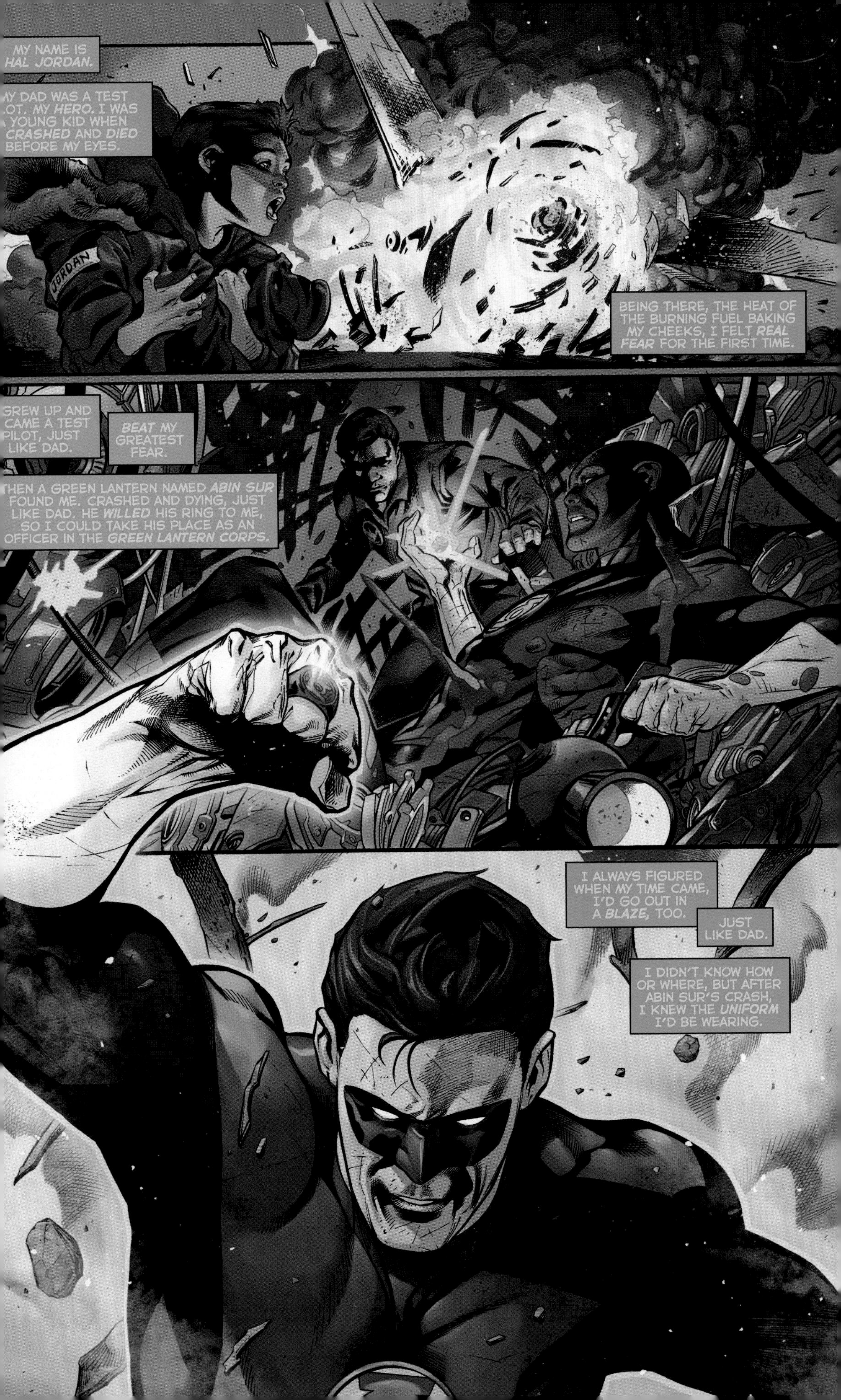
MY NAME IS HAL JORDAN.
MY DAD WAS A TEST OT. MY HERO. I WAS YOUNG KID WHEN CRASHED AND DIED BEFORE MY EYES.
JORDAN
BEING THERE, THE HEAT OF THE BURNING FUEL BAKING MY CHEEKS, I FELT REAL FEAR FOR THE FIRST TIME.
GREW UP AND CAME A TEST PILOT, JUST LIKE DAD.
BEAT MY GREATEST FEAR.
THEN A GREEN LANTERN NAMED ABIN SUR FOUND ME. CRASHED AND DYING, JUST LIKE DAD. HE WILLED HIS RING TO ME, SO I COULD TAKE HIS PLACE AS AN OFFICER IN THE GREEN LANTERN CORPS.
I ALWAYS FIGURED WHEN MY TIME CAME, I'D GO OUT IN A BLAZE, TOO.
JUST LIKE DAD.
I DIDN'T KNOW HOW OR WHERE, BUT AFTER ABIN SUR'S CRASH, I KNEW THE UNIFORM I'D BE WEARING.

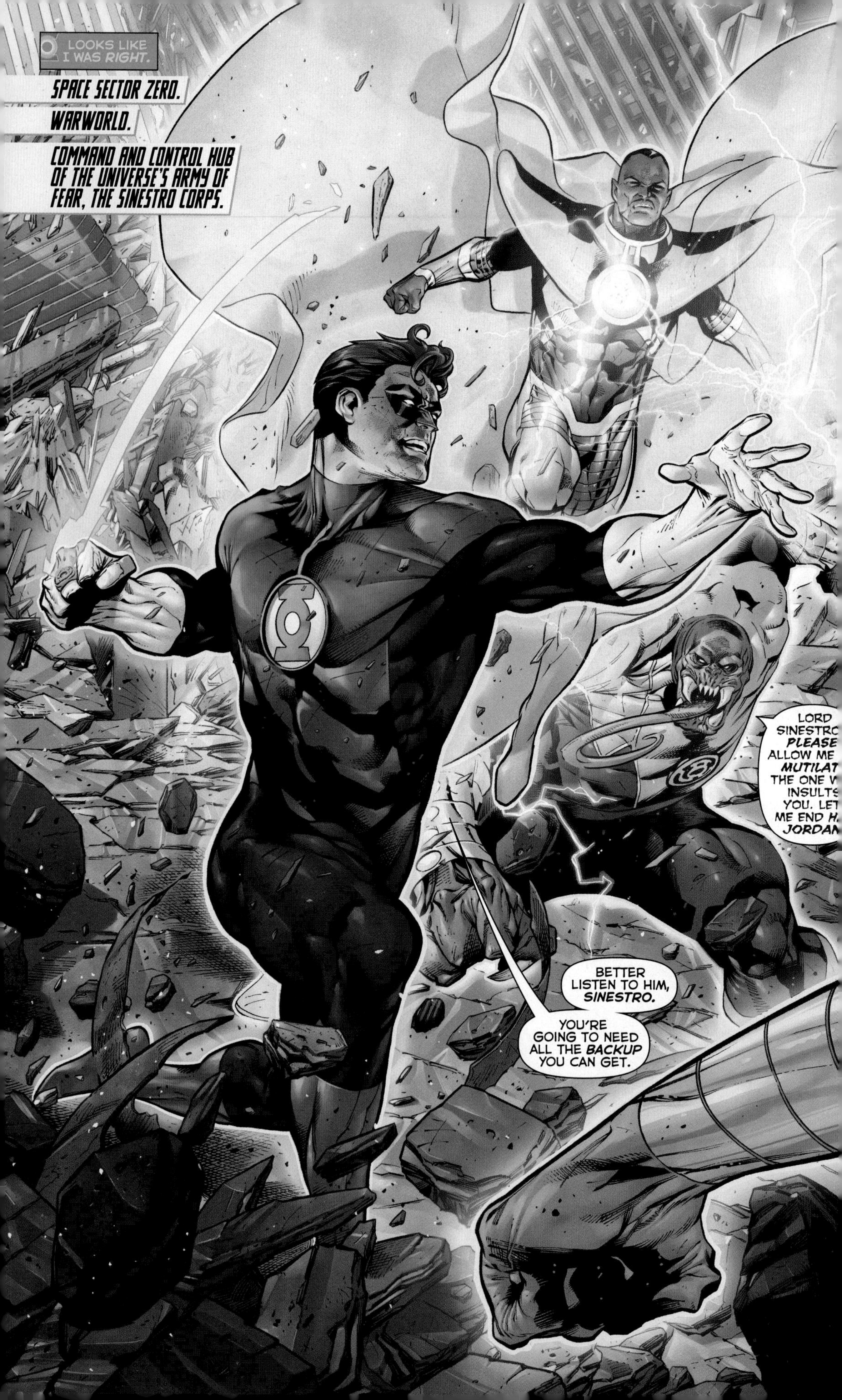
LOOKS LIKE I WAS RIGHT.
SPACE SECTOR ZERO.
WARWORLD.
COMMAND AND CONTROL HUB OF THE UNIVERSE'S ARMY OF FEAR, THE SINESTRO CORPS.
LORD SINESTRO PLEASE ALLOW ME MUTILAT THE ONE W INSULTS YOU. LET ME END HA JORDAN
BETTER LISTEN TO HIM, SINESTRO.
YOU'RE GOING TO NEED ALL THE BACKUP YOU CAN GET.

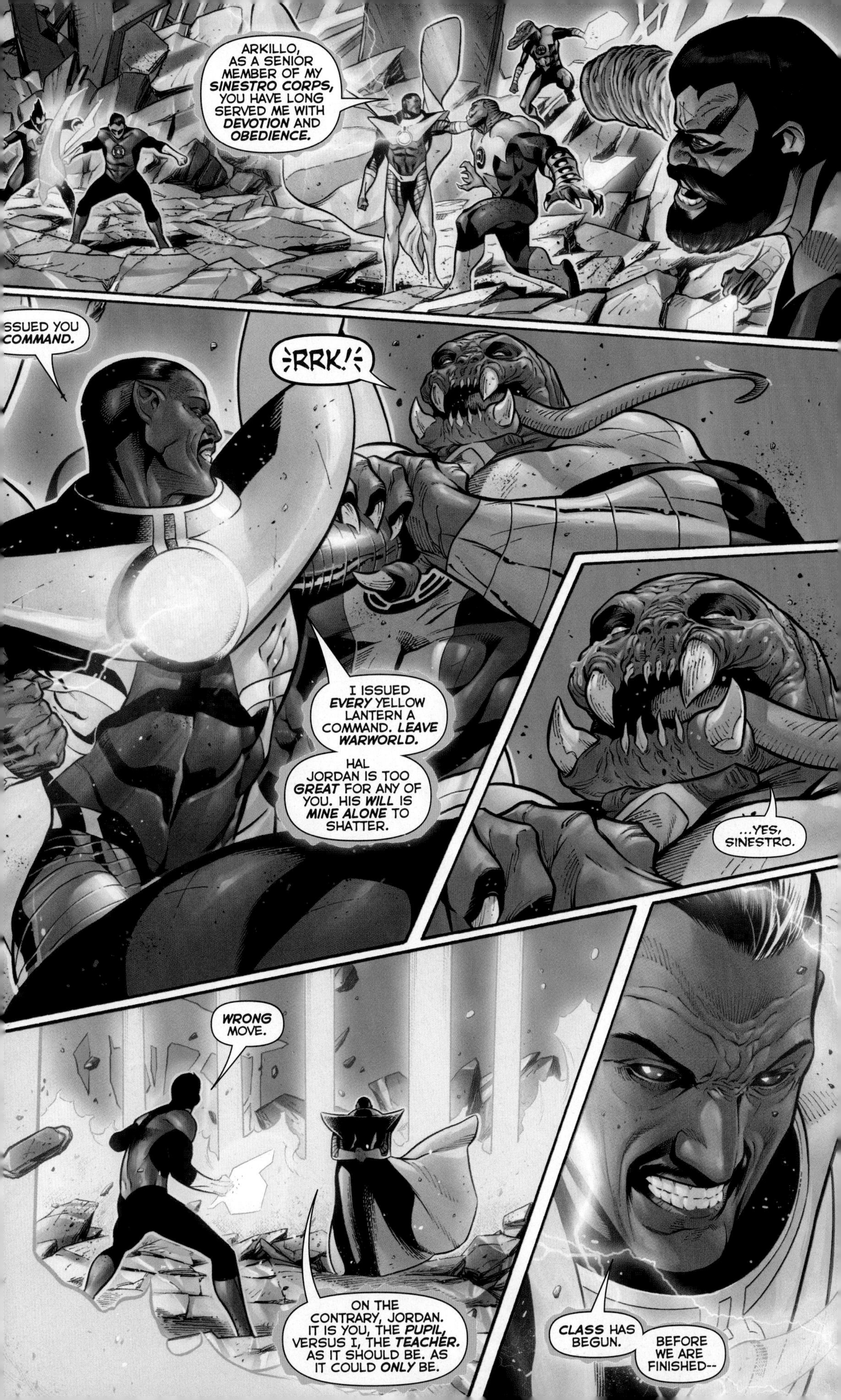

ARKILLO, AS A SENIOR MEMBER OF MY SINESTRO CORPS, YOU HAVE LONG SERVED ME WITH DEVOTION AND OBEDIENCE.
SSUED YOU COMMAND.
RRK!
I ISSUED EVERY YELLOW LANTERN A COMMAND. LEAVE WARWORLD.
HAL JORDAN IS TOO GREAT FOR ANY OF YOU. HIS WILL IS MINE ALONE TO SHATTER.
...YES, SINESTRO.
WRONG MOVE.
ON THE CONTRARY, JORDAN. IT IS YOU, THE PUPIL, VERSUS I, THE TEACHER. AS IT SHOULD BE. AS IT COULD ONLY BE.
CLASS HAS BEGUN.
BEFORE WE ARE FINISHED--

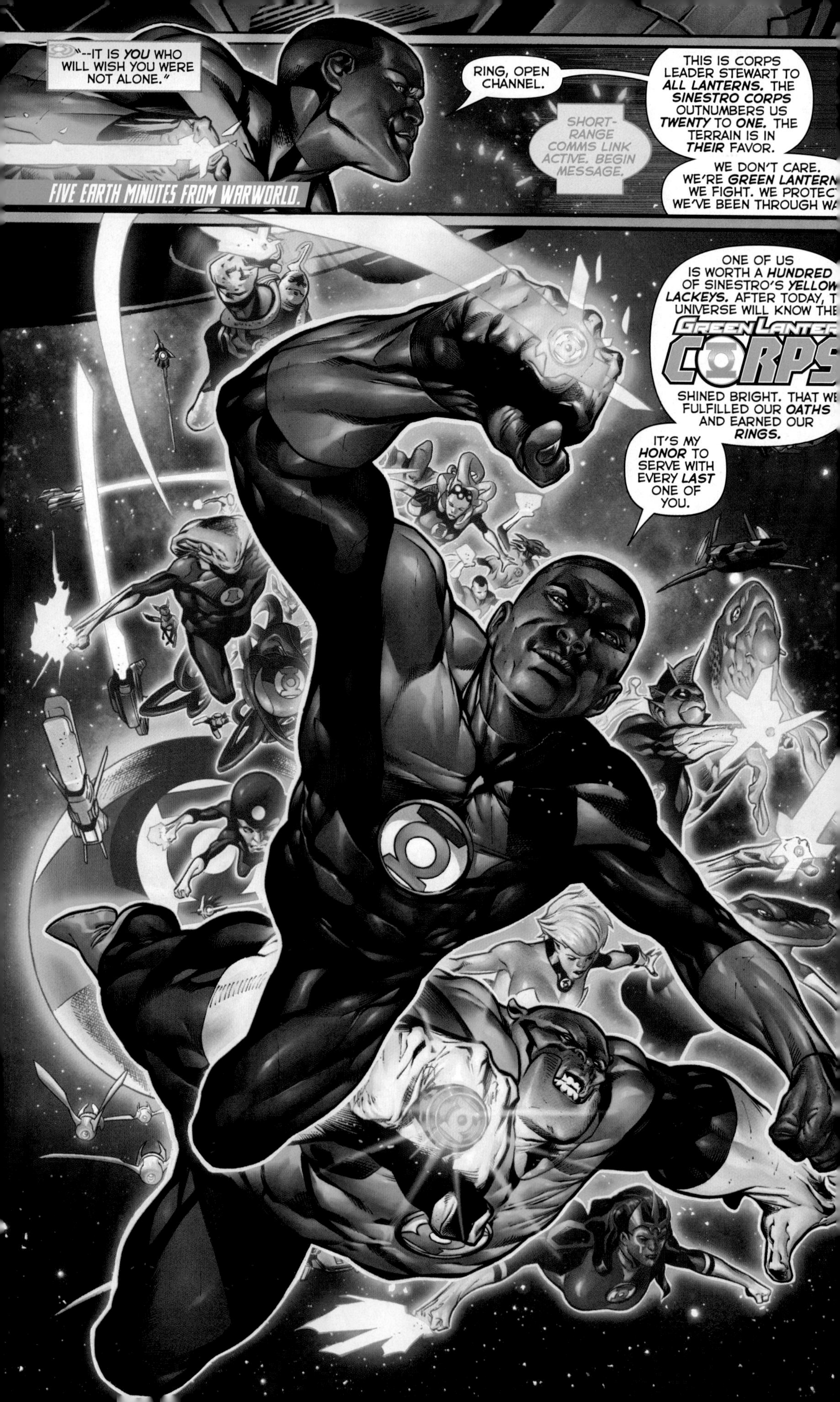
"--IT IS YOU WHO WILL WISH YOU WERE NOT ALONE."
FIVE EARTH MINUTES FROM WARWORLD.
RING, OPEN CHANNEL.
SHORT-RANGE COMMS LINK ACTIVE. BEGIN MESSAGE.
THIS IS CORPS LEADER STEWART TO ALL LANTERNS. THE SINESTRO CORPS OUTNUMBERS US TWENTY TO ONE. THE TERRAIN IS IN THEIR FAVOR.
WE DON'T CARE. WE'RE GREEN LANTERN WE FIGHT. WE PROTEC WE'VE BEEN THROUGH WA
ONE OF US IS WORTH A HUNDRED OF SINESTRO'S YELLOW LACKEYS. AFTER TODAY, T UNIVERSE WILL KNOW THE
GREEN LANTERN CORPS
SHINED BRIGHT. THAT WE FULFILLED OUR OATHS AND EARNED OUR RINGS.
IT'S MY HONOR TO SERVE WITH EVERY LAST ONE OF YOU.

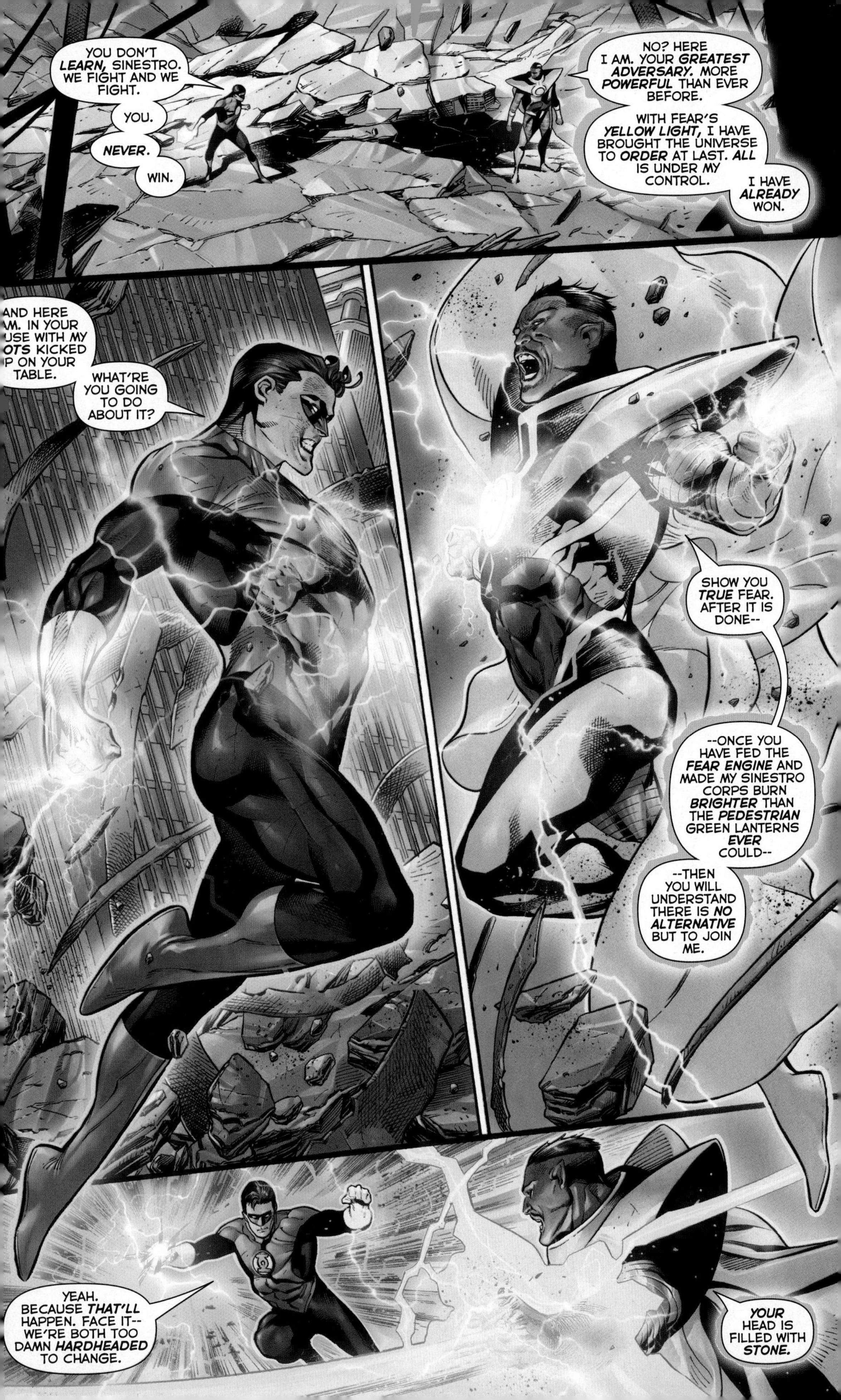

YOU DON'T LEARN, SINESTRO. WE FIGHT AND WE FIGHT.
YOU.
NEVER.
WIN.
NO? HERE I AM. YOUR GREATEST ADVERSARY. MORE POWERFUL THAN EVER BEFORE.
WITH FEAR'S YELLOW LIGHT, I HAVE BROUGHT THE UNIVERSE TO ORDER AT LAST. ALL IS UNDER MY CONTROL.
I HAVE ALREADY WON.
AND HERE AM. IN YOUR USE WITH MY OTS KICKED P ON YOUR TABLE.
WHAT'RE YOU GOING TO DO ABOUT IT?
SHOW YOU TRUE FEAR. AFTER IT IS DONE--
--ONCE YOU HAVE FED THE FEAR ENGINE AND MADE MY SINESTRO CORPS BURN BRIGHTER THAN THE PEDESTRIAN GREEN LANTERNS EVER COULD--
--THEN YOU WILL UNDERSTAND THERE IS NO ALTERNATIVE BUT TO JOIN ME.
YEAH. BECAUSE THAT'LL HAPPEN. FACE IT-- WE'RE BOTH TOO DAMN HARDHEADED TO CHANGE.
YOUR HEAD IS FILLED WITH STONE.

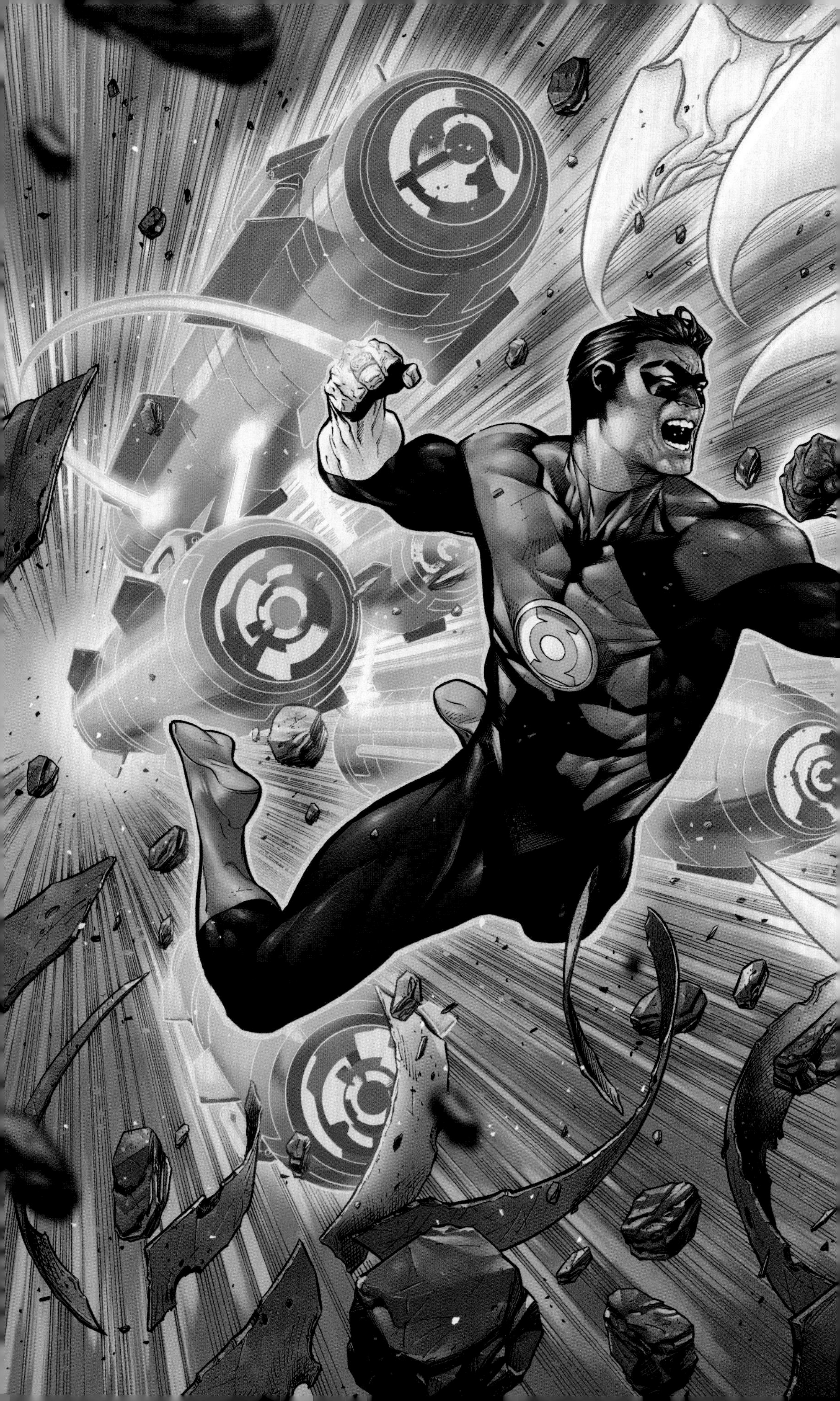

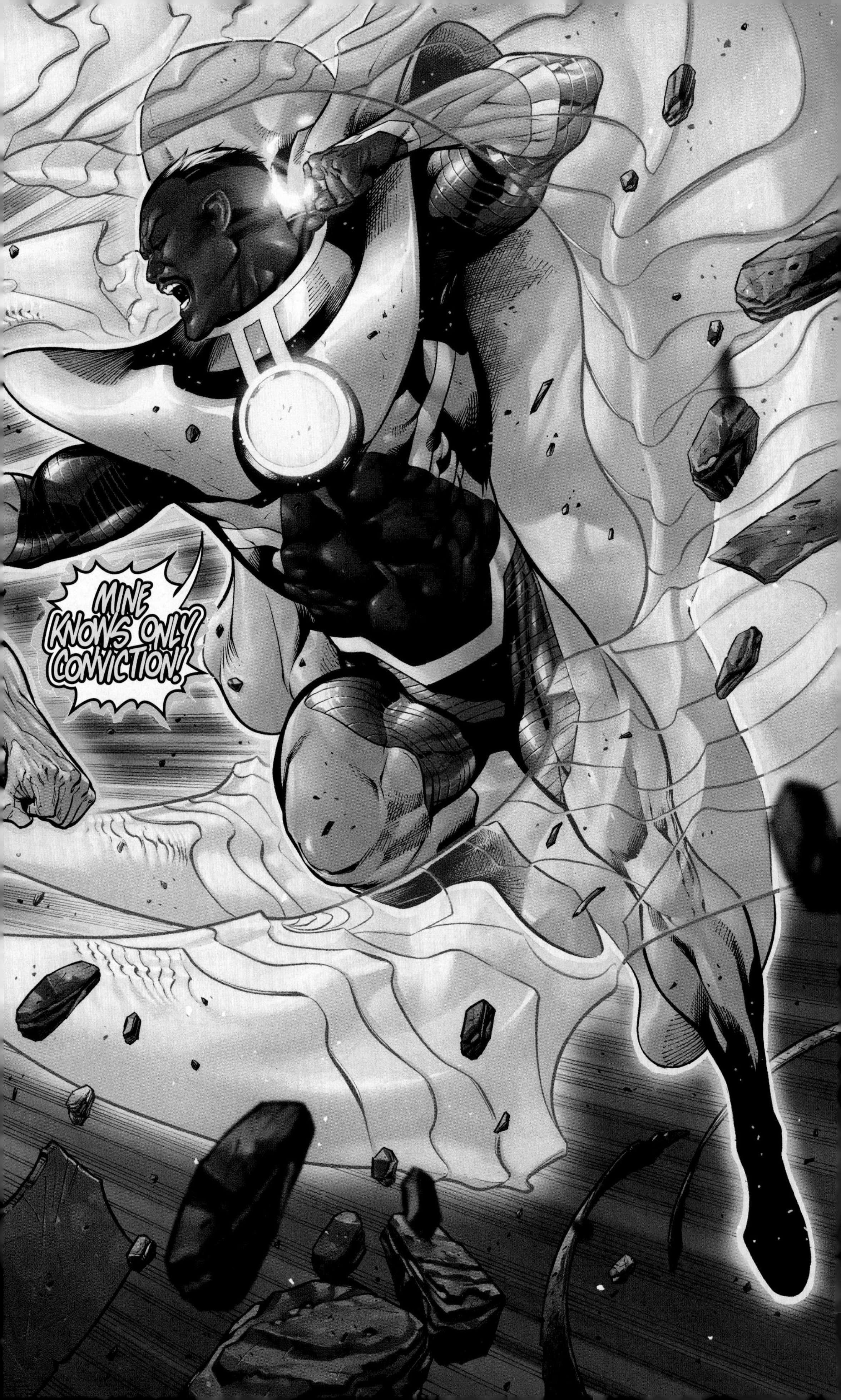
MINE KNOWS ONLY CONVICTION!

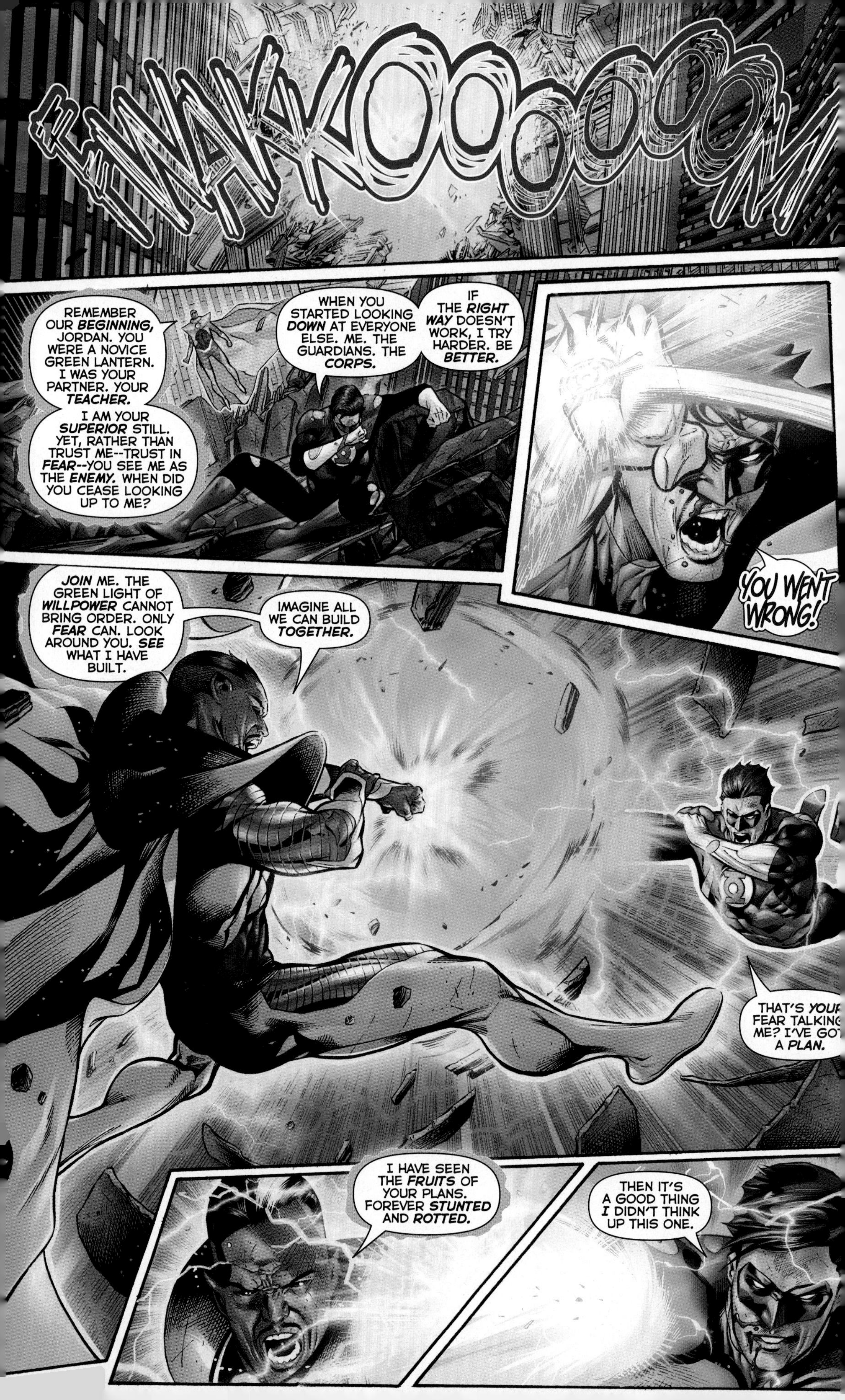

FWAKOOOOOOM
REMEMBER OUR BEGINNING, JORDAN. YOU WERE A NOVICE GREEN LANTERN. I WAS YOUR PARTNER. YOUR TEACHER.
I AM YOUR SUPERIOR STILL. YET, RATHER THAN TRUST ME--TRUST IN FEAR--YOU SEE ME AS THE ENEMY. WHEN DID YOU CEASE LOOKING UP TO ME?
WHEN YOU STARTED LOOKING DOWN AT EVERYONE ELSE. ME. THE GUARDIANS. THE CORPS.
IF THE RIGHT WAY DOESN'T WORK, I TRY HARDER. BE BETTER.
YOU WENT WRONG!
JOIN ME. THE GREEN LIGHT OF WILLPOWER CANNOT BRING ORDER. ONLY FEAR CAN. LOOK AROUND YOU. SEE WHAT I HAVE BUILT.
IMAGINE ALL WE CAN BUILD TOGETHER.
THAT'S YOUR FEAR TALKING ME? I'VE GOT A PLAN.
I HAVE SEEN THE FRUITS OF YOUR PLANS. FOREVER STUNTED AND ROTTED.
THEN IT'S A GOOD THING I DIDN'T THINK UP THIS ONE.

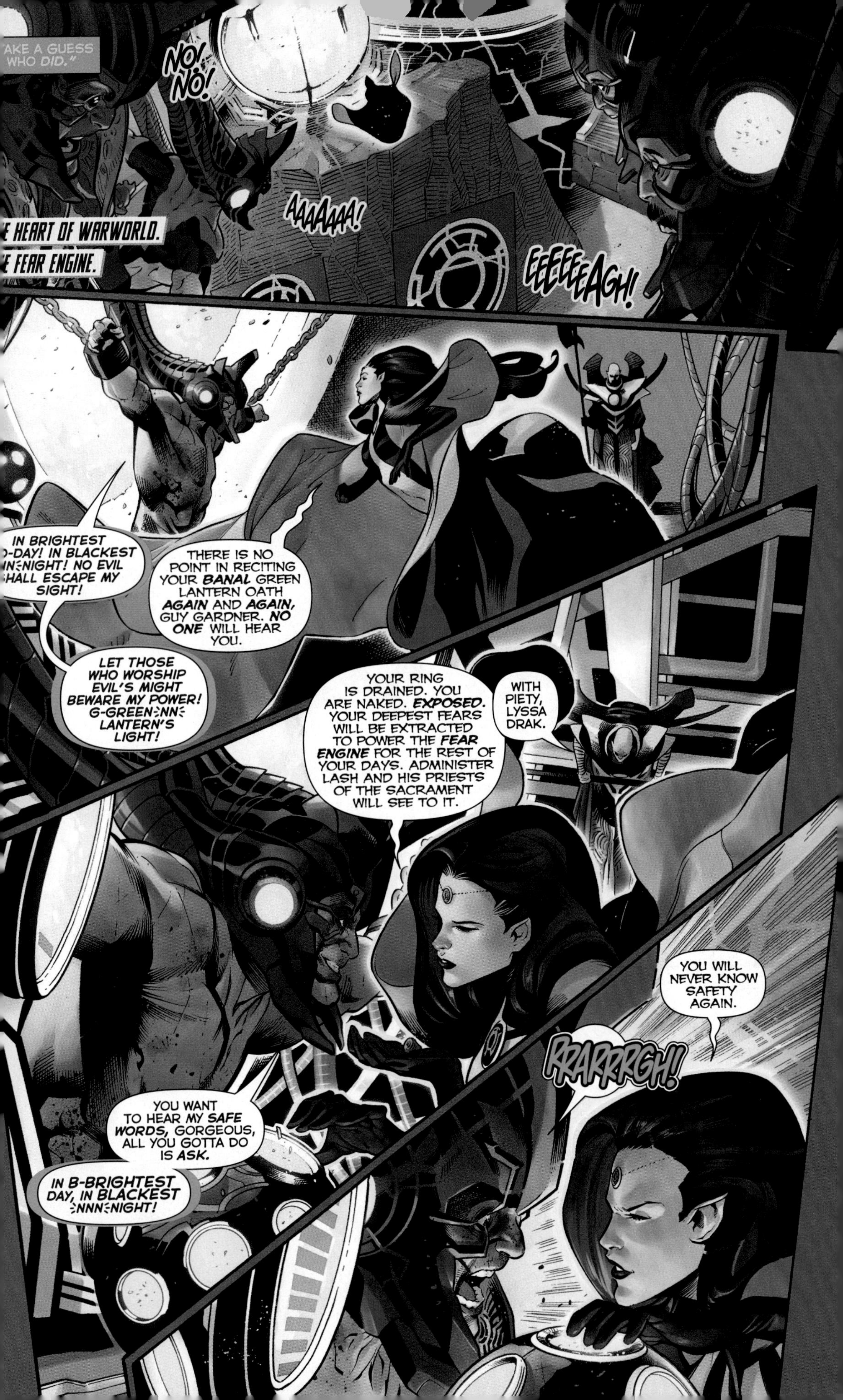
"AKE A GUESS WHO DID."
NO! NO!
E HEART OF WARWORLD.
E FEAR ENGINE.
AAAAAAA!
EEEEEEAGH!
IN BRIGHTEST D-DAY! IN BLACKEST NNN-NIGHT! NO EVIL SHALL ESCAPE MY SIGHT!
THERE IS NO POINT IN RECITING YOUR BANAL GREEN LANTERN OATH AGAIN AND AGAIN, GUY GARDNER. NO ONE WILL HEAR YOU.
LET THOSE WHO WORSHIP EVIL'S MIGHT BEWARE MY POWER! G-GREEN-NNN-LANTERN'S LIGHT!
YOUR RING IS DRAINED. YOU ARE NAKED. EXPOSED. YOUR DEEPEST FEARS WILL BE EXTRACTED TO POWER THE FEAR ENGINE FOR THE REST OF YOUR DAYS. ADMINISTER LASH AND HIS PRIESTS OF THE SACRAMENT WILL SEE TO IT.
WITH PIETY, LYSSA DRAK.
YOU WILL NEVER KNOW SAFETY AGAIN.
RRARRRGH!
YOU WANT TO HEAR MY SAFE WORDS, GORGEOUS, ALL YOU GOTTA DO IS ASK.
IN B-BRIGHTEST DAY, IN BLACKEST NNN-NIGHT!

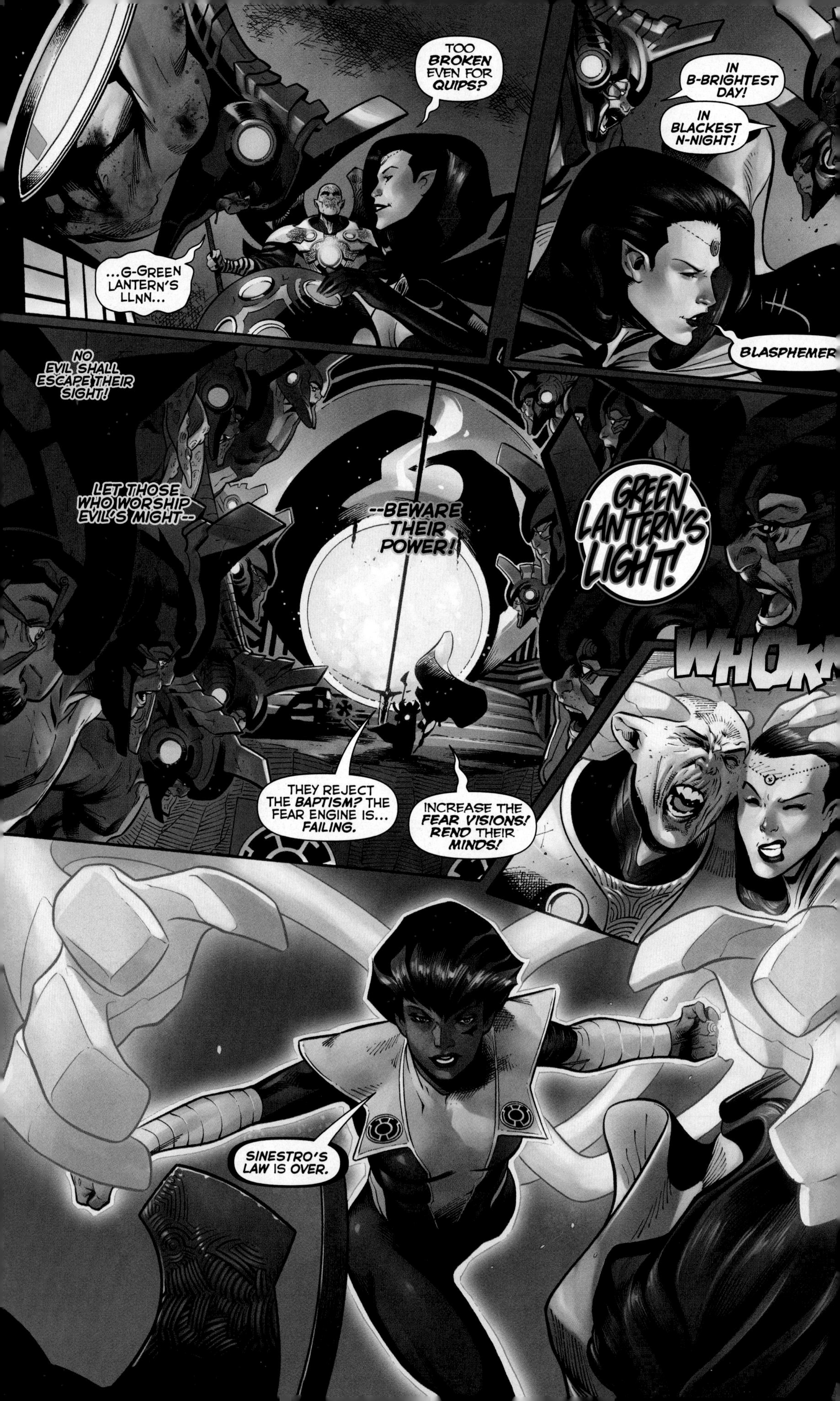

TOO BROKEN EVEN FOR QUIPS?
...G-GREEN LANTERN'S LLNN...
IN B-BRIGHTEST DAY!
IN BLACKEST N-NIGHT!
BLASPHEMER
NO EVIL SHALL ESCAPE THEIR SIGHT!
LET THOSE WHO WORSHIP EVIL'S MIGHT--
--BEWARE THEIR POWER!
GREEN LANTERN'S LIGHT!
WHOR
THEY REJECT THE BAPTISM? THE FEAR ENGINE IS... FAILING.
INCREASE THE FEAR VISIONS! REND THEIR MINDS!
SINESTRO'S LAW IS OVER.

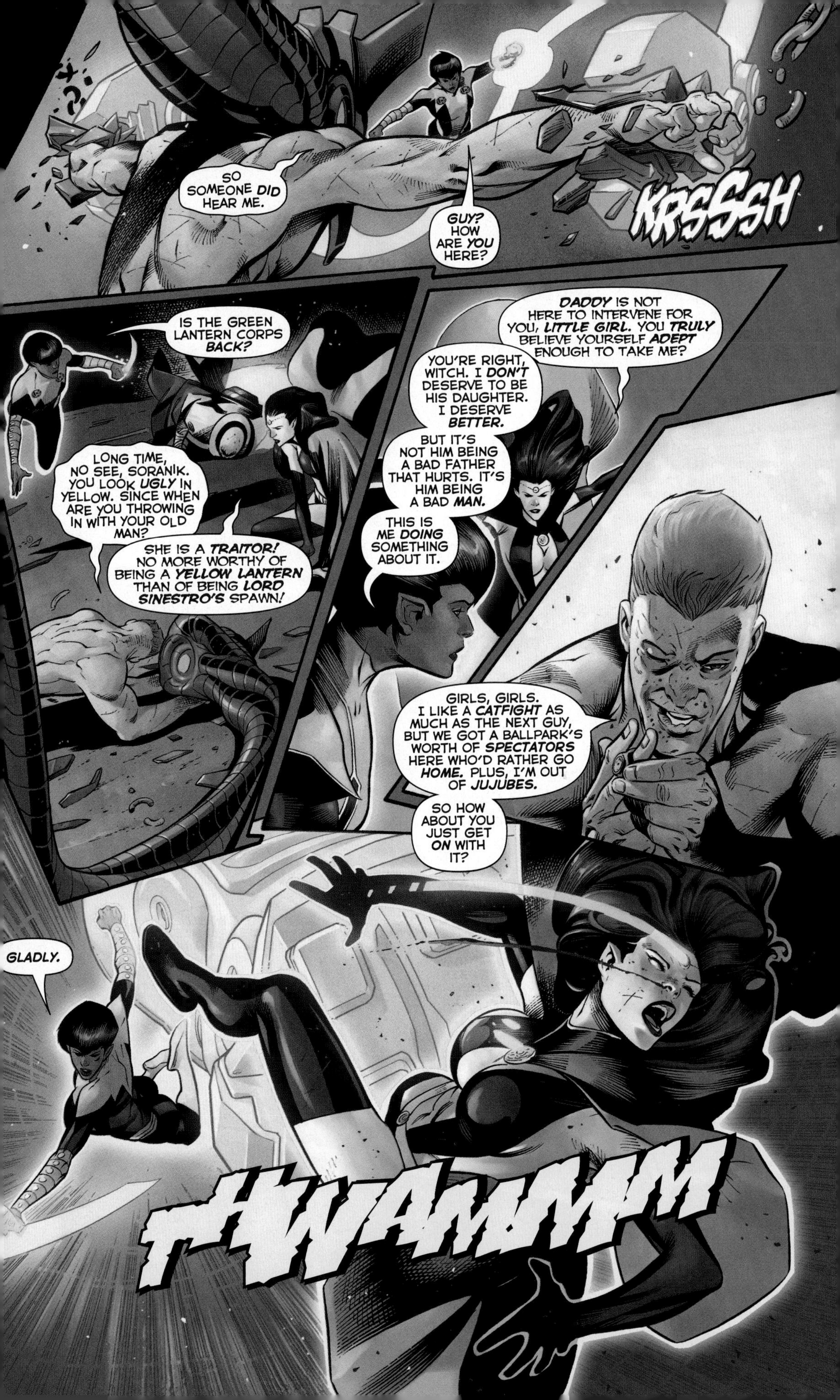
KRSSSH
SO SOMEONE DID HEAR ME.
GUY? HOW ARE YOU HERE?
IS THE GREEN LANTERN CORPS BACK?
LONG TIME, NO SEE, SORANIK. YOU LOOK UGLY IN YELLOW. SINCE WHEN ARE YOU THROWING IN WITH YOUR OLD MAN?
SHE IS A TRAITOR! NO MORE WORTHY OF BEING A YELLOW LANTERN THAN OF BEING LORD SINESTRO'S SPAWN!
DADDY IS NOT HERE TO INTERVENE FOR YOU, LITTLE GIRL. YOU TRULY BELIEVE YOURSELF ADEPT ENOUGH TO TAKE ME?
YOU'RE RIGHT, WITCH. I DON'T DESERVE TO BE HIS DAUGHTER. I DESERVE BETTER.
BUT IT'S NOT HIM BEING A BAD FATHER THAT HURTS. IT'S HIM BEING A BAD MAN.
THIS IS ME DOING SOMETHING ABOUT IT.
GIRLS, GIRLS. I LIKE A CATFIGHT AS MUCH AS THE NEXT GUY, BUT WE GOT A BALLPARK'S WORTH OF SPECTATORS HERE WHO'D RATHER GO HOME. PLUS, I'M OUT OF JUJUBES.
SO HOW ABOUT YOU JUST GET ON WITH IT?
GLADLY.
THWAMMM

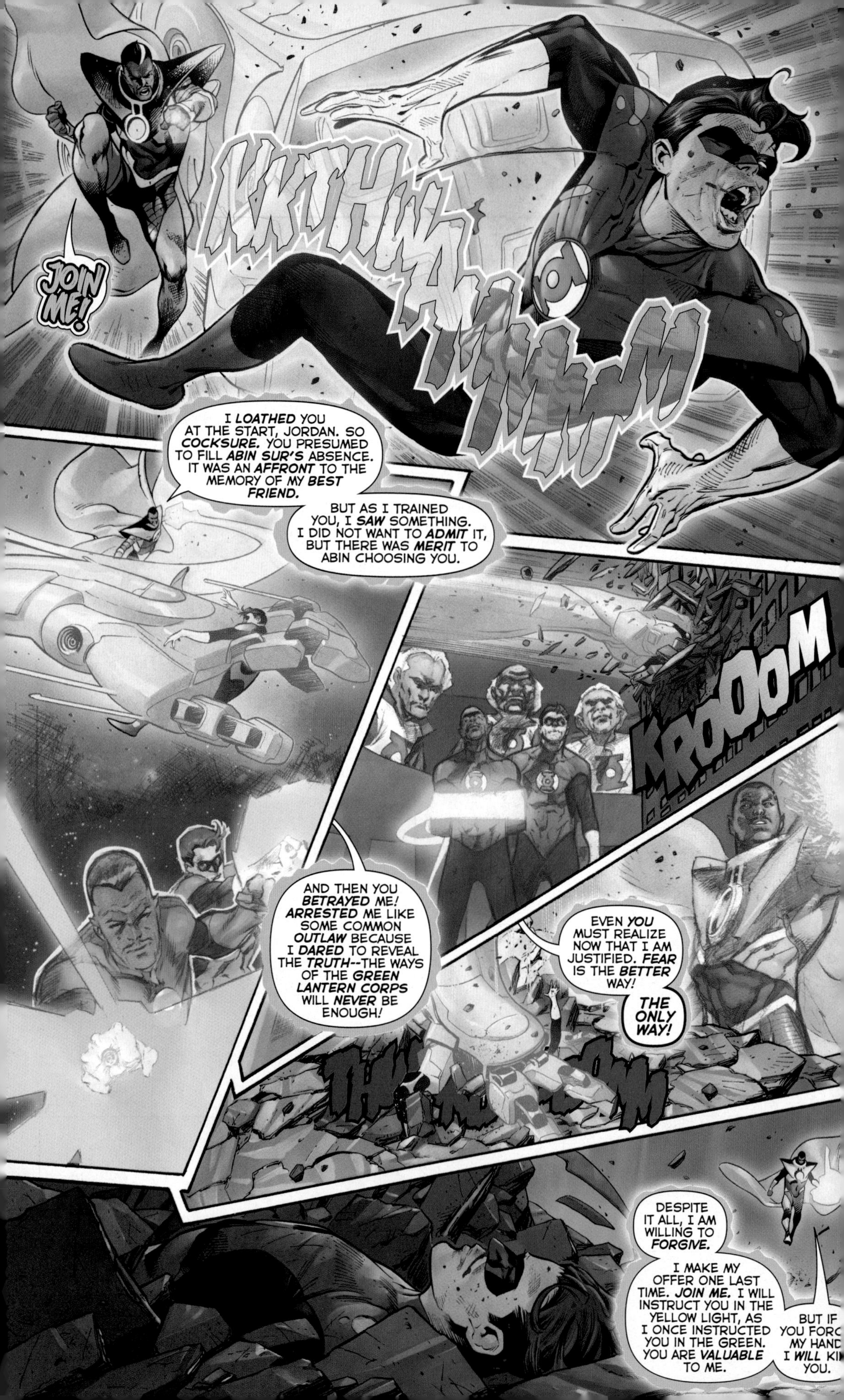
JOIN ME!
I LOATHED YOU AT THE START, JORDAN. SO COCKSURE. YOU PRESUMED TO FILL ABIN SUR'S ABSENCE. IT WAS AN AFFRONT TO THE MEMORY OF MY BEST FRIEND.
BUT AS I TRAINED YOU, I SAW SOMETHING. I DID NOT WANT TO ADMIT IT, BUT THERE WAS MERIT TO ABIN CHOOSING YOU.
KROOOOM
AND THEN YOU BETRAYED ME! ARRESTED ME LIKE SOME COMMON OUTLAW BECAUSE I DARED TO REVEAL THE TRUTH--THE WAYS OF THE GREEN LANTERN CORPS WILL NEVER BE ENOUGH!
EVEN YOU MUST REALIZE NOW THAT I AM JUSTIFIED. FEAR IS THE BETTER WAY!
THE ONLY WAY!
DESPITE IT ALL, I AM WILLING TO FORGIVE.
I MAKE MY OFFER ONE LAST TIME. JOIN ME. I WILL INSTRUCT YOU IN THE YELLOW LIGHT, AS I ONCE INSTRUCTED YOU IN THE GREEN. YOU ARE VALUABLE TO ME.
BUT IF YOU FORC MY HAND I WILL KI YOU.

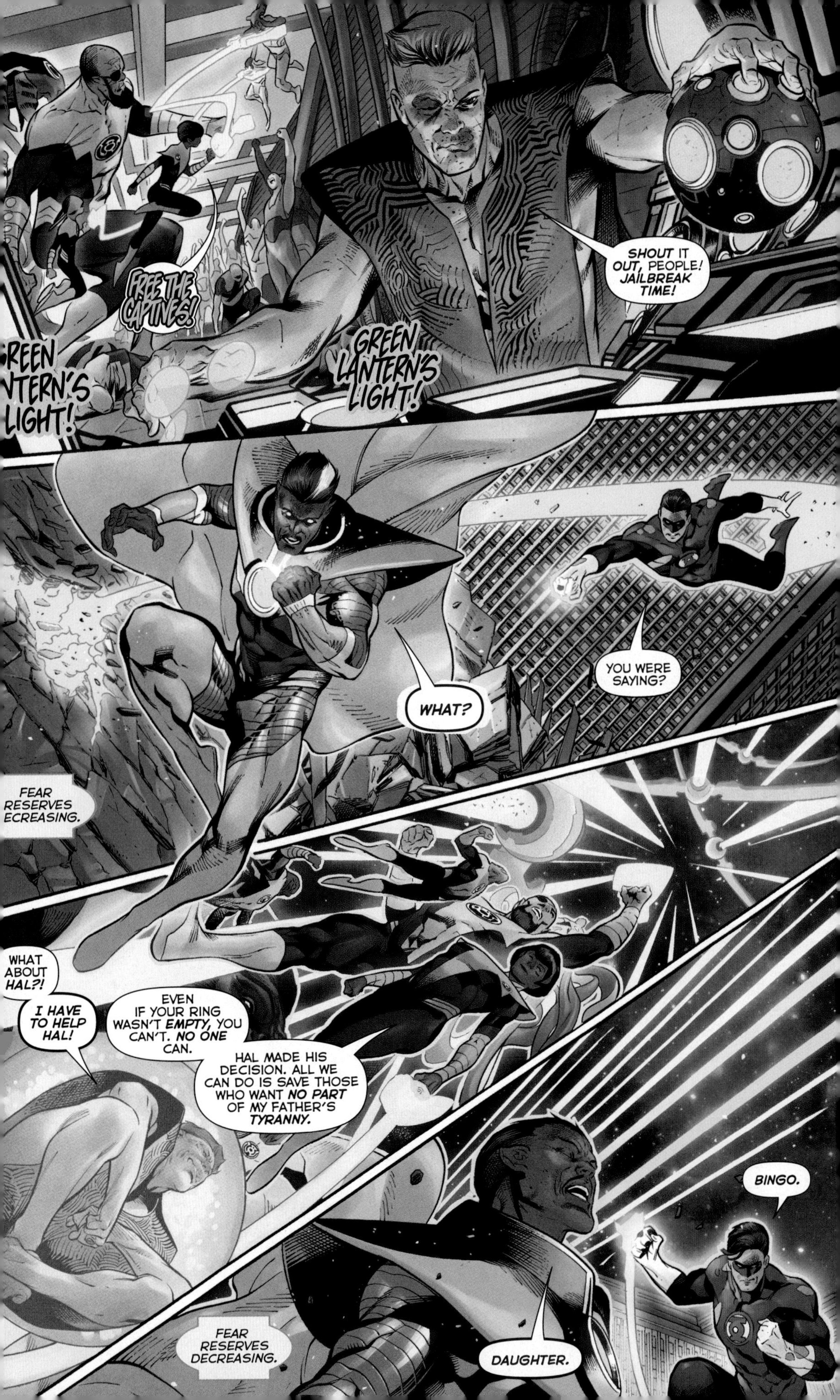
SHOUT IT OUT, PEOPLE! JAILBREAK TIME!
FREE THE CAPTIVES!
GREEN LANTERN'S LIGHT!
GREEN LANTERN'S LIGHT!
YOU WERE SAYING?
WHAT?
FEAR RESERVES DECREASING.
WHAT ABOUT HAL?!
I HAVE TO HELP HAL!
EVEN IF YOUR RING WASN'T EMPTY, YOU CAN'T. NO ONE CAN.
HAL MADE HIS DECISION. ALL WE CAN DO IS SAVE THOSE WHO WANT NO PART OF MY FATHER'S TYRANNY.
BINGO.
FEAR RESERVES DECREASING.
DAUGHTER.

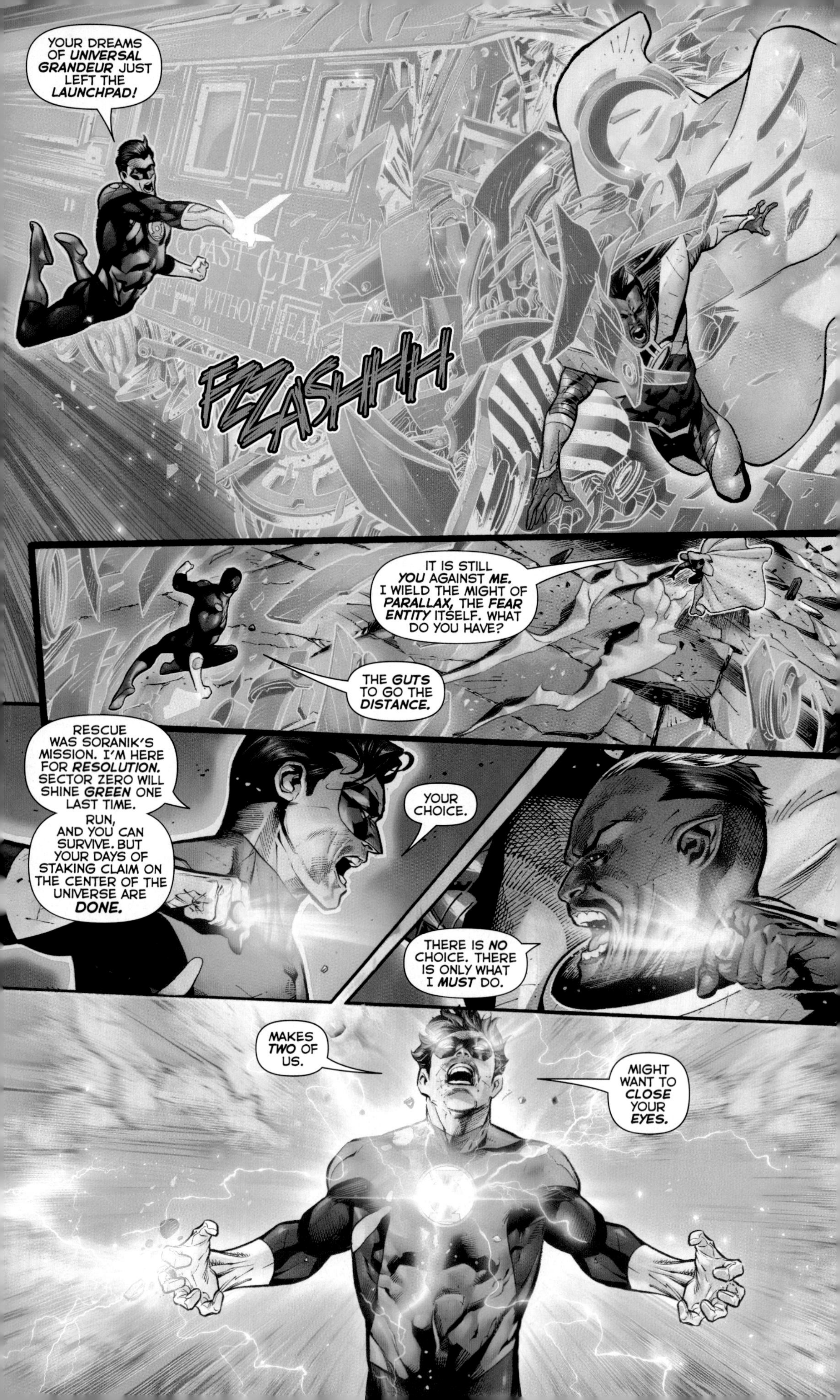
YOUR DREAMS OF UNIVERSAL GRANDEUR JUST LEFT THE LAUNCHPAD!
COAST CITY
THE CITY WITHOUT FEAR
FZZASHHHH
IT IS STILL YOU AGAINST ME. I WIELD THE MIGHT OF PARALLAX, THE FEAR ENTITY ITSELF. WHAT DO YOU HAVE?
THE GUTS TO GO THE DISTANCE.
RESCUE WAS SORANIK'S MISSION. I'M HERE FOR RESOLUTION. SECTOR ZERO WILL SHINE GREEN ONE LAST TIME.
RUN, AND YOU CAN SURVIVE. BUT YOUR DAYS OF STAKING CLAIM ON THE CENTER OF THE UNIVERSE ARE DONE.
YOUR CHOICE.
THERE IS NO CHOICE. THERE IS ONLY WHAT I MUST DO.
MAKES TWO OF US.
MIGHT WANT TO CLOSE YOUR EYES.

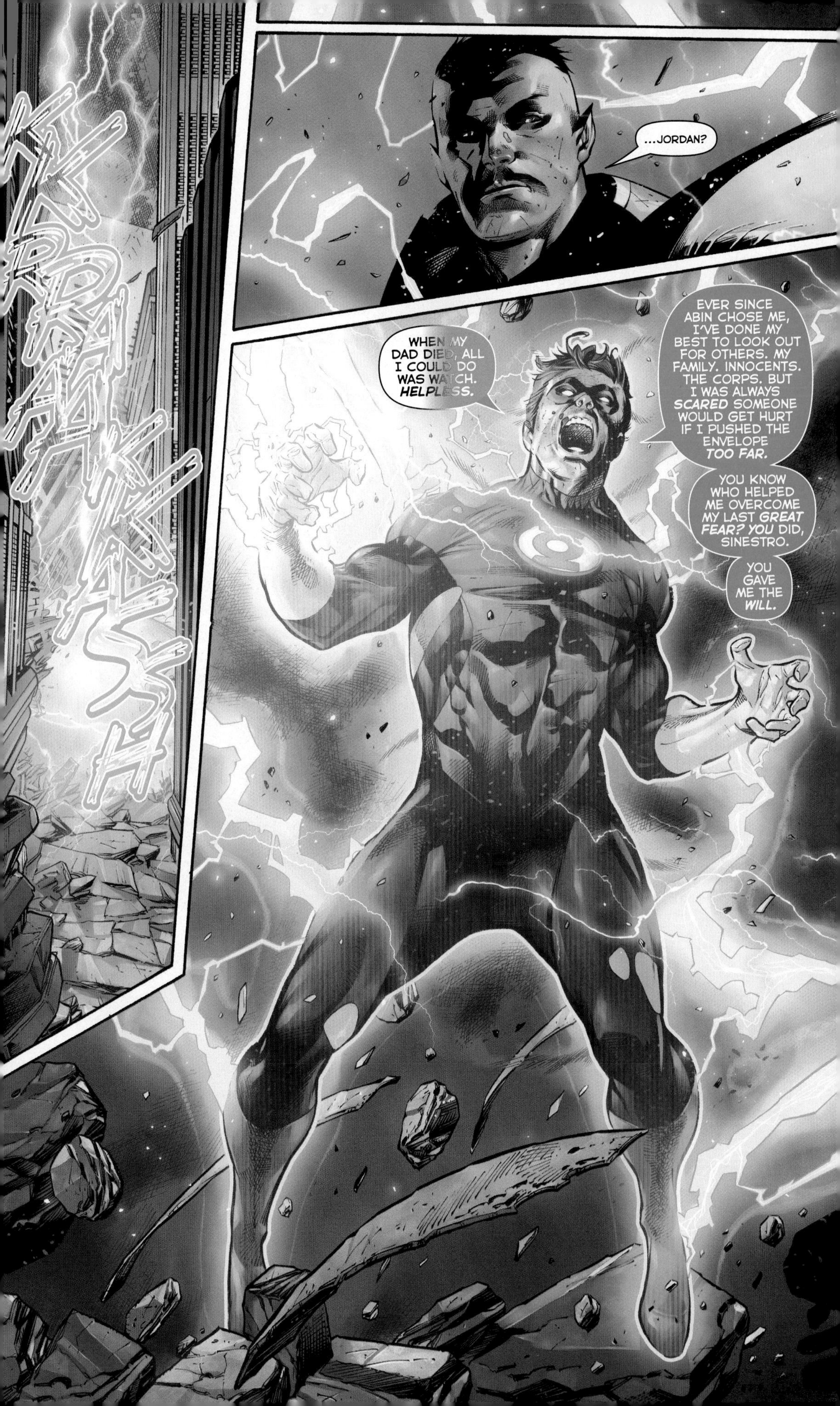
...JORDAN?
WHEN MY DAD DIED, ALL I COULD DO WAS WATCH. *HELPLESS.*
EVER SINCE ABIN CHOSE ME, I'VE DONE MY BEST TO LOOK OUT FOR OTHERS. MY FAMILY. INNOCENTS. THE CORPS. BUT I WAS ALWAYS *SCARED* SOMEONE WOULD GET HURT IF I PUSHED THE ENVELOPE *TOO FAR.*
YOU KNOW WHO HELPED ME OVERCOME MY LAST *GREAT FEAR? YOU* DID, SINESTRO.
YOU GAVE ME THE *WILL.*

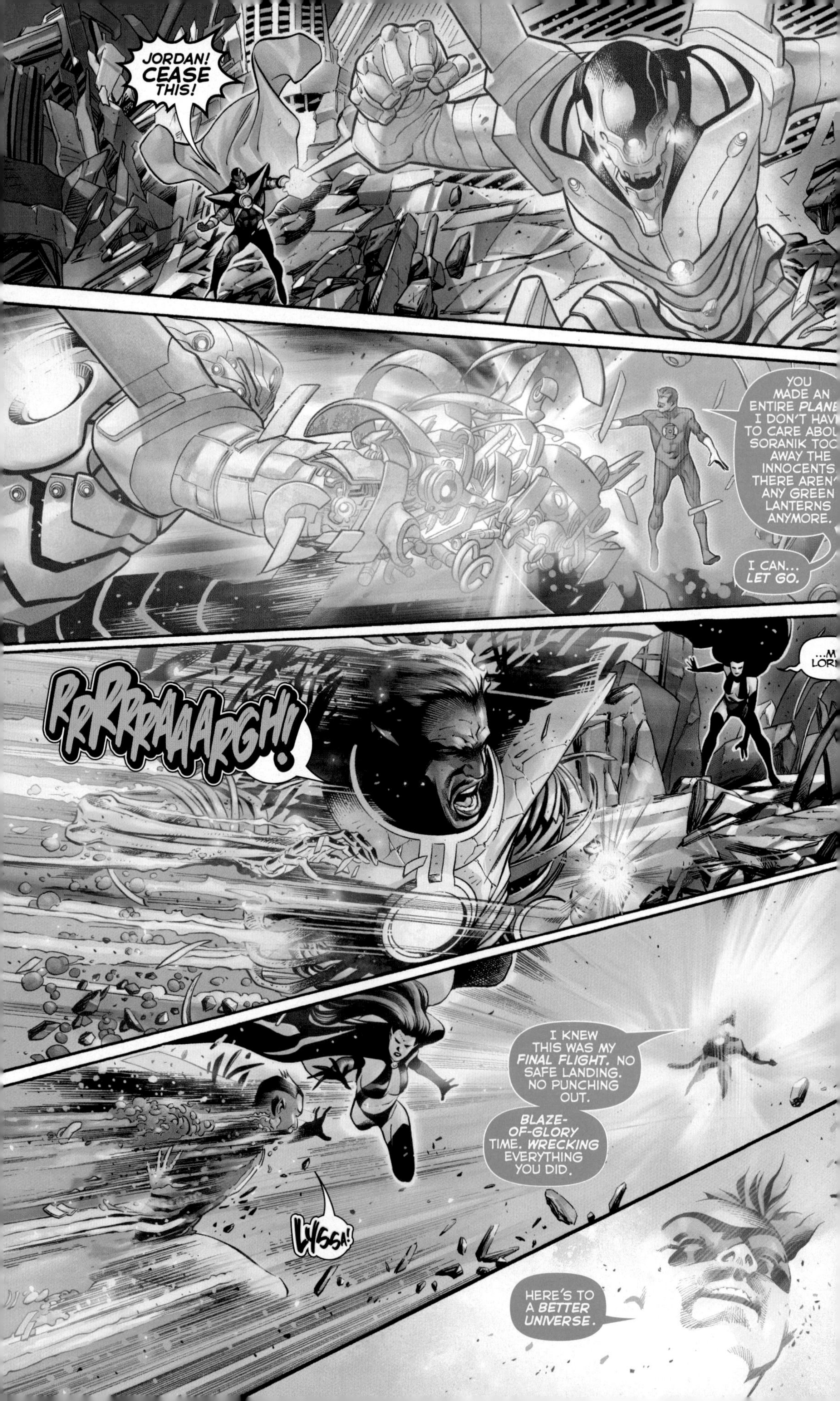
JORDAN! CEASE THIS!
YOU MADE AN ENTIRE PLANE I DON'T HAV TO CARE ABOU SORANIK TOO AWAY THE INNOCENTS THERE AREN' ANY GREEN LANTERNS ANYMORE.
I CAN... LET GO.
RRRRRAAAARGH!
...M LORI
I KNEW THIS WAS MY FINAL FLIGHT. NO SAFE LANDING. NO PUNCHING OUT.
BLAZE-OF-GLORY TIME. WRECKING EVERYTHING YOU DID.
LYSSA!
HERE'S TO A BETTER UNIVERSE.

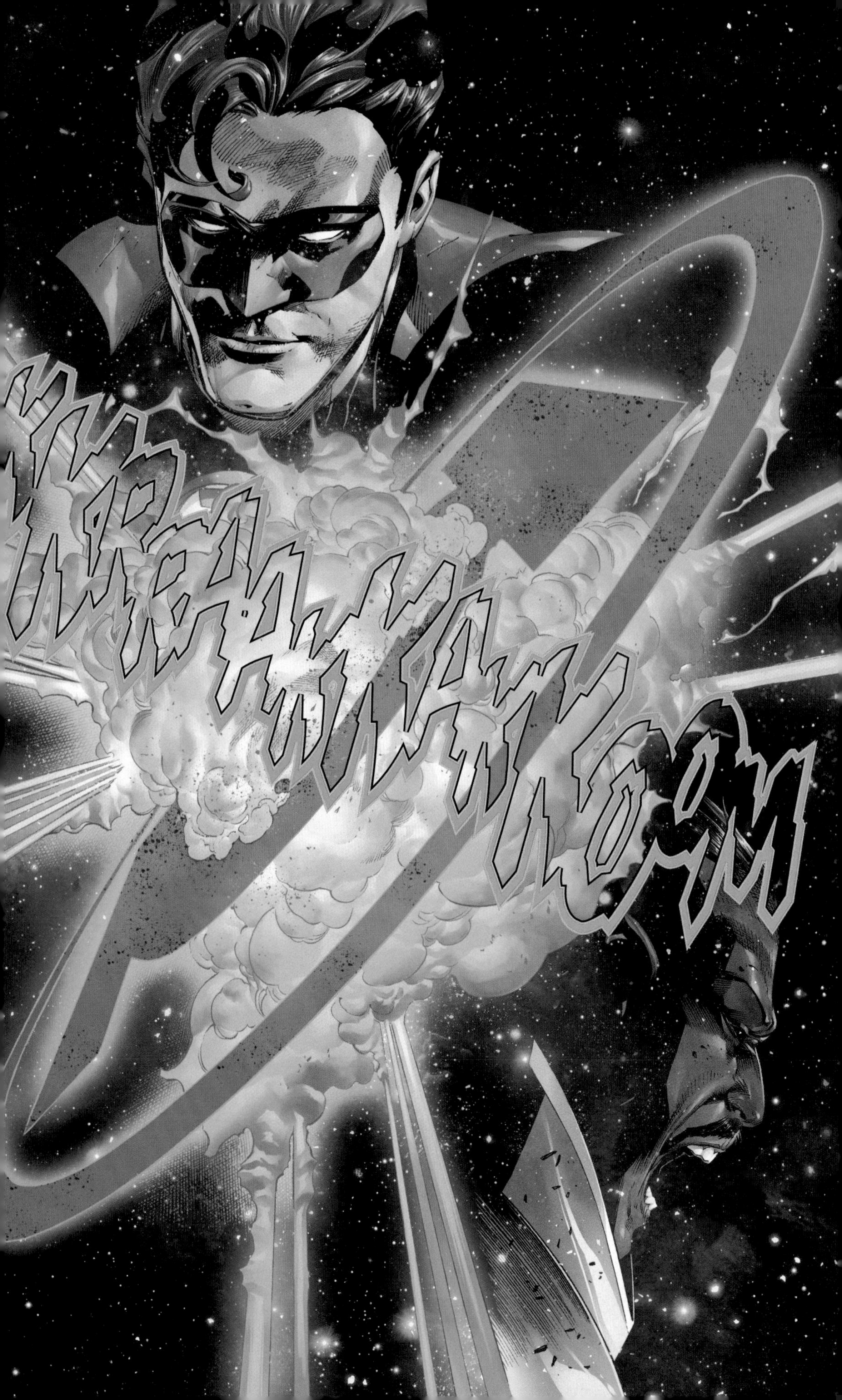

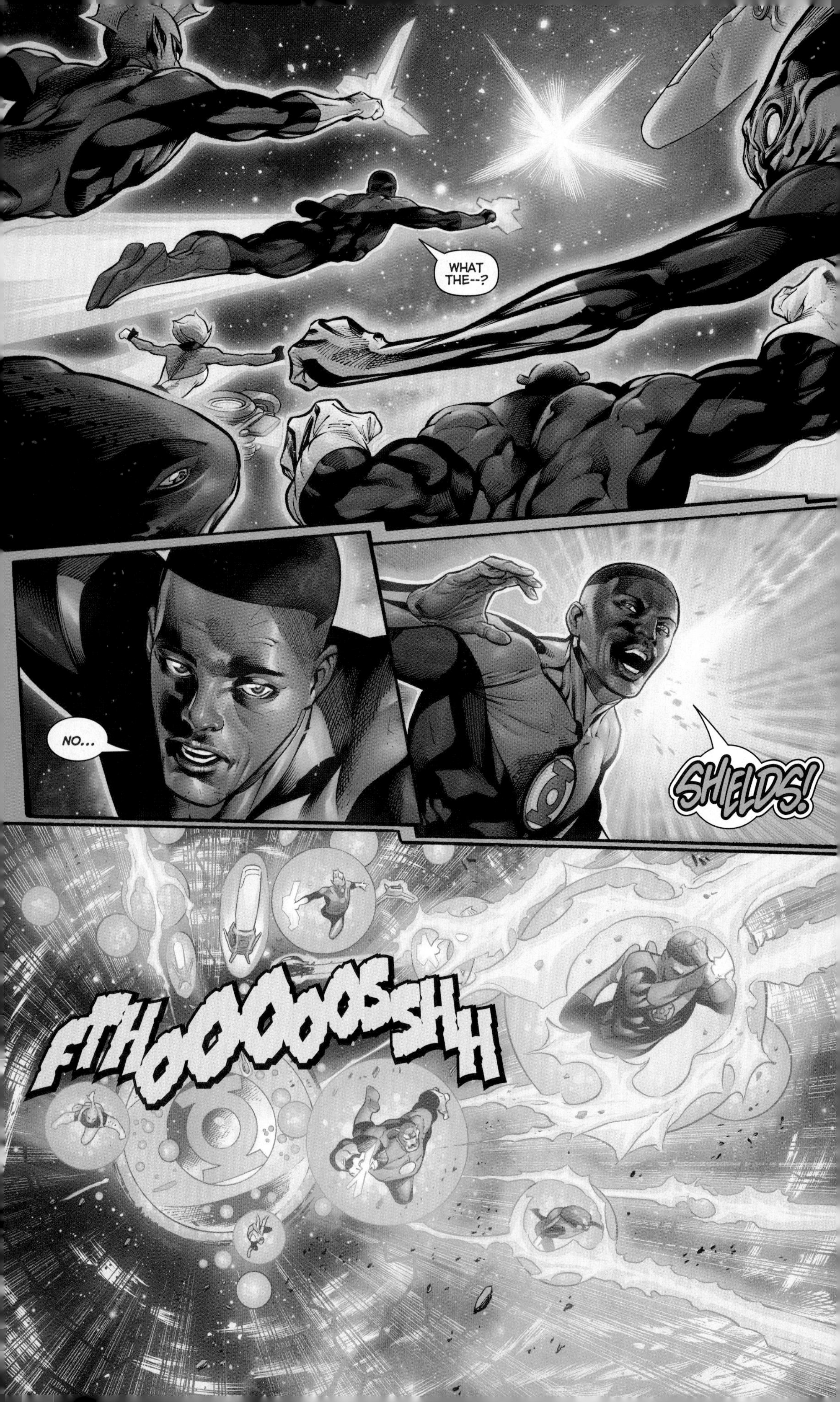
WHAT THE--?
NO...
SHIELDS!
FTHOOOOOOSHHH

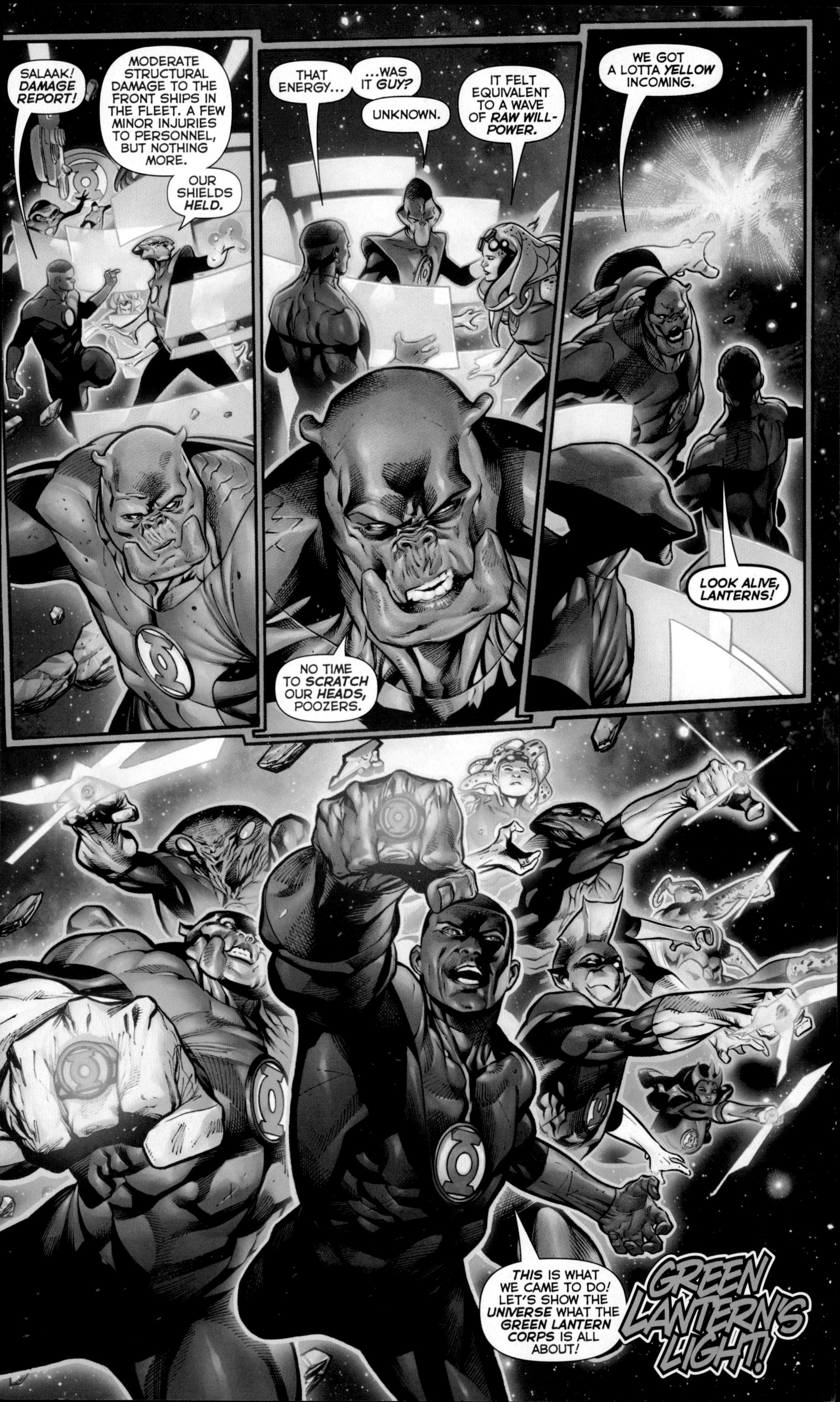

SALAAK! DAMAGE REPORT!
MODERATE STRUCTURAL DAMAGE TO THE FRONT SHIPS IN THE FLEET. A FEW MINOR INJURIES TO PERSONNEL, BUT NOTHING MORE.
OUR SHIELDS HELD.
THAT ENERGY...
...WAS IT GUY?
UNKNOWN.
IT FELT EQUIVALENT TO A WAVE OF RAW WILL-POWER.
NO TIME TO SCRATCH OUR HEADS, POOZERS.
WE GOT A LOTTA YELLOW INCOMING.
LOOK ALIVE, LANTERNS!
THIS IS WHAT WE CAME TO DO! LET'S SHOW THE UNIVERSE WHAT THE GREEN LANTERN CORPS IS ALL ABOUT!
GREEN LANTERN'S LIGHT!

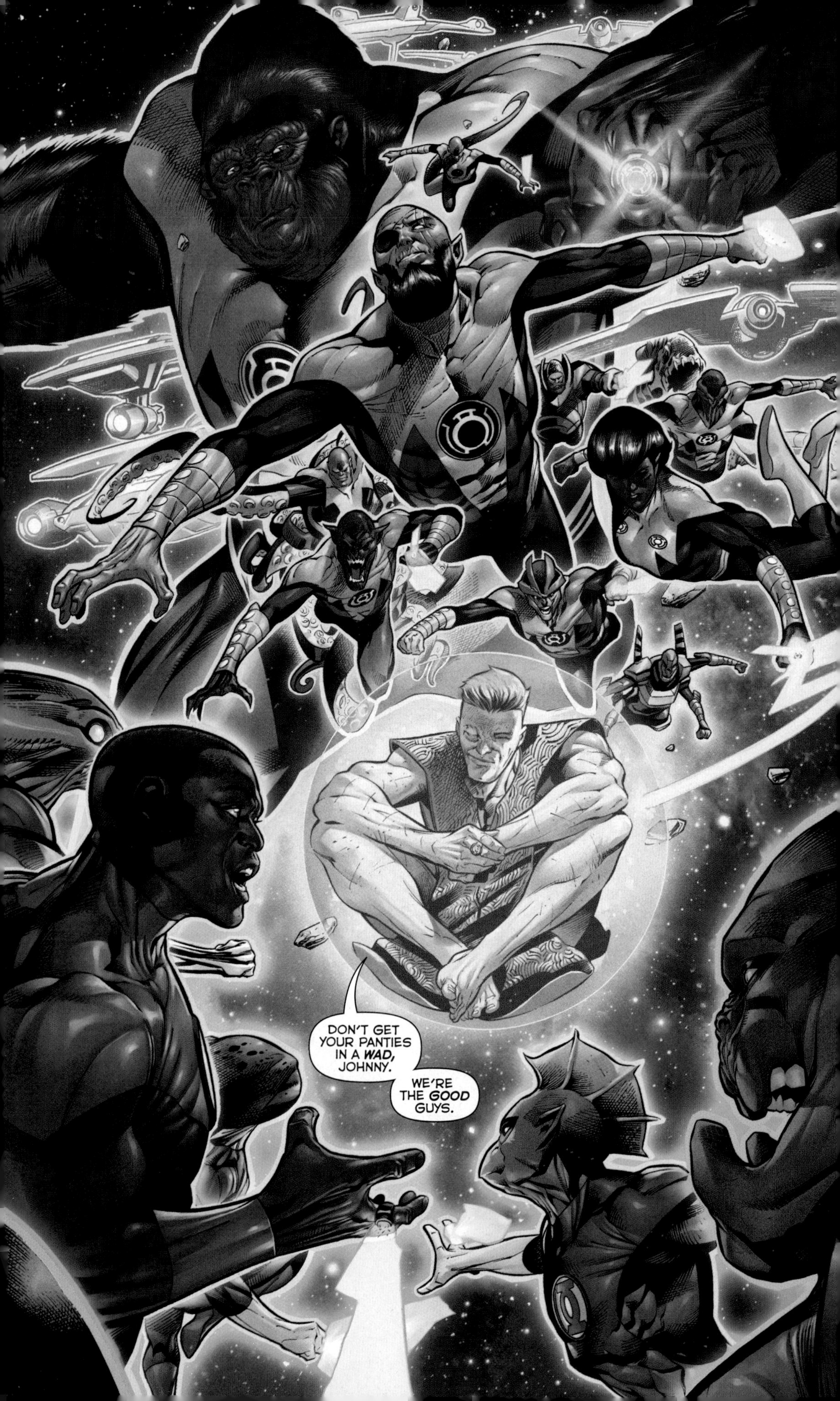
DON'T GET YOUR PANTIES IN A *WAD,* JOHNNY.
WE'RE THE *GOOD* GUYS.

HAL JORDAN AND THE GREEN LANTERN CORPS

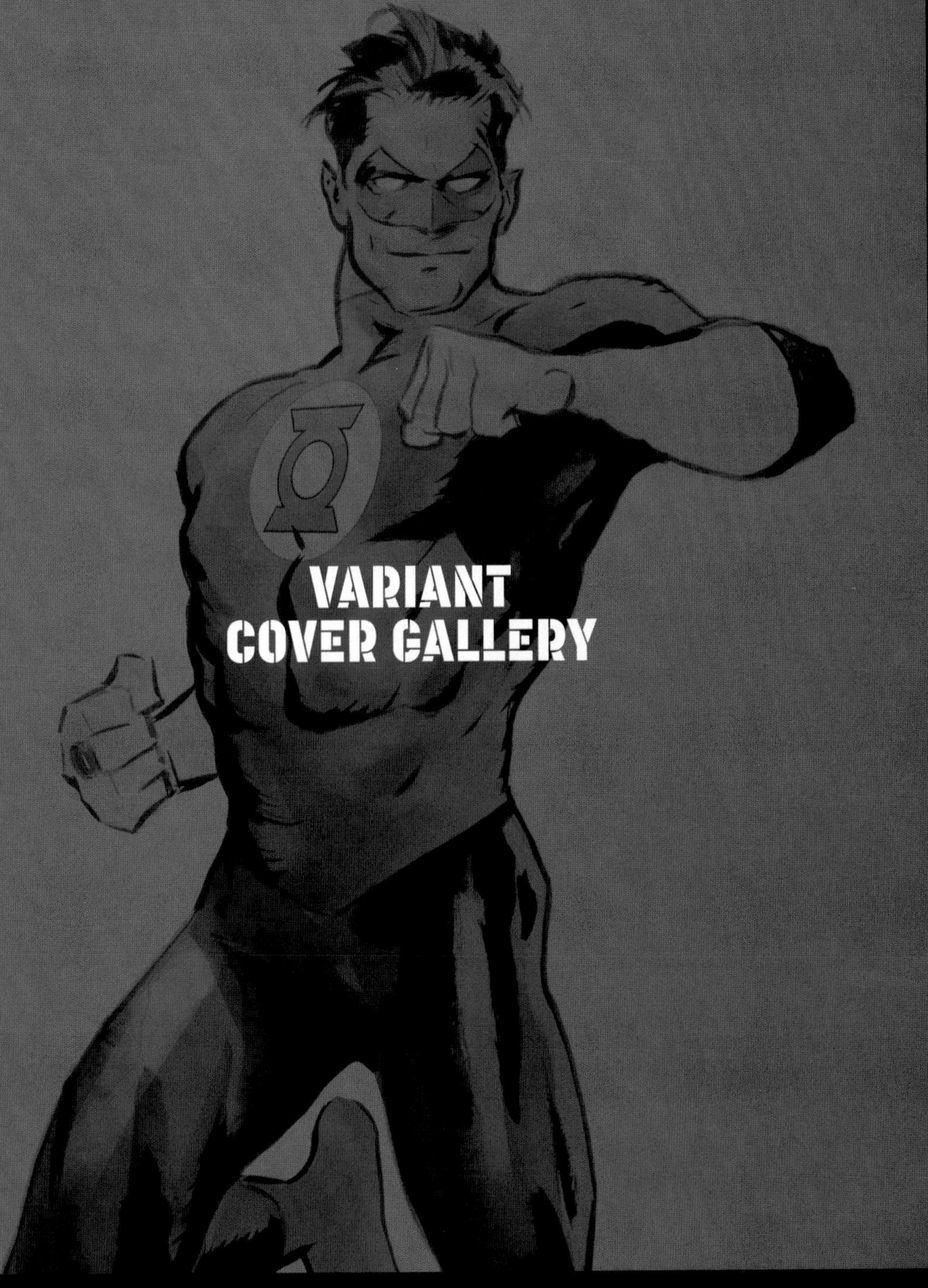

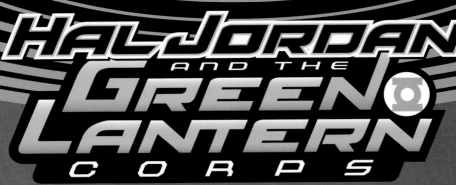

VARIANT COVER GALLERY

HAL JORDAN AND THE GREEN LANTERN CORPS: REBIRTH #1
Variant Cover by CARY NORD

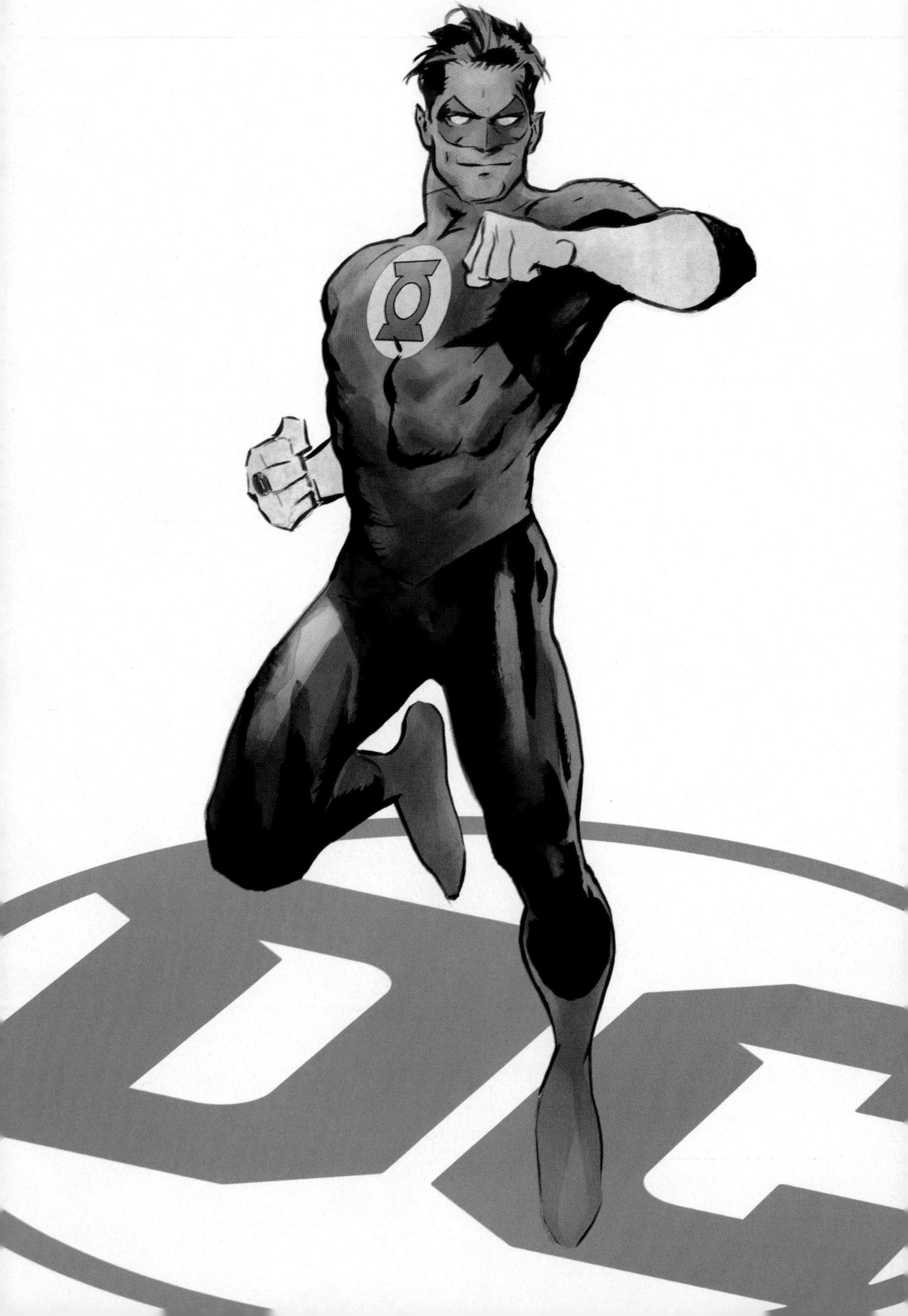

HAL JORDAN AND THE GREEN LANTERN CORPS #1
Variant cover by KEVIN NOWLAN

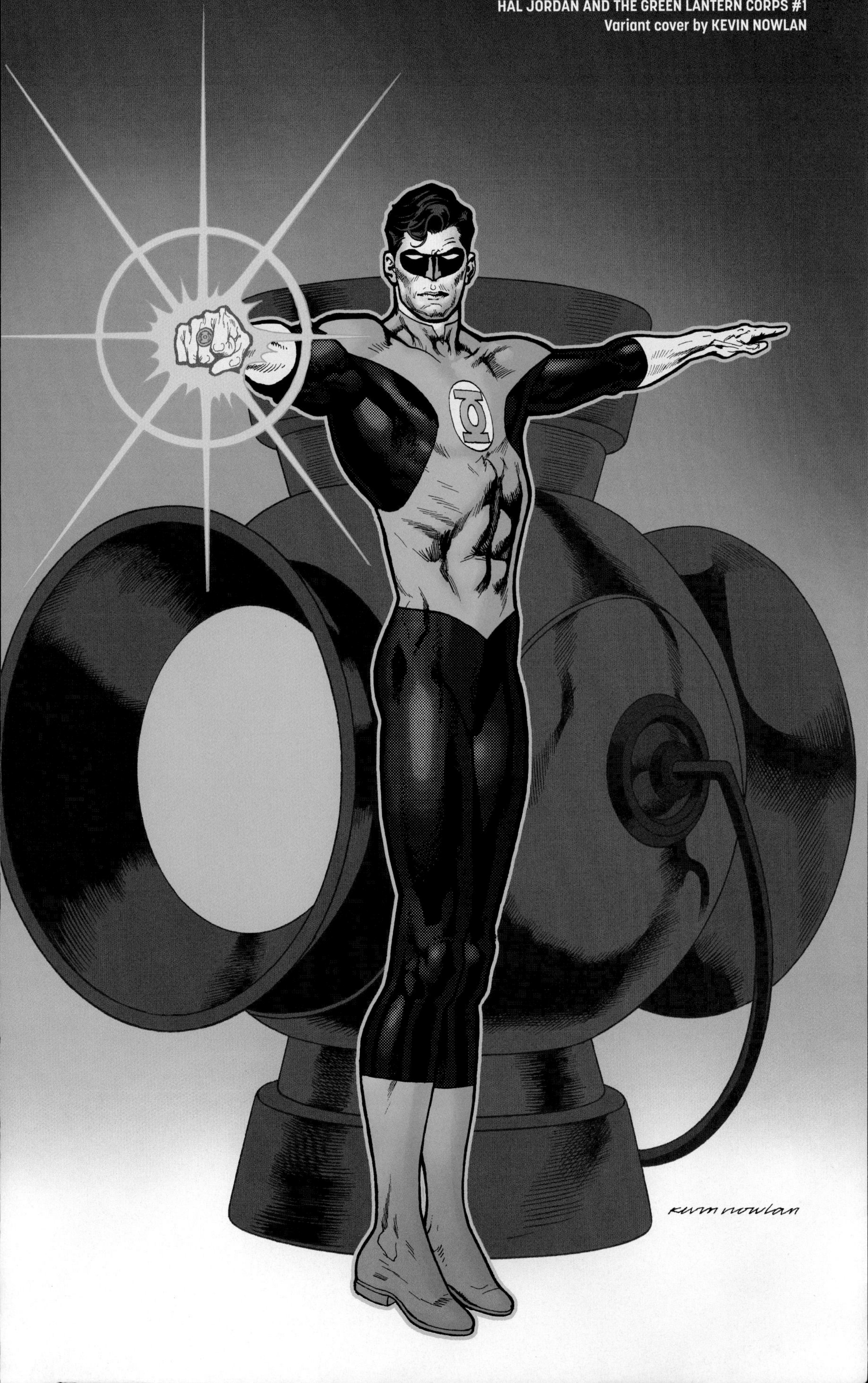
kevin nowlan

HAL JORDAN AND THE GREEN LANTERN CORPS #2
Variant cover by KEVIN NOWLAN

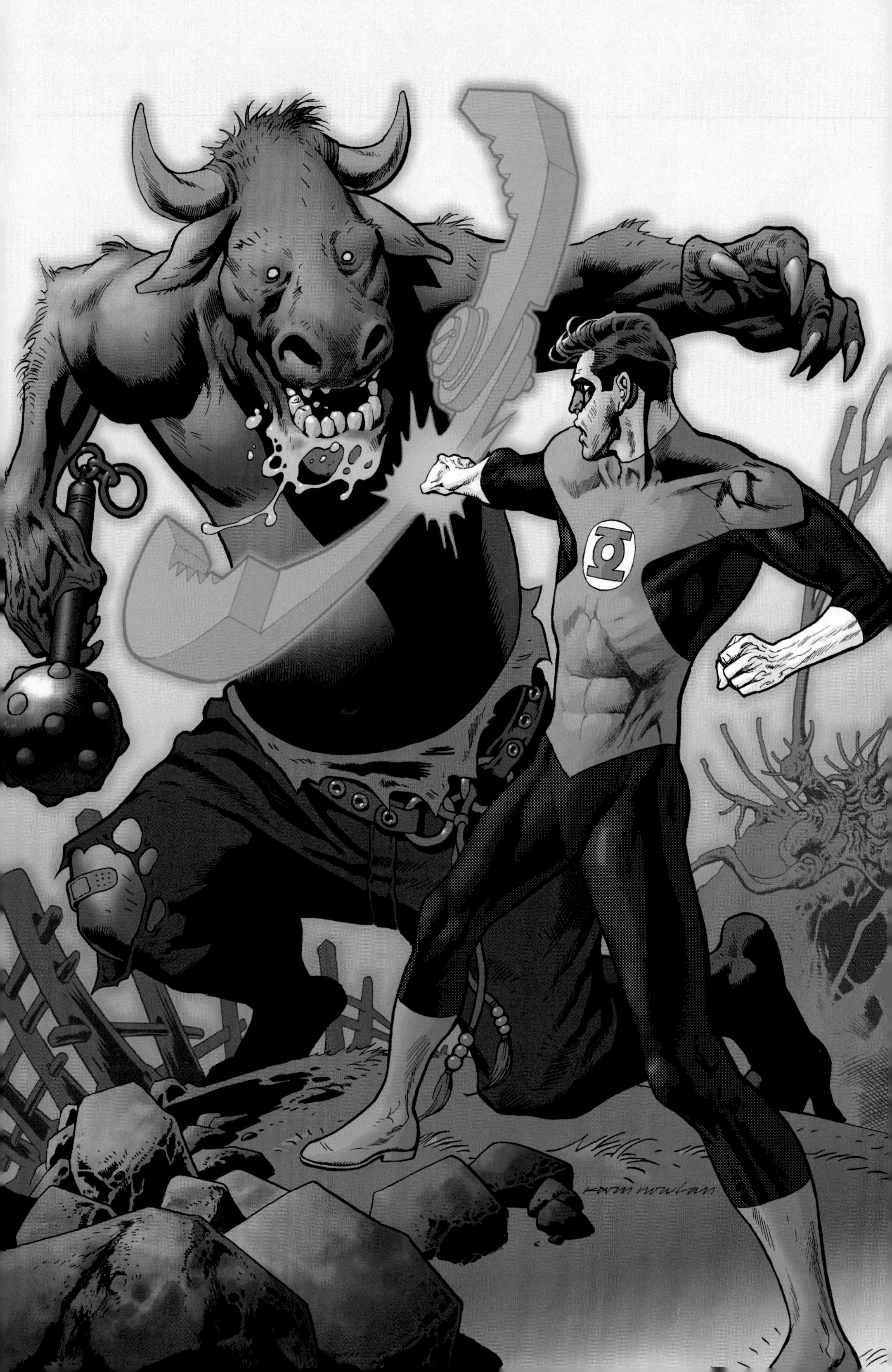
kevin nowlan

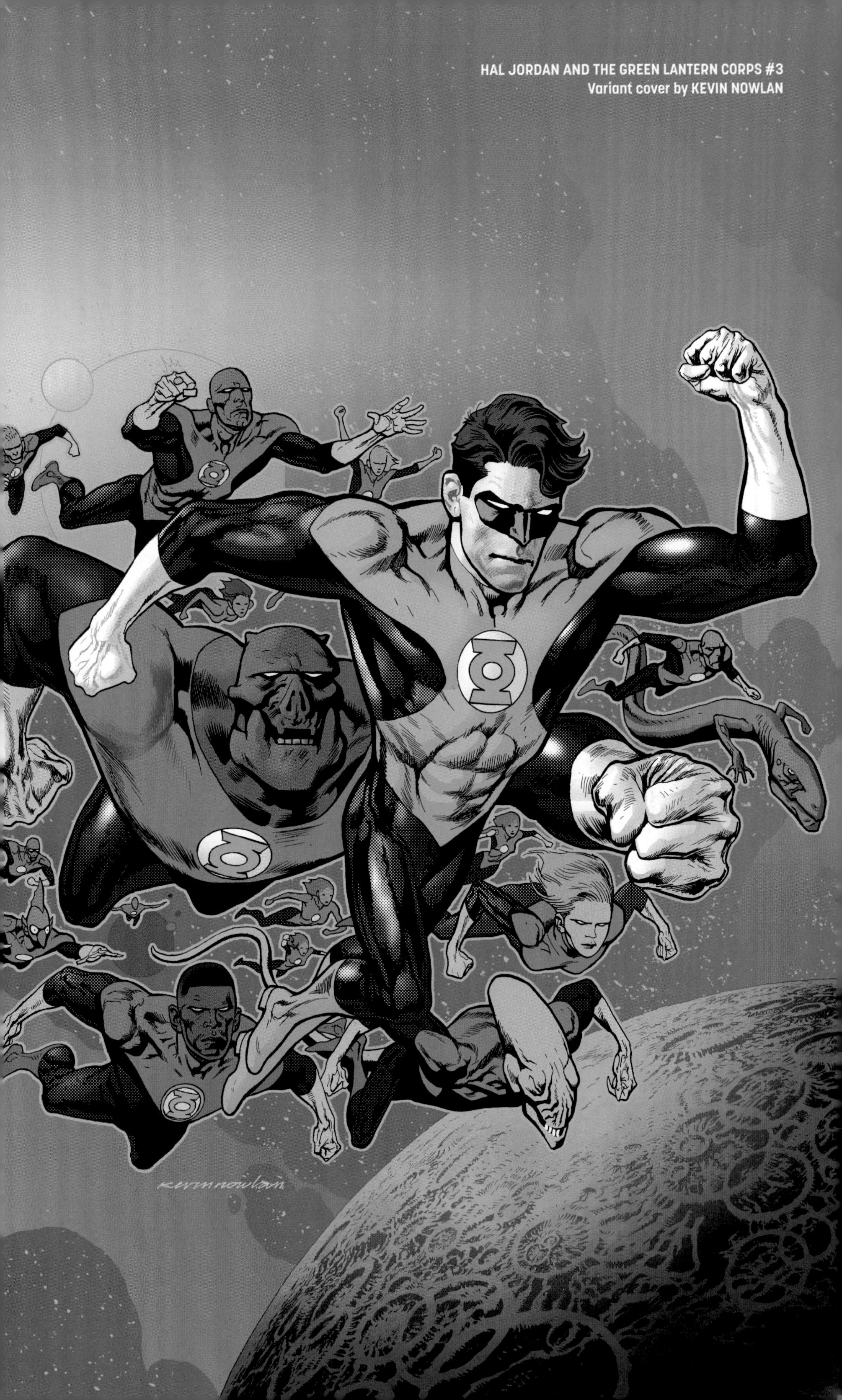

HAL JORDAN AND THE GREEN LANTERN CORPS #3
Variant cover by KEVIN NOWLAN

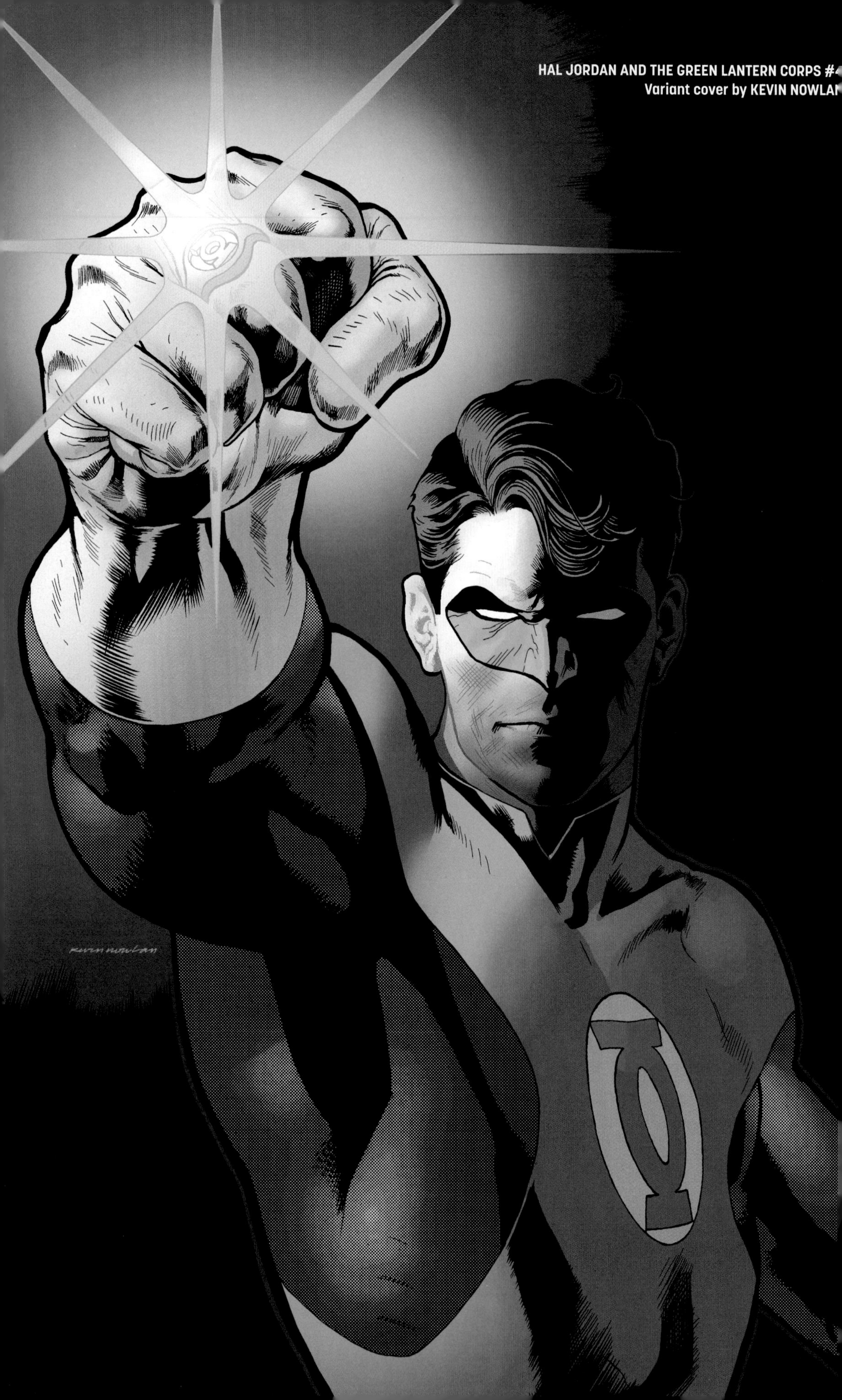
kevin nowlan

HAL JORDAN AND THE GREEN LANTERN CORPS #4
Variant cover by KEVIN NOWLAN

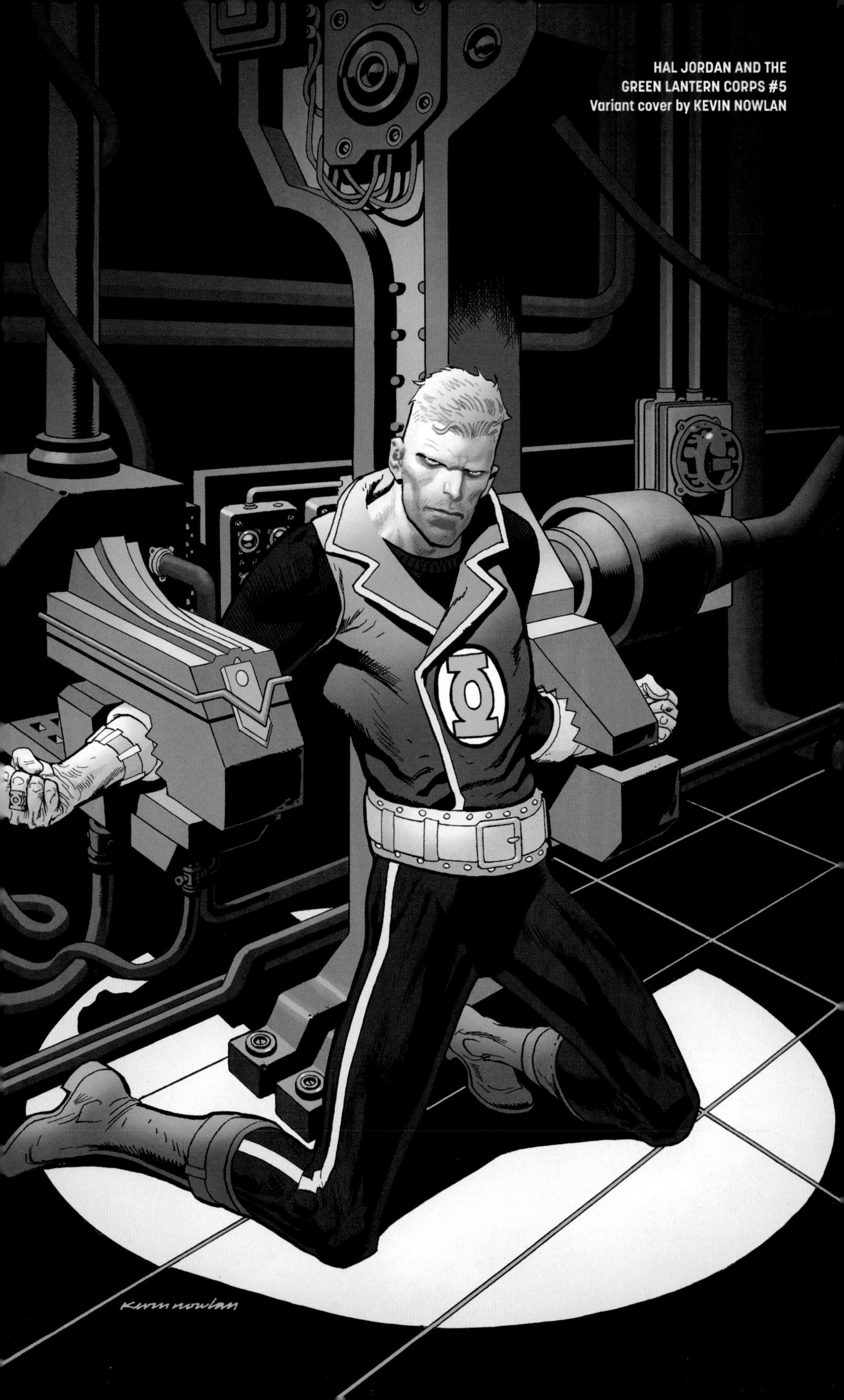
kevin nowlan

HAL JORDAN AND THE
GREEN LANTERN CORPS #5
Variant cover by KEVIN NOWLAN

HAL JORDAN AND THE GREEN LANTERN CORPS #6
Variant cover by KEVIN NOWLAN

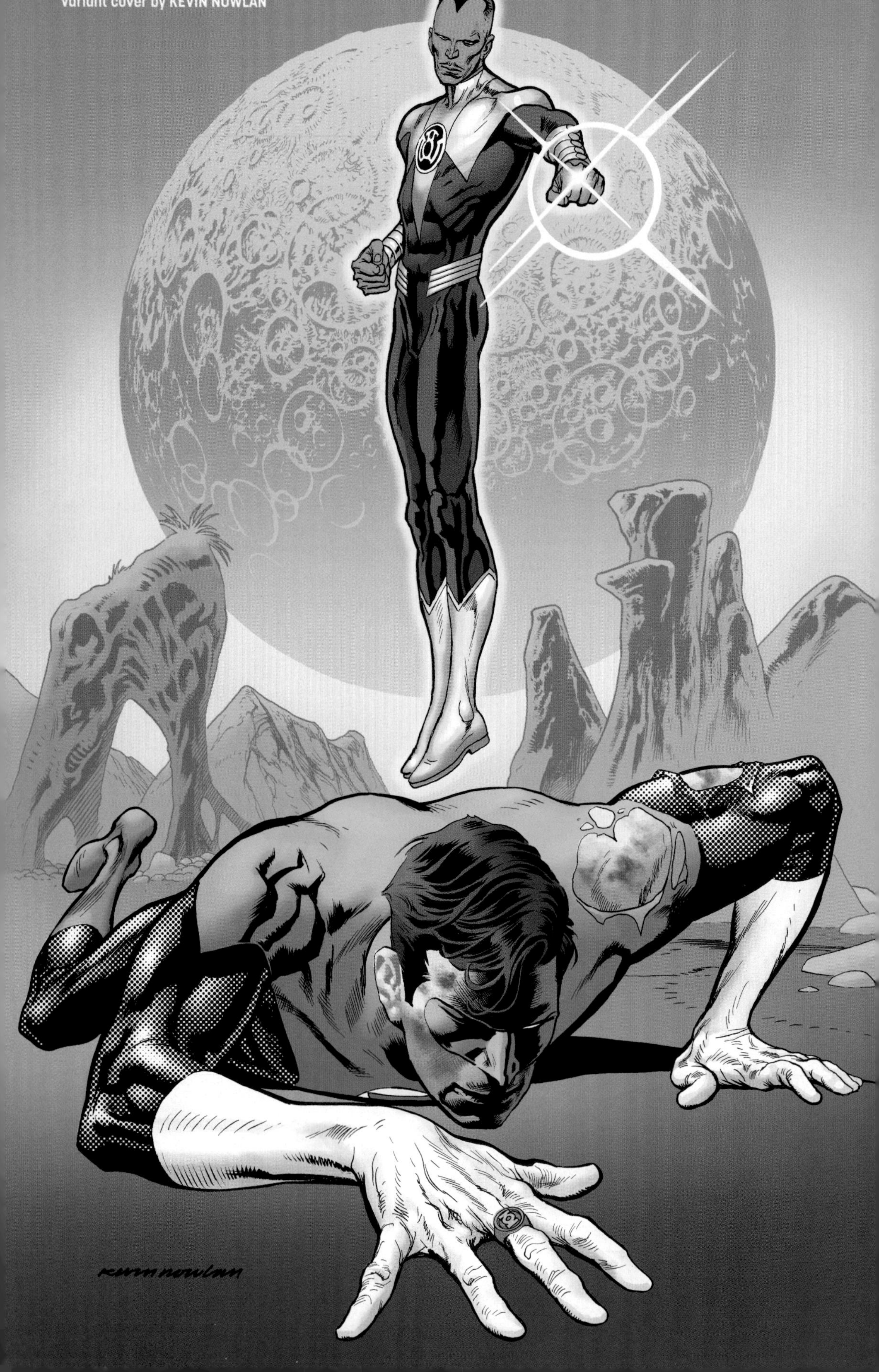
kevin nowlan

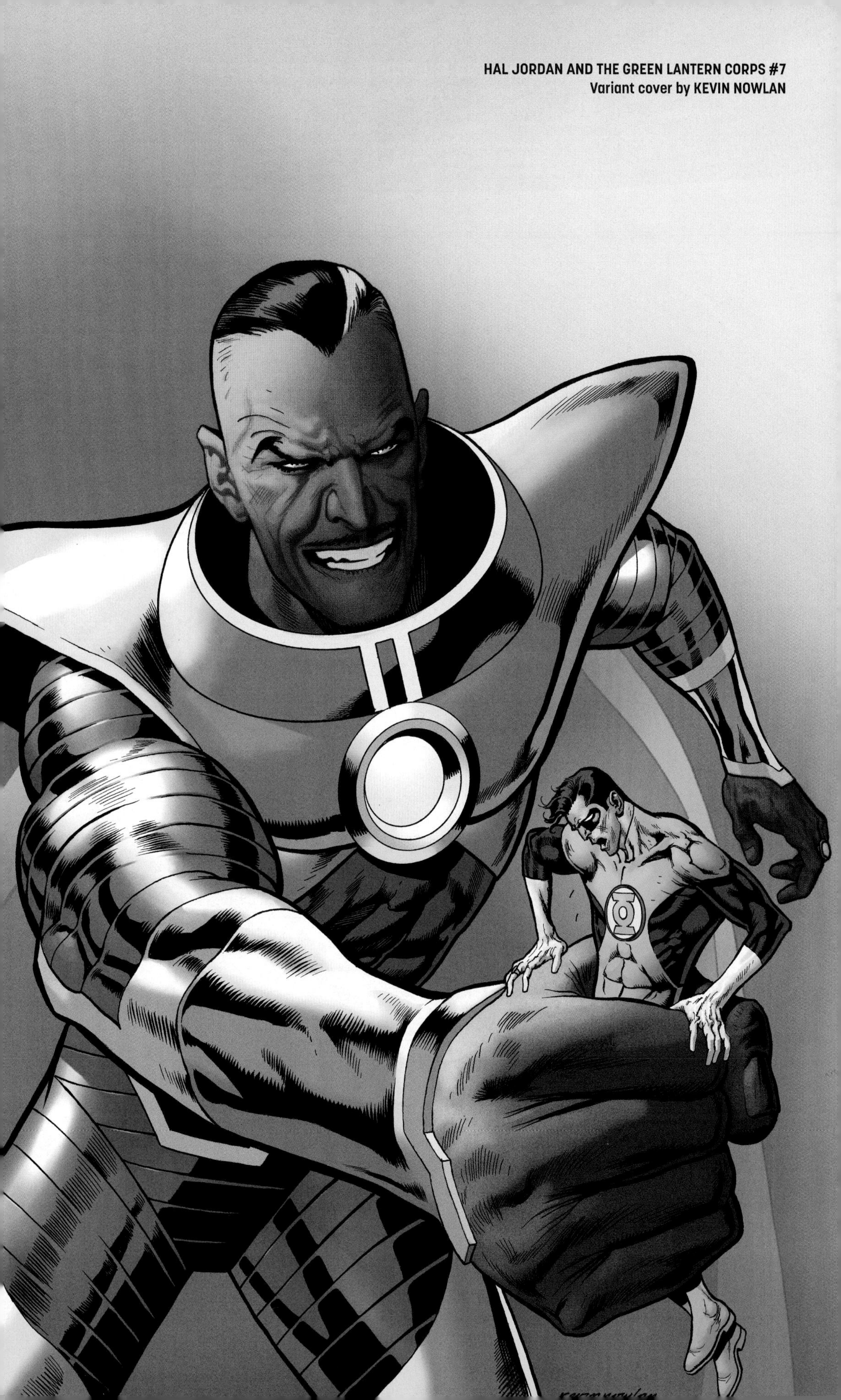

HAL JORDAN AND THE GREEN LANTERN CORPS #7
Variant cover by KEVIN NOWLAN

HAL JORDAN AND THE GREEN LANTERN CORPS #7

Pages 6-7 pencils by Rafa Sandoval

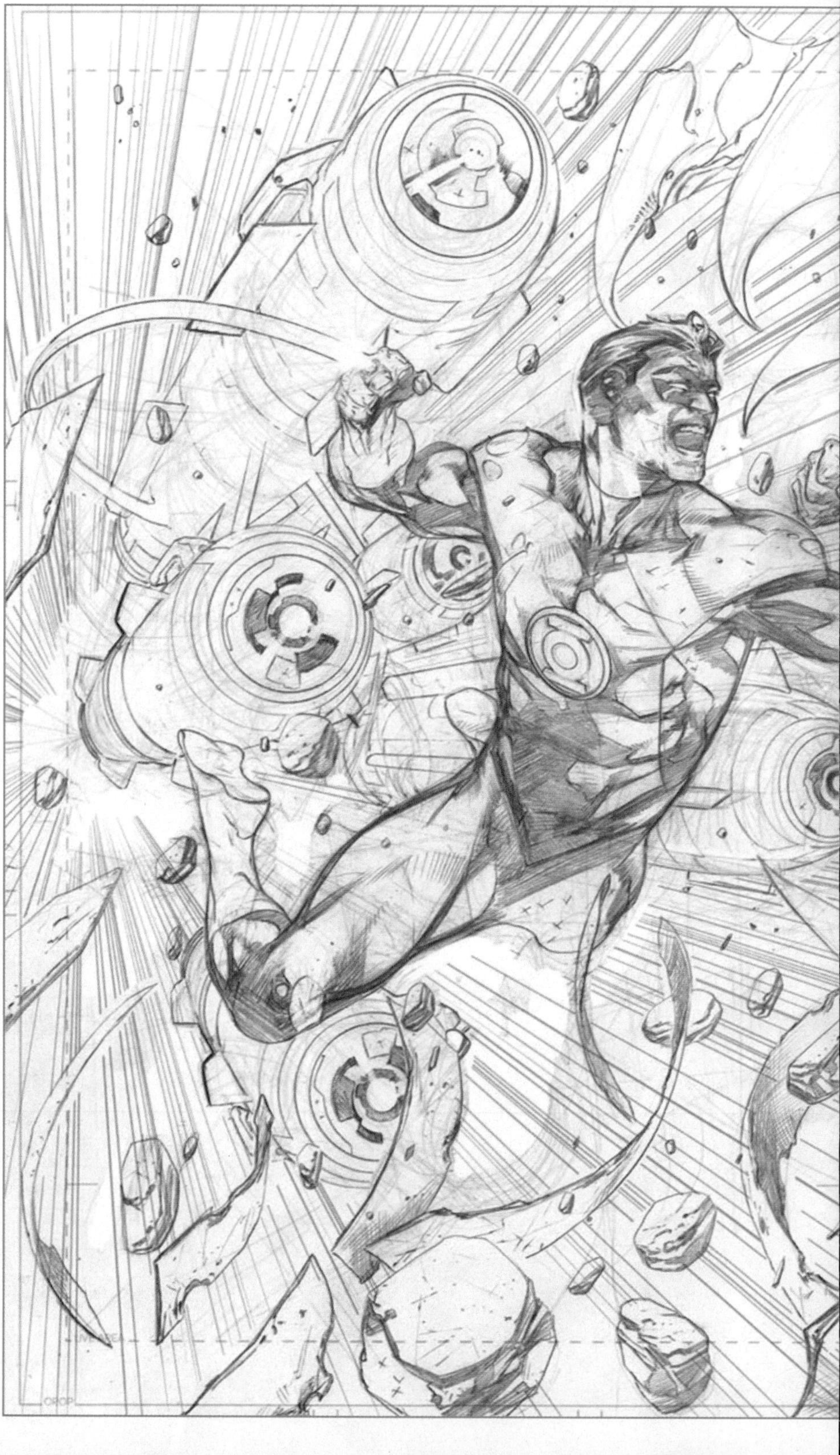

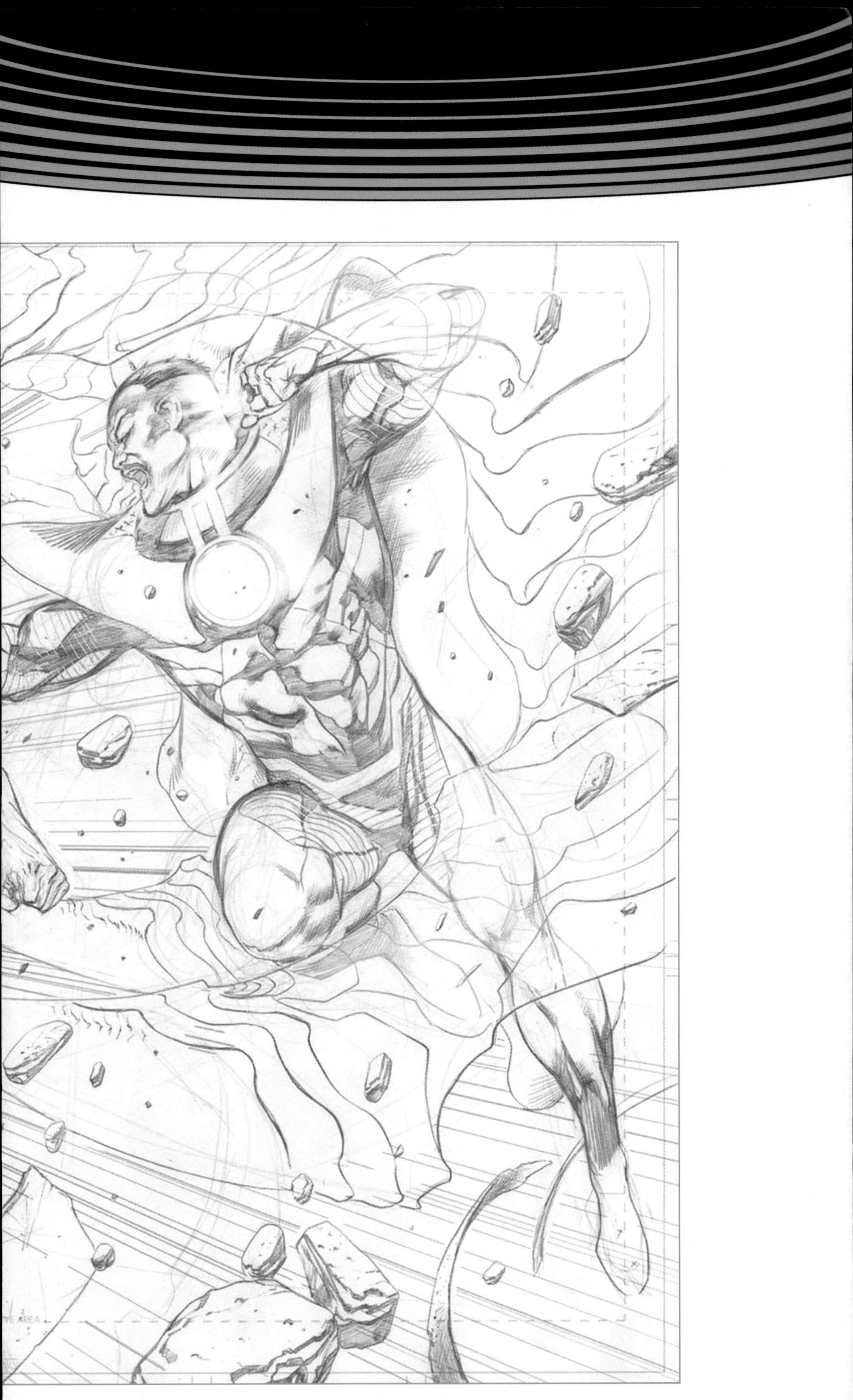

HAL JORDAN AND THE GREEN LANTERN CORPS: REBIRTH #1

Page 20 art by Ethan Van Sciver

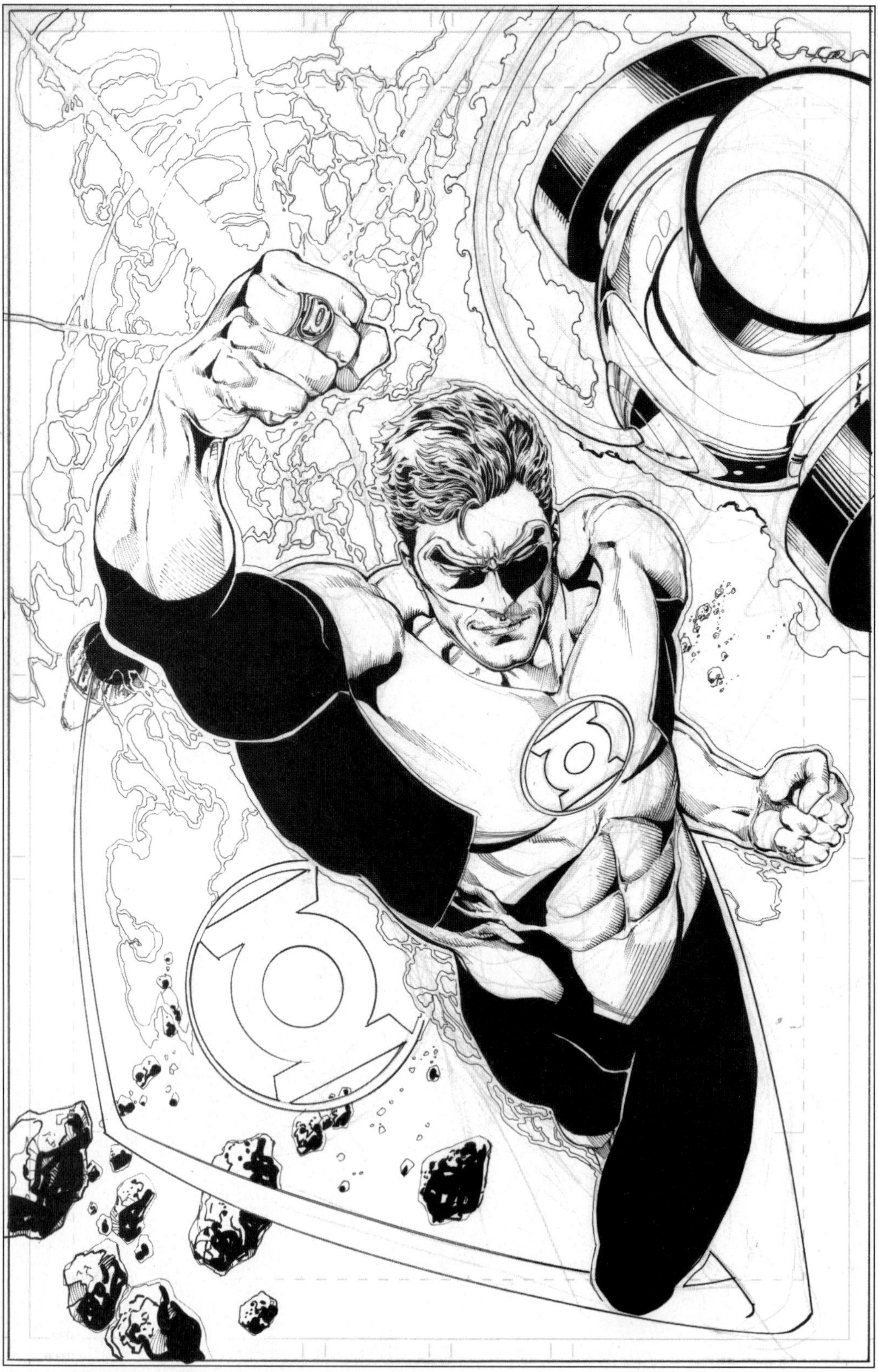